China's Development

China is entering a phase where deep structural changes will arise throughout society. These multi-fold processes will be intertwined in a globalized world, impacted by the transformation of capitalism in the aftermath of the financial crisis and under the threat of severe environmental damage.

Focusing on sustainability, this book explores China's future with insight of Chinese history which enlightens the successful reforms undertaken in the last 30 years. It combines Chinese economic history and up-to-date macroeconomic theory in order to show how economic transformations and institutional changes are intertwined in developing capitalism under state sovereignty. The book is divided into three parts:

- Part 1 shows why rural China was so resilient but why it impaired the development of industrial capitalism. It explores historically and theoretically the causes of the demise of imperial China and of the social disruptions due to political warfare in the twentieth century.
- Part 2 examines the reasons why the last 30 years of reform were successful but fostered deep structural disequilibria requiring a dramatic mutation in future decades.
- Part 3 develops a theoretical model of sustainability that seeks to address the question: what type of political economy can support the purpose of achieving "harmonious society"?

China's Development will be of interest to students and scholars of Chinese economics, politics, history, and development.

Michel Aglietta is Professor at the University of Paris-X Nanterre and Scientific Advisor for the Center of International Studies and Forecasting (CEPII), Paris, France.

Guo Bai is a PhD candidate at HEC Paris, France.

Rethinking Globalizations

Edited by Barry K. Gills, University of Newcastle, UK

This series is designed to break new ground in the literature on globalization and its academic and popular understanding. Rather than perpetuating or simply reacting to the economic understanding of globalization, this series seeks to capture the term and broaden its meaning to encompass a wide range of issues and disciplines and convey a sense of alternative possibilities for the future.

China's Development

Capitalism and empire

Michel Aglietta and Guo Bai

Routledge
Taylor & Francis Group

LONDON AND NEW YORK

First published 2013
by Routledge
2 Park Square, Milton Park, Abingdon, Oxon OX14 4RN

Simultaneously published in the USA and Canada
by Routledge
711 Third Avenue, New York, NY 10017

Routledge is an imprint of the Taylor & Francis Group, an informa business

British Library Cataloguing in Publication Data
A catalogue record for this book is available from the British Library

Library of Congress Cataloguing-in-Publication Data
A catalog record has been requested for this book
Aglietta, Michel.
  China's development: capitalism and empire/Michel Aglietta and Guo Bai.
  p. cm. – (Rethinking globalizations; 40)
  Includes bibliographical references and index.
  1. China–Economic policy–1976-2000. 2. China–Economic
  policy–2000- 3. Capitalism–China. I. Bai, Guo. II. Title.
  HC427.92.A64 2012
  330.951–dc23
  2012014071

ISBN: 978-0-415-53502-1 (hbk)
ISBN: 978-0-203-08588-2 (ebk)

Typeset in Times New Roman
by Sunrise Setting Ltd

Printed and bound in the United States of America
by Edwards Brothers Malloy

Contents

Figures

Tables

Boxes

Introduction

From imperial history to *sui generis* development of capitalism

Since the beginning of what is conventionally known as China's economic reform in 1978, mainstream Western economists have been puzzled by the sustainability of China's economic performances. They gauge the mix of China's achievements, discrepancies, inequalities, and acute social tensions against a specific model of social institutions dubbed universal – the model of economic liberalism. This model has become more and more influential intellectually with the monetarist counter-revolution in the 1970s and has become hegemonic since the rise of the rational expectations school, which proclaimed the efficient market theory *urbi et orbi*. Economic liberalism has risen to prominence politically in the Anglo-Saxon world with Reagan's and Thatcher's counter-revolution in the 1980s.

This theoretical insight equates capitalism and market economy entirely. Furthermore, it is conceptually totalitarian insofar as it claims that the market is the universally most effective mode of coordination of social interactions. As much as people are rational and forward-looking, it pretends that market coordination always delivers the best outcome. It follows that government interactions with the market should arise as little as possible and, when they occur, they should themselves be market-like to be as predictable as possible.

This intellectual mood was given an impetus after the fall of the Berlin Wall and the collapse of the Soviet Union. In the early 1990s "the end of history" was predicted by Francis Fukuyama, a political philosopher at Georgetown University (Washington DC). The whole world was going to embrace Anglo-Saxon market institutions: private property rights, rule of law, market flexibility, full opening, and the like. The bundle of these predicaments was labeled the Washington Consensus. Many developing countries adopted this agenda until a string of devastating crises between 1997 and 2002 burst out in Asia, Russia, and Latin America.

Within this ideological mood, China figured as a kind of maverick. It obviously did not follow the liberal recipe, while it went on posting staggering growth. Confronted with such oddity, Western economists trained in the new neo-classical thinking split between optimists and pessimists. The optimists point out the magic of the market to explain growth performance. They believe that market reforms are underway and consequently that China is converging with market capitalism. The country will become progressively more like Western market economies including representative democracy, the latter equating to representative parliamentary regimes. The pessimists behold the gap between the Chinese political system and what their ideology has taught them about the proper institutions of a market economy. Any time the country faces a crisis situation in the course of transitions between stages of its development, they prognosticate social and political collapse. Those doom watchers were fashionable after the tragic events of Tian Anmen Square in 1989 and again in the aftermath of the Asian crisis. They raise their ugly heads again in the present time, surmising that China will not be able to find its own way to sustainable development.

This book is quite at odds with these contrasting views of Chinese reforms because it rejects basic theoretical tenets of new neo-classical economic theory. It is based upon different theoretical prerequisites that do not equate capitalism with market economy.

Capitalism is a system of power relations whose regulation involves non-market social institutions

Capitalism and market economy are not the same, though they are closely connected, because labor markets and financial markets are not like standard commodity markets. Market economy is based on the division of human activities, whereby individuals are separated from one another without any a priori knowledge of others' needs and desires. A social medium known as money – external to all individuals – is generated by common trust to make exchanges possible. It creates a common metric, called value, to measure the products of individual activities according to the desires of others to buy them against money. Access to money as universal purchasing power and ability to spend it in specific ways determines values. Individuals are equal in status. Quantitative differences arise with modulations in the intensity of individual desires. They do not give rise to systematic inequalities.

Capitalism is based upon a second separation quite different in substance which creates a power relationship between capitalists and workers. Capitalists are those who have access to money in order to fund the acquisition of means of production. Workers are those who have access to money in renting their working capabilities. This separation crucially changes the rationale of the system. The purpose of capitalists is to accumulate money for its own sake, since it entails power over others. The more money that can be mobilized, the greater the power over society. Conversely the status of labor is not that of market participants in pure market exchange economy. Because they are deprived of the means of production, workers are unable to become private producers for the market. In principle they are individually free to rent their capabilities to any capitalist they choose. It is why there is a labor market. But the whole class of workers is subordinated to those who own the means of production. It follows that the wage is not the price of work done. It is the money price for letting out one's capacity of work for a definite time.

One can understand now that labor contract and exchange contract are strikingly different notions. Individuals are autonomous in executing exchange contracts. Independent producers undertake economic risks, owing to uncertainty in consumer demand for products or services sold, because income depends on the validation of the activity of producing by the sale on the market against money. When successful, technological innovations enhance demand supporting higher margins. They provide extra profit to the lucky inventor who can exploit its position in the market. By contrast, labor contract entails subordination of workers in executing the contract because workers have sold to capitalist firms the right to use their capabilities as they see fit under the command of managers who maximize capitalist interests. They have sold a number of hours' work, not the actual work done whose value over the wage accrues to the firm's profit. Intensity of work, which increases the quantity of labor for a given working time, is a function of work rules that are unilaterally determined by management. Work compensation is based on working time, eventually modulated by incentive to work, called efficiency wage, against a standard benchmark. Technological innovation often deepens subordination to reduce labor costs with productivity gains and higher work intensity that accrue to firms' profits. To magnify those profits, capitalist firms resort more intensely to debt finance, which boosts intensive capital accumulation.

Finance is the core of capitalist coordination since every firm must resort to it to accumulate capital and expand employment. But credit markets are not like ordinary markets. They are markets of future promises, irremediably plagued with uncertainty. Prices are not determined by supply and demand, which are well separated. In ordinary markets, such as that of cars, suppliers and customers are quite different people. Price variations are bounded objectively by the inertia in production costs, by the purchasing power of potential buyers, and ultimately by the decreasing marginal utility in the use of cars. This is not so in financial markets. Anyone can be buyer or seller at any time, depending on his or her expectation about the expectations of others. Prices can fluctuate from zero to infinity. Money being not only the medium of exchange but the purpose of the transaction, demand can push prices under the evil of euphoric mania. Interdependence between market participants determines a fleeting collective mood, called a market convention. It is why financial markets are the loci of money games that often degenerate in speculative bubbles followed by collapses. They are the places where capitalism appears unveiled: just money making money. Because money knows no saturation, greed knows no inner bound. It is why financial markets cannot regulate themselves. They must be bounded by state institutions.

Therefore, for capitalism to be viable, society must develop a web of social institutions to regulate the markets that are the linchpins of capitalism. There must be social institutions to regulate labor markets, enact labor laws, protect workers' rights, mitigate the violence inherent to the power relationship, and organize bargaining between collective interests of employees and their employers. The state is involved directly or indirectly in non-market social relationships. Not only is it required for providing market infrastructures, it must also regulate the distribution of income, because labor market coordination is far from being able to achieve social cohesion. As Douglas North (North 2005) has demonstrated in his monumental work, the nexus of social institutions, which evolves throughout history, impinges upon economic agent behaviors and shapes market mechanisms in different ways in different countries. However, a welfare view of market economy is dramatically incomplete because Arrow's impossibility theorem demonstrates that there is no way to aggregate individual preferences into a social welfare function. The common interest, without which no society can hold up, stems from political deliberation processes that are not akin to market processes.

The social cohesion in a country springs from the consistency of its institutions, which determines its mode of regulation in a definite time span. Even if the institutions containing the social tensions inherent in labor and financial markets are similar, their complementarities differ among countries. Modes of regulation always interact with the potential disruptions generated by capital accumulation. As long as the mode of regulation can channel the tensions and move forward the power game from one compromise to another, it achieves a growth regime that has a measure of stability. When the renewed tensions tilt power too heavily for too long in favor of capitalist interests through the medium of finance, the established institutions are no longer able to maintain the coherence of the growth regime. The mode of regulation goes astray and a crisis erupts. It opens a transition to institution rebuilding until the new innovative forces of capital accumulation can be reordered into a new growth regime. Therefore capitalism is embedded in growth regimes that are both diverse among countries and path-dependent in history.

To sum up, a mode of regulation is a set of mediations that ensure that the distortions created by the accumulation of capital are kept within limits which are compatible with social cohesion within each nation. This compatibility is always observable in specific contexts at specific historical moments. The salient test for any analysis of the changes capitalism has undergone is to describe this cohesion in its local manifestations. It also involves understanding why such cohesion is neither universal nor perennial in the life of nations, why the effectiveness of a mode of regulation always wanes. And it requires grasping the processes that occur at times of crisis and the changing behavioral patterns. Lastly, it involves trying to perceive the seeds of a new mode of regulation in the very midst of the crisis afflicting the old one.

Diversity of capitalism in historical perspective

Because basic social institutions and cultural underpinnings of behavior can be long-lived, even if the consistency of a mode of regulation lasts a shorter period of time, long-run history is the best guide for the future. It can test the analytical principles of regulation theory and make scholars aware of the diversity in the models of capitalism and in their path-dependency.

Basic analytical principles of regulation theory exposed above are compatible with the teachings of Fernand Braudel who made an outstanding contribution to the understanding of the rise of European capitalism between the thirteenth and eighteenth centuries. From his vast historical research, Braudel has drawn five principles. First, capitalism has always been both global and embedded in social structures. In the same vein the sociologist Karl Polanyi has forcefully emphasized that the embedding of economic relationships in social structures is a key feature of their working. It is what produces ever-renewed structural differentiations in capitalist models. Second, market economy and capitalism are intrinsically linked, but they should not be confused, as we argue above in defining the capital labor relationship. Capitalism is a momentum of accumulation. Its logic is money making money, not social welfare. It is why capitalism is not self-regulating and not converging toward any predetermined ideal model. It is path-dependent. Inequality is its essence. Third, there is no independence of markets, let alone primacy, because money is a public good and wage labor is far from being reducible to a commodity. Capitalism is a total social phenomenon whereby institutions and market structures co-evolve. Fourth, in history institutions prevail because they guide the overall regulation of societies. The most important ones, because they are the longer lasting, are informal collective beliefs. They embody the common good of a society, e.g. the sense of togetherness in the culture of the people. Cultural beliefs differ from one society to another and permeate the institutions of sovereign states. It is why the state has the common good as its *raison d'être*. Only the support of the people through their common belief, whichever way expressed, makes state power legitimate. Fifth, world capitalism is a confrontation of asymmetric power politics. It has nothing to do with a general competitive equilibrium model. The interdependencies among nation states are both hierarchical and mediated by finance. It is why dominant financial centers are the privileged loci of value capture.

China: a capitalist nation?

Twenty-first-century capitalism was born within the Asian crisis, shattering the phantasm of universality of Western capitalism. An incipient bifurcation has been waxing since the global financial crisis in 2007–8, like the many that have punctuated the history of capitalism.

Therefore global finance must not be apprehended as a process of homogenizing capitalism. Indeed, the magnitude of the financial crisis that started in 2007 and that rebounds throughout the Western world has rebutted this delusion. Finance is a tool of political power that China can use in protecting its domestic economy, in securing its supply lines, and in acquiring critical technology. Our book will emphasize how China develops its domestic financial system largely sheltered from world market instability and builds up a powerful financial center in Hong Kong to project its financial strength worldwide.

Therefore the rise of China's power in the last 30 years or so must be understood within the analytical apparatus of regulation theory. To get insights on the roots of the self-sustaining process of growth one must probe into the formidable cultural and political heritage of China's past. Indeed, hard questions must be faced and answered that are not elicited from the market miracle view of Chinese reform. As Dany Rodrik (2011) and others have shown, adopting market institutions is far from being enough to launch a sustaining growth process in a developing country. Indeed, Chinese history provides a vivid counterfactual example. After the fall of the Qing empire in 1911 the Republic of China was created. All the ingredients of liberal capitalism were formally present: a ruling bourgeoisie, parliamentary elections in 1913, capital opening, and willingness to modernize the country. However, nothing much happened as far as deep-rooted industrialization was concerned. The huge rural masses were not concerned. They were so deep in the traditional imperial order that vast resources in rural China could not be mobilized for the initiation of a nationwide industrialization process. An important question we must solve in our book, which has never been answered in the myriad economic books on Chinese reform, is thus: why did a momentum arise in the 1980s that did not in the early decades of the twentieth century?

Indeed, this question had haunted historians for a long time in modified form: why did China fail to engulf the stream of the industrial revolution at the end of the eighteenth and early nineteenth century despite its cultural refining, its technological advance up to the middle of the eighteenth century, and its long-standing political institutions? A new book by Rosenthal and Wong (2011), who use a political economy approach in a comparative way for China and Europe, brings forth persuasive explanation that runs from politics to economics. We will use similar methodology to revisit the historical question of the so-called "backwardation" of China in industrialization and the breakthrough in the 1980s. We build a formal model in Chapter 2 upon the assumption of a self-sustaining rural economy based upon a tightly knit family structure to explain why such social structure strongly hampered the transfer of labor from the rural countryside to large-scale urban industry.

Dialectics of Chinese reform: a *sui generis* brand of capitalism

Following Braudel's methodological findings, our book exposes the co-evolution in economic structures and social institutions. For theoretical reasons explained above, the reform is put in historical perspective backward and extended forward in a two-decade prospective. In the following outline we provide the Ariane thread for reading the book in highlighting the fundamental principle and logic of the reform, summarizing the stages of reform so far and sketching our hypotheses on the future direction to sustainable growth.

The most fundamental principle is the perpetuity of imperial sovereignty through more than two millennia. China is a central unitary state in the continuity of the empire. The Communist Party has restored the legitimacy formerly personified by the Emperor. The Party must preserve its absolute control on the political system. To achieve this overall objective it must align the interests of the bureaucrats on the common political good of stability and provide the people with growing real income and improved conditions of life. Therefore the state must be strategist and developmental. The political leadership must run the economy so that it produces growing wealth more efficiently. Two consequences follow: first, market economy is a tool, not finality; second, opening is a condition of efficiency and leads to an operational economic directive: "catching up and overtaking the West."

Chapter 1 explains the amalgam of tradition and modernity in the culture of the people that helps us to understand the resiliency of social institutions. Throughout imperial history the pervasiveness of social networks grounded in family structures interacted with the central structure of the empire that stood up most of the time thanks to the mandarin bureaucratic system. A light political and administrative structure was able to provide the collective goods that linked together numerous communities scattered in the countryside.

Drawing from this characterization of the social structure, Chapter 2 revisits the works of the historians who have long debated on the reasons why it has hampered the drive to industrialization. It then provides a formal macroeconomic model to show why this social structure prevented the concentration of labor force in the cities as a prerequisite to the rise of industrial capitalism.

Because the unitary state was undermined after the demise of the empire, the first half of the twentieth century was an era of social chaos and dramatic economic setback overall with an average real income that regressed in absolute terms over 50 years. Sovereignty was restored with victory in the civil war by the Communist Party led by Mao Zedong. The socialist period that followed is studied and revalued in Chapter 3. Contrary to what is asserted on superficial economic analysis, it is shown in Chapter 3 that the socialist period 1950–78 is crucial to understanding the political economy of reform and the success of the first stage in the 1980s. The forceful concentration of resources under Communist Party rule and central planning was able to mobilize the labor force and industrialize the country with positive side effects on the productivity of agriculture in the 1970s.

Part of Chapters 3, 4, and 5 study the rationale of the reform, its contradictions, and how they were overcome. As explained above, our understanding is widely different from standard economics. The reform is the joint transformation of economic structures and institutions. It is pluralistic and feeds on the contradictions it generates in an endless process. It has no reference to any ideal model whatsoever. The meaning of reform is not teleologic; it is immanent to practice. Thanks to the continuity of the political leadership, the reform can be gradual, informed by a long-run view and tested in pragmatic experiment. Strategic planning aims at harmony, which is the balance of forces that contributes to strengthening the sovereignty of the state. Subsequently capitalist interests will never be so powerful that they threaten the paramount supremacy of the state. It is why the state will keep a large domain of sovereign ownership and regulate finance tightly.

Because it feeds on its own contradictions, the reform goes through crises which are transitions from one stage to another. It changes from one step to the next but it remains the same in the legitimacy of its political goal. The dynamic of the reform is a kind of spiral. At stage n a path of growth is under way that fosters latent contradictions which are endogenous but can be magnified by external shocks. They surface in the open in social tensions, while growth has been slowing down, which threatens harmony. The contradictions reverberate politically within the

Party of 84 million members, fostering an opaque process of deliberation, until a compromise is reached with eventual shifts in power among groups of interests, all being united by the overall objective of the integrity of the unitary state.

Chapters 3 to 5 show that there have been two very different stages of reform with a difficult and bitterly conflicting transition between 1989 and 1993. Chapters 3 and 4 deal with the domestic economy. Chapter 5 deals with the foreign opening in trade, then in finance. The second stage of reform being overwhelmingly biased toward heavy intensive accumulation after World Trade Organization (WTO) entry, endogenous contradictions have grown, leading to over accumulation and induced social tensions. The apex of the world financial crisis in the fall of 2008 has magnified the inner contradictions of the ongoing growth regime, giving rise to a new and perilous transition. Because every transition is an open process, the Chinese reform enters a stage that can only be researched in building prospective scenarios based upon dynamics induced by the working of social contradictions. These prospects are studied in Chapters 6 and 7. According to our knowledge, the systematic analysis of policy changes in Chapter 7, guided by a macro view of the direction of the reform encapsulated in a model of sustainable growth described in Chapter 6, is an original attempt to get a comprehensive understanding of strategic planning in China for the present decade and beyond.

The transition to a sustainable growth regime is based upon less capital and energy intensive growth and a social compact to reduce inequalities and provide universal health coverage. The provision of public goods and the drive to environment-friendly urbanization are the linchpins of strategic planning to transform the growth regime in the next two decades. The political implications are pinpointed in the structure of government. The conflicts of interests to overcome are emphasized. The scope of the reforms to accomplish in the price structure, in the tax system, in land ownership, and in social transfers should not be underestimated.

Finally Chapter 8 comes back to where the book has started: the diversity of models of capitalism and their dependency on political institutions. It argues that the culture of social networks in China is strong enough to enhance civil society in ways that can inform and put pressure on the political mechanism within the Party, so that a viable form of capitalism can emerge and enhance social harmony. All in all, the whole book justifies the title: China's development: capitalism and empire.

Part I

Putting China today in historical perspective

1 The role of history and culture in the resilience of China's institutional framework

In the 30 years of reform most Western economists not acquainted with China have repeatedly announced its doom. A return to state planning or the opposite, a collapse of the political regime, Soviet style, was foreseen. Policies and performances have often been gauged against the ideology of the perfect foresight market equilibrium fostered by unbridled individual rationality. Reality, however, has put this flawed perspective into question. Obviously, Chinese reform is not a convergent process toward any normative concept of an optimal economic equilibrium. It is an ongoing co-evolutionary process of economic structures and social institutions.

The theory of regulation of capitalism, contrary to orthodox economic thinking, which elevates the market as an all-powerful coordination mechanism, acknowledges that institutions of civil society, in-between markets and the state, interact constantly with the economic dynamics. Not only do they play an important role in alleviating tensions between economic actors, setting conventions and informal rules of behavior that foster trust and reduce uncertainty, their consistency or their conflict with one another contributes to defining a mode of economic growth that evolves over time. Such institutions are rooted in the past and, anchored in the culture of the people, transmitted through generations. They shape beliefs and patterns of behavior, and make valuable contributions in absorbing shocks. Therefore understanding and exploring China's path today requires us to recognize the peculiarities of China's historical trajectory, its social fabric, and collective memories that derive from very ancient cultural traits but still exercise strong influence on the behavior of its population and the configuration of its society.

Stemming from the distinct process of state formation of imperial China, this chapter attempts to identify the basic social institutions in Chinese tradition that have played eminent roles in stabilizing social orders while being conducive to creativity and continuous change. These social institutions evolved over time but, together, they formed a self-consistent system that has contributed strongly to the relatively uninterrupted continuity of Chinese civilization. They are of essential importance for us in understanding where the sense of togetherness lies in China and how this sense of togetherness translates into a mode of legitimization of the state that is profoundly different from the democratic Western states and logic of economic dynamics divergent from the classic growth models based on European experiences.

Early history of state formation of imperial China

Chinese civilization is far from being the most ancient in human history. Both Egypt and ancient Mesopotamia emerged much earlier than China. However, for one recognizably similar civilization to remain from pre-Christian age down to modern times, China stands out distinctively. Especially long-lasting was the Imperial Age of China, which started after the unification under the Qin (221–206 BC) and consolidated during the Han dynasty (202 BC–AD 220). The succeeding regimes in the following 2,000 years maintained key Han imperial institutions. Many so-called "Chinese" cultural, social, and political features were formed during this long imperial age and have far-reaching influences on the behaviors of Chinese people even today. Most of the traits synthesized in this chapter would be oriented on this historic period.

Imperial China is not simply a centralized and united empire. Its true identity lies with the maintenance and reproduction of certain social and political orders. The formation of these orders was a complex and ever-evolving historical process shaped by both the given circumstances and chance factors. In this part of the book we display the earliest formational stages of imperial China's basic orders by outlining the history from Western Zhou (1122–770 BC) and especially Eastern Zhou (770–256 BC) to the early Han Empire (202 BC–AD 220). During this historical period, especially around the turning point of Qin's unification (221 BC), Chinese civilization experienced fundamental socio-political developments which altered how Chinese people interact and coordinate. These developments eventually enabled the emergence of macro orders with which we identify imperial China, or even today's Chinese civilization.

The decay of the feudal system

Under the reign of Western Zhou, China resembled much of feudal Europe. The first kings of Zhou parceled out the kingdom as large fiefs among the king's sons and brothers, who assumed titles equivalent to duke, marquis, and count. The king (also called "the son of heaven") had strong feudal monarchical power and was able to allot newly conquered territories to his faithful followers or kinsmen.

However, in the Eastern Zhou period this feudal system began to collapse. Certain vassals grew more and more independent along with the increment of their powers. They defied the authority of "the son of heaven" by annexing the smaller fiefs and warring among themselves. This was a period of political fragmentation. The first half of the period is referred to as the Spring and Autumn period (770–404 BC) when the Zhou kings continued to reign by default. Over time, military conflicts became fiercer and more frequent to an extent that the second half of Eastern Zhou is vividly named the Warring States period (403–221 BC). By then the Zhou king had completely lost his power and all smaller fiefs were conquered and absorbed by the seven largest states whose rulers began calling themselves kings in 335 BC as a symbol of total denial of the sovereignty of Zhou.

The Warring States

During the Warring States period China exhibited completely different behaviors compared with the later imperial one. In fact, it is far-fetched to call the Warring States "China," as a unified Chinese identity was purposefully dismantled. Brutal and continuous wars required the people of each state to seriously consider the question of who belonged to "us." Strong national identities were developed with the state one came from rather than with the Zhou kingdom. Hence each of the major states had its distinct identity based on its own history and specific culture. The uniqueness of these identities was accentuated in order to arouse sharp patriotic emotions and foster tighter military unity. The natural family ties were intentionally cut or minimized in particularly aggressive states like Qin. Constant warfare required iron control by the governments over people and land. Family-based societal organization was too loose to serve this purpose. Often strong family attachments would even hinder direct commands from the state to individuals, thus sabotaging the efficiency of military and economic mobilization. The most famous case against family ties in the Warring States period was the reforms applied by Shang Yang (390–338 BC) in Qin state. Not only did he apply a strict direct domicile registration system to every individual Qin resident, he also forcefully broke the patriarchal lineage. No two male adults, given they were father and son, or brothers, were allowed to live in the same household. Tax contributions were doubled for those who did not follow that policy. The warring states usually took active roles in supporting trade and other commercial activities, with the purpose of seizing higher fiscal revenues to sustain their armies and to build massive defense walls. The emergence of government-led coin casting serves as proof of this pro-commerce attitude. Politically, centralized bureaucratic control began to be favored and thus created demands for professional administrators. For the aristocrats who had lost their fiefs and status, the opening of those positions served as great opportunities for social advancement. Many of them started different schools carrying diversified socio-political proposals and travelled from court to court in search of a wise king to implement their theories, or at least give them a job. Philosophical thinking and political theories flourished. Among those wandering scholars were the most influential philosophers in Chinese history, such as Confucius (around 551–479 BC), Mencius (around 370–290 BC), Laozi (around 600–470 BC), and Zhuangzi (around 369–286 BC).

Regardless of how deeply Confucianism and Taoism were ingrained into Chinese civilization in the imperial age, they were by no means the dominant schools of philosophy in the Warring States age. The chief early competitor of Confucius was Mozi, born around or soon after the death of Confucius. In Mozi's theories we can easily pick up elements that resemble Christian teaching, or even Puritanical ones. Mozi preached "universal love" as against the "graded love" endorsed by Confucius, which was dependent on the specific relationships among individuals. Mozi believed that the interest of all would be better served if "everyone would love every other person as much as he loves himself" (Mozi, IV, 14). He was also strictly utilitarian. He advocated measures to enrich the country, increase the population, and bring order to the state. He envisioned rigidly disciplined organizations in which the subordinate at each level would follow the lead of his superior in all matters. It is believed that, for a while, his ideas may have had greater currency than Confucianism (Fairbank and Reischauer 1979: 51).

Another school that prevailed first in Qin state and then the whole of China after the unification under Qin was the Legalists. They were hard-core. The only thing that mattered for them was how to make a prosperous and militarily strong national state. And the only way to achieve this objective, in their mind, was by setting up strict laws and harsh punishments. All aspects of life should be regulated so as to produce maximum wealth and military might. Counting on people's moral virtues was regarded naïve. This school reached its ultimate triumph at the famous "Burning of the Books" event, which took place immediately after the centralized Qin Empire was founded. During this event, all works of other schools were destroyed, and only those of the Legalists remained.

Had Chinese history and civilization gone on with the trend described above, it would be plausible to envision a China (more possibly in plural form) similar to European-style national states. Constant external threats to the regimes of the ruling class would have inspired strong political ambition and nationalist sentiments. The domestic societal organization within the state would have been much more compact than a family-based agrarian society. A more pluralist society would have emerged. The core social relationship would not have been that among the members of organic families but that among clearly institutionalized organizations (such as religious cults, city states, or national states). Cities, with heavy walls for defense purpose, would have taken a central role in the construction of a state, instead of the poorly protected rural area. A sharp division between citizens and peasants might have emerged, with quite possibly a superior class composed of warriors. Political power would likely have turned to local military and financial powers to strengthen the regime, but at the same time been hijacked by the voices of those local powers. Formal rules, including written laws, would have quite possibly been the main mechanisms to regulate the coordination among the population, instead of the often arbitrary and amorphous regulatory mechanisms that prevailed in imperial China such as authoritative persons, "*guanxi*" (social networks), and moral values. And, of course, Confucianism would have never achieved its prominence, as it was so impractical in gathering the population to counter external threats. A better-organized school such as Mozi's would have served well as a uniting ideology. At some point in history, China could have even had its own version of "renaissance" or produced its own Montesquieu.

Yet, it so happened that Chinese history did not go that way.

The unification under Qin and Han

In 221 BC Qin's king, Ying Zheng (259–210 BC), united China. He called himself Shi Huang Di (literally "the First Emperor"). Following the advice of his Legalist chief minister Li Si (?–208 BC), the First Emperor was determined not to divide the country up again. He carried out harsh reforms to foster a united Chinese identity and a centralized political structure. All feudal states were abolished but new, small provinces were established and were under the direct command of the emperor. Weights, measures, coinage, and even the axle lengths of wagons were standardized. Thanks to him, the Chinese written language was consolidated in a single form, which is practically the same as it is today. He laid out a radiating system of roads throughout his empire, beat back the barbarians of the north, and built up the Great Wall as a permanent defense and explicit mark of China's northern frontier. He conquered the far south, the Canton region, which had never before been part of China. Although the harshness of his reign finally devastated his own dynasty shortly after his death, China was radically transformed during the 11 years of his reign.

After several years of civil wars, when Liu Bang, better known by his post-humous title, Han Gaozu, established the Han dynasty (206 BC–AD 222), the first long-enduring dynasty of the new unified China, a new era in Chinese history opened. The Chinese people, rulers and farmers alike, found themselves in quite different circumstances from those faced by their ancestors. A massive population (59,594,978 was the reported population of a census carried out in AD 2) sharing the same language cohabiting in so vast a territory had never been achieved before.

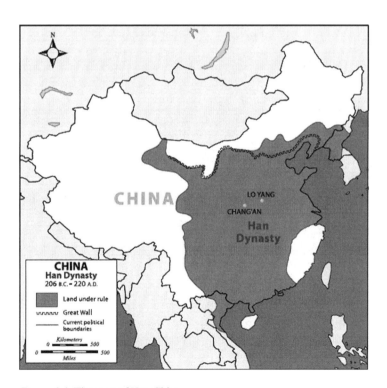

Figure 1.1 The map of Han China.

Source: Minneapolis Institute of Arts. Accessed from http://www.artsmia.org/art-of-asia/history/pdf/china-han-dynasty.pdf (February 2012)

The once frequent life-or-death battles suddenly disappeared from the everyday life of the ordinary Chinese. The only dangerous neighbors of China, the nomadic Tartar peoples, were concentrated on the northern frontier. Central government allocated heavy military strength to guard it with the help of such defense works as the Great Wall. But in the west China was naturally guarded by the Himalaya Mountains, inhabited then by harmless or weak savage tribes. The long coast on the southeast side was also naturally calm as, at that time, travelling through the Pacific Ocean was still infeasible. To the south the Chinese advanced into what is now Vietnam, absorbing smaller tribes along the way.

When wars became remote, identity became united and government singular, the logics of Chinese social and political structuring altered, and civilization had the opportunity to evolve on a fundamentally different path.

The predominant issue for the survival of the empire and the continuity of a royal family's regime was no longer to increase military strength but to sustain domestic order. The Han dynasty inherited the Qin's centrally controlled bureaucratic system. A large body of bureaucrats[1] was selected for their merit, not birth. The emperor had direct and absolute power over the personnel system of this vast bureaucracy. Integrating educated elites into a centralized bureaucratic system was a stone that hit two birds. Not only did the emperor gain considerable help with his rule, but he also deprived local elite groups of their human resources and political independence. For most of imperial history, the Chinese royal house endeavored and succeeded in establishing direct political control over its population while curbing the powers of other institutionally distinctive groups, which could have grown into independent political identities. This extreme centralization of formal political organization removed the root of political fragmentation and the basis of a pluralist society. Instead of searching for compromises with aristocratic, religious, and financial groups as their European counterparts did, the imperial Chinese emperors instead preferred and were able to rely directly on farmers, especially scattered small-scale, self-sufficient rural families. Agricultural taxes were always the main source of fiscal revenue for the imperial regimes in China. Except for the slim layer of scholar-bureaucrats, farmers made up the overwhelming majority of the population. The larger part of private wealth was in the hands of landlords. There was no caste system or any blood-determined aristocracy system to define who would be farmers and who would be landlords. All depended on the natural order of market, work, merit, and a little spin of the wheel of fortune.

The family-based social fabric

No matter how many scholar-bureaucrats a Han emperor employed, with the technological limitations of 200 BC any hope of managing everything in such a vast geographical area as China was frantic. Thus the Han government was not constituted to provide what we today would consider the full services of government. Apart from sustaining the ruling and living of the royal house, Han administration concentrated their resources in providing public goods and services that were of national importance. To be more specific, the bureaucracy managed tax-collecting (mostly poll tax and agricultural tax); national defense; arbitration of some civil disputes; performing ceremonies; and undertaking large public projects such as flood control, major roads, and canal constructions. The only contacts the vast population had with the government was to pay taxes and, for the peasants, to schedule one month of free labor in addition for the government every year. The micro-organization of Chinese society was somewhat spontaneous under these circumstances. As formally institutionalized organizations between state and the people were strictly watched, a strong civil society based on informal institutions and organic organizations, especially lineage-related ones, prospered. The key for understanding traditional Chinese society is, therefore, the understanding of the role of families and lineage systems in societal organization and quotidian life. Even in contemporary China these informal institutions still play an indispensable role for local governance (Tsai 2007).

In other words, *imperial* China had two major layers. The Han imperial government, and the succeeding imperial governments in the next two millenniums, were in fact this concentrated group floating above a sea of self-organized local agricultural communities (Fairbank and Reischauer 1979: 61), most of which were based upon families, or to be more specific, a patriarchal lineage system dominated by the father–son relationship. Apparently, this type of societal organization does not fit into any "modern" national state configurations developed under the European tradition. As a result, examining the corresponding economic structure, political arrangement, and legitimacy of imperial China according to European experiences would be ill advised.

Why patriarchal families?

The reasons why Han Chinese adopted the patriarchal family as their spontaneous way of societal organization could be manifold. Minimized state intervention and relatively fewer external threats, thanks to the geographical and political features of China, had definitely created space for the growth of the family system. The economic structure may have also contributed. Han civilization was based much more profoundly on crop agriculture than European civilization was. The fact that animal husbandry and commerce played a lesser role in the overall economy means that the Chinese population had fewer opportunities for geographical movements. Crop agriculture fixed the population with their land. As Professor Feng Youlan (1895–1990) pointed out,

> The farmers have to live on their land, which is immovable, and the same is true of the scholar landlords. Unless one has special talent, or is especially lucky, one has to live where one's father or grandfather lived, and where one's children will continue to live. That is to say, the family in the wider sense must live together for economic reasons. Thus there developed the Chinese family system...
>
> (Feng 1948: 21)

Deeming economic structure the only determinant of social fabric is debatable, but we agree this influence cannot be excluded.

Organizing the whole society on a family-based system is also consistent with the socio-political ideals of several main philosophical schools that emerged in the Eastern Zhou period and have influenced Chinese civilization ever since. The most extreme would be Laozi, founder of Taoism, who advocated total laissez-faire, so that families could control their own lives with no pressure from any other social or political group larger than a village. However, the school that had most influence on consolidating the family system in China was Confucianism, which elaborately connects patriarchal family order to social and even political ones.

As with many other Chinese philosophers in history, the highest political objective for Confucius was peace and social stability for everywhere "under the heaven" ("tian xia"). Confucius believed that long-term social stability could not be achieved without respecting the innate psychology of human beings. "Sympathy" ("ren") was thus identified by Confucius as the key human affection to bond people with and to base his ideal society upon. And the strongest sympathy is usually felt among those who are closest, such as family members. The farther away and more unfamiliar people are, the less they would feel for each other. Thus a Confucian society can be envisioned as billions of overlapping circles. Every individual is at the center of a circle. The intensity of sympathy (social bonds) he can feel for others wanes with the radius distance of these others from him. This is the "graded love" we mentioned before. Extremely self-centered as it may seem at first glance, this concept actually represents altruistic goals, because no one is alone in this world and everyone falls into certain social relationships, the most basic of all being family relationships: "Ren consists in loving others" (Analects, XII, 22). If every father can behave as a loving father to his sons, and every son acts as a son who loves and respects his father, if elder brother and younger brothers, husband and wife, elder and junior, ruler and subject, and so on, really love the ones they care about and do what they should do for their loved ones, then people are able to fulfill all their obligations in society and be a worthy member of it. Moreover, as everyone is in different social circles, carries different social roles, and has different people close to him, this graded love can hence weave a complex net encompassing the whole society, and serve as a universal bond among people and lay down the foundation of social stability and peace.

Thus the logic of structuring an ideal society, in Confucius's mind, is based upon families, and to be more specific, patriarchal ones. Social relationships outside a family are often translated into personalized terms too. The Chinese often compare their teachers to their father and call their best friends brothers and sisters. The political system is also an embodiment of family order. The emperor has supreme authority over the country just as a father does over a family. This might be the reason why Han Wudi (156–87 BC), one of the most influential Han emperors, who was in fact Legalist in nature, chose to use Confucian principles as criteria in selecting his bureaucrats.

It is amazing how Chinese history completely changed its tide in less than a hundred years. The Legalists, who enjoyed exclusive power in Qin, were barred from any official position in the court of Han Wudi, while Confucianism was established as the official teaching for the empire. This ideological and political arrangement further boosted the legitimacy and popularity of patriarchal families as the major design of societal organization in China. The predominance of Confucianism and the prevalence of the family system in China were two mutually reinforcing historical processes. The moral foundation Confucianism laid down solidified the Chinese family system, made it the most resilient societal organization yet known and, in turn, family-based social fabric enabled China to mature its distinctive civilization based on Confucian ethical ideals.

The lengthy description above tries to explain one thing: why it was that a family-based social fabric instead of any other form triumphed in China. Yet we know we would be unable to enumerate all the reasons for this. History cannot be fully reflected on paper; and the formation of any culture is not a lineal or mechanical process. Chance played its role here and there. But whatever the chances were, after the Eastern Zhou period Chinese civilization increasingly formed upon families and other lineage systems. A complete Confucian moral system provided theoretical guidance to this societal organization and expanded it to other domains, such as economic, legal, and political organizations in China. From Song (960–1279) times on, this civilization and its social institutions became so embedded and compact that even the Mongol and Manchu conquests could not cause significant social changes, until around the mid-nineteenth century. And this unique social fabric has led China onto a historic trajectory of its own kind.

Implications of the family-based social fabric

The implications of this family-based social fabric are profound. The following three sub-parts closely examine the key features of this family-based imperial Chinese society, relating to political structure, social mobility, economic units, and the relating concept of property right. But before that we would like to remind our readers again that the logic and mechanisms of structuring imperial China are disparate from the European paradigms we often take for granted. As family became the center of everyone's life, social units that are of great significance to the European tradition, such as the individual, the church, the guild, the city, and even the national state, receded considerably. Instead, an extended civil society compactly woven by overlapping economic and social ties became the main form of societal organization in China.

This means, first, the functions of family were much broader, encompassing also the services that we now consider "public" or "social." Very different from the nowadays-popular "nuclear families," ideal traditional Chinese families were extended. If the parents were alive, no children, however old they were, could live separated from them. If the grandparents were alive, then all three generations of people would live together. Within this extended family almost all properties were owned in common. If one family member was in difficulty or need, the rest of the family had unavoidable obligations to help solve the problem or fulfill the need. Outside the immediate family there were still other relatives that could be traced back five generations. Terminology of all these kinships was extremely complex. In the oldest Chinese dictionary, Er Ya, more than a hundred terms can be found for various kinships (Feng 1948: 21). Other than the families, there were still clans and other lineage systems, which often maintained ancestral temples, common estates, granaries for charity uses, and clan schools. It was from within those family systems and the interpersonal networks embedded in them, instead of churches or states, that a Chinese individual living in the imperial era obtained his/her main source of economic sustenance and security, as well as necessary social services such as education and medical care. It was also those systems that provided social contacts and psychological support/consolation, mediated conflicts, helped the poor and lonely, and even served as the religious body through ancestor worship.

Second, in many cases family substituted individuals as the smallest unit of society,[2] thus blurring the identity of each individual. Direct contacts between an individual and a formal and institutionalized organization such as the state were therefore minimal. This altered both the behavior of individuals and the nature of the state, relative to their European counterparts. Unlike a citizen of ancient Athens, a Chinese who lived in the imperial era did not need to go to the city assembly and vote on legislations and executive bills. The Chinese were not used to institutionalized organization and hence were usually shy in claiming their social rights. Political decisions were left to the scholar-bureaucrats and "the dictatorship of majority" was not a favored decision-making mechanism inside a family either.

Moreover, the family system also distinguishes the logic of social coordination in imperial China from that of European tradition. For a Chinese individual who lived in the imperial era, human relationships ("*guanxi*"), especially the relationships among family members, were the center of life. In this inescapable net woven by extremely complex personal ties into which every Chinese was born, harmony is crucial. The coordination among people in a family hence was achieved by negotiation, compromise, and, most importantly, through moral virtues which demanded that everyone "behave properly" and fulfilled their obligations to the family according to their positions in it, given either by birth or marriage. This propriety of behavior is what Confucius called "li." As Fairbank and Reischauer observed:

> In a pluralistic society, like that of the modern West, the many forces of church and state, capital and labor, government and private enterprise are balanced under a rule of law. Instead, in Chinese life the personal virtues of probity and loyalty, sincerity and benevolence, inculcated by the family system, provided the norms for social conduct. Law was a necessary tool of administration; but personal morality was the foundation of society. Far from being anarchic because of the weakness of the legal concept, Chinese society was firmly knit together by Confucianism. This great ethical institution occupied in China much of the place filled by both law and religion in the West.
>
> (Fairbank and Reischauer 1979: 16)

Even if modern China has significantly transformed, and father–son relationships may no longer be the dominant social tie, the 2,000 years' prevalence of family system and this interpersonal network-based view of society is still influencing people's perceptions of self, values, government, rights, social inequality, etc. Understanding this system is the cornerstone in understanding Chinese history and China today.

A bureaucratic political system with absolute central authority and decentralized administration

Tracing European history for a while, one would quite possibly conclude the irreconcilability between autocratic regimes and decentralization. Ever since the fifth century European history has been plagued with the power struggles of myriad political entities (aristocratic lines, ecclesiastic units, and the later urban bourgeoisie). All these institutionally distinctive organizations were able to challenge national authority for the preservation and expansion of their own forces. They had the ability to weaken a ruling house's claim over certain land and corrupt the tax base by claiming local taxes themselves. They also succeeded in integrating their influences over the national authority into the political process itself. Oftentimes the switching monarchies relied on the support of certain power groups to establish their ruling over a territory, and in return those monarchies' political legitimacy would require the acceptance of those supporting groups through principles such as political representations to ensure that those groups' voices could be heard and interests be attended. When the delicate balance between the autocratic regime and the other distinctive entities was broken in the labyrinth of a power grid, either the regime would be devastated because of a lack of legitimacy, or the power relations among all entities would be reshuffled. From this perspective, centralized regimes and other institutionally distinctive local groups are competitors and the monarchy would be reluctant to delegate more authorities to local elites, especially when the resources available for central government were already limited in meeting military expenditures.

However, under different circumstances central authority and decentralization are not necessarily incompatible. If the society is not pluralistic, if the legitimacy of political power has an alternative basis, and if the central authority is strong enough and unchallenged, central authority and decentralization can co-exist in a mutually reinforcing way. When properly managed and aided by particular institutions, delegating certain political powers to the local level can emancipate local economic forces, hence increasing the tax base and fiscal revenue. At the same time, administrative burdens on the central government can be mitigated to local groups that master the local situation and have the potential of delivering high-quality social services. Improved welfare levels of the population in turn could enhance the legitimacy of the central power. Imperial China, especially the second half of imperial China, may serve as one example of such an alternative.

In the following, we closely examine the political system of imperial China. Although the system has been through significant evolution in a period of more than 2,000 years, the key features of political logic and institutional design remained consistent. We discover the basis of political legitimacy, ruling mechanisms, and institutions that were unknown in the European tradition. The unchallengeable authority of the emperor and the effective centralized, hierarchical bureaucracy eliminated step by step the existence of any formal entity that bore independent political identity and authority outside the bureaucratic system. Yet it is precisely because of this absence of competitors for ultimate authority that the central government's relation with local elites was so distinct from that in Europe. The Chinese central government felt more and more at ease in delegating local social responsibilities.

Sole and absolute central authority

The absolute authority of a Chinese emperor was based first on the traditional Chinese view of family arrangement. The patriarchal hierarchical order inside a family also spilled over into the political realm. Just as the family order was centered on the father, the ideal political order was centered on an authoritarian ruler. The emperor was unquestionably the father of the whole population and stayed at the apex of hierarchy. As the most basic moral virtue in a traditional Chinese family was filial piety, the indispensable political morality in imperial China was loyalty to the emperor, who would make hierarchical cooperation as it is in a family. The position of emperor was further elevated by the cosmological theories of an important Confucian philosopher, Dong Zhongshu (179–104 BC). In those theories, the emperor was deemed unique among human beings for his capacity to link the realm of heaven, which symbolizes the natural order of the universe, and earth, which symbolizes secular society. Agricultural harvests, high welfare levels of the population, and uninterrupted peace were accredited to the emperor, even if he did not directly interfere in everyday affairs. However, if he was morally corrupt or did not accomplish his role, the balance between heaven and earth would be damaged and natural calamities, such as floods, droughts, and earthquakes, would occur. Ever since the Han dynasty, the double roles of emperor as the father of the whole population and as the link between heaven and earth had become an intrinsic part of Chinese imperial ideology. Both roles put the emperor in a superior position to other citizens of the country, and gave him unrivaled authority.

The question is: why was the Han emperor able to foster the political ideology described above which favored his authority in such an exclusive sense? To answer this question, we need to look at the following issues: power repartition within the country; the logic and legitimacy of imperial order; and the mechanisms for maintaining domestic social order.

The foremost is the issue of power repartition within the country. As mentioned above, in Europe political power was divided among three main groups: the aristocrats, the church, and the urban elites. State-makers had to compete with them or compromise with them in order to keep his legitimacy and his claims over land and taxation. The situation in imperial China was utterly different. Ever since the unification of China under the First Emperor, Chinese rulers lost legitimate competitors for state power. The scholar-bureaucrats and military generals were clear subordinates to the emperor in a bureaucratic system. Aristocracy waned. Religious bodies had never been totally separated from the secular power[3] and even potential foreign intrusions were contained most of the time. The claim of the emperor over the whole territory was absolute. And that was not just any territory. The imperial Chinese territory had no borders: it can be every inch of soil "under the heaven." In the Chinese perception, whenever the Chinese government succeeded in incorporating a territory into the political and cultural order of imperial China, it was considered part of the country. And, once it was integrated, the emperor would be the ultimate owner of this piece of land. This concept rooted out the possibility of unrestricted independent power of any locality, especially toward the later stages of the empire. In the early eras of imperial China, central government still faced serious threats from overwhelmingly powerful localities. Some of them even enjoyed recognition from the central government. Han Gaozu, for example, rewarded his old comrades with large territories to govern. In the Tang dynasty, military towns also enjoyed strong autonomy. But, as imperial institutions evolved to their maturity, these cases became rarer over time. In the year 969, the first emperor of the Song dynasty eliminated the power of all the generals of the remaining autonomic military towns over a banquet. After that, independent local authorities in China totally died out.

The emperor also had total control over taxation. No one else had the legal capacity to impose formal fiscal claims. Throughout imperial China, fiscal revenue depended mostly on agricultural and poll taxes. In the later period the monopoly of salt also brought in considerable income. The composition of fiscal income reflects the agrarian economy of imperial China as well as the political intention of the ruling house. Anchoring farmers as the major providers of fiscal revenue posed the least political threats to the emperor's regime. Scattered, organically organized, small land-owning families had much less possibility of challenging the central regime than magnate families that possessed concentrated wealth and power. To illustrate this point, the European states could serve as a perfect counter-example. Confronted with continuous fiscal shortage because of heavy military expenditures, European states tended to seize as much fiscal resources as they could. However, as local aristocrats or clergies usually claimed land, agricultural tax collection was not always effective. Hence the ruling houses of Europe frequently relied on commercial taxes or fell prey to public debts. The result was either the loss of political independence of their regimes to the urban bourgeoisie and financiers, or endless expansion for new unclaimed resources. Chinese rulers suffered from neither of these outcomes. Even when China suffered fiscal crises, the government could still largely maintain the structure of its fiscal revenue. Thanks to the relatively small burden of military spending, Chinese royal houses were usually able to solve the problem of fiscal deficiency by shrinking expenditures. The most frequently applied measures included cutting administrative costs and subsidies for the royal family, as well as suspending large-scale constructions. Higher taxes would also be imposed in times of financial difficulty. Owing to an effective bureaucratic system and firm control over land, the imperial Chinese governments more or less succeeded in meeting their financial needs under such a land-based tax regime. The Song dynasty might be an exception. With constant military threats from the north, the Song dynasty relied on commercial sources, which provided over half of its administration's fiscal income (Wong 1997: 95).

Although the structure of taxation did not change dramatically, concrete mechanisms of tax collection evolved over time. The key variations surrounded the tax rate, types of tax settlement, and the form of imposition. Generally speaking, the agricultural tax rate throughout the imperial period was kept low for the purpose of protecting the tax base. In the Han dynasty, agricultural tax was a certain percentage (1/15 or 1/30) of production of the year; and later dynasties often charged a quota according to the surface and quality of land. Types of tax settlement evolved with the development of commercial economy. The general trend was from labor, to primary products, to handicrafts, and finally to money after tax reform in the sixteenth century. Tax imposition could take individuals as the unit or households and other kinds of local groups, depending on the policies.

Following the analysis above, the fundamental divergence between the nature of a European state and that of imperial China should be evident. Under the perplexing network of heterogeneous political powers and facing endless competition from neighboring countries, European states had to seek compromises with noble, religious, and urban groups, and negotiate with them in order to obtain maximum fiscal income to achieve their core objective; i.e. to increase their military forces and secure their reign over a territory. Thus the legitimacy of a state government depended on the acceptance of those powerful elite groups mentioned above. Their interests and political claims had to be heard and addressed. This pattern served as the root of a number of modern political principles, especially the political representative system.

However, imperial China was built on profoundly different principles. The key objective of imperial China was the maintenance and reproduction of a social order. "…the emperor worked to develop and sustain a bureaucracy able to meet routine tasks of administration and respond to crisis swiftly and effectively" (Wong 1997: 102). The legitimacy of the imperial Chinese regime did not come from the political representation of key political actors, but from the delivery of basic welfare for the population, especially farmers, who were the principal providers of fiscal revenue. The importance of agriculture was repeatedly accentuated by most of the imperial dynasties, emperors, and the scholar-bureaucrats. Protection of agriculture was sometimes achieved at the expense of other sectors, especially commerce. In the Han dynasty, in order to allow rural areas to recover from years of warfare, the agricultural tax rate was reduced to 1/30. In order to make up fiscal deficits, heavy taxes were levied on merchants instead. Key and lucrative industries, such as iron and salt production, were monopolized by the state. To enhance the performance of the agricultural sector, elevate the welfare level of its population, and sustain social stability, Chinese imperial governments also devoted great efforts to constructing and maintaining large-scale public infrastructural projects than did their European counterparts in the same era. The most notable were irrigation systems, flood-prevention projects especially those along the Yellow River, and the Great Canal that connected the fertile Yangtse Delta with Beijing. The imperial Chinese government also mediated the commodities markets that were of critical importance to people's lives and resultantly to social stability. Large-scale government-run grain dealing originated in the Han dynasty and developed hugely in the Qing dynasty. A sizable national granary system was built accordingly. At the peak of the Qing dynasty, this national granary system had the ability to store several million tons of grain (Will and Wong 1991).

To consolidate this centralized and supreme authority, imperial Chinese sovereigns developed elaborate ruling mechanisms to enable the maintenance and reproduction of endorsed domestic political and social orders. The failure of the First Emperor demonstrated vividly that extreme concentration of administrative power, dictatorial decision-making, and overemphasis on sovereignty over human welfare in fact increased the fragility of an empire and jeopardized the long-term ruling of a royal house. As soon as a charismatic leader died, the whole system would crumble. Han rulers learnt lessons from their antecessors. They realized that building a sustainable political order over such a large territory as China, one could not only rely on rigid top-down fiats and unconditional obedience from the populace. What they needed was a system of political institutions that permitted absolute central authority over executive, fiscal, and juridical exercises, but which, at the same time, took advantage of supervised administrative delegation to civil society. And all should be under the guise of governing for the welfare of the people. To this end, the imperial Chinese political order features three main entwining ruling mechanisms:

1   A singular yet massive bureaucratic system with strictly centralized control over personnel management;
2   Extensive moral instructions over the officials and common people alike according to Confucian doctrines;
3   Strong coercive measures to ensure central authority and established social order.

The formal structure of government varied little throughout the imperial era of China. Unlike in Europe, a bureaucratic system was developed early. The country was run by a hierarchy of more than 10,000 professional bureaucrats who had no innate superiority in blood like the hereditary aristocrats in Europe. The emperor was at the vertex of this pyramid and every bureaucrat was subject to his immediate disposal. There were three main divisions in the central government: the executive, the military, and the censorate. The executive branch handled all daily administration; the military managed military deployments and actions; and the censorate was responsible for conveying complaints to the emperor, criticizing policies, and supervising the actions of officials and the emperor himself. Early Chinese empires only had two levels of local administration. The highest sub-national administrations were commanderies ("zhou").[4] Then each commandery was further divided into counties ("xian"). The numbers and geographical compartmentalization varied from period to period, but Chinese local administration kept this two-level structure until the Tang dynasty, which added a level ("dao") above the commanderies. The numerous Chinese towns and villages under counties did not have any formal form of government and thus were largely autonomous.

Except for certain routine tasks, no officials, either at the central level or local level, were empowered to make major decisions alone. As a matter of fact, even the emperor himself, who might have a final say, did not dictate policy formation. Nevertheless, every official had the obligation and right to propose and criticize policies. Those proposals and criticism passed through formalized channels all the way to the Imperial Court where every morning collective discussions, headed by the emperor, would take place until consensus was reached. After decisions were made, each official shared full responsibility for their enforcement. The performance of these officials was closely supervised through comprehensive regulations, agreed administrative codes, and disciplined reporting requirements. The conformity of their actions with the central directions was a major standard of evaluation and the bureaucrats would be promoted, transferred, demoted, dismissed, or even subjected to criminal punishments accordingly. The central government's – or, to be more specific, the emperor's – absolute control over personnel management of officials was the key in guaranteeing the implementation and enforcement of centrally made policies and the smooth execution of other crucial state functions such as military arrangements and tax collection; this in turn was the key in maintaining the central authority of the imperial Chinese emperor over this immense bureaucratic system.

Profound and extensive integration of moral instructions into the sustaining of sovereignty was another salient feature of the ruling mechanism of imperial China. A major reason why Chinese rulers were able to exploit ideological persuasion as a tool for enhancing their rule more than their European counterparts in similar historical periods might be related to the fact that, in imperial China, religious power and secular power were not separated. The emperor, who was the ultimate ruler on "earth," also served as the sole connection with "heaven" and acted as the only eligible priest in major national religious ceremonies, such as ancestral or heaven worship. As a result, there should be no fragmentation of the governance of people's physical presence and people's minds. Education, incontrovertibly, fell to the task of imperial government and would bolster the secular regime. The correct ethics to fulfill such a need, therefore, would be those that advocate stable hierarchical political and social orders where each individual behaves properly according to their position in this hierarchy. After the regimes of several Han emperors, Confucianism gradually emerged as the best fit. Wu emperor of Han (Han Wudi), who was ironically Legalist in nature, established the predominant position of Confucianism over other schools by setting up a state educational system and official selection system around Confucian studies. Five Confucian classics (*Book of Changes, Book of Documents, Book of Songs, Book of Rites*, and *Spring and Autumn Annals*) were chosen as the official textbooks in the Imperial Academy, the highest educational institute in the country; and candidates for government positions with a Confucian background were favored in the selection process. As Confucian learning became the gateway to political power, its popularity soon spread to every corner of the country. At the end of the Han dynasty, the notion that officials should be men trained in the Confucian classics had been taken for granted and the number of students in the Imperial Academy increased from a few dozen to more than 30,000 (Ebrey 1996: 78).

The advantages of Confucian doctrines for bolstering imperial rule in China were numerous. Except for the obvious good, such as the fact that Confucians officials were diligent, committed to principles, and loyal to their superiors, Confucians were also highly devoted to education, thus providing imperial China with an ample supply of educated men to carry out bureaucratic functions, and ardent educators to persuade the vast population to be obedient, dutiful, and hard-working. However, one of the greatest contributions of Confucianism to the sustainability of imperial rule in China might not have been a conscious choice for Han Wudi. Confucian teachings persuaded officials to view their appointment not only in terms of an employment relationship with the emperor but as a moral obligation to serve the welfare of the nation and the people. Accordingly, the loyalty they held towards the emperor was a disciplined one. It meant the highest respect but not blind compliance. The integrity of Confucian officials lay in their ability to stand against the emperor, to offer pertinent criticisms on the policies and behaviors of the ruler and fellow officials, and to actively seek measures for enhancing the level of welfare of the populace and underpin political stability. In consequence, Confucian morality created a countervailing factor over the seemingly unconstrained power of the emperor and a drive to protect the welfare of the seemingly unrepresented farmers. It was this balance of power that eventually sustained the political legitimacy of the imperial regime. When this balance deteriorated, cyclical renewal of regimes often occurred for their restoration.

The moral instructions in imperial China covered the whole population. Except for the Imperial Academy, imperial Chinese governments sponsored a network of Confucian schools all over the country. Every young man of good character had the right to enter them. Those who excelled in their studying of Confucian classics would be selected into the government through mechanisms such as sponsorship and examinations. This network of public schools declined in the Ming and Qing dynasties but were only to be replaced by ones that were financed by local elites or communities. Throughout the imperial history of China elite education was firmly oriented to Confucianism. For the less ambitious population, easily understandable booklets were drafted to explicate Confucian virtues and demonstrate what should be proper behavior for each member of a family and society. The people were also taught to respect scholarship; thus Confucian scholars were widely treated as local leaders even if they failed to be integrated formally into the administration. And these Confucian scholars had responsibility for cultivating local residents and guiding their behavior. To sum up, imperial Chinese government succeeded in manipulating the content of education for both the elites and common people; and morality was a crucial component of ruling.

Most certainly, Chinese emperors did not just rely on soft powers such as moral standards to rule their country. Various coercive measures were also applied to strengthen central authority. Similar to most other sovereignties, any action of treason or defiance of the emperor's authority would be severely punished, often with the death penalty. Geographical movements and institutionalized associations were also deemed as instable elements because they provided grounds for nurturing strong oppositional groups. Thanks to the Legalist tradition, the Chinese empire had a fairly complete system of written laws to regulate economic, social, and political orders. The imperial Chinese government also cleverly utilized the family-based social fabric to facilitate its supervision of people's behavior, amplifying the punitive consequence of a wrongdoing by targeting the family, instead of an individual, as the smallest legal unit. If one member of the family committed a crime, the whole family, or even the whole neighborhood, could suffer from joint liability. This institutional arrangement greatly fortified the coercive control of government over its population. Even with limited juridical resources, pressures from family and neighbors efficiently confined the behaviors of an individual and largely decreased the number of criminal cases or any moves that could undermine the imperial regime and other established social, political orders.

Decentralized administrative system (both formal and informal)

The relationship between centralization and decentralization in imperial China resembles the frequently mentioned Chinese notion of "yin" and "yang." Extreme concentration of authority and power, paradoxically, led to a decentralized pattern of behavior both within and beyond the bureaucratic ruling system of imperial China.

Within the system the extremely centralized administrative code and regulations created practical problems for local officials. On the one hand, they had to conform to central directions for their own career development; on the other hand, regional differences were often so significant that many centrally made policies were simply not operative at the locality. While local officials had no power in formally adjusting the policies in the centralized bureaucratic system, they learnt to develop an informal code of behavior. Central policies and regulations were often treated only as a formality. Genuine operations were decided by the compromise between central orders and local customs, so both the emperor and the local residents could accept them. As long as the attitude of local bureaucrats was cooperative, the censorial organs mostly turned a blind eye to the wide variety of "interpretations" of policy at different localities over the country. Consequently, imperial Chinese local administrations were by no means uniform, and de facto policy-making was decentralized.

At a first glance the fiscal system of imperial China was also highly centralized. Local governments acted as mere collectors of national taxes, hence they had no say over the tax rate or the usages of these fiscal incomes. On the expenditure side, local operational budgets were also determined by central government and these budgets were covered by central finance. However, this was only the formal system. In reality, the central provision of funds was not sufficient to meet even the most basic local administrative expenditures, including tax collection, as this budget only covered limited items such as the nominal salaries for officials, wages for runners, and sacrificial expenses (Ch'u 1962: 193–9). As a consequence, local governments of all levels depended heavily on various fees. This off-budget fee system widely existed in different dynasties in imperial China and in practice made the public financing system decentralized too.

Even in the matter of personnel, which was supposed to be the most centrally controlled, decentralization was also extensively present in an informal way. As local administrations in imperial China were in fact "one-man government," the officially hired clerks and runners were often not sufficient support. Most local authorities hired personal advisors and servants as assistants in accomplishing their administrative responsibilities. As these personal advisors and servants were not government employees, their relationship with the local official was personal and informal. Personnel management of this group was totally in the hands of local officials, thus decentralized. However, they were an indispensable component of Chinese local governments. Their professional services played an important role in the smooth operation of many Chinese local governments.

When we move our viewpoint from within the formal bureaucratic system to the whole of imperial China, the administration of this country would appear further decentralized. Although towns and villages had no government they were in fact run by informal organizations such as lineage temples and other "solidary groups," as Lily Tsai called them (Tsai 2007). In extreme cases, no clear organizations of any sorts existed at all. Local elites, who were often well-off Confucian scholars highly respected by the locals for their moral and intellectual superiority, were the actual leaders of China on a micro level. This leadership was not generated through an election system or any legal procedures, but its legitimacy derived from similar political rationale as the national sovereign and was backed up by Confucian moralities. Albeit informal, the prestige of these local elites was recognized by both the local governments and the people, and exercised extensive administrative functions in local communities. They had arbitral power over local conflicts; they were in charge of local collective charity funds; they originated and supervised the providence of local public goods and services; led regional religious ceremonies and served as the link between local governments and the people. On one hand, local governments would delegate administrative functions to the local elites in order to minimize their own expenditures. Taxes, for example, were often collected first by those elites in the local communities and then given to the local officials. On the other hand, local elites behaved as a supervisory power over the behavior of local officials and urged them to deliver proper public goods and services. With the consolidation of central authority and the deepening of Confucian moral persuasion, the Chinese empire was more and more at ease in delegating administrative powers to these local elites and, correspondingly, the degree of administrative decentralization of imperial China deepened down the ages.

To conclude, the political structure of imperial China was not strictly vertical, as often assumed. Undoubtedly the central authority was exceptionally strong. However, imperial China's formal political system targeted more or less only on macro stability. Its responsibility was to maintain and reproduce a certain social order on the national level and decouple the negative effects of major crises that were beyond the competence of small communities. On the micro level, decentralized and autonomous administrations, combining formal and informal institutions, were the mainstay. Imperial China demonstrated how informal institutions and interpersonal networks are of irreplaceable importance to the smooth operation of the state, and can be complementary rather than contradictory to the formal bureaucratic structure. These decentralized informal structures were not only widely used in imperial China, but can be broadly traced in contemporary Chinese governance too.

Mobility of social prestige and wealth

The biggest nightmare for the imperial emperors of China, as we could assume from the discussions above, did not come from within the political structure. The royal family, the scholar-bureaucrats of all levels, and the local elites, despite miscellaneous tensions among them, shared common basic interests in sustaining the stability of existing social and political orders. The foremost domestic threat to the imperial regime came from the farmers. When their dissatisfaction accumulated to such a point that one rallying cry could ignite sweeping actions of rebellion, imperial rule would truly suffer heavy damages. When Chen Sheng, leader of the first peasant uprising in imperial Chinese history, phrased his rallying call in 209 BC, he yelled, "王侯将相，宁有种乎?" This slogan was basically a rhetorical question, asking: shall blood (one's birth) decide the destiny of men? If one person exerts himself and excels his fellow men, this person should not be denied access to greater powers and higher prestige, no matter what his origin. This slogan won immediate resonance throughout China. Although Chen Sheng's gang failed after a mere six months, successive riots finally devastated the Qin dynasty and Liu Bang, a son of peasants, ascended the throne and founded the Han dynasty, a strong monarchy that lasted over 400 years.

Chen Sheng's slogan offers us at least two important insights into imperial Chinese society. The question and its long-lasting popularity in China suggested the Chinese people's conviction that the true value of a man does not rely on his birth. Moral and intellectual superiority decides real nobility and should be rewarded with corresponding social status, political functions, and material wealth. The main standard for the classification of human society should be merit, and the formation of an individual's merit, albeit related to the environment he grew up in, is primarily determined by hard work, discipline, and education. Therefore it is possible for any man, given the chances and efforts, to rise to higher, even the highest, positions in society. The even more fascinating point about Chen Sheng's question lies with the attention and responses it drew from imperial Chinese rulers. What imperial China inherited from feudal times was a highly hierarchical social and political order, which the ruling class intended to maintain for their own benefit. However, Chen Sheng's blatant interrogation demonstrated vividly to these rulers that if the innate inequality and injustice of this strong hierarchy could not be properly addressed, such order would not have the vigor of reproducing itself, and hence would inevitably perish. In convincing each member of society to behave properly, i.e. to respect the pyramid of authorities, society should offer sufficient justification for these authorities. If such authorities were based solely on one's birth, similar frustrations as Chen Sheng felt would brew and eventually become landmines threatening the stability of the hierarchical order that the empire aimed to sustain. The Legalist style suppressions of these frustrations, as the First Emperor executed, might work with a charismatic leader but, in the long run, the best solution was to establish institutionalized channels to guide the release of such frustrations.

A united bureaucratic system with centralized authority provided perfect conditions for nurturing this official channeling. For effective and sustainable ruling, the bureaucratic system needed to select its members according to moral and intellectual merits instead of family prestige or wealth. This merit-based selection standard had at least three benefits for the emperors of imperial China. First, capable and loyal bureaucrats could enhance the governing ability of the empire; second, no family or other social groups would enjoy unconditional superiority independent from the emperor. Last but not the least, this merit-based selection standard, combined with Confucian moral persuasions, justified the bureaucratic authorities, and endowed the common people unprecedented chances of advancing in the social hierarchy by learning and working hard. The existence of scholar-bureaucrats meant that imperial China's so-called "ruling class" was no longer a fixed class, but merely a profession to which everyone had equal right. If observed at a static historical moment, imperial Chinese society was full of sharp social and material disparities. However, when observed from a longitudinal perspective, as Professor Ping-ti Ho's comprehensive research on late imperial China suggested, "effective legal barriers to the movement of individuals and families from one status to another" was virtually absent. "Institutionalized and non-institutional factors which had a bearing on mobility, the long-range social and economic leveling of prominent families and clans, and the permeation of segments of the population with certain social concepts and myths conducive to social mobility" (Ho 1960: xii) existed extensively. It was exactly this high vertical social mobility of both wealth and political status that justified the injustices of the imperial hierarchical system, encouraged the suppressed common people to hope and act for the better, and created a new hierarchical political and social order with super resilience.

The mechanisms for upward and downward mobility in political power

The mechanisms of selecting the morally and intellectually superior for bureaucratic offices evolved over time. Many Chinese rulers and philosophers offered their deliberations on this matter. Three individuals, however, should be accentuated for their contributions. The foremost is Confucius himself. In order to guarantee that a maximum of intellectually and morally superior men could be distinguished from the rest, Confucius advocated firmly equal opportunities for education no matter what the financial and social conditions of one's family. Following his line of argument, later Confucians urged the state to set up schools at all levels and educate children of all origins at state expense. Many scholars also sponsored private schools or taught themselves just as Confucius did. Those spontaneous educational institutes became the major source of educational provision in the late imperial ages after the decline of public schools. This extensive educational system served as the basis for any selection mechanisms.

The other two essential persons for the development of merit-based bureaucrat-selection mechanisms were Dong Zhongshu, a Confucian philosopher who proposed several important techniques in personnel selection, and Han Wudi, an emperor who adopted the proposals of Dong. Before the reign of Han Wudi, bureaucratic selection process in the Han dynasty was primitive and still contained features of feudal times. Bureaucrats came from three major sources. The first group included people close to the emperor himself, such as his relatives, personal servants, secretaries, etc.; the second was the offspring of current bureaucrats. This group resembles somewhat the hereditary aristocratic system. Finally, there were the ones who obtained their offices through purchases. From Han Wudi's time on, these methods were gradually restricted and only revived at times of dynastic decline or state financial difficulty.[5] What Dong Zhongshu proposed and Han Wudi adopted was an institutionalized talent sponsoring system. Officials above a certain rank were obliged to recommend two young talents per year for service in the government. Those sponsored talents would be put into examinations set by the emperor himself and sent to minor official posts to test their true administrative ability. Once they demonstrated satisfactory performances, they would be officially appointed to offices. Although a sponsoring system could not exclude the possibility of abuses and favoritism, moral and legal regulations were employed to minimize such phenomena. Morally, as bureaucrats were supposed to be men of high competence and integrity, recommending an incompetent man for office would humiliate not only the protégé, but also the patron. Legally, the ability of these young protégés was crucial in evaluating the administrative performance of those who recommended them. The political careers of the patrons and protégés were thus tied up together and one had to be responsible for the behavior of the other. Therefore sponsoring someone with low moral integrity and administrative ability meant significant personal loss and danger and thus was not usually in practice. This sponsorship system spread official selection to the national scale with minimum transaction costs and it played an essential role in early imperial China.

Also on the advice of Dong Zhongshu, Han Wudi founded a national school to obtain and train more and better men for his use – the Imperial Academy mentioned earlier. Students of this school served as a major source of talent in the Han and succeeding dynasties. They were promoted according to their performance in written examinations on Confucian studies and to their moral behavior.

In middle imperial China the examination system became the most prominent method for official selection. Each year national examinations were held which all men were eligible to take part in. Those who achieved most highly in those exams would be promoted to certain official positions. This system originated in the Sui dynasty (581–618) and advanced in the Tang (619–907). In early Tang the examination system generated less than ten graduates each year (Kracke 1964). The scale of examination system was greatly boosted in the reign of the female emperor, Wu Zetian (624–705), as she found this method effective in harvesting talent from newly integrated territories. At the peak of the Song dynasty, annual graduates from the examination system averaged more than 250 (Kracke 1964). The detailed subjects, forms, and organizations of these examinations evolved from period to period and sometimes altered according to the personal preferences of emperors. But the main content always consisted of Confucian classics and thinking. This examination system lasted altogether 1,300 years (605–1905) and served as the most common institutionalized selection method of bureaucrats in imperial China.

Once selected into the bureaucratic system, individuals and their families were elevated from the masses to the ruling class and enjoyed superb privileges in society. Both social prestige and material wealth were skewed to these members of imperial rule. However, such prestige and wealth required great efforts to maintain. As the political power of scholar-bureaucrats was solely accorded for their competences, it could also be taken away for the lack of such competence at any time. One key principle of Confucianism was the "ratification of name" ("zheng ming"). It applied to the whole population, including the emperor. The principle of ratification of name means that any social position (i.e. the name) must correspond to certain social rights and obligations (the actuality). To match the name and actuality, a person holding a position not only enjoys the rights and privileges endowed by this position, but also has to fulfill the responsibilities required by this position. Failing to deliver such required responsibilities indicates the failure to ratify this person's name and thus he should be disqualified for enjoying his privileges accordingly. The emperor, for example, enjoyed supreme and unchallenged authority, prestige, and power. He was provided by heaven to govern the earth, and hence his responsibility was to use his capability and influence to foster the wellbeing of his people. If he failed in this endeavor, not only would heaven punish him with natural catastrophes, his people also had the right to overthrow his regime. Because he failed to ratify his name as an emperor someone else who could better fulfill these commitments should replace him and so ratify his name. Similar logic applied to officials of imperial China. As assistants to the emperor, imperial bureaucrats had full responsibility for faithfully executing the administrative powers delegated to them, and offering their considered proposals and criticisms to the emperor for the welfare of the people. Any mistake or failure in fulfilling these duties endangered not only the political power and social prestige they enjoyed, but also the material wealth and even the lives of their families.

Even if an official were to survive his whole political career without any dissatisfaction, the prestige and wealth of his family still faced serious challenges from various factors leading to downward social mobility. The political status of a family lacked hereditary mechanisms to guarantee its sustainability. If the father had been an eminent political figure, certainly his sons would have had much better opportunities to receive quality education and better connections to be recognized and sponsored by other officials. However, these were only factors that could facilitate the sons' political success, but not guarantee it. If the sons could not demonstrate intellectual excellence, or failed in the examination systems, most of them would not be appointed to any official positions. The concept of "yin" (蔭), the entitlement of sons to minor officialdom owing to the achievement of their fathers, did exist but such nepotism was limited only to officials in extremely high positions. Not only did the offices given through this mechanism normally possess no real political power, they could not be extended to further generations infinitely.

Factors hindering long-term accumulation and tenure of property

As regards material wealth, its concentration was also particularly vulnerable in imperial China. The core reasons for this vulnerability came from ambiguously defined and ill-protected property rights and the lack of primogeniture. As mentioned earlier, imperial China was not a pluralist society. It was composed of mainly two layers: the ruling bureaucrats surrounding their absolute leader – the emperor – and the scattered, unorganized small property-owning common families. This structure generated difficulties for the clear definition of private property rights both on the micro and macro levels. On the micro level, property was never owned by an individual but by the whole of an extended family. This created legal confusion when trying to identify property ownership. On the macro level, the two-layered societal structure meant that no entities were strong enough to form a countervailing power against the state. Thus, although land was privatized and traded freely at market, scattered property owners could not be organized enough to obtain protection of their property rights against state power.

In a sense the state became the ultimate owner of everything. Everything was bestowed on a family as a gift of the emperor. To signify the emperor's ultimate ownership, a rent was paid to him unconditionally. Legally, most of the properties including land could be exchanged freely in the market and, from the Han dynasty, was registered as personal wealth. Yet, in practice, property rights were only protected against other individuals/families whereas, as the ultimate owner, the imperial government had full power to charge land taxes, to seize private land for "public" uses, or simply expropriate private properties as punishment. Unlike the central position of private property protection in the Western European legal system, the legal system in imperial China had great difficulty in defining what "private" meant. Instead, the legal system in imperial China focused entirely on criminal law. For the imperial Chinese rulers, maintaining political stability and order was their foremost concern. The protection of private property rights from the violation of the state though was of least interest on their agenda.

Ambiguous and ill-protected property rights, in fact, served the interests of imperial Chinese rulers, as it was thus easier to dismantle concentrated material wealth. Because of their political preferences for small ownerships, imperial Chinese rulers were averse to overly concentrated properties. This propensity could be demonstrated by their policy choices. In the early and middle imperial age, various mechanisms could be spotted for distributing public land to landless peasants. Dynasty shifts were also often used as opportunities for shuffling the distribution of wealth, normally more equably. Meanwhile, the state's efforts in breaking down overly concentrated wealth never ceased. Punishment for a political mistake by one official often resulted in the complete loss of his family's properties as well. Extreme cases even involved the exile of influential landlords and their families for the sole reason of eliminating potential political threats. Even if the extremely wealthy families could escape the intervention of the state, the absence of the law of primogeniture always served as a constant factor in breaking down wealth concentration. In Chinese tradition, before both parents passed away, a family had to co-habit and all properties and expenses were put in common. However, after both parents died, the property of the family would be equally distributed among all the sons, rather than inherited only by the oldest one. The strong dispersing effect of this institutional arrangement affected both wealthy families and common farmers alike.

Compared with agricultural activities, it was easier for those engaged in commercial activities to accumulate wealth over a shorter period of time. Could commercial capital escape the fate of downward mobility in imperial China? The empirical examples showed a negative answer. The two-layered power structure not only left no space for the emergence of strong and long-lasting landlords: it hindered the development of commercial capital even more. In imperial China there were four major categories of professions: officialdom, farming, handicrafts, and commerce. Commerce came last. As we explained above, the Chinese empire, for most of the time, did not depend on commercial activities for fiscal income. Rather, merchants were treated as unstable elements of society and thus were often discriminated against. Similar to farming families, merchants in imperial China were often too weak to bargain with the state. The merit-based selection methods further stopped wealthy merchants from translating their money power into political power.[6] Furthermore, the imperial state could seize a business and form a monopolistic control whenever that business turned large profits. Ever since the Han dynasty, numerous businesses fell captive to state monopoly, such as salt production and distribution, alcohol dealing, iron making, water transportation, and financial operations. Chinese commercial capital was seriously damaged by this process of state monopolization and never grew strong enough to escape the downward cycle of wealth accumulation.

What deserves clarifying is that, although imperial Chinese society behaved briskly in both upward and downward vertical social mobility, this movement was realized in a dispersed and individual mode. That is to say, the movement never involved an entire class of people, but only the movement of individual families. As a result, this volatile social mobility had more significance to the behavior of individuals than to the transformation of social order. By diverting people's attention from the social injustices of the hierarchical system to individual aspirations for better social and material status, such social mobility was an integrated institution in stabilizing the political order of imperial China instead of leading to its demise. This contrasts greatly with the social mobility resulted from the class struggle that could be observed in the formation and development of capitalism in the Western world. As a matter of fact, high vertical mobility, scattered ownership, and family-based production units created difficult conditions for imperial China to exploit the advantage of economy of scale and develop a capitalistic system of production both in rural and urban areas. In rural parts, a Chinese village did not have a collective productive organization as did many European villages. Instead of being vertically integrated, a Chinese village was merely a cluster of parallel family-based production units. This structure was not favorable for the emergence of technological advancement in agriculture, because of the large scale of land. For the urban area, family-based agricultural production possessed much stronger flexibility regarding the relationship between land and population than a village-based one. As long as the yield from land could still support the existence of family members, no one was compelled to leave the rural areas for making a living in the city. This structure constrained the supply of labor for centralized commercial production in the urban areas, hence jeopardizing the opportunity for imperial China to develop concentrated large-scale production for commercial goods too. Production of both agricultural products and commercial products were conducted in a scattered way in the countryside. Only trading was done in the urban area. This arrangement could be closely related to the absence of an endogenous industrial revolution in imperial China. In the following chapter, we explain the relationships in more detail.

Conclusion

A peculiar two-layered societal structure

Resulting from a peculiar trajectory of state formation, imperial China had a very specific two-layered societal structure. One layer was constituted by the ruling, i.e. the scholar-bureaucrats surrounding an absolute central authority. The other layer was composed of the vast population with minimum formal association, but densely knitted together into a gigantic net of social relations. The major difference between this societal structure and that of a typical Western state was the lack of influential groups, such as aristocratic families, churches, or cities, which could oppose state power. Stemming from this difference, the source of political legitimacy and mechanisms to maintain the political orders diverged greatly.

A two-layered political power structure freed the state from constant negotiations with countervailing groups. The legitimacy of state power thus was not dependent on the compromises made with various representative powers. Instead, the sovereignty's legitimacy was based directly on people's satisfaction with general social welfare. The imperial Chinese state was not hijacked by the interests of these power groups and, in theory, should have been in a better position to make their policies impartially for the improvement of the welfare of its people. However, with the absence of institutionalized opposition, the authority and power of the state was highly magnified. The state had the ability to interfere heavily in the private domain. Any groups with substantial social status and material wealth independent from the state would be considered as threats and might be dismantled by the state. Such state behavior was extremely detrimental to the development of private capitalist accumulation and enticed merchants to bind with state power for the pursuit of profits.

The single most substantial challenge to state power in imperial China was the collective actions of farmers. When basic welfare of Chinese population was not satisfied, bottom-up uprisings would exhibit extraordinary power to devastate the regime, or at least damage its legitimacy, and hence impair the interests of the whole ruling class. To avoid this severe consequence, even in the absence of obvious countervailing powers, wise rulers still developed self-censoring mechanisms.

In imperial China, the most significant constraints were the moral rules and the censorate branch within the bureaucratic system. These self-censoring mechanisms normally functioned better at the debut of a dynasty when the emperors were still wise and conscientious enough. When the dynasty decayed, the effects of these mechanisms were much weaker.

As pluralistic competition was absent in such a two-layered society, even if a bottom-up mass uprising succeeded in overthrowing an old regime, the "revolutionists" would only elevate themselves into the ruling class while leaving the overall pattern of societal and political structure intact. This is one of the key reasons why, in more than two millenniums, imperial China experienced only cyclical changes. Although the institutions of imperial China matured and evolved considerably over time, there were no authentic revolutions in the political system or societal structure during this historical period.

Nevertheless, this is not to say that imperial China did not possess intense vigor for creativity and change. Contrary to common impressions, imperial China was not an extremely centralized authoritarian country. The formal bureaucratic system inclined to manage only macro problems with national importance. An active civil society composed of multifarious families, social networks, and spontaneous organizations expresses the true dynamisms of this country and were most influential in people's everyday lives. A large body of historical research supplies evidence that markets were eminently dynamic for the most part in imperial China. Dynamic vertical social mobility endowed individual families enough incentive to work hard, to invest (especially for their children's education), and to increase their productivity. Such traditions can still be observed in today's China and have contributed greatly to the success of China's reform that began in 1978.

China, Western nations and the challenge of democracy in the twenty-first century

China and the West share a common belief about the foundation of democracy: the people are the ultimate source of sovereignty. Contrary to theocratic regimes, political authority is legitimized by the will of all citizens of the nation, not by the supposed will of God. Contrary to an aristocratic regime, legitimacy does not proceed from a class that has inherited the wisdom to lead other people. However, this holistic philosophical principle has always raised a formidable and unsolved difficulty: how should the collective will of the people be represented? Since it is impossible in large and complex mosaics of people that make a nation to celebrate unity and common will in a single gathering, there should be accepted rules to delegate sovereignty so that effective government can be legitimized. It is where China and the West differ.

As demonstrated in the present chapter, the political representation of unity in China has been legitimized by a bi-millennium tradition that instituted the central authority of the emperor. The People's Republic has continued to rest upon the tension between the central authority of the Communist Party and the diversity of the society. In the West the principle of sovereignty deposited in the people does not have such a long tradition. It was established as the outcome of the long intellectual elaboration of first principles by French and British liberal philosophers in the eighteenth century. They asserted that the common will was grounded in the freedom and equality of individuals. These principles were only established after bloody revolutions in the United States (US) and in France. But the tension between the holistic principle of sovereignty and the autonomy of the individual was resolved only in procedural terms by the elective principle instituting the majority rule. The principle of majority rule as the outcome of the procedure of periodical pluralistic elections pretends that the government of the majority is worth the will of the totality. This is a congenital shortcoming that has become exacerbated, as much as the contest between irreconcilable political views on more and more complex societies has become entrenched. The US democracy, for instance, is becoming paralyzed by unrelenting conflicting conceptions of the wellbeing of people that undermine the design of policies. In Europe, the promise of sovereignty, embedded in the long-standing construction of the union, has vanished in the bitter conflicts of interests that have devastated the continent ever since the fall of the Berlin Wall.

To overcome the fiction at the root of democracy, pretending that the majority could rule legitimately for the totality, an administrative power developed in the twentieth century to express the common good and to realize it in the production of infrastructures and public services. Founded on competence and capabilities the public administration has become largely autonomous from the political mechanism. It guarantees the continuity of the common good, thus being an essential part of reconciliation between the whole of the nation and the diversity of society. As we have forcefully emphasized in this chapter, the very long tradition of a competent bureaucracy, grounded on individual merit and strictly controlled selection, was a linchpin in the social cohesion of imperial China and is still a crucial condition for the legitimacy of the Communist Party. In both the West and China, the effectiveness of the public administration is an indispensable pillar in the welfare of the people. It differentiates these countries from most developing countries with broken states and incompetent, even non-existent, administrations.

However, in the last two decades, the legitimacy of the public administrations has been undermined by the dynamic of capitalism it had helped regulate beforehand. Globalization has unleashed forces that have promoted a bitter neo-liberal ideology, desperate to disparage the state and to brandish the market as the best vehicle for the general interest. The destabilizing process of globalization against national sovereignty has produced a fragmentation of public authority with the creation of two types of Western institutions: independent public institutions, whose emblematic figures are independent central banks, on the one hand, and European constitutional courts on the other. Such institutions have no counterparts in China, although regulatory authorities, separated from the hierarchical structure of administration, have been created in different sectors of social activities, especially in finance.

However, none of those increasing numbers of institutions by way of expressing the principle of totality are capable of solving the contradictions that threaten to tear contemporary societies apart. The impact of globalization has been devastating in exacerbating social inequalities in both the West and China, while weakening the authority of public institutions whose responsibility is to deal with them. Globalization has also intensified rivalries between the West and China in magnifying global imbalances and worsening environmental problems, while entailing radically opposite views on their causes and on the responsibilities to address them. Therefore the institutions legitimate in fostering democracy and preserving national sovereignty are contested at both the sub-national and supra-national levels.

At the sub-national level the challenge is a deepening of democracy with concrete participation in civil society. It is not yet evident to foresee which of the political regimes – Western or Chinese – will be better equipped to legitimize the intervention of social networks on problems that impinge upon sustainable growth. In Part III of this book, devoted to the new stage of the reform that will be inaugurated with the 12th five-year plan, we will show that China has the political assets to make this transformation.

At the supranational level the rise of China as a world power raises the question of its participation in international governance, which must be improved in order to address the dangerous worsening of world threats to fossil resources, climate change, widening inequalities in development, and financial and monetary instability. To answer this it is necessary to understand in depth what has been achieved by the reform so far at both the domestic and international levels. However, the conditions for reform were sown both by the political and social structures of the country, explained in the present chapter, and by the history of China's international endeavors, retreat, and setbacks prior to the post-World War II revolution. The latter will be dealt with in the next chapter.

2 Growth regimes in capitalist history

What happened to China after around 1820 up to 1950 is a conundrum that has attracted much controversy among historians and economists. Why did the East and the West, more specifically for our purpose China and Western Europe, have diverging trajectories from the early nineteenth century to the mid-twentieth century? Why did the industrial revolution that propelled Anglo-Saxon countries to economic dominance occur at all? Why did China miss it? What is the nature of the restraints on industrialization that were unsurpassable obstacles in some societies yet overcome in others? Did the dramatic divergence derive from state policies or from basic social institutions that shaped incentives, aspirations, and entrepreneurial spirits?

These questions are relevant for understanding Chinese reform, its achievement, its contradictions, and the direction of its progress, all the more so since the reform is conceived as a catching-up process. However, this way of thinking might be a false track. Chapter 1 has shown that the social underpinnings of property rights and wealth distribution in China are very different from the European philosophy of a natural order and the associated Bill of Rights elaborated in the late eighteenth century. The peculiar state formation trajectory of China had abiding influences on the economic behavior of not only the imperial age, but post-imperial Chinese regimes as well. Correlatively the ideal model of the optimal general equilibrium in a pure market economy is not the relevant yardstick to assess the achievements and the setbacks of Chinese reform.

The long-run history of China's economic growth, lengthy decline, and spectacular recovery before the launch of the reform in 1978 is a better guide to put the reform in the right perspective. A rough measure of the divergence in economic growth between China and Western powers between 1850 and 1950 shows that tentative reforms to boost modern industry in the late nineteenth and early twentieth centuries were not effective. By contrast, the Maoist Revolution, with all its vagaries, social upheavals, and human tragedies, sowed the seeds for the powerful 30-year reform that has now reached the dawn of a new stage.

Analyzing and interpreting the historical material leads to theoretical questions of the growth of institutional innovations to overcome the limits of a defined growth regime and to set the basis of another. These are the tools that we will apply to highlight the stages of the reform in Part II of this book.

Five centuries of Chinese economic history: a bird's eye view

As explained in Chapter 1, Chinese traditional society was almost totally rural, with more than 90 percent of the population living in the countryside. It was also a small-scale household-based agriculture, with no stable large estate or share-cropping systems. This was a very efficient, labor-intensive agriculture. Farmers achieved high crop yields per unit of land. They used a three-factor farming technology: careful selection of seed varieties, organic fertilizers, and dense irrigation systems. Such a production function delivered a high average product per unit of land, but a low average product per unit of labor employed (Naughton 2007: 34). In the lower Yangzi, the yield per hectare for corn crop was 2.7 times that obtained in England in the eighteenth century (Huang 2002). Furthermore, the rural economy was not limited to agricultural activities. There were micro enterprises manufacturing handicraft such as textiles, leather goods, food products, and iron tools. There was even a vertical division of labor in silk cloth production. Raising silk worms, spinning raw silk threads, and weaving silk cloth were carried out by specialized households or small firms. These "industrial" activities were, however, largely scattered in rural areas rather than concentrated in cities.

Such a dense small business economy was coordinated by networks of markets run by a large number of merchants. The Californian School of global history calls this highly marketized rural society a proto-industrial economy (Wong 1999). It was highly flexible in the allocation of human and material resources. Because there was no aristocracy, no castes, and no accumulation of inherited wealth, there was no institutional barrier to social mobility upwards and downwards. This small market economy used silver and paper money extensively. It was regulated by written contracts, courts of justice, and merchants' associations long before Western Europe was. Funds were transferred nationwide through letters of credit as early as the ninth century.

Therefore China's rural society was the best proxy of Adam Smith's natural market economy. In such an economy trade expands within nations, driven by population growth and capital accumulation, with a larger number of and more specialized business firms. The economy will prosper until competition on the supply side and limits on demand in the countryside in absorbing products of manufacture reduce the rate of returns. This is the famous high equilibrium trap, which we say more about later in the chapter. For the time being, let us say that Smith's solution lies in international trade that comes naturally from the search for new channels of trade to absorb overproduction of handicraft and industry.

Regarding handicraft and manufacture, fragmented activity in small-scale businesses prevented the increase of productivity because concentrated capital was lacking and the household ownership of the land protected rural workers from proletarization. Therefore the Marxian submission of free unprotected labor to the ownership of the means of production in the hands of a bourgeoisie did not arise (Wong 1999). Even if cotton was woven almost all over the country, large-scale textile mills did not emerge. The proto-industrious economy, efficient as it was according to its own yardstick, lacked the institutions to give the impulse to transform itself into a full-fledged industrial economy. China was unable either to generate its own brand of industrial revolution or to import it from the West.

China, Japan, India, and Western powers: comparative quantitative analysis

Thanks to the lifetime's work of the outstanding British historian economist, Angus Maddison, we can muster rough figures of population, gross domestic product (GDP), and GDP per capita for large countries and regions of the world that make comparative analysis possible over a long period of history. These figures are shown in Table 2.1 and tell a fascinating story. According to Maddison (2007), China was the world's leading economy in terms of per capita income prior to 1500. It outperformed Western Europe in every aspect of economic performance: level of technology, mobilization of resources, and government capacity. After the beginning of the Ming dynasty (1368–1644), the population grew at a rate of 0.4 percent a year for more than 400 years. It quintupled between 1400 and 1820. As a result of this much faster demographic expansion than in Western Europe, China reached the apex of its weight in world GDP in 1820. But its GDP per capita had already long stagnated, having been overtaken by Western Europe as early as 1500 and had stayed the same between 1500 and 1820. Consequently, even if China remained by far the biggest economy of the world in terms of GDP in 1820, it lost ground in terms of GDP per capita against Western Europe all through those 300 years (Table 2.1). It kept abreast with India whose GDP per capita also stagnated.

Table 2.1 GDP and GDP per capita

Countries or regions	1500	1700	1820	1913	1950	1973	2003
GDP (bn of 1990 PPP$)							
- China	61.8	82.8	228.6	241.4	245	739.4	6187.9
- Japan	7.7	15.4	20.7	71.7	161	1242.9	2699
- India	60.5	90.7	111.4	204.2	222.2	494.8	2267.1
- Western Europe	44.2	81.2	159.8	902.3	1396.2	4096.5	7857.4
- USA	—	—	12.5	517.4	1455.9	3536.6	8430.8
GDP per capita (1,000 of 1990 PPP$)							
- China	0.60	0.60	0.60	0.55	0.45	0.84	4.8
- Japan	0.50	0.57	0.67	1.39	1.92	11.43	21.22
- India	0.55	0.55	0.53	0.67	0.62	0.85	2.16
- Western Europe	0.71	1.00	1.20	3.46	4.58	11.41	19.91
- USA	—	—	1.26	5.30	9.56	16.69	29.04
GDP ratio:							
- China/Western Europe	1.40	1.02	1.43	0.27	0.18	0.18	0.79
- China/USA	—	—	18.29	0.47	0.17	0.21	0.73
GDP per capita ratio:							
- China/Western Europe	0.85	0.60	0.50	0.16	0.1	0.07	0.24
- China/USA	—	—	0.48	0.10	0.05	0.05	0.16

Source: Maddison (2007: 117 and 174)

Then China began its 130 years demise. From 1820 to 1913 average yearly GDP growth was an anemic 0.06 percent and 0 percent between 1913 and 1950. In 1950 China was by far the poorest country in the world. Its GDP per capita was about half the average level in Africa and less than three-quarters the level in India. In contrast, the industrial revolution was in full swing, while the aftermath of the Napoleonic wars had been absorbed in the 1830s in England and in the 1840s in France. All in all, when measured in constant PPP$ (Purchasing Power Parity expressed in dollars), GDP grew a robust 4.8 percent on average in Western Europe all through the century to World War I and GDP per capita almost tripled. The takeoff in the US was explosive especially in the half century bridging the end of the civil war and World War I. Despite the depression in the 1930s, and thanks to World War II, the US gained absolute predominance in 1950, the apex of its worldwide hegemony. Between 1913 and 1950 European growth slowed markedly to 1.5 percent a year on average, largely overtaken by the US at 4.9 percent.

These trends have been foreshadowed by Western economists who have commented on China's long-run trends, using piecemeal indicators. It has become common to minimize the collapse of the country after the disintegration of the Qing empire in 1911 and to denigrate the Maoist era. However, for all its chaotic politics, the Socialist Revolution stemmed the economic shrinking of China, in relative terms, at least in GDP weight, if not in GDP per capita. The ratio of GDP in China to Western Europe stabilized at 0.18 and rose to the US 0.17 to 0.21. Since the years 1950–73 were the fastest growing years ever in Western Europe at about 6.0 percent in PPP$, it was not that bad a performance in pure economic terms. In GDP per capita China grew at 2.8 percent per year on average, slightly more than the US, while Western Europe enjoyed its golden age at 4.5 percent. Nonetheless, growth was not oriented to personal consumption, to say the least. Therefore the level of GDP per capita was at its minimum ever in relative terms, e.g. 7 percent of the average income level per capita in Western Europe and 5 percent of that in the US.

Moreover, the overall economic performance of China in those 23 years did not match those of other countries in East Asia. Growth exploded at more than 10 percent a year in Japan, which caught up with Western Europe on average in the 1970s for GDP per capita. Other smaller East Asian countries (Singapore, Taiwan, and Korea) were also in full swing. Even if those countries were far different from China in size, their experience in takeoff and convergence with advanced countries showed that politically authoritarian countries, with heavy state involvement, could be highly successful. The lessons drawn from their experience were valuable in shaping the Chinese reform that began in 1978.

Why the long decline of China?

As already mentioned, population growth was putting a strain on the limited size of arable land. More and more labor had to work on the farms to prevent productivity from declining. Land-intensive rice production was developed along and around the Yangtse River, where population had concentrated since the thirteenth century.

Maintaining a stable per capita income from the fourteenth to the nineteenth centuries in the face of a four-fold increase in population was a remarkable achievement. Consistent with Smith's theory, China turned to foreign trade to enlarge the outlets for its manufactured goods. Already the Song, then the Yuan, emperors had created navies in the thirteenth and fourteenth centuries. The third emperor of the Ming dynasty, Yonglu, enlarged the scale of international trade in ordering six of the seven naval expeditions between 1405 and 1433 (Needham *et al.* 1971). These were all commanded by Admiral Zheng He, a eunuch from the Ming imperial household.

The mystery was: after such triumphs in these navy expeditions, why did Ming rulers finally decide to disband the fleet, close the shipyards, and even impose a ban on private foreign trade in general? Why did the late imperial dynasties not seek their chance to break the Smithian trap by enlarging their overseas markets and advancing their naval and military technologies?

One possible perspective for interpreting these strategic choices of the Ming dynasty draws on the specific trajectory of state formation in China (see Chapter 1). Chinese governments, imperial and post-imperial ones alike, have an essential political claim: constructing a unitary state. The Chinese definition of a unitary state requires not only a united and central sovereign but also an absolute supreme authority over any local and non-governmental organizations. Imperial China was so successful in fostering its sole authority that, after the Tang dynasty, hardly any domestic groups had the capacity or legitimacy to challenge the imperial sovereign. What is more, thanks to its large geographic scale and long-term superiority in economic and technological performances, imperial China also enjoyed relatively few immediate external threats for much of the time. Thus the logic of ruling in imperial China was not based on opposition or competition with domestic or external groups over territory or fiscal resources, as were its European counterparts over a similar historical period. To sustain such absolute central authority, Chinese imperial governments based their political structure on a relatively egalitarian agrarian economy. Fiscal needs were mainly satisfied by the direct extraction of agricultural tax from farmers with the help of an immense bureaucratic system. By providing the scattered land-owning farmers security, stability, and infrastructural support, the ruling class gained their political legitimacy and financial resources accordingly. In other words, the primary task of Chinese imperial rulers in sustaining their rule was not financial and military expansion, but the sustainability of domestic systems constructed around an agrarian economy.

As a result the expansion of foreign expenditures and trade was not viewed by the Chinese imperial state as a promising new source of fiscal income, nor was it a path leading to faster economic growth. The objective of Zheng He's expeditions was not to create a colonial empire, neither was it to open permanent ports of trade abroad. It was to assert China's soft power, or benign hegemony, via tributary relationships extended over a much wider area, from Korea and Japan in the east to the eastern coast of Africa in the west. Trade subsequent to these expeditions was strictly regulated. Private merchants embarked on the vessels and could exchange commodities in the places they visited, but not on their own terms. They were supervised by officials of the imperial administration. Indeed, trade was not a pure economic objective. Rather, it was a way to exchange gifts with foreign rulers and to develop the accreditation of ambassadors. It was very formal, being one of the means of asserting China's suzerainty in establishing tributary relationships in vast territories. It was subordinate to the quest for security.

But this policy did not last long. The ruling scholar-bureaucrats soon noticed contradictions of such expeditions with established domestic order. One potential problem was the rise of economic entities associated with foreign trade, notably the merchants. Because of geographical mobility and their propensity to accumulate large sums of wealth in a short period of time, throughout imperial Chinese history merchants' related commercial activities were regarded as a destabilizing factor in agrarian society, and hence a threat to the unitary state. Another concern was the increased exposure to external threats. Although China faced no threat against its sovereignty from the West prior to 1820, Ming and Qing bureaucrats instinctively felt averse to the increasing piracy and inflow of foreign religions. The most acute controversy concerned the allocation of fiscal resources. There were conflicting views between the Ming imperial household and the mandarin bureaucracy over the cost of financing the expeditions. At the same time as these expeditions decisions were taken to move the capital from Nanking to Peking and rebuild the Grand Canal. Both of these two projects had critical importance for the maintenance of domestic order, which the imperial rulers deemed the basis of their governance. The displacement of the capital to the north strengthened the defense of the northern border against potential invasions from Mongolia and Manchuria, where the usual and, at that time, more immediate foreign enemies of China came from. The Grand Canal was vital for domestic stability because it linked the food-surplus lower Yangtze to the food-deficit Northern Plain (Naughton 2007: 36). Both projects, especially the reconstruction of the Grand Canal, were large investments. To alleviate the fiscal burden, emperor Yonglu printed a lot of paper money. Hyperinflation in paper currency ensued, which actually destroyed the value of paper money in private transactions, seriously disturbing the economy. As a consequence paper money all but disappeared. From the 1430s on silver became the accepted instrument of exchange both in private transactions and in tax payments. The fiscal and monetary crisis gave the upper hand to the bureaucracy in the debate about foreign expeditions. As mentioned in Chapter 1, imperial Chinese governments relied more on cutting marginal expenditure than aggressively seeking new fiscal resources when facing fiscal crisis. Compared with maintaining domestic security and stability, everything else would seem marginal. Therefore the mystery questioned above happened. Imperial China gave up foreign exploration and trade for better financial ability in maintaining domestic order and compromised with European merchants by granting trading posts in order to concentrate its defense against the northern enemies, regarded as more dangerous at the time.

If Ming emperors could have had hindsight, they might have regretted their decision. The termination of naval expeditions became an important reason for the stagnation of technological improvements in late imperial China. What is more, they might have discovered that European capitalism had a much more aggressive nature than the Tartar tribes, since what it coveted was not just territory but a forceful integration of China into a global capitalist economic order. Thus this foreign force posed not only a direct threat to independent authority whose magnitude was unprecedented throughout the course of China's imperial history but, more importantly, an unavoidable and constant destroyer of the established imperial social order. Unfortunately, Ming emperors did not have hindsight. They made the correct choice at the time to put domestic order first. But by their failure to respond actively to the emerging European forces, it was just a matter of time before the empire's final fall.

As early as 1557 the Portuguese were allowed to establish a base in Macao. The trading post became the main locus of European trade with China; Portuguese imports mainly consisted of pepper and other spices. They were first financed by bullion shipments, then by the profit of trading Chinese silk against Japanese silver, which lasted almost a century after 1550.

Portuguese trade declined in the seventeenth century. The Dutch, followed by British and French merchants, took over. The composition of trade changed from traditional pepper and spices to raw silk and tea. By 1750 the British had superseded the Dutch. They financed their tea purchases in Canton with opium shipments from India. China did not react to the European challenge. Enjoying a trade surplus for most of the time before the massive inflow of opium, the Middle Empire underestimated the Europeans throughout that time. Its bureaucracy was not interested in the scientific achievements of the West. The Chinese elite disposed of ample income that might have been invested productively. But the way social status was recognized and individual endeavors were rewarded within the elite was alien to the money gains that work as entrepreneurial incentives according to Max Weber's spirit of capitalism.

Notwithstanding this, until the mid-eighteenth century imperial China was still successful in maintaining its order and the sovereign had firm control over its territory and fiscal base. The total outbreak of crisis only arrived when the late Qing government gradually failed to provide sufficient infrastructural support for the welfare of its people. The essential public goods necessary to unite such a vast empire were not properly maintained. The reserves of food in public granaries diminished after 1790. The irrigation networks began to deteriorate (Elvin and Liu 1998). With the pressure of population growth, ecological vulnerability increased in rural areas. With the diminishing efficacy of the public system, the rural population became victims of floods and droughts, which provoked terrible famines. In 1855, owing to the neglect of irrigation maintenance, the Yellow River burst its banks, causing devastating floods. With shrinking government involvement, the economy was no longer supported. Because the rural economy became more fragile and faced a relentless population pressure, social stresses fell disproportionately on poor areas. The marginal product of labor plummeted in farms too small to support family life, causing recurrent starvation and population decline in the most affected provinces.

The hardest blow to the Manchu regime was the Taiping rebellion, which raged over half of China from 1850 to 1864. This rebellion was one of the typical peasant uprisings that plagued Chinese imperial regimes in their downward cycle. It erupted out of the farmers' accumulated dissatisfaction with the government's failure to maintain material support for its population. The purpose of such uprisings was clear: to overthrow a sovereignty that was no longer legitimate. Suppression of the Taiping rebellion was on top of the agenda of the Qing royal house, and it seriously affected the financial balance of the country. On the one hand, the suppression of this rebellion required extremely high military expenditure. The recorded annual military expenditure during this time was over 20 million taels, roughly half of the national fiscal revenue. From 1850 to 1875 the aggregate expenditure on military uses was estimated to be 850 million taels (Peng 1983: 137). On the other hand, the Taiping rebellion significantly eroded the fiscal base of the Qing government. At its apex Taiping leaders occupied more than 18 provinces, including the richest Yangzi Delta. In order to make up for the loss of these provinces and meet the increasing financial needs, the Qing government ruthlessly taxed the regions still under its sovereignty. The agricultural tax rate increased at least 50 percent. In Sichuan province, taxes on agricultural activities increased 4–9 times from 1850 to 1877 (Li 1957: 306). From 1853, Qing began to extract the "lijin" tax, which was a kind of commercial tax. At its origin, it was a temporary tax designed to respond to one-shot military expenditures against Taiping. The tax rate was set low at 1 percent. However, before long the extraction became institutionalized and the tax rate inflated. For certain commercial operations the tax rate could reach as high as 20 percent. From 1870 taxes from "lijin" made up 25 percent of all fiscal income. Heavy tax extraction further degraded the domestic order under the Manchu regime.

As the domestic crisis escalated, foreign intrusion became more persistent. Catastrophic defeats arrived in quick succession, starting with the first Opium War in 1839 against Britain whose motive was the free access to Canton to secure the profitable trade of Indian opium for Chinese tea. The British faced little resistance and imposed the treaty of Nanking in 1842, forcing China to cede Hong Kong and to open five Treaty Ports to foreign control. A second Anglo-French attack in 1858–60 destroyed the Summer Palace in Peking and imposed a treaty that opened up the interior of China to free trade imperialism, far into Manchuria up to Harbin and along the Yangtze River up to Chongqing. China was forced to maintain low tariffs, the opium trade was legalized, and foreigners enjoyed extraterritorial rights.

Apart from the Western encroachments on Chinese sovereignty, new rapacious invaders appeared after 1860. The network of China's tributary states was completely dismantled and vast territorial losses were inflicted on the country. Russia captured a huge portion of land on the Pacific coast and founded Vladivostok. It also increased its empire in Central Asia. Then the breaking up of the empire accelerated. Indochina was ceded to France in 1885 and Burma to England in 1886. Japan took over Taiwan and made a protectorate of Korea in 1895 as a prize for its victory in the Sino-Japanese war, concluded by the treaty of Shimonoseki.

The Boxer rebellion in the 1890s was the pretext for Western powers to mount a punitive allied force from eight countries, which occupied Beijing and forced the Chinese government to sign the 1901 Boxer protocol. In all practical matters concerning its revenues the Qing government was placed under foreign tutelage. Tax extraction became ferocious. Fiscal revenue doubled from around 40 million taels per year in early Qing to more than 80 million taels in 1886–96. In 1908 annual fiscal revenue exceeded 200 million. Yet all this was not enough to pay off massive military expenses and a gigantic amount of indemnities.[1] The collapse of the Qing government came as no surprise. When it happened in 1911 Tibet proclaimed independence and expelled its Chinese population. Russia extended its sovereignty over Outer Mongolia in 1915. Militarist Japan occupied Manchuria in 1931–3 and established the Puppet State of Manchukuo. Finally, in 1937 the Japanese army invaded China and committed unimaginable atrocities until its defeat in the Pacific War.

After the end of the Qing regime, completely undermined by continual disruptions without sufficient breathing space to recover and to restore authority, and after the proclamation of the republic, the country was ravaged by a bitter power struggle intermeshed with civil wars. From 1911 to 1927 the country suffered from political fragmentation and warlord rivalries. In 1927 the Guomindang, a nationalist autocratic party under the dictatorship of Chiang Kai-shek, took over and unified the country until the Japanese conquest in 1937.

The mixed legacy of modernization prior to the Communist Revolution

After this short account of Chinese history, it should be no surprise that real income per capita declined in absolute terms and slumped in relative terms from 1820 to 1950, as shown in Table 2.1. This does not fit with the benign account of globalization, however, viewed from the economist's point of view. When the industrial revolution was well underway after the 1830s, capitalist expansion in Europe gave rise to the globalization of the classical era of industrial capitalism that lasted until World War I. The international division of labor brought about by the flow of capital was supposed to spread benefits to peripheral countries with the help of foreign investments. China, however, was not a peripheral country: it was the Middle Empire. The interference of foreign powers weakened basic institutions and provoked severe social crises. In trade, the forced change of opium for silver to pay for Chinese exports deprived China of its monetary metal and created a serious opium addiction. There are better ways to show that trade is always mutually beneficial! Furthermore, China waged repeated wars to try to stem its loss of territories. The empire lost all of them, losing much of its legitimacy internally with the Taiping, then the Boxer rebellions. It also lost its revenues because it had to pay for reparations and was deprived of the most profitable parts of its economy, seized by the foreign powers as economic enclaves, called Treaty Ports, which were entirely under foreign control. Shanghai was the most important.

The question is: what attempts of industrial modernization were made both before the end of the empire and after the promulgation of the republic, especially under the guidance of the Guomindang in the 1927–37 decade? Were seeds sown for future growth? This question is much more than factual: it provides insights about the nature of capitalism in China. Thus it will serve to understand better the dynamic of the ongoing reform described in the second part of this book.

Where did the impetus to modernize come from? Until the defeat of 1895 it did not come from the central government. One impulse was given by high officials in some provinces, vice-kings and governors who sponsored military industries on the one hand, and from the comprador merchant elite in the Open Ports on the other hand. The collaboration between both strands gave rise to mixed ventures between local government officials and private interests (Bergère 2007). This was an incipient bureaucratic capitalism motivated by the doctrine of self-reinforcing which started after 1860. The leaders of the modernizing move were members of the mandarin elite who were distinguished in successfully fighting the Taiping uprising. Because taxes on trade were levied in the provinces, the governors of the provinces which hosted Open Ports had the fiscal means to finance the industrial projects they promoted. They financed the creation of shipbuilding and arsenals, but development remained limited because military industry requires the backing of the mining, iron and steel, and machinery industries that were not available. The weakness of the Chinese industrial structure was blatantly revealed.

The failure of the self-reinforcing drive gave way to the only feasible route at the time: industrial modernization within Open Ports benefiting from technology transfers from foreign capital and producing for export. A modern urban civilization emerged on the eastern coast, pioneered in the cities of Tianjin, Canton, and Shanghai. This industrial activity was completely cut off from the huge, backward, agricultural countryside. It was an alien protuberance with no capacity to awaken the economy of the whole country. On one side, foreign enterprises met fierce resistance whenever they unsuccessfully tried to penetrate the interior of the country. On the other side, compradors were despised as the pet dogs of the hated foreigners, all the more so as their activities as middlemen allowed them to pile up the largest private wealth in China.

Nonetheless, an intellectual move emerged between 1872 and 1895 (Bergère 2007). This was the movement of Western Affairs, which wanted to draw lessons from the failure of self-reinforcing. The motive was nationalistic against the humiliation inflicted by foreign penetration. The idea was to raise mixed enterprises associating state officials and private shareholders in heavy industries, transport, and finance. The new firms should imitate Western companies in technology and organization in order to compete on the same footing. To do this, business elites were to be raised in modern specialized schools. To be accepted as members of the traditional intellectual elite, the newly trained experts had to be recruited as technical advisors to very high mandarins who endorsed the idea of modernization. These mandarins fixed the general orientation of the business, appointed directors, and negotiated state privileges, but they did not interfere with management, capital raising, and shareholder control of profitability.

Despite the relevance of the concept, the movement of Western Affairs failed. Few enterprises were created or were viable. They were not able to instill modernity in Chinese society. Shareholders demanded high guaranteed dividends, which thwarted profitability and investment capacity. Nepotism and corruption were widespread. The most overriding obstacle to their development was the weakness of the state. Provinces had loosened their ties with the central power so consequently modernization depended too much on the rivalries between provincial governors and on the vagaries of their careers. In other words, the early attempts of industrial modernization in China were restricted to the coastal urban areas. Unlike the urban elites who began to foster strong nationalistic sentiments for all the years of foreign humiliation, the vast rural interior of China was still deep in imperial logic and tradition. Not only did rural gentries hold speculative attitudes toward these "modern" enterprises, there was a silent battle between the interior rural China symbolizing the old imperial order, and the new capitalist urban one. As regards the late Qing state, not only it did not have the capacity or "know-how" to mobilize rural resources into an industrialization process, it could not take a clear-cut stand either. After all, Qing rulers were trained to be emperors. Rebuilding a unitary state upon an industrialized economy in a perplexed and bellicose international environment was too arduous a job. As long as the regime still had a strong grip over the major parts of its territory, the Qing central government was inert to change.

The shock came with the defeat of China against Japan in 1895 and the ensuing treaty of Shimonoseki. This failure rallied the central government to the policy of reform. But the will to modernize came too late to save the Qing dynasty.

In July 1901 an imperial decree launched a new policy inspired by the Japanese Meiji reform. But the government was too weak and too poor to implement it. All functions of government were affected by the reform. One of its most important institutions, the imperial system of examinations, was abolished in 1905. However, the core of the reform was the recentralization of government authority, the strong intervention of the state in the economy, and the coordination through state agencies under the sole authority of the central government in dominating the conflicting interests of local governments. But central government simply did not have the resources to impose its reforms any more. Rivalries erupted everywhere, making new companies unmanageable, many of them lacking vital financing. The empire finally crumbled in 1911, opening a new chaotic era in which an ephemeral blossoming of private capitalism, confined to the coastal regions, sprang from nowhere.

The years 1911 to 1927 made a strange epoch. The republic founded in 1912 was never able to impose a unified authority and disappeared as early as 1916, leaving the country divided between conflicting warlords in the north and the centre and a revolutionary government run by Sun Yat-sen in the south. The removal of the unitary state somehow enabled a period of spontaneous and vibrant private capitalism, entirely focused on exports and without any connection with the depth of the rural Chinese economy.

In April 1927, Chiang Kai-shek's coup reunified the country under Guomindang rule until the Japanese invasion of China in 1937. The capital was transferred to Nanking. The coup launched the long-standing endemic civil war between

Guomindang and the Communists under Mao Zedong's leadership, which lasted until 1949. It became an open war for power all over the country between the surrender of Japan in August 1945 and the proclamation of the People's Republic of China on October 1, 1949. Because Guomindang's ideology had no sympathy for private capitalists and because the Great Depression began to hurt the Chinese economy in 1932, bureaucratic capitalism made a comeback in a mixed economy that severely limited the freedom of private enterprise.

Let us sketch the most salient economic traits of these two contrasted periods to pinpoint their legacies for the contemporary reform.

The growth of private capitalism in the anarchic period (1912–27)

A dual industrial system developed without much linkage or spillover effects. In Manchuria exploitation of coal and iron ore led to heavy industrialization and construction of a dense network of railroads to serve Japanese military interests. Equipment and managers came from Japan and sub-contracting to Chinese firms was very limited. In and around the Open Ports, World War I provided considerable opportunity to create clusters of private firms in light industries.

Because of the war, foreign competition declined dramatically. Chinese firms that were prevented before from producing for domestic markets by the unequal treaties now indulged in import substitution in textile and food industries. Simultaneously exports benefited from world demand in primary commodities and goods produced by light industries. Because Asian countries (primarily China and India) had silver currencies, the jump in foreign purchases of Asian countries increased the world demand for silver. The increase in the relative price of silver raised the real exchange rate of the tael (the Chinese currency), augmenting its purchasing power over foreign goods.

The big push to private Chinese enterprises continued after the war and into the roaring twenties. It was a Confucian capitalism, an achievement of extended families, drawing resources, competences, and customers from network solidarity that is the root of Chinese society. The entrepreneurs of this "golden age" were able to effectively combine tradition and modernization. The families provided finance and human capital. Business confidentiality was a must. Most firms did not register, or else they did under partnerships instead of shareholding companies. The ultimate authority was patriarchal, exerted by the chief of the family who controlled the sensitive commercial information and finances with the help of a close private bureau. Within firms, social relationships were based on Confucian principles. Hierarchy and reciprocal obligations, loyalty and obedience on the side of employees, benevolence and protection on the side of the boss, were the ties that amalgamated business and family culture.

How did this brand of capitalism impact rural areas? Not much, except in the vicinity of the big coastal cities. Even in those privileged areas, agricultural production was not elastic enough to provide both the city population with enough food and firms with primary commodities at times of increased demand. Many more regions lost out. New weaving machines ousted hand-weaving. Only in suburban areas were there both increased opportunities for industrial employment and increased demand for agricultural products. In the rest of the country real rural income went on decreasing. Because the traditional economy weighed much more in GDP, the decline in real income continued unabated, as depicted in Table 2.1.

Another source of fragility in these enterprises was finance. Wealth owners were wary of lending. They demanded guaranteed interest and very high dividends. Financial costs absorbed most of the profits, leaving firms vulnerable to downswings in demand. Their cash flow depended on short-term bank loans. Widespread speculation in the Open Ports upset the business cycle. Industrialists and merchants did not cover their foreign exchange receipts and expenses. They preferred to speculate on the world price of silver, benefiting from short-term gains just after the war, but suffering catastrophic losses in 1923. Therefore this financial environment was not conducive at all to the long-term strategies that Chinese development needed most.

In addition, the political regime was utterly uncertain. Not only was there a scramble for power among warlords, but a powerful labor movement arose under the guidance of the newly created Communist Party. At its start in 1921 the Party participated in an anti-imperialist coalition with business associations strikes in foreign firms, and boycotts of foreign-made goods were means of an economic nationalism aimed at weakening foreign competition and ultimately getting rid of the wicked treaties. Politically the nationalist movement was led by the Guomindang. In 1926 the Communists mobilized labor unions and peasant organizations to help Chiang Kai-shek defeat the warlords and conquer the provinces in the centre of the country, de facto unifying China, but Manchuria was occupied by the Japanese. However, on April 12, 1927, Chiang Kai-shek abruptly betrayed his Communist allies. Financed by bankers, he recruited yobs from secret gangs to murder union leaders in Shanghai and crushed the strikers. In financing Chiang Kai-shek's coup, business interests killed two birds with one stone: they broke the threatening insurrectional strikes once and for all and helped restore a unified state that could establish some political stability. Nonetheless, the aftermath proved disappointing for business interests: capitalists were entirely subject to the government and the Guomindang bureaucracy.

State capitalism and Japanese occupation (1927–49)

The world economic crisis was the proximate cause that put an end to the "golden age" of Chinese capitalism. From 1928 to 1931 the value of silver collapsed on the world market, pulling down the value of the tael. The huge unintended devaluation (about 50 percent) sheltered Chinese foreign trade from the impact of plummeting world trade in the first few years of the crisis. However, the depression struck in 1932. The value of silver recovered after sterling abandoned the Gold Standard in September 1931, bringing about a revaluation of the tael at the worst time. Meanwhile, government policy did not uphold private firms. Guomingdang's regime was a partial unitary state. It had to co-exist with regional warlords, and most of its resources came from urban China (Wong 1997:164), the only places they had effective control. Moreover, Guomingdang failed to propose, let alone implement, congruous national ruling mechanisms. Their leaders lacked the will to apply parliamentary rule, nor could they inject new vigor into Confucian traditions. The partiality of unity brought about the worst outcomes. On the one hand, the state was too weak to shield foreign influences and domestic rivalries, and thus military goals were still the most crucial, hijacking the economy. On the other hand, unitary logic squashed the private economy which had already had an arduous time. For firm political control and thorough exploitation of economic resources, state capitalism became the best choice.

Facing a worsening war against Japan, the Guomindang was determined to centralize economic resources. A planning agency (the National Defense Commission, then the Natural Resource Commission) was set up in 1932 with the objective of building up heavy industries under state control. Banks were nationalized in 1934. In other industries the government forced the transformation of private into mixed enterprises supervised by bureaucrats. In 1934 the tael was abolished and the link with silver ended. The monetary system was placed under an inconvertible paper currency (dollar-fabi). The government could freely finance its deficit with inflationary money expansion.

The Japanese invasion started in the summer of 1937. The battle for Shanghai lasted three months, the city falling in November followed by Nanking at the end of the year. The nationalist government retreated to the central provinces, but the enemy carried on its offensive and took over Wuhan in October 1938. Chiang Kai-chek was obliged to settle in Chongqing, far in the west. Even this far-away city was not protected from the devastating Japanese bombing. China was de facto cut in two until 1945. This was also the fate of the capitalists. Some stayed in the occupied regions and collaborated, voluntarily or not, with the Japanese. Others transplanted their enterprises in the free zone with heavy costs. During the war, industry in the free zone rested entirely on the public sector. After the Japanese surrender, Shanghai recovered its predominance, all the more so since the imperialist enclaves had been swept away. However, the nationalist government faced two deadly threats: hyperinflation, and the civil war that resumed in the summer of 1946.

After the end of the war, chronic high inflation increased, disrupting economic activity entirely. All investment gave way to hoarding every precious metal or scarce commodity instantly tradable. The closer to Shanghai the battlefields, the higher the inflation rate. In August 1948 a feeble and desperate government attempted a monetary reform. The valueless paper currency was replaced by a new currency, the gold Yuan at a conversion rate of three million to one. The issuance of notes in the new currency was to be strictly controlled. Attendant measures to discourage speculation and to control prices were taken. However, the government was soon to break its commitment and abandoned the reform at the end of October. From that date on trust collapsed completely. The overall defeat of the Guomindang and the takeover of the country by the Communists was just a matter of months away. The dawn of a new era that would reveal a radically different economic regime was breaking.

The Maoist era: forced industrialization under political instability

Despite the multiple bifurcations in policy, the Communist leadership was inspired by two pervasive ideas: capital-intensive industrialization in heavy industries and inward growth cum minimal exchanges with the outside world. Some scholars label it "Big Push industrialization" (Naughton 2007: 55–9). It was essentially a command economy where market forces were curtailed and even disappeared entirely at some stages. Agriculture and industry were treated differently. In 1950 a radical land reform collectivized production in agriculture all over the country, although it took until 1956 to enroll farm households into the cooperative. Markets for agricultural products decayed and the state became the sole buyer. Compulsory procurement quotas were established over basic goods. Farmers had to sell a defined quantity of goods to the grain monopoly at low prices, keeping wages low and stable. Only informal exchanges remained, kept alive by peddlers who were tolerated at the fringes of the planned economy.

When the Communist Party took over the country, the economy was at its nadir. Industrial production had slumped 50 percent and agricultural production 25 percent. The industrial equipment in Manchuria had been plundered by the Soviets in 1945–6. Many owners and managers of private firms in the main cities of the eastern coast had fled. The newly established currency, the renminbi, was not immediately accepted. Facing such difficulty, the Communist Party envisaged a lengthy transition to the Soviet model of industrial planning. Mao Zedong explained the doctrine of the United Front guided by the Democratic Dictatorship of the People. National capitalists, who had chosen to help fight the anti-imperialist war, were welcome to participate in the reconstruction of the country. Private firms willing to cooperate were assured of loans from the People's Bank of China, of allocations of scarce primary commodities, and of state purchases. The government also mitigated the claims of the workers for the sake of the reshuffling of the national economy. Committees gathering representatives of workers and business managers negotiated working conditions and production objectives under the arbitrage of Party officials.

Between 1949 and 1952 the policy worked wonders. The investment rate as a share of GDP increased to 26 percent, a high level for such a poor country; 80 percent of investment went to heavy industry, so that industrial production rose 54 percent. Meanwhile, state enterprises achieved a much higher speed, with the result that the private sector declined relatively from 63 to 39 percent of industrial production between 1949 and 1952 (Bergère 2007: 201). Encouraged by a better-than-expected performance and worried by the threat of American imperialism following China's involvement in the Korean War in 1950, the Party leadership decided to speed up the transition to a fully socialist economy. From that time on, the Chinese development strategy deviated markedly from the Japanese post-war growth model (Table 2.2).

In 1952 the Party launched the campaign of the Five Anti (bribe, fraud, fiscal evasion, embezzlement, and illegal capture of secret state information). This campaign ended in the full nationalization of private businesses in 1956. In the interim

Table 2.2 China and Japan's contrasting industrialization strategies (1952–78)

Characteristics	China	Japan
Political regime	Democratic dictatorship of the people but instability within Communist Party	Representative democracy with a single party in power (Liberal Democratic Party of Japan) throughout the period
Overall strategy	Priority to heavy industries integrating vertically	Start with consumer light industry and integrate upstream
Agriculture	Collectivization and state procurements at low prices	Private with regulated high price of rice
Main source of demand	Government investment projects in public sector	Domestic consumer demand and exports inducing high invest
Household income	Slow growing	Fast growing
Degree of openness	Minimal	Low but increasing with competitiveness
Economic coordination	Central planning under Communist Party guidance	Market with high collusion between the Ministry of Finance, the Ministry of International Trade and Industry, and business associations

period private firms had to transform into mixed ventures. Therefore state control on the economy was immensely increased. In all practical matters the Chinese bourgeoisie had ceased to play a significant social role. In the meantime the Party launched the first five-year plan in 1953, the objective of which was to establish true state capitalism. As acknowledged by Barry Naughton, it was a dramatic success, although growth was far from steady. There were two peaks of investment surge in 1953 and 1956 interspersed by two years of retrenchment. The big boost of 1955–6 entailed the recurrent stresses between agriculture and industry. Millions of workers had migrated from rural dwellings to the cities and agricultural production could not keep pace with the fast increase in demand.

In September 1956 the Eighth Congress of the Communist Party acknowledged the risks of careless change and advocated moderation. This was the "Hundred Flowers" episode, praising a subsidiary role for market mechanisms and the coexistence of different forms of ownership. It was a Chinese brand of New Economic Policy (NEP). However, decentralization of planning rights facilitated irrational investments which dramatized the stresses between agriculture and industry. This reforming attempt eventually degraded into one of the most catastrophic experiences ever, called the Great Leap Forward (GLF) that lasted from 1958 to 1960. By massively reducing the supply of labor and land available for food production and by hardening the compulsory deliveries of food to the state, Mao's leftist drive condemned the countryside to starvation. Outright famine occurred in 1960, and lasted until 1962, albeit 20 million workers had already been sent back to the countryside in 1961. The rural communes were restructured on smaller groups of households and inefficient rural factories were cut back. Meanwhile, industrialization was focused on the creation of an industrial base in inland provinces for military reasons. It was the Third Front that was abruptly halted when Mao launched the Cultural Revolution in 1967. However, as far as the economy was concerned, the Cultural Revolution did not seriously disrupt agricultural production. Regarding industrial production, it declined moderately. After its end in 1969, the imbalance between industrial and agricultural growth re-emerged. Industrial growth was much too fast for the rigid capacity of food supply. Too much manpower was tied up in too long investment projects.

The political struggle within the Party continued on the course of policy with oscillations between the "Leftist" propagandists advocating a big push to fast access to communist society and the "Rightists" who pleaded for a patient lengthier transition. The latter resumed the upper hand when Prime Minister Zhou Enlai cut back the priority of the Third Front and took advantage of the improvement in diplomatic relationships with the US to authorize imports of industrial equipment and to welcome foreign investment to build fertilizer plants. In 1974 Deng Xiaoping was reinstalled in a leadership position. After a final political jolt in 1976, Mao's death in September finally broke the political deadlock. In December 1978 the third plenum of the Central Committee shifted irreversibly the rationale of economic policies. The era of fundamental economic reform had finally come.

Although Mao's era was often used to contrast with the reforms after 1978, it actually laid down crucial foundations for the later dazzling economic performance. Starting from their experiences in the countryside during the Japanese invasion, the Communist Party finally succeeded in mobilizing the rural regions of China. Attempts to profoundly restructure rural China into communist collectives after 1949 completely destroyed the working incentives of the farmers and led to catastrophes, but it did succeed in shaking rural China, so that rural institutions exhibited more willingness to evolve from thousand-year-long imperial traditions into hybrid models and became engines for the first stage of reform (1978–94).

At the same time, through strict central planning and major distortion of prices (especially for agricultural goods and labor), the Communist Party succeeded in breaking the bottleneck that low agricultural productivity imposed on the national dynamic of industrialization. The industrial investment rate was kept high, which enabled the establishment of a widespread industrial base with Third Front projects bringing industrial modernization from the coast to the deep interior.

However, the most fundamental difference of Mao's reign, compared with previous post-imperial regimes, is political. State power was finally strong enough to splinter all external and domestic identities independent from central authority, no matter whether they were military, political, or economic. The old unitary system was re-established. A new unitary ideology was formed based on Confucian tradition with a communist face. The Democratic Dictatorship of the People was a restatement of absolute central authority, which based its legitimacy on the minimum welfare level of its population.

The irony is that both capitalism and Confucianism were the two trends Mao Zedong fought against the hardest for the whole of his life. The Cultural Revolution was his last and most desperate battle to dismantle Confucian bureaucratic tradition and capitalist dynamics in China. He did not win. On the contrary, it was precisely he who sowed the seeds for the revitalization of both in China. Once the total denial to market mechanism was incrementally corrected, China erupted with astonishing momentum with a hybrid of Confucian and capitalist institutions. We will elaborate this argument in Chapter 3.

From China's economic history to growth theory

The legacy of the Socialist Revolution to 1978 prolonged the main characteristic of the long overview of Chinese economic history. As pointed out by Barry Naughton, every time the system began to accelerate, it ran into fundamental problems. The stumbling block was the inability of agriculture to generate sufficient food surpluses to supply a burgeoning industrial sector. Therefore the growth dynamic envisioned by Adam Smith, whereby the social division of labor generates productivity gains that increase income and demand for new markets, which in turn generate a deepening of the division of labor (Figure 2.1) was thwarted early. If labor productivity gains in agriculture do not rise fast enough to provide an expanding surplus for the cities to release manpower to be employed in incipient industries, real income ceases to increase and the economy remains trapped in a high equilibrium, when the growth rate of the economy equals population growth and real per capita stagnates.

What are the obstacles to sustained growth? Did China fall into the trap while Europe avoided it with the industrial revolution? Why did Europe break the Gordian knot in the early nineteenth century and China stayed put? Previously we pointed out some institutional reasons that were specific to China. Below we focus on the economic dynamics, drawing insights from new findings from research by the Global History School.

Kenneth Pomeranz (2000) has shown that neither East Asia nor Europe was ready as late as the eighteenth century to launch the industrial revolution. It was

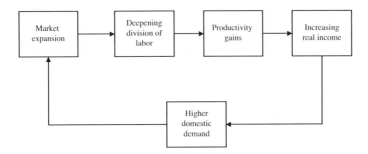

Figure 2.1 Adam Smith's growth dynamic.

a dramatic bifurcation in the course of history due to the expansion of trade towards the new territories of America that effectively eliminated the obstacles in primary resources. Pomeranz shows convincingly that, before the exports of slaves from Africa to America and the huge migration of European colonists there, European national economies had both a limited supply of arable land and a limited supply of timber, then the only source of energy. For that matter, Western Europe was even more handicapped than China. In massively importing food and cotton from cheap land and slave labor, Britain was able to break the increasing cost of agricultural production. Furthermore, Britain was able to exploit coal mines that were close to the new industrial cities of Manchester and Liverpool, while in China coal mines were far from the lower Yangtze and suffered from high costs of transportation. The connection of coal burning and vapor machines was the linchpin of the first industrial revolution.

Apart from ecological obstacles, the high equilibrium trap was fostered by institutional constraints already mentioned by Adam Smith. In China merchants were not at the top of the social elite. Money wealth was not a praised social value, even if markets were buoyant. Fernand Braudel noticed in his insightful history of the European economy that a market economy is not a capitalist economy (Braudel 1985). Capitalism can dawn and develop only behind a state power that embodies the interests of the emerging bourgeoisie. In Western Europe the sovereigns united their national territories politically in waging wars against feudal lords and in securing their borders through endless wars against one another. Technological modernization came in the military. Moreover, to finance strong armies sovereigns were content to fall into debt. They became persistently dependent on financiers who then acquired privileges and political influence. Conflicting alliances between the public prestige of sovereigns and the private interests of financiers upset the ancient ties between the nobility and the sovereign in the British political revolution of the 1690s and the French revolution of the 1790s. In Great Britain, however, the Magna Carta had already placed the finances of the kingdom under parliamentary control as early as 1215.

Sugihara (2003) remarks that a different type of state existed in East Asia. In China a decentralized market economy was loosely coordinated by bureaucrat elites whose recruitment and reproduction prevented the crystallization of a bourgeois class. The spending of central government was a low share of GDP and was financed by domestic taxes and foreign tributes. The military was not a spur for technological innovations after the ending of naval expeditions.

At this point of our investigation let us say that the two pillars of industrialization required to break Smith's high equilibrium trap were strong states mustering finances to build armies that spur technological innovation on the one hand, and long-distance trade and investment that globalize markets on the other hand. In the late eighteenth century China lacked both. Now we need more formal analysis to understand better the linkage between agriculture and industry. A theoretical knowledge about the links between agriculture and industry is necessary to understand why, after 1978, China finally broke the limits that the rural economy had laid upon growth for centuries.

However, as we will show in the second part of this book, China's reform has not stalled but has gone through severe disequilibria. There are questions about the capitalist growth model adopted since the early 1990s. Therefore we first of all revisit Adam Smith's theory of limited national growth within the apparatus of a formal model. Then we examine the Marx–Schumpeter theory of endless worldwide capitalist growth. Their endogenous growth model suffers from the effects of ecological constraints that have reappeared worldwide with the depletion of primary resources and the threat of climate change. This challenge leads us to introduce in the third part of this book the concept of sustainable growth as a guide for the new stage of reform in the next two decades.

Contrasting dynamics in capitalist development: Adam Smith's barrier of limited land and primary resources in national economies

The mainstream theory of growth is the Solow model (Solow 1956). It assumes that all productive activities are represented by combinations of factors of production that are substitutable and freely mobile from one activity to the other. They all exhibit constant returns to scale and decreasing marginal returns in the factors of production. In this framework growth is capital intensive. Capital accumulation raises capital per worker and the latter increases labor productivity. Because the marginal productivity of capital diminishes with capital accumulation, net productive investment diminishes until the net return on capital (marginal productivity minus depreciation) reaches zero. At that point the ratio of capital to output is optimal. If long-term growth subsists, it is fully exogenous, being due to growth in the labor force and to a supposedly costless technological progress.

In a free trade world, where all combinations of the factors of production are available everywhere and capital is fully mobile, trade will bring a single system of relative equilibrium prices. This is the famous Samuelson–Stolper theorem (1941). Subsequently every country will reach the same optimal capital/output

Table 2.3 Disparities of development and conditional convergence

	GDP per capita (1990 PPP$)				GDP per capita (% US)			
	1900	1950	1990	2000	1900	1950	1990	2000
Western Europe	2,893	4,579	15,966	19,256	70.7	47.9	68.8	68.9
US	4,091	9,561	23,201	27,948	100.0	100.0	100.0	100.0
Japan	1,180	1,921	18,789	20,683	28.8	20.1	81.0	74.0
Latin America	1,109	2,506	5,053	5,811	24.4	26.2	21.8	20.8
China	545	439	1,858	3,583	11.0	4.6	8.0	12.8
Other Asia	802	918	3,084	3,997	19.6	9.6	13.3	14.3
Africa	601	894	1,444	1,489	14.7	9.3	6.2	5.3

Source: Maddison (2003)

ratio. Because exogenous technological progress is a free good, GDP per capita will converge steadily all over the world.

This growth model is utterly irrelevant in accounting for historical development. Taken from Maddison's statistics, Table 2.3 exhibits levels of GDP per capita in absolute terms and relative to the US in the twentieth century.

Instead of progressive convergence, Africa suffered persistent divergence throughout the century! In the first half of the century all regions of the world except Latin America lost ground to the US, already by far the most developed region in 1900. However, Latin America diverged in the second half of the century. Convergence occurred in Europe and Japan from 1950 to 1990 and then the process stopped in Western Europe and reversed in Japan. Only in China and other Asian countries was there a sustained catching up, admittedly from very low levels, in the second half of the century. Therefore another growth model is definitely needed to understand the development of societies that are primarily rural and agrarian. Convergence is obviously conditional, but conditional to what? How can capitalism take root in some parts of the world and not in others?

Two basic characteristics of development are alien to the standard theory of economic growth. First, the production system is heterogeneous; activities are more complementary than substitutable. Second, the most important heterogeneity in early stages of industrial development is decreasing marginal returns in agriculture and increasing returns in industry. These characteristics lead to irreversible dynamics whereby the state of the economic system depends on its past history. Contrary to the traditional production function, there is no way to reverse the combinations of the factors of production that have been adopted through time.

Therefore let us consider two sectors: agriculture and industry. In industry there are increasing returns to scale, so that the real wage is an increasing function of labor employed. In agriculture the factor "land" is fixed and there are two sub-sectors. One is exogenous and has a fixed level of production and price. It produces subsistence good primarily for the self-consumption of the rural people, whose surplus is "exported" to the urban economy. The real wage in the rural economy is fixed in terms of the subsistence good. The other sub-sector produces marketable goods that are "exported" to the urban industrial economy (Box 2.1). Conversely, the rural economy imports the manufactured good produced by the industrial sector. We suppose homogeneity in the industrial sector so that the manufactured good imported by the rural economy can be partly a consumption good consumed over subsistence and partly an investment good. The amount of labor that can be employed productively on the land is limited. The limit is partly a natural constraint, partly the result of the mode of appropriation of land. We have remarked that the predominance of household ownership in China allows much more labor intensity than sharecropping and lease farming. Box 2.1 posits the structural equations in the urban and in the rural economy and the reduced equations to be solved.

The main result is the following. The conjunction of an exogenous subsistence wage in the rural economy and of decreasing marginal returns in the "exportable" agricultural good makes the rate of return in the "capitalist" agriculture a decreasing function of the subsistence wage. Conversely, because industry enjoys increasing returns to scale, the urban real wage and the industrial rate of return are both rising functions of industrial production, thus of the level of production of the agricultural good imported as input in industry. Therefore the minimum subsistence wage in terms of the subsistence good in the rural economy entails a constraint on industrial production. A situation can arise in which full employment of the available workforce in industry involves a relative overproduction of industrial products regarding the available supply of agricultural products. This is Adam Smith's high equilibrium trap. It is also the root of the great urban–rural divide acknowledged by Arrighi (2007).

It is possible to understand theoretically why it is a trap. Box 2.1 provides a formal demonstration. The market adjustment to this disequilibrium is a rise in the relative price of agricultural to industrial products. There is a price that gives an amount of rent to the landowners, making them capable of absorbing the excess supply of industrial products. However, this reasoning ignores the specific character of the labor force, whose price cannot decline under a minimum in terms of subsistence. Furthermore, the subsistence sub-sector is not market-oriented but rather a mode of production which preserves the social network of interrelationships within rural communities. It is immune from market influence.

Kenneth Pomeranz has convincingly shown that Western Europe was victim to the same trap as late as the eighteenth century. However, the nature of rival nation states with their emphasis on military strength and their permeability to private financial interests induced Britain, and France to a lesser extent, to improve naval technologies and to develop long-distance trade at lower costs and better security. Leaning heavily on their colonial empires, these countries exported slaves from Africa to America in order to exploit an abundance of new and fertile open land. The trade between Europe and America accelerated after the independence of the United States, dramatically lowering the cost of food and textile products imported in Europe for manufactured goods exported to America. Such was the boost in economic globalization that created a sine qua non condition for European industrialization.

Therefore international expansion of trade and investment into new territories was tantamount to radical technological innovation in agriculture. It broke the

---

Box 2.1 A Smithian two-sector model of the urban–rural divide

Structural equations

Industry in urban economy:

$$Py = (wl + kPy + jP^* y)(1 + r)$$

$$y = l^{\alpha}$$

$$\frac{w}{p} = (l^{\alpha-1})^{\sigma}$$

$$sy = ky + b\left(\frac{P}{P}\right)(1 - s^*)y^*$$

Agriculture in rural economy: one subsistence good exogenous and one good "exported" to the urban economy as both industrial input and consumer good

$$\overline{P}y^* = \overline{P}\overline{x} + P^* x^*$$

$$x^* = l^{*\beta}$$

$$\overline{x} = \left[1 - b\left(\frac{P}{\overline{P}}\right)\right](1 - s^*)y^*$$

$$x^* = jy$$

$$P^*x^* = (w^* l^* + k^* Px^*)(1 + r^*) + R$$

$$R = P^* (1 - \beta) x^*$$

$$\overline{w} = \overline{\varpi}\overline{P}$$

"Balance of payment" equilibrium between urban and rural economies:

$$P^*x^* = k^* Px^* + b\left(\frac{P}{\overline{P}}\right)(1 - s^*)y^*$$

Structural coefficients and exogenous variables:

k and k^* are input coefficients, j is import coefficient from industry to agriculture

α and β are factor elasticities of the production functions. $\alpha > 1$ since industry is in increasing marginal returns, $\beta < 1$ since agriculture is in decreasing marginal returns

s and s^* are the saving rates respectively in the urban and rural economies

σ is the elasticity of the real wage to production in industry

The subsistence sector is entirely exogenous in production, price, and subsistence wage:

$$\overline{x}, \overline{P}, \overline{\varpi}$$

Endogenous variables:

Production per capita: y, x^*, and y^* (total production in the rural economy)

Labor input per capita: l and l^*

Nominal prices: P, P^*, $\overline{P}$

We introduce three variables which are relative prices:

$\varpi = \frac{w}{P}$ is the real wage in industry

$e = \frac{P}{\overline{P}}$ is the real exchange rate of the urban against the rural economy

$\tau = \frac{P^*}{P}$ is the terms of trade of the "exportable" agricultural production to industrial production

r and r^* are the rate of returns in industry and in agriculture respectively

Reduced equations

In eliminating nominal variables, we arrive at a structural model of nine equations in the nine endogenous real variables: y, l, x^*, l^*, τ, e, ω, r, r^*.

$$y = (\varpi l + ky + j\tau y)(1 + r)$$

$$y = l^{\alpha}$$

$$\varpi = (l^{\alpha-1})^{\sigma}$$

$$sy = ky + b(e)(1 - s^*)(\bar{x} + \tau ex^*)$$

$$s^* = l^{*\beta}$$

$$\bar{x} = [1-b(e)](1-s^*)(\bar{x} + \tau ex^*)$$

$$x^* = jy$$

$$\tau ex^* = (\varpi l^* + k^* \, ex^*)(1 + r^*) + \tau e(1-\beta)x^*$$

$$\tau x^* = k^* \, x^* + b(e)(1 - s^*)(\bar{x} + \tau ex^*)$$

In eliminating y, l, l^*, τ, ω, a reduced system of five equations remains:

$(1)\ \dfrac{1}{1+r} = (\dfrac{x^*}{j})^{\frac{(\alpha-1)(1-\sigma)}{\alpha}} + k + j\tau$

$(2)\ \beta\tau e = (\varpi x^{*\frac{1-\beta}{\beta}} + k^*e)(1 + r^*)$

$(3)\ \bar{x} = [1 - b(e)](1 - s^*)(\bar{x} + \tau ex^*)$

$(4)\ \tau x^* = k^* \, x^* + b(e)(1 - s^*)(\bar{x} + \tau ex^*)$

$(5)\ \tau = \dfrac{(s - k)}{j} + k^*$

Resolution

We can see that τ (the terms of trade of agriculture over industry) is the driving variable since it depends only on structural coefficients. They improve with excess saving in the urban economy ($s>k$), with techniques of production in industry that save primary input from agriculture ($j\downarrow$) and with more industrial input to produce a unit of exportable agricultural output ($k^*\uparrow$).

Replacing the value of τ in equation (1) we can see that r (the rate of return in industry) is a rising function of x^* because more input from agriculture means more industrial production that involves lower unit labor costs with increasing marginal returns. But it is obviously a decreasing function of τ.

Equations (3) and (4) determine x^*:

$$x^* = \frac{[s^* +(1 - s^*)b(e)]\bar{x}}{\tau(1 - s^*)e[1 - b(e)]}$$

x^* depends on relative prices. It is a decreasing function of τ and also a decreasing function of e if $s>k$.

Finally equation (2) determines r^*:

$$r^* = \frac{(\beta\tau - k^*)e - \overline{\omega}x^{*\frac{1-\beta}{\beta}}}{\overline{\omega}x^{*\frac{1-\beta}{\beta}} + k^*e}$$

The conflicting capitalist interests in industry and in agriculture are blatant. R is an increasing function of x^* and r^* a decreasing function of x^*. The income due to a higher production in exportable agricultural product is captured by an increase in rents. Furthermore, industrial wages are an increasing function of x^*.

$$\omega = (l^{\alpha-1})^o = y^{\frac{(\alpha-1)\sigma}{\alpha}} = \left(\frac{x^*}{j}\right)^{\frac{(\alpha-1)\sigma}{\alpha}}$$

If x^* expands with international trade $\frac{\omega}{\overline{\omega}}$ rises with x^*. Export-led growth induces wage inequality between urban and rural economy at the expense of the latter.

---

deadlock of declining marginal returns in Britain. Enactment of free trade laws in 1844 heralded the complete victory of the industrial and merchant bourgeoisie over landowners. Imports of cheap food and cotton from slave-labored American plantations worked as a rent-reducing device that diminished labor costs in British textile and food-processing factories.

Income generated in America by the sale of primary products hugely enlarged the demand addressed to British industry. Because the subsistence wage defined a floor price in terms of agricultural products, transatlantic trade generated a foreign trade multiplier for manufactured British goods. The multiplier raised the rate of profit in industry. British industrialists could make the most of increasing returns in raising their investment rate. A new growth regime, grounded on sustained accumulation in industry, could take off and open the era of industrial revolution. China failed to implement it in the Maoist epoch. It had to delay the second stage of its reform until the 1990s and 2000s after a successful land reform and an increased opening to foreign trade in the 1980s.

Contrasting dynamics in capitalist development: Marxian–Schumpeterian ever-lasting growth in the global economy

Marx differs from Smith in his representation of capitalist accumulation in a crucial way: the transformation of money into capital. For Smith the market is modeled according to the simple exchange C (commodity)_M (money)_C (commodity). He does not consider money as something different from a medium of exchange. Marx shows how capitalism transforms the market into M_C_M. The essence of capitalism can be deployed. It is the process of self-increasing abstract value in the form of money for its own sake. This process is limitless in its purpose because there is no limit to the search of money wealth. The reason is that money is power in the hands of financiers. Therefore a necessary (but not sufficient) social condition for limitless growth is a society where the power of money is also state power or it decisively influences state power. A complementary condition is the development of free capital markets encompassing the whole world. It allows a financial elite, managing oligopolistic financial institutions, to circumvent state regulations and (or) to dictate its own interests to government policies. In such societies capitalism is threatened by the class struggle, not by the finitude of natural resources.

In borderless world markets labor itself is completely cut off from its rural roots. Ideally, from the capitalist viewpoint, labor tends to become a free commodity. When this state of affairs is reached by virtue of market expansion, the division of labor within firms supersedes the division of labor among firms as the main source of productivity gains. Marx calls it the search for relative surplus value by virtue of specializing work and coordinating segmented jobs with machinery. In large industrial firms, which had appeared in the US in the late nineteenth century as the outcome of a powerful merger wave, increasing returns to scale within the firms propelled the US to the position of having the most efficient brand of capitalism (Aglietta 1980). "Scientific" management, the basic principle of which was Taylorism, radically changed capital–labor relationships and reverberated in the labor market. A dual labor market settled down. An insider market of skilled workers, enjoying high wages and relatively protected jobs, was separated from the outside market of proletarized unskilled labor. Company rules and union representation of the interests of skilled workers negotiated collective contracts on work conditions and wage formulas linked to labor productivity advances. The resulting institutionalization of labor relationships reinforced the segmentation of the labor market.

Nonetheless, Marx thought that the large masses of unskilled workers, deprived of social rights, would get ever poorer. They would unite internationally in a powerful class struggle that would be strengthened as much as capitalism would conquer the whole world. Therefore Marx did not consider that Smithian limits to capital accumulation, stemming from primary resources, would reappear worldwide. He was convinced that the class struggle waged by anti-capitalist forces would trigger world revolution and abolish capitalism before any scarcity in natural resources had raised overriding obstacles to runaway growth. The reason for Marx's optimism was the understanding that growth is endogenous, as opposed to exogenous growth depicted in the Solow model. The most popular theoretician of endogenous growth is Schumpeter who agreed with Marx on the self-fulfilling logic of capital accumulation, which was capable of generating increasing returns without being thwarted by natural limits. However, he disagreed with the outcome of increasing mass poverty of workers and pending world revolution.

Marx viewed the worsening class struggle as a side effect of the way capitalists increased surplus value by exploiting labor. To get ever-higher surplus value, firms have to introduce more and more capital-intensive technologies. Surplus value is generated by the work process in which labor sets fixed capital in motion, while the latter transmits only progressively its value to the product through depreciation. Therefore a higher surplus value means a rising share of profit in GDP. But, thanks to competition between capitalists, profit is accumulated not consumed. When capital accumulation is underway, investment in fixed assets increases faster than profits. Subsequently capital rises faster than profit and the rate of return plummets, triggering a crisis of over accumulation in fixed capital. Because most capital accumulation is financed by credit in expectation of higher returns on invested capital, the self-inflicted barrier to steady growth launches a full-fledged financial crisis. In the subsequent recession fixed capital is massively devalued. After the destruction of excess capital, the rate of profit recovers and a new wave of capital accumulation is generated. However, since the scale of capital accumulation mounts in one financial cycle after another, financial crises get more and more destructive, throwing large numbers of people into abject poverty giving ground for further bitter class struggles.

Schumpeter viewed technological innovation differently. He thought that the field of innovations is very broad, encompassing not only process innovation, which raises productivity in augmenting the share of profits, but also modes of consumption, organizational methods, and social rules. Instead of being excluded the labor class is included, achieving higher real wages, better work conditions, and social benefits. True innovations are both creative and destructive but, in the aggregate, the overall impact is not necessarily conducive to a falling rate

---

Box 2.2 Underpinnings of endogenous growth

Endogenous growth: the AK model

As explained above, processes of production change over time but are complementary rather than substitutable at any particular point in time. There is no reversibility in combinations of factors of production once some combinations have been chosen and others discarded.

Complementarities are captured in the following production function:

$Y_t = \min (AK_t, BL_t)$. K is the stock of capital and L is the amount of available labor. As long as capital is scarce regarding average productivities A and B, the function is $Y_t = AK_t$

Capital accumulation depends on depreciation (δ) and on the saving investment equilibrium with (σ) the aggregate rate of saving:

$$\dot{K}_t = -\delta K_t + I_t$$

$$I_t = \sigma Y_t$$

The potential growth rate is:

$$g = \frac{\dot{Y}_t}{Y_t} = \frac{\dot{K}_t}{K_t} = \sigma A - \delta \text{ as long as } AK > BL$$

This is the AK model of endogenous growth. It is path-dependent since a higher saving rate is conducive to a permanently higher growth rate, due to the non-declining marginal return on capital.

Schumpeterian innovation sustains the marginal productivity of capital

Technological innovation is a social phenomenon. It surges from the exchange of knowledge and learning that weaves network externalities between enterprises. It is a mix of institutional organization to develop advances in research and informal exchanges.

The impact is felt in network externalities between participating firms. Individually each firm would have had a production function with decreasing marginal productivity:

$$Y_{it} = A_t K_{it}^{\alpha} \text{ with } \alpha < 1$$

But the marginal productivity of capital of each firm belonging to the network is enhanced by the technology embodied by the capital of the whole bundle of firms which is a rising function of the accumulation of the aggregate of firms in knowledge technology:

$$A_t = AK_t^{\beta}$$

Consequently the production of each firm depends on its own capital and on the capital accumulated in the whole network:

$$Y_{it} = AK_t^{\beta} K_{it}^{\alpha}$$

In the simple case where all the firms have the same size, the aggregate production of the whole network of firms is: $Y_t = AK_t^{\alpha + \beta}$

If $\alpha + \beta = 1$, the marginal return on capital is constant. This is the AK model.

of profit. New processes and new products that embody a change in knowledge and that are intensive in human capital can save fixed capital as well as unskilled labor. In this way innovation boosts total factor productivity so that the aggregate capital/output ratio stays put (Box 2.2).

Table 2.4 Exogenous and endogenous growth

Exogenous growth	Endogenous growth
Marginal productivity of capital decreases with accumulation in aggregate	Marginal productivity of capital constant with accumulation in aggregate
In long-term equilibrium the rate of growth per capita depends only on exogenous technological progress	Growth is path-dependent: a permanently higher investment rate gives rise to a permanently higher growth rate
Diffusion of exogenous technological progress leads to universal convergence of all countries	Convergence is conditional to social processes that assimilate available technologies and raise productive investment

Table 2.4 sums up the opposition between exogenous and endogenous growth. Endogenous growth makes capital accumulation a process that is not automatic opposite to the Solow model. Innovations spring from the mind of entrepreneurs and are encouraged or discouraged by formal and informal social institutions. It follows that countries can assimilate new knowledge, follow the leaders and converge, or be left behind. What the Schumpeterian teaches are the conditions of conditional convergence. Furthermore, as long as innovation can combat the scarcity of natural capital, the virtuous circle between total factor productivity, real wage, and consumption growth may lead to sustainable growth.

Conclusion: China on the eve of reform

The Socialist Revolution forced China to industrialize. However, as long as the above-analyzed constraint of agricultural output over industrial persisted, China was unable to ride on a dynamic path of industrialization. In the 1970s, a "green revolution" was quietly breeding in China. The trap of low productivity in agriculture could finally be mitigated. Chances for a brand new regime of growth were emerging.

In the urban economy, the socialist era put most investment into heavy industries. Consumption was thwarted both in light industries and services. However, assets for future growth were enhanced health and education for the whole population. Furthermore, despite political instability, the unity of the country was preserved and state institutions remained strong. Thus contrary to the failed attempts to modernize in the early years of the twentieth century, the foundations for a takeoff had now been laid.

Part II

Understanding Chinese reforms in the past 30 years

3 On the political economy of reform

In the past 30 years the world has increasingly marveled at the economic achievements of China. During those 30 years the Chinese economy has been growing at a spectacular rate. The average GDP growth was over 9.7 percent from 1978 to 2009. Thanks to the curbed population growth, GDP per capita also increased rapidly at an average annual growth rate of 8.5 percent during the same period. Investment rates were constantly high and productivity improved steadily as well. The population in absolute poverty decreased from 75.7 percent of the population in 1980 to 12.49 percent in 2001. Virtually every indicator of the Chinese economy has shown significant improvement in the reforming years.

However, the most remarkable achievement of those 30 years is that China, after more than a century's endeavors, finally succeeded in starting a long-run dynamic industrialization process. Thus, to analyze the true "magic" of Chinese reform, the key is not just about comparing the differences before and after 1978, but about identifying the guiding mechanisms encompassing China's dynamism in order to answer the following two questions successively: how did China finally succeed in riding on the path of industrialization on a national scale? How has the rapid growth been sustained for more than 30 years?

To answer the first question, we believe that re-examining the history between 1949 and 1978 is necessary. Looking back at the year 1978, it is surprising how "ordinary" it was. Steven Cheung (2008) once synthesized the decisions made at the 3rd Plenary Session of the 11th Central Committee, which is widely regarded as the official start of Chinese reform, as: (1) China would open up in order to advance economic development; and (2) Deng Xiaoping would be restored to power. However, neither of these two proclamations could augur the mysterious transformation of China in the years that followed. Similar ambitions for a developing economy had been expressed before, and this was the third time Deng Xiaoping was back in power. At the time, no one could be certain about how the policies were to be deployed and what would happen to Deng in the years to come. There is no evidence to suggest that the Communist Party of China (CCP) discovered a magic therapy in 1978.

Of course, one may argue that China's reform is a gradual process. Therefore what happened in 1978 was not the most significant. The decisive impulse stems from a change in political direction and the following flow of policies, which brought in, or permitted, more and more "free market" characteristics into the Chinese economy. A typical argument is as follows: "Chinese socialism held the economy far below its production frontier while severely restraining the frontier's outward movement. ... limited reform that even partially ruptures the shackles surrounding incentives, marketing, mobility, competition, price flexibility, and innovation may accelerate growth" (Brandt and Rawski 2008: 8). This observation may explain the sharp contrast between a socialist planning economy and a market system. However, if we expand the historic horizon of our observation, hard questions arise. As we explained in Chapters 1 and 2, both the traditional Chinese economy and the contemporary Chinese economy before 1949 were full market systems. Yet not only was China unable to kindle its own industrial revolution in its glorious imperial times, it also failed to "catch up" and industrialize the country despite continual endeavors from 1850 to 1950.

Therefore we have to understand that market economy and industrial production are two distinct concepts. Although a market economy provides economic stimuli that can play a strong role in promoting industrial development, industrial production is not the necessary and obvious offspring of a market economy unless social and political institutions pose the need for, or open the possibility of, accumulating massive resources (both capital and labor). Such accumulation may then possibly interact with the emergence of new technologies able to create a capitalist system of production and distribution, hence supersede the limits of the Smithian model and initiate the industrialization process. Similarly, to introduce China into self-generating industrialization, the concentration of material and human resources and the emergence of industrial innovations are also indispensable, in addition to market mechanisms.

Unfortunately traditional Chinese institutions posed severe obstacles to industrial transformation, one especially being the limited flow of resources from rural to urban China. The constraint of agricultural production over the development of urban industrialization is not unique to China. Land, the key input of agricultural production, is often considered as a given factor. Diminishing marginal productivity lays down limitations for economic growth and leads to an equilibrium trap in the Smithian model (see Box 2.1 in Chapter 2). Yet, unlike the sharecropping system of European villages, traditional Chinese economy was based on scattered families, which were either small landowners or tenants with fixed rent contracts. In a sharecropping system, the village was typically the unit of organization and tenants had to pay a proportion of their agricultural output to landlords. Thus, when productivity improvements occurred, the landlords expropriated most of the gains. Farmers could not obtain more food and the rural population remained relatively stable. The rural families in China, though, were fully autonomous in productive activities and, thanks to fixed rent and self-ownership, they were usually able to retain all productivity gains. In this case, as long as the output of a certain piece of land was sufficient to meet subsistence requirements, Chinese families preferred to keep all members together on this land, no matter how much labor surplus there was. Such an arrangement meant that rural China had a much higher tolerance for rural population growth than Europe, and was thus more vulnerable to the Smithian trap. This explains why, although China was able to achieve high productivity per unit of land in the late imperial age, labor productivity remained stagnant. From the beginning of the Ming dynasty (1368–1644), population had been growing at a rate of 0.4 percent a year for more than 400 years. This steady growth quintupled Chinese population between 1400 and 1820. Such demographic expansion was supported by the improvement of productivity per unit of land. During the same period, China's GDP also quintupled. However, the hand-in-hand increases in population and productivity put the growth of GDP per capita at a standstill.

High tolerance of surplus labor in rural China had three major effects that jeopardized China's opportunity for industrialization. The first concerns labor. When most of the labor supply (even labor surplus) was kept scattered in rural regions, urban areas could not attract large concentrated labor forces. The second is the limitation of "exportation" of agricultural production to the cities, as the accrual of the rural population absorbed productivity gains per unit of land. In this case, concentration of material resources could not be achieved in urban China either. The third effect of the large surplus labor is low labor costs. It provides no incentive to create and adopt technologies that enable capital-intensive production methods. To conclude, the urban–rural relationship in traditional China hampered major preconditions of modern industrialization. If China were to start a dynamic process of industrialization, this relationship had to be transformed.

China also lacked other social and political institutions beneficial for the occurrence of industrialization. The traditional Chinese political system put emphasis on maintaining domestic order. To sustain the ultimate authority of royal family, no space was left for the creation of a strong bourgeois class. Accumulation of wealth, when exceeding a certain threshold, was regarded as a threat to royal power, and would and could be smashed by imperial rulers. In order to keep its political legitimacy, overseas expeditions were completely cut back in the Ming dynasty (see Chapter 2) so that the central government could concentrate its limited fiscal resources on domestic infrastructure construction, crucial for the wellbeing of the Chinese population. Such an inward-looking political attitude indicated that China could not obtain sufficient state support to break the high equilibrium trap through international expansion either.

To sum up, both the economic regime and political system of traditional China created obstacles to the initiation of the industrialization process. The task of eliminating those obstacles and liberating China from a Smithian trap could not be accomplished by market mechanisms alone. The role of the state is paramount. After the Opium Wars, China was politically disintegrated. No regimes before 1949 had the ability to mobilize resources in the vast rural areas of China, nor to unite the country for an independent position in the international arena. Even in its golden years (1920s–30s), China's national industrial development was confined only to a few coastal cities, and specialized in some light industries. Further industrial growth was severely constrained by the lack of critical resources including natural resources (such as energy supply) and heavy industrial products (such as steel).

If the CCP did not have a magic remedy in 1978, some critical conditions must have been transformed during the period of 1949–78, so that China could finally succeed in getting on the road towards industrialization after 1978 on a national scale. Hence we believe a careful re-examination of China's socialist history is of great value in understanding the initiation of China's industrialization process and the nature of Chinese reform.

As regards the second question posed above, i.e. the continuity of China's rapid growth, we would also like to take an empirical approach. The steady growth tends to give an impression that Chinese reform is a gradual linear process following the country's opening and marketization. A closer examination of China's performance, however, reveals that China's development trajectory is not a converging process towards any universal values or Western ideal forms, but a joint transformation of its own economic structures and institutions. One of the most eminent features of China's reform is that China went through its reforms under a hierarchical bureaucratic regime with a socialistic claim. At its start, the intended purpose of reform was to ameliorate planning economy (Gong 2009). Although the rapid surge of market economy eventually caused the decline of planning and China has gone through a fundamental transformation in every aspect, China's market economy has never, by a long way, fully possessed the full institutional features of a Western market economy and China's political system has consistently played an active role in the reforming process. As Barry Naughton put it:

> During the economic transformation, the CP hierarchy did not sit off to one side, frozen in time while everything else in China changed. Rather, the hierarchical political system shaped the process of market transition, and the political hierarchy itself has been reshaped in the response to the forces unleashed by economic transition.
>
> (Naughton 2008: 115)

In the 30 years of reform, the economic dynamic and state governance went through distinctive phases, or "growth regimes." Each growth regime is based on a specific demographic, economic, social, and political context and demonstrates its special developmental momentum, and each eventually leads to intrinsic tensions and crisis that become the catalyst for the formation of the next regime. Marketization alone cannot answer the question of how China succeeded in reacting deftly to the tensions and crisis, and leading such a large economy into the next phase of growth with transitions featuring extraordinary stability. The inquiry into the endogenous logic behind such relatively smooth transitions among different growth regimes in the past 30 years of Chinese history will give us insights to understanding the nature of China's perennial reform.

Hence in this chapter we demonstrate the *sui generis* path stressing the endogenous features of China's industrialization process. Our discussion starts from 1949. The 60 years after 1949 are analyzed in three phases. The economic dynamics underlying each phase (or "growth regime") features disparate mechanisms in mobilizing both human and material resources for the production and distribution of goods and services. However, continuity can be found in the logic that enables the transitions from a control economy (1949–78), to a Smithian model (the 1980s) that is land-intensive and labor-intensive, and then to a Marxian model (from the mid-1990s to the global financial crisis in 2008), which features capital-intensive accumulation and export-led growth. Analyses of such transitions between growth regimes not only have their importance in developmental economics, but also in understanding the roles of the social fabric and political mechanisms in allowing or even motivating such transitions. This understanding is crucial as a background to thinking of more prospective issues: whether China's reform is indeed a *sui generis* process, how the next phase of reform will be deployed, and what adjustments are needed for the future sustainable development of China.

The basis of reform: China between 1949 and 1978

The myth about the success of Chinese reforms after 1978

The years between 1949 and 1978 are often used to form a sharp contrast with the years after 1978. Indeed, when evaluated by economic performance and economic institutions, such contrast is obvious and undeniable.

On the side of economic performance, careful reviews have shown that the estimated average GDP growth rate was approximately 4 percent during 1949–78; however, this rate increased sharply to 9.5 percent during 1978–2005 (Perkins and Rawski 2008: 855). Productivity growth improved from 0.5 percent (1949–78) to 3.8 percent (1978–2005) per annum. The most significant contrast is about the supply of agricultural and consumer goods. Before 1978 China had never been able to sufficiently feed its large population. The most extreme incident due to such insufficiency occurred in 1959–61. Following the Great Leap Forward, devastating famine lasted three years and caused the death of tens of millions of people.[1] Starting in the 1950s, the purchase of virtually any important consumer goods, especially food stuffs or clothing, were rationed. After 1978 such shortages were gradually relieved.

As for economic institutions, the contrast was also sharp. Ownership changed from almost uniformly public to a much more diverse form. In 2008, 57.7 percent of Chinese enterprises were privately owned; and 95 percent of the enterprises were not state-owned. The rigidly planned price system was replaced by a market-oriented one with governmental regulations. Although the "hukou system"[2] still exists, in the last 20 years massive migration for work and education purposes involved 150 to 200 million people each year. China indeed relies more and more on market mechanisms for mobilizing its material and human resources.

The fact that rapid economic growth and incremental institutional liberalization happened almost simultaneously makes it natural to suspect that the two have a strong causal link. However, why did such a virtuous process not begin earlier than 1978? Are the changes of economic institutions the only keys for the success of Chinese reform, or were there other crucial conditions?

As explained in Chapters 1 and 2 and re-emphasized in the introduction of this chapter, one of the major deadlocks that prevented China from embracing industrialization was not the lack of market economy, but the inability to breakthrough the limits of rural "exportation" of both labor and resources to urban industrial production. This "high equilibrium trap" cannot be broken simply by the development of a market or commercial economy, but requires other conditions often endogenous to specific societies. One of the critical conditions is the support of state. In Europe, the outward exploration and expansion endeavors of many European states, such as Spain, England, the Netherlands, plus the eventual discovery of America, brought in limitless natural resources, labor, and agricultural products. Such geographical expansion was one of the crucial preconditions for capitalist industrialization to be installed in Europe. The Chinese state, however, had its particular regime. Without immediate and constant military competition with neighboring countries, the Chinese empire valued its domestic order above all. Under this system, it sacrificed its advanced naval expeditions in the fifteenth century in order to concentrate the use of fiscal resources on domestic issues.

When CCP founded the People's Republic of China, the constraint of agricultural output over urban industrialization was at its height. After 12 years of continual war, i.e. eight years of the Anti-Japanese War (1937–45), and three years of Chinese Civil War (1945–9), China was by far the poorest country in the world.

Constant war seriously damaged agricultural infrastructures, especially irrigation networks. Such damages jeopardized agricultural production and productivity (Naughton 2007: 50). Rural China was so impoverished that it could barely sustain the survival of its population, let alone support industrial development in the cities. The industrial conditions were even more desperate. Earlier industrial development in the coastal cities had been in light industries only. After the fatal disruptions of the Japanese invasion and the Civil War little was left in workable conditions. The only reliable core of heavy industry was in Manchuria, developed by the Japanese. At the end of World War II, those industrial facilities were seized by the Soviet army, and were handed over to the CCP after 1949.

Internationally, 1949 was in the heat of Cold War. It was highly unrealistic for China to rely on international aid or trade to relieve its lack of agricultural products, or for any other critical resources, technologies, or equipment. As a matter of fact, being a Communist Party, not only could the CCP hardly gain international recognition for its legitimacy, its national security was also under threat from the US and its allies. Such a hostile relationship reached its peak after the outbreak of the Korean War (1950–3).

Although the conditions for industrialization were extremely unfavorable, the need for industrializing China was immediate. Potential threats from Western countries required the young administration to gain sufficient military equipment. The completely destroyed infrastructures (irrigation system, transportation system, housing, etc.) all demanded restoration and further construction. Without international aid, China had to develop its own industrial system, especially the badly needed heavy industries, as quickly as possible.

Other needs that the CCP had to fulfill, though relatively less researched, came directly from China's population. In 1949 the Chinese population was about 550 million. Although in absolute number this population was less than half the Chinese population today, it was 30 percent of world population (today, the Chinese population constitutes 20 percent of world population). The pressure of providing sufficient food for such a large population was already extremely high. Moreover, this massive populace was also unhealthy and uneducated. Because of poor nutrition and sanitation, as well as the prevalence of several serious epidemic diseases, the death rate was as high as 18 per thousand. The average life expectancy was in the low 40s, infant mortality rates were as high as 130–146 per thousand, and illiteracy was as high as 80 percent. To make the situation worse, constant wars and fundamental social changes had almost completely destroyed the traditional networks of medical care and education provision. In order to improve the basic living standards of Chinese people, new medical care and education networks were urgently needed.

Under such severe circumstances, initiating China's industrialization process with market mechanisms and weak state regulation was doomed to encounter great difficulties. At the beginning of the Mao era, the CCP planned to use the following 10–15 years (called the "New Democratic Period") of market economy with mixed ownership to industrialize China and develop the economy. Problems emerged immediately. One of the worst concerned the market of agricultural products, especially grains. Widespread shortage of food induced speculation. From April 1949 to February 1950, in merely 11 months, prices for agricultural products quadrupled throughout the nation. In order to maintain social stability, the young government reacted swiftly. From 1950 to 1952 the Chinese government sold a large quantity out of the strategic reserve of grains to the market (30–40 percent of the whole market volume). Such action was effective. In 1952 grain prices grew by only 2.8 percent compared to the price level in 1950. However, the CCP paid a high cost for such market intervention; in fact, maybe too high a cost. It is difficult to quantify how much a burden such market intervention was for the young CCP government. As a rough idea, we do know that from 1949 to 1952, all agricultural taxes were charged in the form of grains. These taxes were 7.5 percent of total grain production but were about 40 percent of total fiscal revenue of the time.

The limits of grain extraction from the countryside to support the demand in the cities became more and more pronounced after 1953. With the beginning of the first five-year plan, a series of large-scale investments and constructions started. The number of urban residents rose sharply accordingly, with their food demands also increasing. At the same time, as agricultural productivity per unit of land recovered, farmers' survival concerns lessened and it was only natural for them to start expecting a higher living standard. They began to diversify their production from grains to more economic crops and livestock. As the production of economic crops and livestock is more energy-intensive and the majority of this production was for self-consumption of rural residents, the recovery of agricultural productivity did not translate sufficiently into an attendant increase in "exportation" of agricultural products to the urban regions. The contradiction between rural China and urban industrialization became pronounced. Such a contradiction was further aggravated in the distribution sector. As distributors saw food shortages in urban China, they held grains in inventories with expectations of future price rises and a higher return.

In urban China the CCP also began to feel increasing frustration with private ownership. Without the necessary institutions to evaluate and extract commercial and production taxes, the young government could not collect fiscal resources from the private enterprises efficiently. From 1949 to 1953 commercial and production tax revenue increased by less than 20 percent while the profit turned in from state-owned enterprises (SOEs) grew by 171 percent (Ministry of Finance People's Republic of China [MoF] 1987). In Wuhan, a large commercial center in central China, only a couple of large enterprises adopted double entry accounting. It was infeasible for tax bureaus to obtain accurate information about the revenue and profits of private enterprises (Zhang and Wu 2010). Hence, from 1949 to 1953, the profits turned in by SOEs increased more than 180 times in Wuhan yet tax revenue only doubled during the same period (Statistic Bureau of Wuhan 1989).

Under such circumstances, the supporters of the "Big Push" industrialization similar to Soviet style began to win the upper hand in political debates. In 1953, only four years after the establishment of the new China, the CCP abruptly ended the "New Democratic period" and pushed the whole country, urban and rural regions alike, into public ownership and a controlled economy. This so-called "Socialist Transformation" was completed in less than five years (1953–7). The CCP had thus gained full control over the Chinese economy, and was ready to speed up the country's industrialization process at all costs.

Industrialization with visible hand

The key point about "Big Push" industrialization – or here we call it "industrialization with visible hand" – is the absolute control over labor price throughout the nation. The whole population, urban and rural dwellers alike, would receive salaries close to mere subsistence level. By manipulating the salaries of both rural and urban workers, the state could alleviate the constraints of agricultural productivity over urban industrialization by maximizing the "exportation" of agricultural products to the cities through a planning system. According to the model shown in Chapter 2, Box 2.1, the subsistence wage in the agricultural sector was not flexible and had a fixed floor. With a large rural population (and a very large rural labor surplus also because of the family-based organizational tradition), China had to spend a big chunk of its agricultural production to meet the subsistence need of its countryside. Resultantly, the portion of "exportation" to the industrialized areas was fairly limited. To guarantee primary supply to the urban sector, the CCP had to centralize the management of agricultural activities so that the rural population planted only the most needed and energy-efficient grains, and their consumption of their own production, i.e. the agricultural goods, would be kept at the lowest possible level in order to maximize the "exportation" to urban China.

In the urban areas, wages were also regulated at an extremely low level (subsistence level). After the Socialist Transformation, almost 80 percent of urban employees worked for the state in one way or another. This made it possible to deprive enterprises of their power to decide wage compensations. Wage reform in 1956 mandated that wages and other benefits be allocated to workers according to a classification system based on occupations, regions, industry, ownership (state vs. collective), administrative level (e.g. central and local), and type of workplace (size and technological level; Bian 1994). There were eight distinct salary levels for factory workers and technicians and 24 levels for administrative and managerial workers. Under this planning system, industrial salaries would not increase with productivity gains, thus making large profit margins possible in the emerging industrial sector. As the focus of industrialization was in heavy industry (80 percent of new investments from 1953 to 1978 went to heavy industry), the industrial outputs did not have to be absorbed by consumption. All outputs and profits were turned into capital accumulation (which was badly needed at the time). The problem of disconnections between salary and productivity was thus concealed on the macroeconomic level. However, as the whole population did not have the means to afford discretionary consumptions, the underdevelopment of light industry and services was a natural result.

The outcome of such industrialization strategy was noticeable. For the first time in China's history, the Chinese government was finally "able to mobilize its fiscal and other resources to finance a sustained investment effort" (Naughton 2007: 57). Resources began to concentrate steadily into urban China for industrial uses. As shown in Figure 3.1, albeit with big fluctuations due to policy instability, the investment rate climbed to extremely high levels for such a poor country. The investment rate grew from slightly more than 20 percent of GDP in 1952 to an average 35 percent in the 1970s. Between 1952 and 1978 industrial output grew at an average annual rate of 11.5 percent. Such rapid growth in industrial activities transformed the structure of Chinese economy. The share of industry in total GDP climbed steadily from 18 percent to 44 percent, while the share of agriculture dropped from 51 percent to 28 percent. A sizable industrial base was forming.

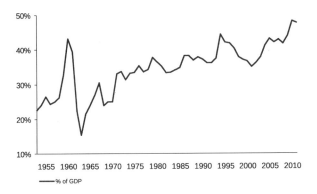

Figure 3.1 Share of gross capital formation in GDP.
Source: CEIC

However, as the key of "Big Push" industrialization was firm control over salaries in both rural and urban sectors, there were two main negative implications of this strategy. On the one hand, without any price mechanism, a strong economic incentive tool was missing. Society had to rely purely on non-material incentives. This explains partially why Chairman Mao was so obsessed with constant "social movements." On the other hand, to maintain the state's absolute control over economic behavior, any means of gaining revenues outside of the planned salary system, such as the "Family Responsibility System," or even the smallest of private businesses, had to be strictly suppressed. Otherwise, strong economic incentives could alter people's behavior away from what was desired in the "Big Push" strategy and collapse the planned salary system. Were the CCP to lose control over salaries, the whole command economy would be devastated and rapid industrial growth, especially the development of heavy industries, would be severely undermined. This explains why the reforming attempts of the CCP before 1978 all took the form of "administrative decentralization" instead of "economic decentralization."[3]

Indeed, contrary to common impression, socialist China initiated several reforms before 1978. Realizing fully the negative effects of the lack of economic incentives on people's working spirits, the CCP was willing to integrate some sort of economic incentives into the planning system. However, the fear of interrupting the forced industrialization process surrounding strict salary control precluded allowing any income outside the planning system. A compromise was to introduce some kind of competition and decentralization inside the system, or, to be more specific, to decentralize the planning right. Yet such an arrangement in fact created distorted incentives because it did not encourage fair competition but struggles for economic rents or political credential. It also diluted badly needed resources for key infrastructure constructions and disrupted important industrial developments. Both the reforming endeavors in 1956 and 1965 followed this pattern. Take the reform that started in 1956, for example. That year Mao Zedong wrote an article ("lun shi da guan xi") discussing "ten important relationships" that he identified as crucial for the further development of the Chinese economy. Special emphasis was given to the necessity of adjusting the relationship among the state, enterprises, and individuals. The article affirmed that economic incentives should be given to enterprises and individuals, so as to enhance economic vitality. In 1957 Chen Yun led the drafting of three documents aimed at reforming management of industries, commerce, and the financial system. The idea was to decentralize decision-making and management power to localities and enterprises. The change was drastic. Central government gave up its direct control over 8,100 enterprises, i.e. 88 percent of the enterprises they originally controlled. Economic planning also relaxed. Local authorities had rights to adjust targets for production of both agricultural and industrial products. Accordingly, fiscal, financial, human resource management, and investment rights were also liberalized and devolved to localities and enterprises.

These reforming attempts unfortunately turned into the tragic farce of the Great Leap Forward. Myriad repetitive and incompetent investment and infrastructure construction projects initiated by localities jeopardized the limited financial and material resources needed for crucial projects with national importance. Due to the decentralization of human resource management, the number of employees working for state-owned enterprises increased from 24.5 million to 45.3 million in 1958 alone. In 1960 the number of urban employees rose sharply to 59.7 million, i.e. 143.5 percent of the number in 1957. The total number of urban residents increased by more than 30 million from 99.5 million in 1957 to 130 million in 1960 (Zhou 1984: 73–5). As industrial enterprises began to hire more and more people, rural areas suffered from a sudden loss of labor. Such massive transfers of labor from rural to urban regions broke the fragile balance between rural and urban China. Rural China had to support a much larger demand for agricultural products with a serious loss of labor force. Such imbalance was a significant reason for the outbreak of the catastrophic famine in 1959–61. As a result, in 1961 the CCP decided to re-centralize most economic powers and re-establish a strict central planning economy.

The unsuccessful experiences of reforms before 1978 demonstrated that, unless there was to be a sharp increase in agricultural productivity or a more accommodating international environment for trade, China had no alternative path of industrialization but the "Big Push" strategy. Yet as long as China stuck to this strategy, the need of a strictly controlling salary system for the whole population would fail to be reconciled with the need to provide effective economic incentives. This innate contradiction is a curse on a planned economy and explains why the "administrative decentralization" reforms before 1978 had all failed. China had to wait for major conditions to change, i.e. a sharp increase in agricultural productivity, or a more accommodative international environment for trade, before it could quit forced industrialization and embrace market decentralization. Fortunately, both of these two conditions were met in the late 1970s and reform of "economic decentralization" finally took place. We will discuss this reforming process in detail later in the book.

A strong unitary state legitimated by the rationale of revolution

Drastic economic changes in China after 1949 were supported by equally radical changes in the political realm. The most prominent of these was the re-establishment of a hierarchical bureaucratic regime with independent sovereignty. More than a hundred years after the outbreak of the Opium Wars (1840–3, 1856–60), China once again had an effective government that possessed the ability to mobilize economic and political resources on a national scale. Although the socialist government was built on entirely different claims, the political system shared many similarities with imperial China. Chairman Mao replaced the emperor as the ultimate authority. Only people did not call him "father" or "son of dragon" anymore; instead, he was compared to "the sun," "the captain" or "the great saver." Claiming to be the faithful representative of the interests of all workers and farmers, CCP and the socialist state under Mao's reign gained legitimacy from enhancing general social welfare levels through better national security, better provision of social services, and equalization of the distribution of land. The Socialist Transformation eliminated thoroughly any landlords or private enterprise owners. De facto, China went back to a two-layer society as in its imperial age. The basis for a pluralistic society disappeared once again.

However, the socialist government also had very distinctive features of its own. The bureaucratic system after 1949 was much more extensive than the traditional bureaucratic system in imperial times. State power, for the first time, reached into the private domain, and controlled economic activities directly. Rural China, which had been left out of the bureaucratic system below township level, was also integrated into the centralized system through the rural collectives. The new sovereignty also put much more priority on fostering military powers than traditional imperial Chinese regimes. During the process much of the welfare people could have enjoyed was sacrificed. Thus the CCP government before 1978 also relied heavily on revolutionary rationale to legitimate itself. The international environment was intentionally depicted as woeful and nationalist emotions were cultivated. Mao was an expert in initiating political movements and manipulating non-material incentives for the control of people. During 1953–78, we could observe such successive movements, with the Cultural Revolution at their frenzied peak.

Later in the chapter we further evaluate the influence of this political system over the trajectory of China's reforming process, but at this moment we wish only to stress the importance of the establishment of a strong and nationally recognized government for the initiation of China's process of industrialization. Without it, any industrialization efforts would have been made in vain.

Other preparations for the 1978 reform

The "Big Push" was not and could not be a dynamic process of industrialization. However, it indeed aided China in laying down the foundations of its dynamic industrialization process by establishing a complete industrial base and a unitary state that could give strong and steady governmental support. Both of these two achievements were groundbreaking in Chinese history. However, the deadlock between rural and urban China still persisted. Were there other preparations made in 1949–78 that helped bring China out of the Smithian trap?

The answer is positive. The most critical concerned the radical change in the production unit in rural China. After the Socialist Transformation, most agricultural production was no longer organized by scattered families, but by so-called agricultural collectives (also called "communes"). This arrangement not only allowed China to farm on a larger scale, but more importantly provided an institutional framework that (1) integrated rural China into a national network that enabled the rapid diffusion of crucial technological achievements; (2) established a framework to provide social services to rural residents; and (3) created the possibility of organizing larger scale industrial production in China's vast countryside. We will see in the analysis of the first stage of reform how crucial these changes were for the success of China's industrialization.

Another crucial improvement concerned investment in human capital. Thanks to the relatively equal distribution of medical and educational resources and the next to zero cost of those services during the socialist era, the Chinese population enjoyed a rapid improvement in their health and education conditions. Life expectancy increased sharply from 42.2 (45.6) years in 1950 to 66.4 (69.4) years in 1982 for males (females; Wang and Mason 2008: 138). The most deadly epidemic diseases were eradicated by nationwide preventive measures. The improvement in education was at all levels but the most salient was the advance in basic education. The proportion of Chinese aged 16–65 who had not completed primary school was reduced from 74 percent to 40 percent between 1952 and 1978 (Brandt and Rawski 2008: 5), and the percentage of population that was illiterate dropped from 80 percent to 16.4 percent. Such accomplishments in human capital investment were remarkable, especially when compared with countries at the same development stage as China.

One very important, yet now less talked about, contribution of the socialist period was the relatively equal distribution of wealth and means of production. Although salaries were kept low, social services were provided for free. And, most notably, in the cities urban workers enjoyed welfare housing. In the countryside farmers were guaranteed availability of land. Therefore the Chinese populace in the socialist era in fact enjoyed a massive totality of implicit wealth. Such equal distribution of wealth and means of production was a crucial factor that allowed the first ten years of reform to be a "reform without losers" (Lau, Qian, and Roland 2000). The real estate reform initiated in 1994 in the urban regions allowed urban dwellers to transform their implicit wealth (welfare housing) into explicit wealth (tradable housing). That transformation injected strong vitality into the second stage of reform. The implicit ownership of farmers over the land they use has yet to be transformed into an explicit form, but we have strong reasons to believe that such a transformation, if it happens, will again promote China's reform and economic growth to a new stage.

To conclude, great achievements were made in 1949–78. Although the industrialization facilitated by the "visible hand" could not set China onto a dynamic path of industrialization, it was the only choice China had at the time. In those 30 years, crucial structural adjustments were made and institutional infrastructure laid down. As soon as there was to be a technological breakthrough in agricultural production, or the international environment eased, a great transition could be expected in China.

Changes in critical conditions at the end of the 1970s

The 1970s was a decade full of tensions, transitions, and opportunities for China. The "Big Push" strategy led to substantial gains. However, the contradictions that stemmed from this growth regime accumulated and radicalized in the 1970s. The inefficiencies of the command economy, due to the lack of incentives for working, innovations and the mismatches in resources allocations, became blatant. After more than 20 years of income stagnation, Chinese people were becoming impatient with the slow improvement in their living standards. The pressure upon the CCP government to provide more and better agricultural and more diverse consumption goods rose. In the meantime, the ten-year craziness of the Cultural

Revolution compelled more and more Chinese politicians to feel averse to using revolutionary rationale in running a country. Indeed, most of them had themselves been direct victims of fickle policies and brutal political movements. The wish was to shift state legitimacy to a more sustainable basis, i.e. enhancing the welfare level of the whole populace. The death of the charismatic leader, Chairman Mao, in 1976 made such a shift possible as well as necessary. Furthermore, the rapid growth of several Southeast Asian countries prompted Chinese politicians to realize how far behind China had lagged and that it would go on being left behind if the country did not open up and converge with the international technological frontier.

Fortunately, other groundbreaking positive changes were also occurring in the 1970s. Internationally, a new phase of globalization was surging and the tensions between the socialist and capitalist blocs were easing. In 1971 the People's Republic of China replaced Taiwan as one of the permanent members of the United Nations (UN) Security Council. In 1972 President Nixon visited China. In 1978 the US finally acknowledged the legitimacy of the CCP government. Thirty years after its birth, Communist China finally felt relief from immediate military threats and the road was paved for China to participate in international economic and techno-logical exchanges while maintaining its political independence. Domestically, a quiet "green revolution" was proceeding in the 1970s, which not only transformed rural China but later transformed the whole Chinese economy as well. Starting in 1964, Chinese scientists began to have substantial success with the breeding of high-yield dwarf varieties (HYVs) of rice. In 1974, Professor Yuan Longping developed a high-yield variety of rice suitable for widespread use in China. In 1975 supporting technologies for planting these HYVs were developed and in 1976 new seeds were introduced immediately for large-scale use under govern-mental promotion. In 1973 and 1974 the Chinese central government also made a serious commitment to developing the modern nitrogen fertilizer industry by purchasing from abroad 13 large synthetic ammonia and urea factories. Starting with these projects, a large domestic fertilizer industry was gradually built up in China (Naughton 2007: 260–1). With irrigation systems gradually restored after 1949, the breakthroughs in seed breeding and fertilizer production completely transformed China's agricultural sector and agricultural productivity experienced explosive growth. Before the 1970s, Chinese agricultural output per capita was capped at 300 kilograms. After the improvements in the 1970s, in 1984, per capita production reached 400 kilograms and this number was to be outrun in the years to follow as well.

The technological breakthroughs and the rapid spread of high-yield seeds were highly related to rural institutional infrastructures established during the socialist era. Seed breeding requires research investment impossible to accomplish at the level of individual farms. During the 1950s socialist China founded a multi-level research system, which is by far the largest in the world. The Chinese Academy of Agricultural Sciences (CAAS) is at the apex of this system. There are also provincial-level academies and an agricultural extension service in every county. As the national research center focuses more on basic sciences, local branches help to adapt newly developed seeds and other technologies to local conditions (Naughton 2007: 261). This extensive multi-level system also carried out the role of distributing the newest generation of seeds to each farm, which is crucial for the application of HYVs because these plants do not have the ability to self-reproduce. Thanks to this system, China succeeded in diffusing high-yield seeds really rapidly. Hybrid maize was also introduced in 1961, and by 1990 about 90 percent of sown areas was sown with the hybrid variety. The technological breakthroughs and expansion of the chemical industry in the 1970s were among the most important causes for agricultural productivity improvements in China.

Another important change that occurred in the 1970s was demographic. In the 1950s and 1960s a sharp decrease in death rate and rapid surge in birth rate triggered an explosion of China's population. From 1950 to 1982, the Chinese population almost doubled from 552 million to 1017 million. In the 1970s population growth did not slow much because a large young population was entering reproductive age. China's demographic pattern had quietly gone through profound transformations. Contrary to the pro-childbirth policies in the 1950s, the Chinese government implemented an effective family-planning program in the 1970s that promoted later marriages, fewer births, and longer birth intervals (Wang and Mason 2008: 137). The mean female age at first marriage rose from 19.7 to 22.8 and the total fertility rate (TFR) declined from 5.7 births per woman in 1970 to 2.8 births per woman in 1979 (Coale and Chen 1987). Thus by the time reform began at the end of the 1970s, China had by and large completed its fertility transition by international standards, even before the enforcement of the "one couple, one-child" policy (Wang and Mason 2008: 138). The other transformation concerned the age structure. As the first generation of baby boomers from the 1950s grew into adulthood, the young active labor pool of China expanded. Coupled with a sharp decline in TFR, such an expansion meant that China entered a period of low dependency ratio.[4] In other words, at the end of 1970s, China started its demographic "golden years" where its working population had the fewest social burdens to carry, regarding either the young, or the old.

These three major changes (ameliorated international environment, a jump-start of the "green revolution", and a young and healthy population) had fundamental significance as to where China's economy and society would head at the end of 1970s. What first changed was China's rural–urban relationship. In the socialist period, as agricultural productivity did not increase, total agricultural output was barely enough to support the subsistence of Chinese people. In order to maximize the "exportation" of labor and material resources from rural to urban China, a planned economy had to be established in order to keep both agricultural and industrial salaries under strict control to ensure that grain production and heavy industrial investments, the two priorities for the CCP, could be maximized. This "Big Push" strategy suppressed the constraints of agricultural productivity over industrialization, but it did not eliminate such constraints. China could not initiate a dynamic endogenous process of industrialization. However, for an extremely poor and isolated country, this strategy allowed China to form the beginnings and necessary institutional structures for next phase of growth.

In the 1970s the diffusion of new agricultural technologies and the restoration of rural infrastructures sharply enhanced the productivity of rural China and, accordingly, increased the "exporting ability" of rural China to support urban industrialization. As the international environment became friendlier, China was also able to turn to international trade to cope with temporary food shortages. The reasons to strictly control agricultural production and distribution started to disappear. In urban China the reduced external threats to the country's national security also allowed China's obsession with rapid heavy industrial expansion to diminish. Meanwhile, the population expansion created an increasingly larger domestic demand for light industrial products, and the young population also provided China greater comparative advantage in labor-intensive industries in the international scene. China's industrial structure in the late 1970s was on the verge of profound change.

To conclude, by the end of the 1970s, fundamental changes in agricultural productivity, international environment, and demographic structure transformed the basis of the Chinese economy. For China to enter into a new growth regime, all that was needed was a policy set that could integrate all these changes into a harmonized process.

The political process of the first stage of China's reform

The guiding political principles of China's reform

In 1978, the People's Republic of China had already gone through nearly 30 years under the CCP regime. Those 30 years were bumpy with dramatic twists and turns both economically and politically. However, a hierarchical bureaucratic system with a centralized authority had been restored and reinforced during the whole period. Even though one of the main purposes of the Cultural Revolution was to rattle such a bureaucratic system, the profound and widespread upheavals of personnel did not alter the basic structure of the hierarchy. Indeed, after the death of Mao, the first response of China's leaders had been to rehabilitate the hierarchical bureaucratic political equilibrium, and the veteran CCP leaders who survived the Cultural Revolution were restored to political power accordingly.

The resilience of hierarchical bureaucracy with strong central authority stems from the long tradition of imperial governance in China. In such a political system, society was stratified into two main layers: the ruling bureaucrats and the scattered family-based society. China in 1978 fitted well with this two-layer society model. The political reasoning of the two-layered society strongly contrasts with that of a pluralistic society. The primary goal of the political regime in the former is not winning political contests in representative elections, but facilitating the following three tasks. First, the regime has to deliver basic welfare for its population. This is the root of its political legitimacy and failing in this task increases the risk of mass upheaval, the most common cause of the collapse of such political regimes. Second, for the regime to guarantee the enforcement of central policies, it needs to align the behavior of its bureaucrats with central guidance. To achieve this purpose, the central committee typically controls the personnel power and, in imperial China, Confucian moral values were diffused to encourage loyalty and integrity. However, the true incentive for the allegiance of bureaucrats usually comes from political patronage. Rewards are given to the regime's loyal supporters, either in the form of material or political assets, so that central government's interest in sustaining the political regime can be translated into the personal interests of bureaucrats as well. The third task of a hierarchical political regime is to suppress the emergence of other organizations that can challenge the authority of the existing bureaucratic system. If these organizations cannot be suppressed, they are tied to the existing political regime in one way or another.

Such was the true rationale of China's reform: sustaining the political regime of CCP administration. Although to do so in 1978, China had (and was able) to introduce market mechanisms to vitalize its economy. This does not mean that the fundamental doctrine of China's reforms was in line with any Western-style "universal values." If necessary, the economy might as well be turned from market-oriented to planning, just as did happen in the early 1950s. The pattern of reforms (in 1978 or before) or, rather, the ruling logic of China, was extremely pragmatic. The ultimate purpose of all policies was to sustain the political regime and to achieve this the government had to improve the welfare level of its people (an explicit purpose) and take political patronage for the bureaucrats (an often implicit purpose) into serious consideration at the same time. Such considerations decided that any policy changes had to take an incremental path with the following purposes: allowing consensus to be formed among the higher-ranked officials, identifying the most vulnerable points in the bureaucratic system, giving rewards to supporters and achieving political equilibrium. Therefore, in such a political regime, although the authority is central and ultimate, the decision-making process is not dictatorial. Critical national policies have to be made collectively. There were certain tensions of mutual restraints both inside the central decision-making body and between central rulers and localities. All these political parties were united under a common interest, i.e. the sustainability of the regime; and the balance among them was often achieved through political rent-sharing. The advantage of such a political system was that (1) it was possible for policies to embody a long-term view, and (2) the violence of the state keeps in check the violence of capital. However, the drawbacks were of course the inefficiencies created by political rent-seeking and the uncertainty about the integrity of national leaders. We discuss the influence of this political regime on China's future and the necessary adjustments required to the political regime itself in the concluding chapter of the book. At present, we focus on explaining the process of China's reforms from 1978 to 2008 using the political principles identified above.

The most immediate problems for political sustainability in 1978

During the 1970s the regime of the People's Republic of China had more and more difficulties basing its legitimacy in certain revolutionary ideals. In order to support a high investment rate, especially high investment in heavy industries, Chinese people had made tremendous sacrifices for the revolutionary passions encouraged by the CCP. Income stagnated for nearly 30 years in both urban and rural China. The frustration of the populace over the lack of improvement in their material and spiritual welfare had become acute. In order to maintain the Party's political legitimacy, the central committee of the CCP faced ever-stronger pressure to enhance living conditions for Chinese people.

Meanwhile, the CCP organized intensive missions abroad. In 1977, 13 top leaders of the People's Republic of China, including Deng Xiaoping, visited 51 foreign countries. In the second half of the year, various ministries also sent out their own delegations abroad. The importance of these trips was immeasurable. China's national leaders finally realized how large the gap was between development in China and the rest of the world. Consensus was forming at the top: new technologies and equipment had to be purchased from developed countries to push China closer to the productive frontier. During these visits, big-ticket contracts for importing agricultural goods, equipment, and technologies were signed. The Central Planning Committee planned to borrow US$18–20 billion over eight years to support those imports. China was in urgent need of foreign currencies.

Hence, in 1978, China did not choose to reform. Rather, domestic and external crises demanded change. Radical measures were needed to incentivize farmers and promote foreign trade-boosting exports of Chinese goods.

The hard questions facing the Chinese leadership were: what changes were needed and how should they be initiated? No one had explicit answers to these questions. Because of the two crises described above, Chinese leaders acknowledged that it was high time to alleviate the burden of Chinese farmers, to allow more autonomy in industrial activities, and to open up China to international trade. Yet as to how to achieve these aims and what changes to pursue, there were no blueprints. What is more, although the need to reform had received wide acceptance, any changes to the existing system still faced strong reservations or even resentment from some bureaucrats. The planned economy protected the bureaucrats' maximum control over the economy and society. With more autonomy given to farms and enterprises, and with the opening up of the economy to foreign players in trade and investment, the monopolistic power of China's bureaucrats would fade and the vested interests of many bureaucrats would be affected. Under these circumstances, the Chinese reforming process was inevitably filled with experiments and more profound changes would be observed in sectors where initial vested interests were weaker.

The great transformation of rural China both in agricultural and industrial activities

Although crucially important to the nation, the agricultural sector was on the periphery of China's power system. Rural organizations were at the bottom of China's hierarchical system and political rents involved were relatively low and scattered. This situation made rural China the most suitable sector for liberalization. The biggest worry for Chinese national leaders about the liberalization of rural China was for grain procurement. However, after the spread of the "Green Revolution" and the easier availability of imported food, the government was ready to take some risks, at least in regions less important for grain procurement. Hence, in the 3rd Plenary Session of the 11th Central Committee, a decision was passed to encourage farmers to pursue a family income outside of the structure of rural collectives. To guarantee food supply to cities the grain procurement price in the summer of 1979 increased 20 percent compared with that in 1978. On this basis, if a rural collective sold more grains to the state, excess sales would be paid at 50 percent higher than the normal procurement price. This large price rise was not confined to grain procurement. All major agricultural products benefited from the same measure. At the same time, thanks to new technologies and equipment acquired from industrialized countries, China succeeded in significantly reducing production costs of key agricultural inputs, such as fertilizers, pesticides, agricultural plastic, etc. Thanks to the planning system, the CCP was able to forcefully translate the cost reductions immediately to price abatements. From 1979 to 1980 prices for those key agricultural production materials decreased 10–15 percent. These drastic price changes definitely enhanced income in rural China. Thanks to the equalized income distribution system, the lives of all Chinese farmers saw significant improvements, and incentives for higher production rose accordingly.

With the loosening up of policies, rural China also went through transformations in production organization. Two important organizational innovations spontaneously emerged. The first was the so-called "Family Responsibility System." Under this system, rural China revived its traditional mode of production, i.e. family farming instead of collective farming. Attempts to return to family farming did not occur only after 1978. With the strong tradition of a family-based economy, similar endeavors to break rural collectives occurred repeatedly before 1978 as well, especially in provinces such as Anhui, Hubei, and Sichuan where population is dense and land is extremely fragmented. But after 1978 the CCP government stopped suppressing such actions, and instead encouraged them. Even without market reforms, the breaking down of rural collectives immediately gave individual families enormous incentives to work harder and more intelligently, because they could, under "Family Responsibility System," retain all the output of the family for themselves. Such motivation greatly increased the efficiency of agricultural production.

These were not the only changes that occurred in rural China. Once the individual families began enjoying the full return of their labor, farmers began to look for all possible ways to use their surplus labor in order to obtain a higher income for the family. This incentive gave rise to the other important institutional innovation in rural China: the Township and Village Enterprises (TVEs). Although they lacked any professional skills in industrial production and business operation, TVEs took full advantage of the void in the domestic market for light industrial products, the cheap cost of labor owing to China's demographic structure and the recent opening up of China to international markets. From 1985 to 1992 the surge of TVEs took China by surprise. If the "Family Responsibility System" was a revival of the traditional Chinese economy, TVEs were clearly relics of the socialist era. Based on the remaining structures of the rural collectives, villagers worked together in commercial production. As the factories were built locally, farmers did not have to leave their families, nor were they required to work for the factories full time. The emergence of large numbers of

TVEs greatly changed the relationship between rural and urban China. Although the workers of TVEs resided in rural regions and were still involved with agricultural production, they were industrial workers with rural homes. In 1993, TVEs in China hired 123 million workers. Such institutional innovation altered all variables in the Smithian model (see Box 3.1). Without any large-scale migration, there was a de facto strong inflow from rural to urban China of both labor and output.

Thanks to all these promising changes, real productivity in rural China rose rapidly and so did the relative income of Chinese farmers vis-à-vis Chinese urban dwellers. Figure 3.2 demonstrates clearly the evolution of the relationship between Chinese urban and rural household incomes.

Box 3.1 Use of the Smithian model for the takeoff of the agricultural sector

In the early stage of reform, the government gave farmers the opportunity of trading their surplus at market prices. Farmers responded positively to the incentive, so that the market output x^* rose relatively to the output $\bar{x}$ in the fixed subsistence sector within the rural economy. Recalling the equation that determines x^*, one can see that it is an increasing function of s^*, e.g. the rate of saving of farmers that market their output.

$$x^* = \frac{[s^* + (1-s^*) \, b(e)]\bar{x}}{\tau(1-s^*) \, e[1-b(e)]}$$

s^* rose because the opening of the market sector for farm products increased their income and gave them the incentive to plow it back into their business. Farmers became the first capitalists of the Deng Xiaoping era.

The rise in x^* launched a virtuous circle. Recall that during the Cultural Revolution, the cities were not catered for adequately in farm products. There was a high-unfulfilled demand, which showed up as soon as marketable farm output became available. In the model it is captured by j, the propensity of the urban sector to "import" from the rural sector.

An increase in j leads to decline in τ since: $\tau = \frac{(s-k)}{j} + k^*$

A decline in $\tau = \frac{P^*}{P}$, the relative price of the "exportable" agricultural goods to industrial goods raises the volume of production x^*. Therefore marketable farm production was enhanced. In turn, the farm sector demanded manufactured goods as agricultural machinery and consumer goods for the demand of the enriched farmers. The demand from the rural sector stimulated the production of manufactured goods y and, with increasing returns to scale, employment and the real wage ω in the urban sector, which is an increasing function of x^*, while the virtuous circle is under way:

$$\omega = (l^{\alpha-1})^\sigma = y^{\frac{(\alpha-1)\sigma}{\alpha}} = \left(\frac{x^*}{j}\right)^{\frac{(\alpha-1)\sigma}{\alpha}}$$

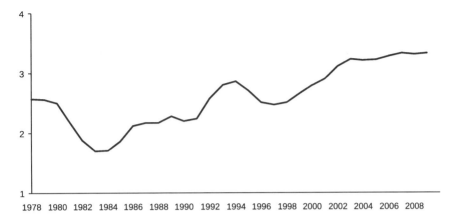

Figure 3.2 Ratio of urban household income to rural household income.
Source: National Bureau of Statistics of China (2011b)

The attempts of urban reforms

As suggested by the relative decline of urban residents' income to that of rural residents, the results of urban reforms in the 1980s were far less rosy compared with what had been achieved in rural China. The sole economic players in urban China in 1978 were state- or collectively owned enterprises. As a result, urban China was a traditional battlefield for political and economic rents, and involved perplexing interest relations among China's bureaucrats. In order to keep the political equilibrium and protect the political patronage in urban regions, urban reforms in China did not start with the lowering of entry barriers to economic activities. In other words, urban China could not allow the free emergence of private small and medium enterprises (SMEs) like the emergence of TVEs in the rural regions. Thus, although reforms started at the same time in urban China as in rural China, the forms were disparate. In urban China, reform was perverted by the traditional mentality of redistributing benefits and increasing managerial autonomy. In 1978 Sichuan Province launched an experiment. It chose six SOEs to try out measures of enhancing the managerial autonomy of enterprises. In 1980, similar measures had been spread over 6,600 SOEs, which constituted 60 percent of all budgetary industrial production in China (Wu 2010). However, the reform did not bring significant productivity improvements. Although certain enterprises excelled in the process, in general this round of urban reform led to economic chaos just like the reforms before 1978.

Although the first round of urban reform was not successful, the outstanding performance of rural China consolidated the attitudes of Chinese bureaucrats toward change. The bureaucrats began to see that new and more lucrative rents could be brought in with economic liberalization. Thus further attempts to reform the urban industrial sector were made and after 1984 the central government deepened urban reforms. Inspired by the "Family Responsibility System," the CCP decided to contract its SOEs out to their managers. With profit sharing contracts, SOEs were able to retain excess profit above the contracted level. At first glance this policy was a profit sharing scheme between enterprises and their supervising governmental bodies. Actually, it was a sharing scheme between the bureaucrats and the state. Naturally, this policy was widely welcomed and gained national popularity in no time. However, those profit sharing contracts did not significantly improve industrial productivity.

To sum up, urban reforming attempts were far from successful. Actually, after the reforms, with the challenges from other players in the market and leaping labor costs under state regulation, more and more SOEs began to suffer operational losses. Before 1988 less than 20 percent of all SOEs suffered from loss, but in the 1990s this percentage increased to about one-third and rose to nearly half in 1998. The situation was even more alarming if we look at the total losses in volume (see Table 3.1).

The deterioration of central government's balance sheet

Although urban reforming endeavors had largely failed, in order to let the higher supply of agricultural and consumer goods benefit the whole population, urban residents needed a higher income as well, despite the absence of obvious productivity gains. As 80 percent of China's urban active population (unemployment rate was next to zero) was employed by the state one way or another, it was possible for the state to raise the salaries of almost the total urban population five times from 1978 to 1984. Such income boosts with limited productivity gains could not be sustained. Although these salaries were paid through the accounts of SOEs and other publicly owned entities, their increases were in a sense subsidized by the state. From the start, such subsidies showed in the decline of SOEs' profits and gradually a large proportion of SOEs were surviving on policy loans. The eventual consequence of the firms' indebtedness was a banking crisis cum runaway inflation.

Table 3.1 Losses and profits of Chinese SOEs (1990–98)

Year	% of SOEs in loss	Total loss of SOEs (billion RMB)	Total profit of SOEs (billion RMB)
1990	30.3	93.2	49.1
1991	28.0	92.5	74.4
1992	22.7	75.6	95.5
1993	29.8	47.9	166.7
1994	32.6	62.4	160.8
1995	33.3	80.2	147.0
1996	37.5	112.7	87.6
1997	43.9	142.0	53.9
1998	47.4	196.0	−7.8

Source: Finance Yearbook of China of various years

In the first stage of reform the Chinese government also subsidized the urban population through the prices of agricultural products. In 1984 Chinese grain production reached a historic high of 400 million tons and the market distributed 30 percent of this production. The CCP considered the time was right to let go its control over grain procurement and prices. On January 1, 1985 the Chinese State Council declared its decision to entirely cancel mandatory grain procurement. This decision triggered a sharp growth (10 percent) of the market grain price that same year. However, at the same time, 80 percent of grain sales in the urban regions were still through state-run grain distribution channels, where the prices were kept low. In other words, there co-existed two "market" prices in China for grains: one was the free market price, and the other government-controlled "market" price. This was a strange market, with the main player, the state, buying grains in the free rural market at relatively high market price, and then selling what they bought at subsidized prices to urban residents. Grain prices were thus lower in the cities than in the countryside.

With increased subsidies to SOEs and urban residents, coupled with the inability to tackle the new economic players as reliable tax bases, the Chinese central government suffered greatly from a deteriorated balance sheet. As shown in Figure 3.3, from 1978 onward fiscal revenue declined steadily, setting off alarm bells by the early 1990s. Ultimately, budget revenues reached a historic low at 10.8 percent of GDP in 1995, leading to a deficit equal to 1 percent of GDP. Although the official deficit was not large, the big losses of revenue showed in the balance sheets of the state-owned banks. A bank crisis together with macroeconomic and even political instability was building up.

From early banking decentralization to runaway inflation (1984–8)

In the socialist period, banking was centralized in a monobank, the People's Bank of China (PBoC), which was a department of the Ministry of Finance. This structure

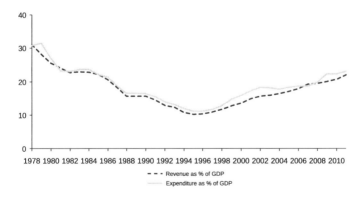

Figure 3.3 Revenues and expenditures of central government as a percentage of GDP (1978–2011).

Source: CEIC

was consistent with central planning. The monobank was more a bookkeeper than a credit system, because central planning defined both prices and quantities produced, the latter determining the demand that could be satisfied. As such it was part of the control mechanism, monitoring the execution of the plan.

A very first act of reform occurred by the end of 1979 when the PBoC departed from the Ministry of Finance to become a separate entity. Meanwhile, four specialized state-owned banks either split from earlier departments of the monobank or were created at the time to finance the sectors of the economy. The China Construction Bank (CCB), originally formed in 1954, was set up to handle the financing of fixed investment in manufacturing. The Bank of China (BOC) was given the mandate to deal with transactions related to foreign trade and investment. Nothing much happened in the 1980s in structuring the financial system for a market economy. The Agricultural Bank of China (ABC) was set up in 1979 to take care of all banking business in rural areas. The Industrial and Commercial Bank of China (ICBC) was created only in 1984 to take care of what remained of the commercial business of the PBoC, while the latter was exclusively assigned the role of central banking.

Therefore in 1984 banking reform had reached the point where the People's Bank of China was completely separate from the sectoral state banks and became nominally a central bank. In 1986 the four banks were allowed and even induced to compete in making credit to all sectors of the economy. However, before 1995 they were not afforded the legal status of commercial banks as this was part of the second stage of reform that began in 1994. On the one hand, the authority of the central bank was reinforced, together with the mission of controlling the money supply. On the other hand, the law on commercial banks granted them the autonomy to manage their credit business and the responsibility for their depositors.

The 1984–6 reform was as incomplete in finance as it was in industry. The four banks did not have the ability to manage their activity in a competitive environment. At the time the principle of responsibility was extended from farmers to businesses in other activities. At the margin, after fulfilling their planned requirements, firms could sell their products for profits. However, the autonomy for the big public enterprises had alleviated central state control, without transforming their managers into efficient entrepreneurs. They became intermeshed with local government officials. The income of managers and local officials increased at the expense of firms' profits. As mentioned above, many SOEs survived by running into debt. Those debts were policy loans granted by banks. The inability of banks to replace planning control by effective financial control allowed those firms to enjoy a soft budget constraint.

As Janos Kornaï forcefully pointed out, this distorted regulation was also prevalent in the former USSR in the late stage of the socialist era. Firms felt released from financial commitments, resorting to unfunded bank loans to socialize their debts, while they privatized profits with accounting manipulations and negotiated prices. However, the opening of the Chinese economy to world markets provided checks against the seizure of markets by monopolies and introduced some competitive restraints, at least in manufacturing.

In banking it was quite another matter. Interest rates were still entirely regulated, so that there was no price competition even at the margin. Furthermore the highly concentrated banking system was completely sheltered from foreign competition. There was no substitute to the guidance provided beforehand by central planning through the monobank. It ensued that the big banks applied the soft budget constraint in letting their local branches loose. The latter withdrew from headquarter control and were exposed without any check to the pressure of local government officials who demanded political loans. Bank officials were eager to comply because fixed interest rates made their revenues a positive function of the volume of loans supplied in collusion with local governments. Meanwhile, local governments encouraged the development of regional banks, which they partly owned, mostly in the coastal areas where the special economic zones were established. A network of rural credit cooperatives was also set up, supposed to be under the supervision of the ABC. Urban credit cooperatives also proliferated.

Such a system could only work on a grand scale with loose overall monetary control and non-existent prudential control. Indeed, the government had provided the banks with the capacity to make credit autonomously, without acknowledging that banks are not ordinary businesses. They are special in their balance sheets. In running the payment system and sheltering deposits, which are fixed-term contracts at indeterminate maturities for potentially the whole population, banks fulfill a public-good function on their liability side. Conversely they are entities taking risks on their asset side in making loans that are both risky and extend to a wide range of maturities. It follows that banks indulge in massive maturity transformation that conveys risks to their depositors who have no way to manage them. Furthermore, banks are intertwined in a network. Any loan gives rise to counterparty interbank risk. Therefore they are systemic in their very nature, especially if the industry is concentrated in just a few banks. Finally, since the aggregate of their deposits forms most of the money supply, they directly impinge on the price level and its variations over time, e.g. on inflation.

If one has understood the nature of banking, one cannot be surprised by the consequences of the 1984–6 halfway banking reform. Bank credit exploded with no consideration for risk and return of the assets financed by those loans. For its part, the newly created central bank had no experience and no doctrine in monetary policy. It validated the loans that had been issued in creating whatever base money was necessary to keep the banks afloat. Hence inflation accelerated sharply to reach 28 to 30 percent in 1988. Also, urban SMEs developed as soon as private activity was tolerated. They partly got credit from the credit cooperative and partly resorted to self-financing and to informal finance. Their expansion in number explains the bulk of the extraordinary spike in national saving in the 1980s, from 20 percent GDP in 1981 to 30 percent in 1988. After 1984 the financing came largely from price increases. Inflation spiked in 1988 and 1989, reaching a peak of 18 percent year-on-year (Figure 3.4).

The impact of inflation was devastating. In 1988 social unrest spread over the country because the win–win game of the first stage of reform was brutally interrupted. Inflation cut heavily into real income because most wages were still regulated by state control and thus stickier than prices. In the spring of 1989 an unlikely alchemy occurred, already seen in France in the spring of 1968 when deep social unrest prompted a student uprising, the most advanced front line of a youth movement demanding more freedom in their life. Unfortunately the drama unfolded tragically in June 1989 on Tian Anmen Square. The reason might be found in the bitter political dissensions within the Communist Party at the time.

The lack of macroeconomic regulation entailed the huge instability in the growth regime. GDP growth jumped from 6 to 16 percent between 1982 and 1986, plummeted to 9 percent in 1987, and rebounded to 12 percent in 1988, before the slump to 4 percent in 1992 followed by a startling recovery to 14 percent in 1994 (Figure 3.5), which reignited inflation with a vengeance. Then China successfully entered the second phase of its reform while taming inflation over the following years.

A rural reform that benefited all and an-ill-conceived urban reform that precipitated a crisis

The unique feature of the first stage of Chinese reform is that it benefited all until inflation raged in 1988. Precisely for this reason, reform gained universal legitimacy in China with all sectors of the Chinese population. The secret for achieving a universal improvement in welfare in that phase was not a transition to capitalism, but what we may call a post-socialist reform. During that phase of reform, rural China experienced genuine increases in agricultural productivity, though less so in industry. Such productivity gains were assisted by the institutional infrastructures established in the socialist era and the benefits of such gains were able to be distributed relatively equally to the whole population, thanks to the principle of equal distribution inherited from the socialist period. Reform also gained acknowledgment from the bureaucrats, who began to notice that liberalization increased their opportunities to translate political power into economic wealth. A new system of political patronage was forming.

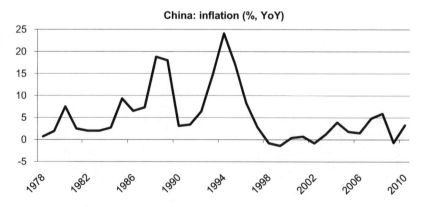

Figure 3.4 Inflation rate.
Source: CEIC

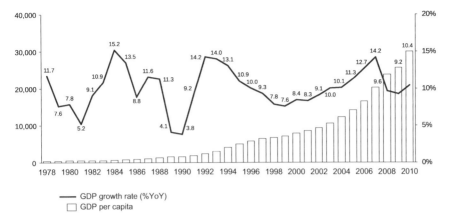

Figure 3.5 GDP growth rate and GDP per capita.
Source: China Statistical Yearbook of various years

However, the incomplete reforms in the urban regions created a fiscal burden for the central government that transferred to the banks, which were not completely reformed. A credit explosion triggered runaway inflation and political upheavals. The first stage of reform collapsed into crisis.

Conclusion

By carefully re-examining the socialist history of China and the initiation of the 1978 reform, this chapter argues that the guiding political principle of Chinese reform was not the convergence towards market liberalization, but the sustainability of China's specific unitary political regime. This pragmatic approach was behind the "Big Push" industrialization, as well as the reforms started in 1978.

In 1949 China faced severe constraints in agriculture output over industry. The country was devastated by continual wars and isolated from the international world. At that time, "Big Push" industrialization was the best strategy to minimize the stresses of agriculture and maximize industrial accumulation. Although the command economy did not and could never lead China onto a dynamic path of industrialization, from 1949 to 1978 China indeed succeeded in establishing an industrial base, enhancing the health and education of its populace, and restoring a strong unitary state.

By the end of the 1970s fundamental changes in agricultural productivity, international environment, and demographic structure provided much more accommodating conditions for initiating a dynamic industrialization process. Meanwhile, the population's dissatisfaction with their stagnant living standards surged and directly undermined the legitimacy of the CCP's political regime. Under the circumstances, introducing market mechanisms was appropriate in order to vitalize the economy and protect the political regime. This move proved to be extraordinarily successful. Nevertheless, it does not mean that the fundamental logic of China's reforms was in line with any Western-style "universal values." If necessary, the economy might as well be turned from market-oriented to planning, just as what did happen in the early 1950s. The underlying purpose of reform (in 1978 or before) has always been the maintenance of a unitary political regime. In the following chapter, we demonstrate how this rationale was at work for the second phase of Chinese reform (1994–2008).

4 The second phase of Chinese reform

As we discussed in the previous chapter, the guiding political rationale of Chinese reform was not the convergence towards market liberalization but the sustainability of China's specific unitary political regime. As a result, the reforming measures did not aim to bring revolutionary changes toward any established ideal, but incremental improvements based on existing conditions and opportunities. The pragmatist attitude of China's reformers could be vividly seen in a series of slogans popular in the early 1980s. Many of them were rumored to be Deng Xiaoping's own inventions. One of the most famous, for example, was the "Cat Theory," asserting that "no matter if a cat is black or white, as long as it can catch mice, it is a good cat." Another was the metaphor that compared the reforming process to "wading across the stream by feeling the way." Both of these sayings encouraged Chinese people to embrace reforms as an experimental process without ideological constraints so as to solve the practical problems of the present day.

With such pragmatic logic, the first phase of reform (1978–93) depicted in Chapter 3 did not cast aside socialist institutions abruptly. On the contrary, it inherited distinctive socialist features, took full advantage of the grounds laid in the socialist era, and also aimed to tackle the most pressing problems resulting from it. One of the legacies that exerted pivotal influence over the deployment of the first phase of Chinese reform was the relatively equalized distribution system of national income.[1] In rural China such equal distribution was built upon the equal distribution of land and collective ownership of TVEs. And in urban China it was based upon a state-dependent employment system[2] with nationally regulated salary schemes. Such an equalized distribution system spread the benefits resulting from any productivity gains to the greatest possible number of Chinese people, and enabled the first phase of Chinese reform to be a "reform without losers." The general improvement of welfare quickly endowed the word "reform" with universal acceptance and political legitimacy, which further endowed the CCP with the political credentials to introduce more drastic measures in the second phase of reform beginning in 1994. However, it was also exactly this equalized distribution system and the strong will of the government to protect the universal improvement of people's welfare that led to the increasingly deteriorated balance sheet of the Chinese central government. With the public debts contaminating the banking system, acute inflation and the resulting political upheaval eventually ended the golden years of "reform without losers" and led Chinese growth down a different path.

In order to understand better why the first phase of reforming measures undermined the fiscal capacity of Chinese central government so much, a revisit to China's fiscal system under the planning economy is necessary. Chinese planning economy, similar to that of the Soviet Union, was a Party–State Inc. The whole of the national economy (especially the urban industrial part) was run as one single corporation, with the state acting as headquarter and SOEs as operational units. Under this system enterprises did not possess any managerial power, their sole task being to fulfill the production commands issued by the central planning body. Resources for both daily operations and investments were allocated to the enterprises when needed and, in return, all outputs were returned to the state also. Prices existed but only as a measurement for internal accounting in this enormous Party–State corporation. Apparently, in the planning economy, the concept of tax barely existed. The state collected all revenues from SOEs and this revenue was the largest source of income for central government. As branches of central government, local governments had a claim on fiscal income through a revenue-sharing system so as to provide the necessary local public goods and services. The sharing rates were set annually after intense political bargaining.

Before 1978 most of the SOEs were profitable because: (1) the price system was made preferential to industrial products and discriminative to agricultural products; and (2) SOEs enjoyed absolute monopoly over all industrial markets. The profitability of SOEs guaranteed that government was quite affluent as well. By the mid-1950s the government could already raise more than a quarter of national GDP as budgetary revenues. This was a stunning achievement considering the low development level of China at the time, and the consistently weak tax extraction capacity of the Nationalist government before the war (Naughton 2007: 60).

After the start of reform in 1978, however, this revenue-based fiscal system began to erode. In 1979 the procurement prices for agricultural products rose by 20 percent, and at the same time market exchanges of agricultural products were made legitimate. These policy shifts indicated the start of the price correction for agricultural goods. The price advantage of industrial outputs over agricultural ones was waning. With the deepening of reform, SOEs' profitability was also challenged by the surge of industrial producers outside the traditional planning economy. These producers included small and medium enterprises (SMEs) in the urban regions, TVEs in the rural regions and foreign enterprises in the costal regions. The emergence of these new economic players outside the planning system demolished the monopoly of SOEs over the markets of industrial goods. SOEs, or even state planning bureaus, lost their absolute control over selling prices. Yet meanwhile the state commanded continual salary raises for all SOE employees. The profit margin of SOEs was eroded from all sides.

With a revenue-based fiscal system, the decline of SOEs' profitability directly led to a sharp reduction in central government's fiscal income, whereas the buoyant economic growth outside of the planning system could not be effectively taxed because of the lack of the necessary taxation institutions. Attempts were made to boost the fiscal capacities of central government, yet most of these failed and put the central government in an even more miserable budgetary position.

One such attempt was the revenue-sharing "contract" systems initiated in the 1980s. In Chapter 3 we introduced the role of this "contract" system in reforming SOEs but what we did not mention was that, in 1988, facing a steep fiscal decline yet lacking the capacity to monitor tax efforts in the provinces, the Chinese central government introduced these "contracts" to regulate the revenue-sharing relationship between central government and local governments as well. This system of fiscal contracts was called the "fiscal responsibility system" (Wong and Bird 2008: 431). Under this system, provincial governments remitted only a fixed revenue to the central government, retaining all the rest for their own uses. These revenue-sharing contracts further undermined central fiscal capacity for, at least, the following three reasons. First, as the remittances to central government were fixed by contracts, the center could not benefit from the rapid economic growth. In 1988 local governments retained 96.7 percent of all increased fiscal income, while central government only got 3.3 percent (Xin 1996: 550). Such disproportionate distribution of new fiscal resources did not change until the fiscal reform of 1994. In Figure 4.1 we can clearly observe the dropping of the central share of fiscal revenue in total Chinese fiscal revenue. Second, the "fiscal responsibility system" failed to take inflation into consideration, despite the years after 1988 suffering from hyperinflation (see Chapter 3). As the remittances were set at nominal values, inflation shrank the real income of central government and increased its expenditures. In 1988, for instance, nominal central fiscal income increased by 6.5 percent when compared with 1987. However, CPI in the same year was as high as 18.5 percent. Therefore central government revenue actually diminished severely in real terms. The third fatal flaw of the contracting systems was that the contracts lacked binding power over the contractors when it came to losses. Both managers and local officials had no problem retaining surpluses when available; however, they could not be held fully responsible for their actions when losses occurred. Such a situation was a typical breeding ground for "moral hazard." As the first phase of reform inherited strong socialist characteristics, bankruptcy and layoff of labor were not politically acceptable. Neither could the central state collect the full aggregate of remissions promised in the contracts, nor could it abstain from acting as "last resort" for both SOEs and localities. Not surprisingly, central fiscal capacity continued to decline (Figure 4.1). At the nadir, the central budget allocated only 3 percent of national GDP (Wong and Bird 2008: 432). In the mid-1990s, half of central government's expenditures were financed by debt. Banks were commanded to issue policy loans without proper risk management. As a result, a banking crisis was brewing with the rise of non-performing loans (NPLs) and in 1993 inflation rocketed with the sharp expansion of the money supply.

All these crises, i.e. the central government's fiscal deficiency, the escalating accumulation of NPLs in the banks, and the runaway inflation, erupted towards the end of the first phase of reform and were translated into a perilous ruling crisis

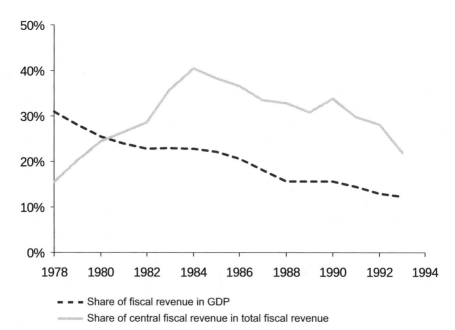

Figure 4.1 The evolution of China's fiscal capacities from 1978 to 1993.
Source: CEIC

for the CCP. Threats toward the unitary hierarchical political regime came from all directions. Chapter 3 expounded three main conditions for the sustainability of a unitary hierarchical political regime in a two-layered society: the delivery of acceptable welfare levels for its people; the alignment of bureaucrats' behavior with the political goals of the central leadership and the banning of organized groups mustering independent political power. In the first phase of reform, the long overdue welfare improvement in the socialist era compelled Chinese reformers to put the priority on the first condition in order to maintain their political legitimacy. That was a period of "reform without losers." The general welfare level of the whole populace was elevated and more than 400 million people were lifted out of absolute poverty. However, from the end of the 1980s to the mid-1990s this growth regime undermined all three conditions necessary for the sustainability of the CCP's political regime. The most seriously threatened condition was central government control over the behavior of its bureaucrats. Under a revenue-sharing contract system, local governments enjoyed a high degree of financial autonomy. This led to central government losing fiscal revenue as local authorities were in charge of tax collection. Weak fiscal capacity endangered the credibility of the unitary political power as the hierarchical bureaucratic system crumbled from inside. Outside the bureaucratic system, a large private economic body was emerging and growing fast. During the first phase of reform the CCP had not yet developed sufficient regulatory institutions to guide the activities of these new economic organizations. As a result these organizations were not only highly independent from the bureaucratic system, but they also enticed bureaucrats to quit the political system and "jump into the sea."[3] In other words, the private economy started to challenge the ultimate authority of the central political regime, and this contest could not be tolerated in a typical political regime based on a two-layered society. Worse, the general welfare level of people eventually declined as inflation went out of control in the later 1980s. The control of the CCP faced a serious challenge: without effective measures to alter the situation, the CCP political regime could have ultimately collapsed.

Such a critical situation called for drastic action and an iron fist to carry it out resolutely. Zhu Rongji, known for his toughness, was named the first Vice-Prime Minister in 1993 and Prime Minister in 1998. Immediately after his ascent to power, Zhu took a series of radical actions, leading Chinese reform into its second stage. The sustainability of the CCP's unitary hierarchical political regime was without doubt the paramount rationale of this second stage of reform. Thus the measures taken were designed to systemically tackle all the challenges to CCP control described above. In doing so, the growth regime was deeply transformed.

Increasing the political control of central government

New tax regime

In order to rescue the weakening control of central government over the bureaucratic system, one of the most pressing tasks was to re-strengthen the fiscal capacity of central government. Consequently the prime purpose of the 1994 fiscal reform was to recentralize fiscal control. This purpose was realized in three steps.

From revenue to tax

The first step was to establish a modern taxation system so that economic activities outside the planning could be effectively taxed. After 1978, although non-state economic actors emerged and grew rapidly, a modern tax regime that could cover both state and non-state sectors on an equal basis did not materialize. The 1994 fiscal reform was the first attempt to systemically transform the fiscal system from revenue-based to tax-based. Although the schemes established were still crude and the system was far from being complete, the birth of an embryonic modern taxation system already had far-reaching significance.

A single-rated value-added tax (VAT)[4] was applied to unify all turnover taxes charged over industrial activities. For the service sector, a business tax was charged on sales. The tax rates ranged from 3 percent to 20 percent depending on business type. In addition to VAT, 11 categories[5] that were considered either luxury or detrimental to public health were subject to consumption tax. A unified corporate income tax[6] was also adopted. Foreign enterprises enjoyed preferential rates for income tax and this differentiated tax treatment persisted until 2008. The rules of personal income tax also underwent adjustments in 1994 to accommodate the changed income structure.

The establishment of modern tax principles was a prerequisite for rationalizing the tax-sharing relationship between central and local governments. Unitary VAT and income tax schemes created a level playground for economic players of different ownerships. The industrial tax base was better defined than before. Tax evasion and the myriad extra-budgetary charges were restrained. The fact that tax regimes were applied on a national level also suggested that the central government obtained the exclusive right to making fiscal policies. Thus, with this step, the central government already recovered the initiative against local governments.

New tax-sharing scheme

The second step of the 1994 fiscal reform was to abolish the "fiscal responsibility system" and establish a well-codified tax-sharing scheme. This change directly shuffled the fiscal relationship between the central and provincial governments. VAT, for example, was defined as a shared tax. Central government claimed a majority of 75 percent and the remaining 25 percent was allocated to the local governments. As VAT was the biggest item in the new tax regime, the 75/25 share gave central government back the upper hand for tax-revenue sharing.[7]

The reform in tax-sharing had immediate impact. The central share of tax revenue jumped from an abysmal 22 percent up to 55.7 percent. Although this share experienced minor downward adjustments in the years that followed, it stayed largely around the same level throughout the second phase of reform. Meanwhile, fiscal expenditure sharing did not go through significant changes before and after 1994. Local governments still had to carry out more than 60 percent of total fiscal responsibilities. Most of them became highly dependent on central fiscal transfers.[8] This

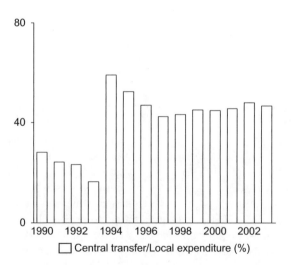

Figure 4.2 Central transfers to total local expenditures (%).

Source: Calculated with data from China Statistical Yearbook of various years

drastic shift in the power relationship was decidedly beneficial to the strengthening of central government's control over localities.

Restructuring tax administration

The final step of the 1994 fiscal reform was strengthening tax administration. After the tax regime and tax-sharing system had been established, an effective tax administrative body that could enforce the schemes properly was essential. In order to protect the central share of tax revenue from local influence, the former local taxation bureaus were split into two. China created a unitary fiscal system with two sets of tax administrative bodies. One set of tax offices was under the direct control of central government and this national tax administrative body was responsible for the collection of central and shared tax items. The other set of tax offices, controlled by local governments, was in charge of collecting local tax items, such as corporate and personal income taxes. Under this "double-track" tax administrative system, central government held a tight grip on VAT, the biggest tax item, and thus guaranteed its fiscal safety against any local encroachments.

Although we explained the 1994 fiscal reform as a three-step process, in reality the application of these three steps was an intertwined political process with one political goal, i.e. to strengthen the central control over the behavior of local administrations through the recentralization of fiscal power. When evaluated with this gauge, the 1994 fiscal reform was a huge success. Not only did the central share of total fiscal revenue bounce up drastically from 22 percent in 1993 to 55.7 percent in 1994, but tax revenue as a share of GDP also experienced steady growth throughout the second phase of reform (Figure 4.3). The central

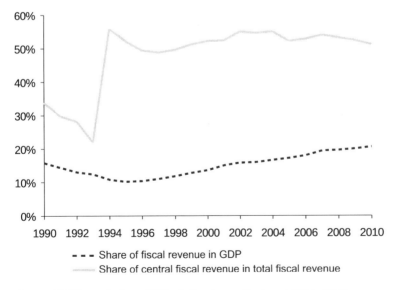

Figure 4.3 The evolution of China's fiscal capacity from 1990 to 2010.
Source: CEIC

government acquired full decision-making power over tax policies and obtained nearly 60 percent of all fiscal revenue. The financial autonomy of local governments, at least on the income side, was much weakened.

It is noteworthy that the 1994 fiscal reform was only a halfway reform in building a modern Chinese fiscal system. As the primary purpose was to recentralize fiscal power, the design of the tax regime, the method of calculating fiscal transfers, the scheme for sharing fiscal expenditures, etc. lacked scrutiny. As time has gone on, the deficiencies of the 1994 system have become more and more pronounced. Further adjustments are surely needed. We discuss these in Chapter 7.

Repositioning SOEs

With the swift implementation of fiscal reform, central government strengthened its financial position on the revenue side. However, the aggregate profitability of SOEs continued to wane (aggregate loss of 7.8 billion RMB in 1998). As owner of these companies, the Chinese government faced escalating financial risks on the expenditure side. More and more enterprises were suffering from persistent losses. As their last resort, central government and the affiliated banking system had to repeatedly bail out these unprofitable enterprises. A large number of SOEs in the mid-1990s had already suspended their productive activities, only lingering as vehicles to deliver basic living allowances and social services to their employees, who constituted a majority of the urban active population. In 1978, SOEs took care of 75 million employees, 78.3 percent of total urban employment. With the economy outside of the state system growing rapidly, this share dropped to 60.1 percent in 1994. Nevertheless, as the active population was expanding fast, the SOEs' total employment actually grew by 49 percent to 112 million. Even if wages were low, the sum of the payrolls was still enormous. What is more, under the socialist tradition, SOEs were obliged to provide free educational services, free medical cares, and often free housing for their employees and their families. To conclude, in the 1990s, SOEs had completely turned from a "cash cow" to a growing tumor damaging the central government's financial health. Unless SOEs underwent drastic restructuring with their burdens transferred to society as a whole, they would persistently keep central government in financial danger. Under these circumstances, the imperative of guaranteeing political sustainability finally won out over the desired full control of economy in the CCP's political arbitrage. Once political consensus had been achieved, the principles and measures of SOE restructuring became self-evident.

Legal preparations for the restructuring of SOEs

As the principal purpose for the new round of SOE reform in the 1990s was to secure central government's fiscal capacity, two main tasks had to be accomplished. The first task was to close unprofitable enterprises in "non-strategic" sectors. The strategic sectors were defined as sectors that concerned national security, sectors that were naturally monopolized, sectors that provided critical public goods and services, and sectors that had great growth potential and possessed high-technologies.[9] By grasping these "strategic sectors" tightly, the CCP would maintain its dominance over the core economy. However, by "letting go" the unprofitable and non-strategic SOEs, the government could substantially alleviate its financial burden. This policy was vividly called "seizing the large and letting go of the small." The other task was of course to lay off a large proportion of SOE employees. These laid-off workers became the first group of population since the start of reform whose benefits were sacrificed. Chinese reform officially ended the "no loser" phase.

To enable "letting go" and SOE downsizing, three types of management decisions had to be made legal. They were: privatization, bankruptcy declaration, and labor layoff. They were made legal under two laws passed successively in 1993 and 1994: a Company Law and a Labor Law. With the enactment of the Company Law, Chinese SOE reform entered a new age. The emphasis of reform was no longer signing revenue-sharing contracts, but turning SOEs into "modern" corporations. This reform act continued to empower firms' managers, but it also provided a legal framework to diversify ownership and deal with bankruptcy. The Labor Law was passed in 1994 and took effect on January 1, 1995. It equalized employment relationships with different ownership types. Total job security, also called the "iron rice bowl," enjoyed by SOE employees was officially repealed. Instead, labor contracts were mandated between workers and their employers. Significantly the law also permitted no-fault dismissal of workers in response to changing economic conditions (Cai *et al.* 2008: 174). It was tantamount to providing the legal basis for large-scale SOE labor layoffs.

The process of "seizing the large and letting go of the small"

Corporatization is a prerequisite for privatization and bankruptcy. For small SOEs and collectively owned entities, corporatization was immediately intertwined with privatization. Usually those companies were sold to their workers and managers at preferential prices. However, for larger SOEs, privatization came much later than corporatization. The Chinese State Council handpicked the first hundred SOEs for corporatization in November 1994. Yet all that changed seemed to be only the company names. Corporate governance evolved slowly and the ownership remained strictly public. However, the restructuring of large SOEs was accelerated after 1997 due to the escalating losses made by SOEs and the stern fiscal status of central government. From that year on, SOEs in the non-strategic sector began to be sold off or declare bankruptcy on a large scale. Simultaneously the massive layoff of SOE employees also began. The whole privatization process of these enterprises was quite messy and highly non-transparent. There were hardly any central directives about which enterprises to let go, when to let them go, or how to calculate their value and sale prices. The local governments were in full charge of carrying out the privatization process and, naturally, this privatization process was full of abuses. A small group of well-connected individuals acquired sizable personal benefits at the cost of state assets, as occurred in Russia. After the birth of the State-owned Assets Supervision and Administration Commission (SASAC) in 2004, some rules were finally established. However, managers could still quite easily evade the rules thanks to their insider knowledge.

For the large and medium SOEs of strategic importance, i.e. the enterprises to "be seized," corporatization was also adopted. However, the purpose of incorporating them was not privatization. It was to improve corporate governance and profitability. After corporatization, the autonomy of management from bureaucratic administrations was further institutionalized and protected. Some of these SOEs went through initial public offerings (IPOs) and became the first Chinese enterprises listed on stock markets. Regardless of how much these measures had indeed improved these SOEs' corporate governance and efficiency, the remaining SOEs enjoyed strong business momentum thanks to their often monopolistic market positions and the now concentrated financial and material support from the state. These SOEs played an important role in controlling the economic lifeline for the state and influenced the entire economic structure in the second phase of reform.

The process of state-sector downsizing

In the early SOE privatization labor layoff had already occurred, but the scale was restrained and the process was slow. Indeed, downsizing was a very risky move for it could harm the welfare of a large population and thus directly undermine the legitimacy of the CCP's political regime. However, with the losses of SOEs amplifying, this painful step had to be taken eventually. Large-scale SOE downsizing accompanied the full fling of SOE privatization and the string of bankruptcies that started in 1997 as a consequence of the economic slowdown provoked by the Asian crisis. The layoff program had a name of its own: xia gang ("stepping down from one's working position").

Table 4.1 The impact of "xia gang" on employment

Year	Stock of laid-off workers at year end (million)	Number of workers laid-off in the year (million)	Number of SOE workers (million)	Registered unemployed workers (millions)	Registered unemployment rate %
1997	9.95		107.70	5.77	3.10
1998	8.77	7.39	88.10	5.71	3.10
1999	9.37	7.82	83.40	5.75	3.10
2000	9.11	5.12	78.80	5.95	3.10
2001	7.42	2.83	74.10	6.81	3.60
2002	6.18	2.11	69.20	7.70	4.00
2003	4.21	1.28	66.20	8.00	4.30
2004	2.71	0.49	64.40	8.27	4.20
Total	32.60	27.04			

Source: National Bureau of Statistics of China (2003, 2006)

In Table 4.1 we can clearly observe the scale of the layoff program. Before 1998 there had already been at least more than 10 million laid-off workers. From 1998 to 2004 the aggregate number of laid-off workers was 27 million. That is to say, in the second phase of China's reform at least more than 37 million workers were downsized. However, this figure was probably an underestimation. SOE employees left their jobs through various mechanisms, and some of them, such as early retirement, were not counted as "xia gang." A comparison of the numbers of SOE workers in 1997 and 2004 gives us a rough impression of the real magnitude of this wave of labor layoff. In 1997 SOEs hired 107.7 million workers and this number decreased by 43.3 million to 64.4 million in 2004. This 43.3 million reduction in labor demand did not even include collectively owned enterprises. Ironically, the registered unemployment rate in all those years stayed roughly the same. From 1997 to 2000, the rate stayed at 3.1 percent for four continuous years. After 2000 this rate rose slightly to 4.2 percent.

To the relief of the CCP, such a massive layoff program did not cause damaging uprisings. Even though complaints and social conflicts were on the rise, generally speaking the transition in the labor market was carried out smoothly. The reasons for such a relatively smooth transition were manifold. One of the major stabilizing contributors was high economic growth, which enabled the quick absorption of laid-off labor in other economic activities. In Table 4.1 we observe that the stock of laid-off workers without new jobs was restrained to a certain threshold, despite the massive number of newly fired. The upsurge of the private sector, especially the export-led labor-intensive enterprises and urban service providers, absorbed a large proportion of laid-off workers.

Besides, the "xia gang" program offered a fairly generous compensation scheme, which typically provided up to three years of living subsidies (and pension and health care benefits) based on 60 percent of each worker's final wage. Before the laid-off workers found their new jobs, they stayed in formal ties with their original work places and were offered free training programs and free employment assistance. The social security programs that were once run by individual enterprises were also taken over by local governments. Although the progress was slow and the recovery rates of these programs were low, they provided a bottom-line security for laid-off workers.

Another important stabilizer in SOE restructuring was the housing reform that occurred in 1994 and was completed toward the end of the1990s. During this reform welfare housing units allocated gratis to urban dwellers before 1994 were sold to their occupants at highly concessional rates. As most of the SOE families benefited from welfare housing, this reform was a large one-shot transfer of public assets to individual families and boosted the universal wealth level of SOE employees. This large wealth transfer had an invaluable soothing effect for the laid-off workers: at least they did not lose everything in the privatization process of their work units.

The role of strong family ties and social networks in China should not be forgotten either in the smooth transition of the labor market in the 1990s. The story in each family or neighborhood varied and it would be hard to generalize, but personal assistance of all kinds helped make up the incomplete social security schemes in the 1990s and it goes on even today.

The effects of SOE restructuring

After the implementation of "seizing the large and letting go the small" and large-scale state-sector downsizing, the Chinese government succeeded in repositioning the role of SOEs in the whole economy. The CCP ended its attempt to control every sector of economic activity. Instead Chinese leaders realized that, as long as the few "strategic" sectors were still firmly held in hand, they could still effectively direct national economic development.

Although the process caused great pains to laid-off workers and their families and created substantial social inequality by transferring massive public assets to a small group of people, all in all SOE restructuring enhanced China's industrial productivity and economic dynamism. Uncompetitive production facilities were withdrawn and the scale of market competition was greatly expanded. Large numbers of experienced workers were released into the buoyant private sector, especially to the coastal regions and, most importantly, the aim of strengthening central government's fiscal capacities was accomplished. Central government could now focus its fiscal resources on what the State Council regarded as of most consequence for the whole nation and the political regime. Its power was significantly boosted.

Increasing administrative control over the economy

When reform started in 1978, the goal was to "supplement planning economy with market mechanism" (Chen and Duan 2009: 51). However, the actual result went beyond anyone's expectation. A large non-state sector grew at amazing speed outside the planning system, eroded the planning economy, and eventually destroyed the whole command system. The private economy was challenging the ultimate authority of the CCP. In the first phase of reform, CCP government had mostly stayed in a defensive position. Fierce in-party political debates made any consensus about critical issues hard to achieve. Under such circumstances, bureaucratic inertia sustained the socialist tradition, which insisted on holding direct control of every economic sector and on safeguarding the benefits of every group of the population. However, attempts to keep direct control of every sector dispersed valuable fiscal resources and endeavors to benefit every group added fiscal burden and eventually sparked an inflationary spiral. After learning hard lessons in the early 1990s, the CCP finally realized that it was impossible and unnecessary to continue with the old planning approach in regulating the economy. The private sector can grow rapidly in output and employment without harming the political authority of the state if proper mechanisms are developed to regulate the flow of critical inputs and the rules of the game for a mixed economy.

Fiscal resources

Recentralized fiscal control after the 1994 fiscal reform was the first weapon to deploy. When necessary, the CCP seldom hesitated to use its strengthened fiscal capacity to guide investments and to supervise macroeconomic trends. This attitude was first tested in 1998. When the economy faced the threat of the Asian crisis, the Chinese state resolutely instigated large government-guided investment plans. Similar fiscal stimulation was also applied in 2008 to counter the global financial crisis.

Government-guided investments exerted strong influences over the behavior of the whole Chinese economy. Bureaucrats were avid supporters of these investment plans, providing them with both the political credentials for promotion and opportunities for rent seeking or corruption. SOEs served as an important vehicle in carrying out government-guided investments. Thanks to their ambiguous financial relationship with the government, Chinese SOEs could receive fiscal supports for investments yet keep the return on those investments almost entirely to themselves. Undoubtedly, they also supported investment plans wholeheartedly. The government-supported investment projects also attracted private investors. With government backing, private investors perceived lowered risks and guaranteed returns. Such economic stimuli compelled many of them to network with government officials in the hope of gaining participation in those projects. Consequentially, the active role government played in investment was one of the critical elements that made the economy more and more investment-dependent in the first ten years of the twenty-first century. Meanwhile, it also strengthened all Chinese economic players' dependency on government decisions and guidance, thus strengthening the political authority of the CCP.

Financial resources

One can never stress enough the importance of finance for business. Thus understanding the allocation of financial resources provides useful insights in apprehending the Chinese state's control over the economy.

The Chinese financial system is notorious for being bank-heavy. Banks, especially the largest four state-owned banks – Industrial and Commercial Bank of China (ICBC), Bank of China (BOC), China Construction Bank (CCB), and Agricultural Bank of China (ABC) – altogether constitute about 80 percent of deposits. As a result, governmental directives have a strong influence over the flow of bank credit, the most common source of funding. Although the operation of the large banks became much more independent from the bureaucratic system, after they had been listed on the stock market and after they had centralized credit assessment and authorization to their headquarters, we can still observe significant political influence over the behavior of banks.

Bank credits, as a result, flew disproportionally to SOEs and to the financing of urban real estate development via loans to local governments through special vehicles, such as the urban development investment corporations (UDIC). These are analogous to the special investment vehicles used by investment bankers to finance the securitization of mortgage loans in the US. They receive bank credit against land earmarked for real estate development, which has been transferred by local authorities to be posted as collateral for the loans. They lend the money

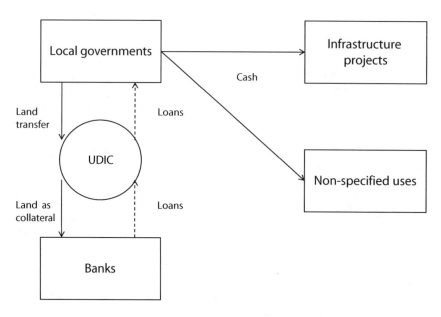

Figure 4.4 Financing local governments with off-balance-sheet vehicles.

to the local authorities. The quality of the loans is speculative in as much as it depends on the anticipation of rising real estate prices (Figure 4.4). Therefore it exposes the Chinese banking system to the danger of real estate price reversal. Nevertheless, the size of such loans has never ceased to increase. Yet, for private enterprises, financing became the most serious bottleneck. Surveys made by the All-China Federation of Industry and Commerce continued to report how difficult it was for SMEs to gain access to bank credit. Under these circumstances, SMEs had to rely heavily on informal finance and self-finance, severely hampering the development of their businesses.

The banking system was too heavily regulated: what about the capital markets? Capital markets are composed of the bond and equity markets. Capital markets in China made great strides both as a consequence of the 1998 stimulus plan and of the restrictive monetary policy that followed. However, the evolution in the structure of total social financing shows that the main beneficiaries of the change are still the banks in offering acceptance bills and trust companies in making unsecured loans. It is not that banks buy all the bonds that are issued: they buy roughly half government bonds and short-term private bonds. It is more the problem of the price. Interest rate regulation restrains both supply and demand for bonds, because the secondary market is virtually non-existent, although the Ministry of Finance formally introduced a secondary market for government debt in 1994 in the wake of the fiscal reform. It is why, despite its growth since the mid-2000s, Chinese bond outstanding is still much smaller than those of more mature markets in East Asia (Korea, Malaysia, Singapore), even leaving Japan aside.

On the supply side, because interest rates are heavily regulated, the PBoC de facto guarantees the profit margin of banks on their loans. The PBoC sets the whole yield curve from one month to five years, with the exception of the short-term money market since the introduction of the Shibor in 2007. The money market is the only deep market because it is a repo market used by banks for acquiring liquidity against government bonds pledged as collateral. However, it does not impinge much on the pricing of capital for longer maturities. Therefore corporate bonds are largely confined to the short-end of the maturity structure. As far as government bonds are concerned, the central government has wanted to minimize its own deficit and has tolerated the debt financing of local governments, backed by land values and performed by hazardous vehicles.

On the demand side, the market of bank deposits is captive because deposits are the primary resource of the banks. When interest rates are changed, bank debtor and bank creditor rates move in tandem to keep the interest rate margin steady. Only recently, with the leakage of deposits to trust companies, were interest rates on deposits raised slightly more than lending rates for maturities of three to five years.

Regulated interest rates preclude the secondary market from playing its role of price discovery. Public bonds are issued at rates that are higher than bank lending rates for the same maturities. Banks are the main holders of those securities. Because lending rates are strictly controlled to ensure low capital costs, banks have every reason to keep those bonds on their books to maturity. Therefore the secondary market hardly exists. Because the pseudo-market yield is systematically lower than the yield on issue, it does not attract investors. Thus trade on the secondary market makes losses. Consequently bonds are held to maturities on the books of banks and other financial investors. Still the large SOEs and central government itself have the financial strength to get an interest rate on issue lower than the bank lending rate at the same maturity. This is why the China bond markets have developed to finance the government and the SOEs cheaply without pricing risk adequately.

In developed financial systems, bond financing and bank credit are substitutes for each other. Asian financial systems are too heavily tilted towards banks. This feature was the consequence of their fast government-led growth and of their high household saving. Governments found it convenient to facilitate extensive branch networks by commercial banks. In so doing the banks were able to tap savings from remote corners of the economies and extend loans at stable interest rates to both the public and the private sectors in financially closed economies. High levels of investment, conducive to fast-sustaining growth, could be financed at minimal costs. This is what liberal economists call "financial repression."

Two structural changes undermined the consistency of those closed and regulated financial systems. The first was financial globalization that reached smaller Asian countries in the 1990s and China after the change in the exchange rate regime in July 2005. The second was the diversification of the growth regime, when the stage of middle-income countries had been reached. Both structural changes raise problems of capital allocation different from maximizing accumulation. With new sources of funds, competition brings about concern for risk-adjusted returns. With the widening of consumer opportunities following the ascent of a middle class, financial decisions become more decentralized. In complex financial systems, encompassing multiple layers of access to credit, and managing and disseminating risk become all-important.

The benefits of well-functioning bond markets are five-fold. First, debt-issuing capital markets help to smooth investment cycles in eschewing credit crunches and creditors' runs, while the banking sector has been loaded with problem loans. The corporate bond market provides a "safety valve" in permitting solvent economic agents to continue borrowing. Conversely, commercial banks backed by central bank liquidity can forestall the flight to quality triggered by disrupted corporate bond markets. Second, as opposed to bank credit, which involves private risk assessment and monitoring, bond markets improve the efficiency of resource allocation in laying out a mechanism of public risk assessment and dissemination. Deep and liquid government bond markets will provide a yield curve that in turn will help pricing credit risk at each maturity. A well-defined yield curve, extending to long-term bonds, opens a new source of finance for long-run investment projects. The use of credit derivatives will further allow splitting the spread between elementary factors of risk: credit risk, liquidity risk, risks embedded in specific contracts (callability), and eventually tax differences.

Third, bonds make a basic asset class in the strategic allocation of long-run institutional investors. For long-run investors, the riskless security in strategic asset allocation is not a short-term bill but a long-term bond. The reason is that long-term bond yields exhibit mean-reverting processes, while rollover short-term bills do not in an uncertain interest rate environment. Therefore enriching capital markets has the subsequent advantage of enhancing institutional asset management in countries like China where the population is aging and the government is establishing compulsory retirement plans. Fourth, the more public information is gathered in credit markets, the sooner the central bank will be able to shift from direct credit control to the price channel of monetary policy. By being able to communicate to the financial markets a forward view of the future path of the economy, the central bank will be able to smooth out fluctuations in real variables and make the growth path steadier. However, to abandon direct quantity and price control in monetary policy, the government must be sure that the use of market-oriented instruments would not attract more capital inflows from abroad without being offset by capital outflows from Chinese institutional investors. This is why, since the decision to let the Yuan drift against the US dollar in July 2005, the Chinese government has significantly opened the capital accounts. Financial institutions and the state pension scheme have been allowed to invest abroad. Fifth, an efficient domestic market is a precondition for safely phasing out capital controls. This is a step forward to link the domestic capital market to global markets. The short-run range of the yield curve is the domestic leg of the forward foreign exchange market. Commercial banks will be able to supply hedging instruments to foreign trade operators and to investors eager to diversify abroad. Conversely, it will be possible to borrow abroad in domestic currency, reducing the dependency on the dollar. With a broader and more diversified capital account, it will become possible to move to a more flexible exchange rate regime. In the next chapter we consider the move to internationalize the Yuan offshore since 2010 as an important preliminary step to liberalizing domestic interest rates.

The bond markets have the potential to expand dramatically in the years ahead. On the supply side, a new stage of reform is being launched by the 12th five-year plan starting in 2011. This stage will be driven by public expenditures to build up infrastructures, invest heavily in education, and set up a public welfare system and a universal public pension system. The financing of the public debt that will increase markedly will hugely enlarge the supply of government bonds. On the demand side, the likely steady increase in household income, the large and expanding size of the working population, and the huge pool of savings looking for diversification may all create demand for bonds. This will become a strong pillar in broad and deep capital markets, serving growth well.

Equity markets are more speculative playgrounds than temples of Chinese capitalism. The Shanghai and Shenzhen stock markets were created respectively in 1990 and 1991. The number of listed firms has expanded tremendously together with market capitalization, but their contribution to financing the firms has always been modest. Except for a once-and-for-all spike in 2007, the equity funds raised every year have always been less than 10 percent of new loans (Figure 4.5). The position of state sectors in those markets is dominant. Roughly two-thirds of the shares are owned by the Ministry of Finance, by public financial agencies and by other state-owned enterprises. They are not marketable and do not have the same value as marketable shares. Therefore state owners and firm managers do not care much about the market value of the firms. Correlatively the secondary markets are not only illiquid: they are rife with embezzlement, insider trading, creative accounting, and conspiracy. This is why the State Council decided to reform the market in setting up the China Securities Regulatory Commission (CSRC) to monitor a reform in 2005. The overall objective was to establish a competitive stock market, able to deliver safe diversification in assets and wealth

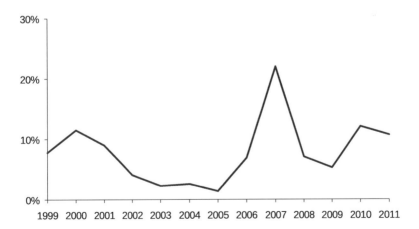

Figure 4.5 New equity financing on domestic markets to new credits (%).
Source: CEIC

enhancement for households, reliable information to financial investors for efficient capital allocation, and a source of long-term funds for companies. The
reform is still underway and far from achieving all its objectives yet. In undertaking this huge task the CSRC first had to police the market in order to create
a climate that could give confidence to retail investors, favor the market-making
role of institutional investors, and attract foreign capital. Judging by the volatility
of these markets and the sharp 2007 speculative bubble, the goal is far from being
reached (Figure 4.6). The segmentation of the market and the scarcity of shares to
be traded might be one reason. Listed companies can issue three types of shares:
A shares issued and registered in Yuan on domestic markets for domestic investors, B shares issued and registered in dollars on domestic markets for foreign
investors, and H shares of two kinds: shares issued on domestic markets in HK
dollars but traded in Hong Kong and so-called Red Chips, e.g. shares issued in
HK dollars, traded in Hong Kong and subjected to Hong Kong law. The latter are
preferred by foreign investors. Few firms are entitled to be listed on Chinese stock
markets. Neither medium-size public firms nor private SMEs have been authorized
to issue public shares. Implementing solvency law in effective court litigations,
normalizing accounting and auditing, are processes that have no tradition in
Chinese law-making and will take a long time before becoming widespread.

To increase the demand for stocks, the China Insurance Regulatory Commission
(CIRC) is considering more flexible regulation to permit insurance companies more
investment in A shares. However, supervisory authorities do not want to give direct
access to the market before financial institutions have built reliable risk control systems and have reformed their governance so that the alerts and checks provided
by the internal audit departments impinge effectively on higher management. One
way to move forward is to authorize trading and investment through fully capitalized asset management subsidiaries. The same goes for banks: authorization to

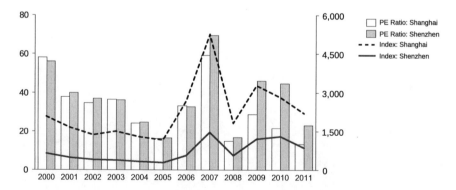

Figure 4.6 Indexes and average price/earnings ratio on domestic stock markets.

Note: PE ratio refers to the "price/earnings ratio." It is calculated as the market value of a firm divided
by its net profit.

Source: China Statistical Yearbook of various years

create securities houses is conditional upon substantial improvement in their own governance. The types of funds that have exploded in 2007 and triggered the bubble are public-offered funds providing accounts to individuals in the largest cities where an affluent middle class has been thriving. These people invest an excessive share of saving on equities because of a lack of opportunities for investing in bonds. In an unstable market they are exposed to heavy losses. A potentially very large investor is the National Social Security Fund, which is the pillar of the compulsory stage in the three-tier retirement funding system based upon the Singaporean model. With the development of retirement saving, it will become the largest pension fund, an outstanding instrument for long-term investment.

On expanding supply, the challenge is how to make non-tradable shares tradable. The reform has the twin advantage of creating fiscal revenues and improving the liquidity of the stock markets. The government must decide the perimeter of the public sector it wants to keep according to its overall strategy in promoting long-run growth. Then the parties involving the Ministry of Finance, the National Development and Reform Commission (NDRC), SOE managers, underwriting banks, and investing communities must agree on the method to engineer IPOs that depend crucially on the process of valuation. The complexity of the problem and the conflicts of interests it raises have slowed down IPOs after a boost in 2007 that aroused expectations and fed the bubble. The feedbacks of the global financial crisis burst the bubble in 2008. A short rally occurred in 2009, pulled by the expansive economic policy of the time, and then the restrictive monetary policy to fight rising inflation has since hampered the markets in 2010 and 2011, keeping the markets substantially undervalued.

Fixed assets: natural resources and land

It is not uncommon for state to have property rights to key natural resources. However, as a country just going through the transition from a completely public ownership to a mixed economy, the Chinese government has an uncommonly large stake of such resources at its disposal. The allocation of them, including land, is also an important tool in directing economic development. In China, royalties, rents, and taxes charged for the usage of natural resources are extremely low. The right to exact natural resources was often given for free. According to an incomplete survey of 150,000 mining companies, only 20,000 paid for their mining rights (Fan *et al.* 2010: 146). The rest obtained the mining resources free of charge through administrative allocations. Subsequently the state decides who is able to attain lofty profits. This is a powerful system of patronage.

After the housing reform started in 1994, land transfer became not only a large ticket income for local governments, but also a tool to direct regional economic development. Industrial land usage was often transferred to enterprises for free when local governments wanted to attract them either for fiscal reasons or for economic structural reasons. The strong administrative power over the allocation of key natural resources, especially land, provided strong incentives for enterprises to woo local administrations. Such a situation hampers the efficient allocation of resources and created a hotbed of corruption. What is more, the overly low resource prices undermined the property rights of the whole Chinese population because, legally, these assets are publicly owned and should be allocated according to the common interest of the Chinese populace. In reality, however, administrative allocation mainly favored heavy capital-intensive accumulation. Local authorities captured collective rural land at extremely discounted prices for the development of industrial parks and commercial housing, which were much more lucrative tax-wise.

The result of the biased mechanism of resource allocation was the increasingly capital-intensive growth mode in the second phase of Chinese reform from 1994 to 2008. If the Chinese government is serious about economic rebalancing and environmental protection, the scheme for natural resources and land allocation has to be reformed. We discuss this matter in more detail in Chapters 6 and 7.

Guaranteeing general welfare level by maintaining rapid growth and macroeconomic stability

The political legitimacy of the CCP regime is based on the welfare improvement of its population. In the first phase, this improvement process was equal and simultaneous for the majority of the population. In the second phase of reform, such equalized distribution of income could no longer be maintained. In order to sustain the CCP's political legitimacy and China's political stability in face of increasing income inequality, rapid economic growth and improved macroeconomic stability are the two key factors to watch. Earlier in the chapter we mentioned the role of stronger fiscal capability in stabilizing the economy, especially the fiscal stimulus plan in 1998. In this part, we examine the measures related to financial and monetary stability and the importance of the export-led sector in absorbing China's labor surplus and over capacity.

Increasing financial stability and curbing inflation: from banking laws to bank consolidation (1994–2008)

The legal and institutional basis of financial regulations

The runaway inflation toward the end of the 1980s almost cost the CCP its political regime. The crisis persuaded the Chinese government of the importance of monetary and financial stability to the economic growth and general welfare of people and, accordingly, public opinion as well. In 1993 and 1994 a steep rise in inflation again occurred, although the social consequences were minimized by an immediate sharp rise in salaries. Chinese politicians finally agreed that systemic changes had to be made concerning financial and monetary institutions.

In 1994 and 1995 China enacted two important laws. In 1994 the Statute of the People's Bank of China was strengthened in its twin missions of ensuring price stability and supervising banks. The purpose was to give the central bank the authority to implement the macroeconomic policy determined by the State Council against the overbids of local governments on credit demand, resulting in large oversteps of credit objectives. In 1995 the banking law was implemented, which granted the status of commercial bank to the four state-owned banks (SOBs). They acquired complete autonomy in running their businesses as well as responsibility for the risks involved. Correlatively the government created three development banks to take charge of the financing of large infrastructure projects formerly financed by the SOBs.

While the central bank had been rapidly successful in avoiding spikes of inflation, the progress of reform faced a tough and protracted problem, the solution of which was a priority for the authorities. This was the problem of the huge accumulation of non-performing loans (NPLs) which lasted about ten years before the four leading banks could be consolidated. The NPL problem was largely inherited from the late 1980s and was severely aggravated by the consequences of the Asian crisis.

In 1994 the Chinese leadership had overcome its inner dissensions following the Tian Anmen crisis. After Deng Xiaoping's tour of the coastal provinces in the spring of 1992, reform was revived. The line to be followed was export-led growth, the characteristics and impact of which are studied in the following chapter. Let us observe here that the new growth regime was launched by a huge devaluation, boosting the profitability of the traded goods sector. Subsequently a new wave of credit was launched to finance expanding production capacities in industry and to develop new industrial parks.

In July 1997 the Asian crisis erupted in Thailand and in October it spread to Hong Kong, Taiwan, and Korea, China's closest trading partners. Their currencies depreciated heavily, while the Chinese government took the political decision not to devalue. The profitability of many firms slumped both with the contraction of foreign trade and the loss of competitiveness. Insolvencies hit the private sector. To protect employment, local governments pressed the banks to finance expenditures that were encouraged by the central government. Problem loans swelled and the situation became alarming as early as 1998, persuading the government to embark on a long-standing battle against non-performing loans.

FIRST STAGE: CREATION OF BAD BANKS AND LOAN TRANSFERS

The process started in 1999 for the four state-owned banks. The Ministry of Finance issued special bonds worth 270 billion Yuan (US$33 billion at the time), while reducing the required reserve ratio from 13 to 9 percent deposits. With the released liquidity, the banks bought the bonds to reshuffle their capital base. In the meantime the ministry invested 40 billion Yuan to create the capital base of four bad banks, called Asset Management Corporations (AMC), to take care of the four state-owned banks in buying problem loans: Huarong for ICBC, Cinda for CCB, Great Wall for ABC, and Orient for BOC. The financing of the bad banks was completed by issues of 820 billion Yuan bonds bought by non-bank financial institutions and 570 billion Yuan loans from the central bank. This financing permitted the AMCs to buy NPLs for 1,400 billion Yuan.

The AMCs were placed under the triple authority of the PBoC, the CSRC (China Securities Regulatory Commission), and the Ministry of Finance. Their job was to buy and restructure the non-performing loans in order to sell them over time. Not much is known of the special investors willing and able to buy the NPLs because those investors (vulture funds and private equity funds) operate underground in China. The restructuring was arduous because of the political nature of the NPLs. They were made of myriads of loans in small amounts resting on the personal relationship of the borrowers. In so doing, the AMCs got back about 20 percent of the face value of the loans, thus generating fiscal losses.

SECOND STAGE: RECAPITALIZATION

Recapitalization was a long and tortuous process that lasted ten years. The first step was the 1999 purchase of special bonds mentioned above. The government reinvested the proceeds from the sale of the bonds in the banks' equity base. Starting in 2003, bank losses were identified more precisely following the creation of the China Banking Regulatory Commission (CBRC) in 2003. In February 2004 a very important law assigned to CBRC the responsibility of regulating and supervising all banks and other deposit institutions. The CBRC has played a decisive role in improving bank safety. It is a supervisory institution whose competence has nothing to envy in its Western counterparts. It has compelled the banks to strengthen their balance sheets, it has performed evaluations of their creditworthiness, it has forced them to learn the techniques of risk management, and it has cut their incestuous dependence on local governments. Recapitalization proceeded systematically to bring back non-performing loans to normal levels. The result of CBRC guidance can be seen in Table 4.2.

At 2003 year-end, nearly 500 billion Yuan capital investment was made out of foreign exchange reserves. For that purpose a government holding called Huijin was created to receive the funds from the central bank and invest in equity in three big banks: 174 billion Yuan in both BOC and CCB, 124 billion Yuan in ICBC. In 2004 and 2005 the central bank bought for 780 billion Yuan NPLs of the three banks and sold them back to the AMCs. Finally ABC, whose NPLs had reached the colossal amount of 815 billion Yuan, was recapitalized in 2008 with another investment of foreign exchange reserves by Huijin, amounting to 130 billion Yuan, supported by 150 billion Yuan zero-interest credit from the central bank

Table 4.2 Non-performing loans of the main commercial banks

NPLs	2003	2004	2005	2006	2007	2008
Total (billion Yuan)	2,104.46	1,717.56	1,219.69	1,170.30	1,200.99	486.53
Sub-standard	320.11	307.47	294.96	227.07	184.43	224.89
Doubtful	1,113.07	889.93	460.90	485.03	435.75	212.15
Defaulting	671.28	520.16	463.84	458.19	580.81	49.49
NPL ratio (% credits)	17.90	13.20	8.90	7.50	6.70	2.40
Sub-standard	2.70	2.40	2.20	1.50	1.00	1.10
Doubtful	9.40	6.80	3.40	3.10	2.40	1.10
Defaulting	5.70	4.00	3.40	2.90	3.30	0.20

Source: CBRC

and the rest by a loan from the Ministry of Finance at a 3.3 percent interest rate. This policy was pursued with an impressive persistence. The result, as Table 4.2 shows, is that the largest commercial banks have become solvent and are now able to attract foreign ownership and raise capital in international financial markets.

Strategic partnership with foreign investors and equity issuance

Equity investment in Chinese banks by qualified foreign investors began in 2005 up to the limit of 20 percent of the stock required by the CBRC. The state holding Huijin sold over-the-counter US$2.5 billion CCB shares to the Bank of America. The latter then successfully made an IPO to issue H shares on the Hong Kong stock market in Q4 2005. BOC followed the same procedure in Q1 2006 and then issued A shares on the Shanghai stock market in July 2006. The Bank of Communication (the fifth Chinese bank) proceeded with capital restructuring as early as August 2004 after an over-the-counter deal with HSBC. Bank of Communication issued H shares in the Hong Kong financial center in June 2005 and in Shanghai in May 2007.

Restructuring the mammoth ICBC was quite another matter. Because it was heavily involved in industrial lending, ICBC depended on the reform of state enterprises, e.g. their transformation into shareholding companies. Nonetheless, its risk management had already improved. Its NPL ratio had diminished in mid-2005 to 4.6 percent on its overall loan portfolio and only 1.6 percent on the loans granted since 1999. ICBC succeeded in the double capital fostering: over-the-counter share purchase by Goldman Sachs, Allianz, and American Express for 10 percent of ICBC's stock in 2006 followed by double IPO in Hong Kong (H shares) and Shanghai (A shares) in October.

Table 4.3 sums up the participation of strategic foreign investors in Chinese banks. When restructuring was completed, the largest Chinese state-owned banks entered the club of the top ten world banks by amount of capitalization.

Table 4.3 Participation of foreign strategic investors in Chinese banks in 2007

State-owned banks	Foreign investors	% of shares
Industrial and Commercial Bank of China	Goldman Sachs	4.9
	Hong Kong Securities Clearing Company Nominees Ltd	12.9
	Allianz (Dresdner Bank Luxebourg S.A.)	1.9
	American Express	0.4
China Construction Bank	Temasek Holdings	5.1
	Bank of America	9.0
Bank of China	The Royal Bank of Scotland (RBS)	8.3
	Asian Financial Group	4.6
	UBS	1.8
	Asian Development Bank	0.2
Bank of Communications	HSBC	18.6

Source: Banks' Annual Reports

The incentive for foreign investors to buy into the capital of the large Chinese banks under the conditions set by the CBRC was compelling. Chinese banks needed a lot of capital to create branches in the fast-growing inner provinces. Foreign banks acknowledge that the government wants to keep majority control on these banks and they will never be able to establish a network of branches on their own to tap Chinese saving. With the enthusiastic response of foreign investors and the subsequent public issues, the five leading Chinese banks are now among the best-capitalized banks in the world.

Consolidation of urban commercial banks

Apart from the big banks, the larger reform of the banking system also applies to urban commercial banks. These are more vulnerable than the SOBs to the influence of local governments. The latter can more directly jawbone city banks to thwart the culture of risk. As long as local governments are able to finance their favorite projects against tax advantages and land sale, such mutual interest is an obstacle to financial discipline. So are connected loans to the shareholders of the banks. Nonetheless, CBRC wants to promote the banking system and has real power over all banks to achieve this goal. It can intervene in bank management if regulatory requirements are not respected. It has the authority to close banks or force consolidation to create larger banks.

Consolidation is a means to strengthen the governance of smaller and more fragile banks deprived of market niches. More concentrated city banks can attract foreign banks, which have not yet been able to set up a stronghold in China. In diversifying their participation in the Chinese banking system, foreign banks can diffuse modern methods of governance. Better equipped after mergers and cross-shareholding, city banks can find their comparative advantage in financing SMEs.

Some local governments have helped recapitalize city banks. Local AMCs were created. At the end of 2004 local governments had withdrawn around 35,000 non-performing loans in transfers and replacement in bank balance sheets. Private funds have also played an active role in some provinces. This is the case in Zhejiang province. Wenzhou is a city where private businesses are very active. Private funds hold more bank share than the municipal government. Commercial banks are well performing.

Cooperation and merger between city banks is useful in expanding business beyond the limits of the city in order to capture increasing returns to scale and to diversify risk. The CBRC has gradually permitted such moves. Another approach is to allow city banks of sufficient size and robustness to open branches in other regions. Banks that adopt this strategy (Bank of Beijing, Bank of Nanjing, and Bank of Ningbo) are authorized to issue shares on the stock market to finance their expansion. Those banks have become very strong with capital adequacy ratios reaching 17 to 20 percent.

When they have been able to establish efficient risk management systems, urban regional banks can find competitive advantage in retail banking. They can take advantage of urbanization, which nurtures the development of prosperous middle-class people demanding a range of customized financial services.

Reforming Agricultural Bank of China and restructuring rural credit cooperatives

Reforming ABC is much more than a banking problem. It could not be done by enhancing market mechanisms cum prudential rules. ABC had social commitments in supplying special credits to support the poor. It also made very small credits to individual farmers, which are not profitable. Special credits should be made by a dedicated non-commercial development bank and would shrink with a vigorous social welfare policy towards the countryside. Therefore ABC's financial health depends on the effectiveness of policies aimed at improving rural income. In 2004 the outstanding special credits of ABC was 200 billion Yuan, most of which became non-performing. Therefore ABC could not become a commercial bank unless it was discharged from making these credits. Similarly small credits should be the responsibility of reshuffled credit cooperatives, because they have been loaded with non-performing loans, lightly capitalized, and badly managed.

In 2006 the government showed concern and announced an overhauling program for credit cooperatives prior to recapitalizing ABC in 2008. The grand design was to reallocate the multiple functions in financing agriculture. The first step was to recycle rural saving that flees to safe havens, namely the postal service the funds of which are deposited in the central bank. This saving should be used to finance credit cooperatives via loans from the rural development bank, which would either issue bonds subscribed by rural saving or be granted low-interest credit by the central bank. Whatever the scheme, it should exclude ABC. Apart from recycling rural saving, financing agriculture requires different types of banks: agricultural development banks to finance rural infrastructure, ABC to finance inputs destined to raise agriculture productivity and profitability on larger, recast land plots, and rural cooperatives to make loans to individual farmers.

In more developed regions, trade between countryside and cities is strong. Credit cooperatives are profitable and can be transformed into commercial or cooperative banks. Commercial bank status can be granted for cooperatives of at least 1 billion Yuan assets, 50 million equity, and 8 percent minimal capital adequacy ratio. These new banks are supervised by CBRC. Cooperative bank status is granted with at least 1,000 members, 20 million equity, and core capital adequacy of 4 percent. In areas around medium-sized cities, joint ventures of cooperatives and a city bank make institutions able to finance both the city and the countryside if the value of their assets is over the value of their debts and if they have equity of more than 10 million Yuan. In the poorest region the reform is very difficult. The method consists in merging cooperatives whose assets are over their liabilities and closing those whose financing agriculture is insufficient.

Bank performance, new problems and unfinished reform

Since 2003 CBRC has made a good job of reducing the gap between Chinese practices and international standards. The purpose is to achieve the status of modern competitive banks. This is why the CBRC has emphasized basic rules of bank governance: systems of risk assessment and control, separation of responsibilities between initiative and evaluation of loans, and credit rating inspired by international rating agencies. CBRC has hardened the accountability of top managers for their loan approvals and imposed sanctions on large bank CEOs who do not respect the objective of reducing non-performing loan ratios. Table 4.4 shows that the policy has worked. The performance of the five state-owned banks improved tremendously until the global financial crisis with a caveat for ABC whose restructuring was belated.

In late 2008 the US-engineered financial crisis spread worldwide through the collapse of liquidity in international money markets and the slump in foreign trade. The Chinese government reacted speedily in announcing a huge stimulating plan, worth 4,000 billion Yuan. The plan was two-thirds financed by bank credit. The central bank made credit available in accommodating liquidity. Moreover, local governments competed to propose projects well over the central plan ceiling. Many projects, not approved by the NDRC, were nevertheless financed by different devices circumventing the local government budget constraints. They involved banks in tortuous devices using special vehicles reminiscent of the shadow banking in the financing of the US sub-prime mortgage. This process alarmed Western commentators promptly to conclude that the Chinese banking system was once again on the verge of collapse. It is likely that new NPLs have been generated on a large scale. But they are much more manageable than the losses in the balance sheets at the turn of the century. The spur of an off-balance-sheet financing teaches another, more important lesson, showing that the financial reform is incomplete, as long as it has not touched capital markets and interest rates are rigidly regulated. However, the principle of free capital markets, proclaimed the best institutions to allocate saving efficiently, is not self-evident. In pretending to conform to this principle Western finance grossly undervalued risk and was driven to excesses leading to financial disaster.

Besides, the role played by the financial system in China is much more complex. It can only be understood in adopting the economic policy approach suggested throughout this book. Financing provincial, municipal, and local governments is at the core of the distortions of the financial system. At the county level tax revenues are very much lower than fiscal expenditures for producing essential public goods. There is no common mechanism to redistribute state revenues nationwide. Discretionary transfers from central government to poor regions have been grossly insufficient up to now. It is the main reason why local governments resort to debt finance. The mammoth stimulating plan launched in November 2008 led local governments to resort to off-balance-sheet debt to finance approved infrastructure projects and other unspecified expenditures. Local governments created 8,800 UDICs in the 18-month period after November 2008.

At year-end 2010 the outstanding debt of local governments due to this mechanism was estimated around 10,500 billion Yuan. Thus a sharp downturn in real estate prices would create large new non-performing loans. This is why the central government is careful to discourage the debt financing of high-end housing in the largest cities, while investing heavily in social housing. Furthermore, the government has decided to tackle the problem of new NPLs. It is part of the new

Table 4.4 Performance indicators for the largest commercial banks

Indicators (%)	ICBC			BOC			CCB			BC			ABC
	2006	2007	2008	2006	2007	2008	2006	2007	2008	2006	2007	2008	2008
Net return on assets	0.71	1.01	1.21	0.95	1.09	1.00	0.92	1.15	1.31	0.80	1.07	1.19	0.84
Net return on equities	15.18	16.15	19.39	14.19	14.22	13.72	15.00	19.50	20.68	14.42	17.17	20.86	—
Cost/income	35.68	34.84	29.54	38.60	35.59	33.55	43.97	41.83	36.77	46.04	40.26	39.38	44.71
NPL ratio	3.79	2.74	2.29	4.04	3.12	2.65	3.29	2.60	2.21	2.01	2.06	1.92	4.32
Capital adequacy ratio	14.05	13.09	13.06	13.59	13.34	13.43	12.11	12.58	12.16	10.83	14.44	13.47	9.41
Provisions/NPL	70.56	103.50	130.15	96.00	108.18	121.72	82.24	104.41	131.58	72.41	95.63	116.83	63.53

Source: CBRC and Banks Annual Reports

approach in the reform starting with the 12th five-year plan aiming at liberalizing service sectors. We look at this in Chapter 7.

From bank credit to total social financing

The PBoC is also taking care of the diversification of the sources of credit supply outside standard bank credit. Indeed, the share of bank loans has been shrinking in total social financing. To measure and to adjust to the phenomenon, the PBoC introduced a new credit aggregate in early 2011. The means of finance that have increased the most are debt market instruments (banks acceptance bills and corporate bonds) and non-bank intermediated credit (entrusted and trust loans). The share of loans in foreign currencies is fluctuating but still strictly limited by capital controls (Table 4.5).

In 2009 total social financing more than doubled in absolute terms and almost doubled in percent of GDP. Every category of credit expanded to finance the stimulus plan and other unauthorized credits to local governments. In 2010 the PBoC began its restricting stance in raising the required reserve ratios about ten times to 21.5 percent and 19.5 percent for smaller ones, so as to stem mounting inflation. Even so, the momentum of credit expansion accelerated until Q1 2011 with bankers' acceptances supplementing straight bank loans and SOEs circumventing credit restrictions in floating corporate bonds.

On the one hand, non-financial corporations have been in search of unofficial financing. On the other hand, affluent households had been in search of yield, all the more so since regulated deposit rates had become negative in real terms with higher inflation. For their part trust companies are in the grey area between official and shadow banking. They are intermediaries between essentially private companies in need of finance and cash-rich households in search of returns. The big banks play the same unofficial investment-banking role regarding trust funds as they do regarding UDICs. They sell to trust companies, shifting off their balance sheets the loans they would have made directly to corporations or real estate developers in a less constrained environment. Indeed, local governments often own trust companies. Others are set up in Hong Kong by the SOBs themselves. The reason why they are eager to do it is the same as in the US: regulatory arbitrage. All non-bank financial entities are lightly regulated if at all. They are in the realm of informal finance. Correlatively the trading book of the SOBs does not face the drastic capital adequacy ratios imposed upon the banking book.

Shadow finance counteracted for some time the credit tightening engineered by the central bank. The ratio of total social financing/GDP increased from 41 percent in 2009 to 43 percent in Q1 2011, while bank credit/GDP declined from 28 to 23 percent. In doing so shadow finance distorts the cost of capital in the economy. Because the five major banks that make 80 percent of bank loans do not care for lending to the private sector, the latter depends either on lending by smaller banks or on informal finance. Because small and medium banks get in aggregate a small share of household deposits, they are severely squeezed when required reserve ratios increase systematically as the privileged means of restrictive monetary policy. They react with credit rationing their business clients. It follows that the private sector (especially the SMEs) is disproportionally affected.

Table 4.5 Amount and structure of total social financing

Total social financing	Total social financing		Of which (% of GDP)				
	RMB (billion)	*% of GDP*	*Bank loans in RMB*	*Loans in foreign currencies*	*Entrusted and trust loans*	*Bank acceptance bills*	*Corporate and other non-financial bonds*
2006	3,977.00	18.00	15.00	0.5	1.3	0.7	0.4
2007	5,917.00	22.00	14.00	1.1	1.9	2.5	0.9
2008	6,850.00	22.00	16.00	0.2	2.4	0.3	1.8
2009	14,087.00	41.00	28.00	2.7	3.3	1.4	3.8
2010	14,275.00	36.00	20.00	1.0	3.0	5.8	3.0
2011 Q1	4,192.00	43.00	23.00	1.5	3.4	7.8	4.7
2011 Q2	3,573.00	33.00	18.00	1.7	4.3	5.2	1.9
2011 Q3	2,036.00	18.00	13.00	1.2	3.1	−3.0	1.6
2011 Q4	3,030.00	20.00	12.00	0.6	2.3	0.3	3.5

Source: CEIC

To counteract the credit crunch, private firms rely on informal credit based upon interpersonal networks. The size of financing is limited by the involvement of contributing wealthy people who gather in private trust companies. The cost of borrowing is much higher than in formal banking. Therefore the allocation of capital depends on the personality of the borrowers, much more than on the objective assessment of returns and risks.

This is why financial reform must move forward. Because interest rates are rigidly regulated, the present state of affairs constrains monetary policy to use quantitative tools excessively at the expense of the price mechanism in order to tame the surge of liquidity. Correlatively it distorts the allocation of capital in providing an implicit subsidy to SOEs. The distortion shows as too much investment in heavy industries, giving rise to over accumulation, and too little in light industries for domestic consumption and in services. Furthermore, the shadow banking must be reintroduced in formal finance and subjected to prudential regulation.

The significance of exportation to China's rapid growth

As Chapter 5 is fully dedicated to explaining the evolution of China's relationship with the rest of the world, here we wish only to point out the importance of exportation for China's rapid economic growth, domestic macroeconomic stability, and even political stability.

In the first phase of reform, the prosperity of TVEs was based upon the huge gap between demand and supply in the domestic market at administered prices. In the second phase of reform, however, China's supply–demand relationship went through structural changes. Productive capacity was greatly enhanced, yet at the same time, the restructuring of SOEs put a large proportion of urban residents in financial difficulties; and the state-led allocation of resources (with distortedly low prices) drove investments (especially from SOEs) into capital-intensive industries where the importance of labor was overshadowed. Therefore both labor demand and the price of labor were dampened. As a result, the share of household income in national income distribution began to decline since 1997–8. From 1997 to 2007 this share declined more than 10 percent from 68.6 percent to 57.5 percent. Correspondingly, both governments' share and enterprises' share in national income distribution increased.

The disadvantageous position of Chinese households in primary income distribution directly led to a marked decline in domestic consumption in the second phase of reform despite the rapid GDP growth rate. This structural mismatch would have created overcapacity and underemployment in a closed economy.

What was worse, the business environment for Chinese private enterprises, especially SMEs, also had a lot to be desired during the second phase of reform. Private enterprises were treated discriminatively with the allocation of critical resources (including bank credit), entry barriers to certain industries, and extensive administrative interferences. Under these circumstances, if Chinese private economic actors play only in the domestic market, it would be reasonable to expect certain suppression of their growth.

Fortunately, the second phase of Chinese reform coincided with a strong wave of globalization. The negative impacts of all these structural problems mentioned above were concealed, or at least alleviated, long enough thanks to China's large increase in exportation. In other words, the Chinese economy depended on exportation to rebalance itself. The vast international market absorbed China's overcapacities. It provided Chinese entrepreneurs with a business environment relatively independent from state regulations. All the three most vibrant productive zones in China, Yangtse Delta, Pearl River Delta, and Wenzhou region are all export-led. Surplus labor was largely digested by the coastal labor-intensive enterprises.

The root of so-called "imbalances" in China's trade relationship with the rest of world was indeed China's domestic structural imbalances and opposite US structural domestic imbalances, i.e. a distribution of income that was unable to sustain consumption growth without ever increasing debt. Because of the tremendous significance and complexity of the issue, in Chapter 5 we examine the interplay of China and the international world in depth.

Conclusion

To conclude, the rationale behind China's second phase of reform remained the same as in the first phase, i.e. to sustain a bureaucratic hierarchical political regime with the ultimate authority of the CCP. However, as the major contradictions faced and the conditions available at the beginning of these two phases were disparate, the measures taken exhibit different features and emphasis.

At the end of the first phase of reform China encountered a serious governing crisis. The ultimate authority of central government was challenged from both inside the bureaucratic system and from independent economic forces. Resultantly, the emphasis of the second phase of reform was to strengthen the ruling power of central government by consolidating the bureaucratic system, hardening the grip of state control over the economy, and guaranteeing macroeconomic stability and rapid economic growth. This rationale is the logical reason behind all achievement from 1994 to 2008, as well as all the structural problems that emerged and aggravated at the same time. Toward the end of the second phase of reform those structural problems, including the rising investment rate, the bias to capital-intensive industrial structure, the declining share of domestic consumption due to the declining share of household income, widening income inequalities, surging current account surpluses, and the enlarging regional disparities were magnified. How the CCP should solve those problems and contradictions is the subject of Chapters 6, 7, and 8. Before undertaking that task, though, we must complete the broad picture of China's three decades of reform in explaining the importance of opening up China to the world.

5 China's economic opening to the world

China's economic opening is a process closely intertwined with the gradual changes introduced in the domestic economy. Domestic and foreign transformations have multiple interactions and mesh together in the strategy of development. This strategy, introduced in 1978 and explained in Chapter 3, was meant to release the economy from the fatigue of the Cultural Revolution and the lack of social progress in the 1970s. Technological progress in agriculture, available in the late 1970s, could only be converted to rural income if farmers were able to sell their surplus upon planned output.

Chapter 3 has demonstrated how and why reform started in the rural economy with the establishment of a dual track. The market economy was introduced and enhanced in the countryside alongside central planning by means of contracting pieces of land to farm households. After they had fulfilled the commitment of delivering defined amounts of agricultural production at prescribed low prices, farmers were free to sell their surplus at market prices. Land contracting to households spread all over the country and profitable prices allowed farm households to buy fertilizers and machinery. The success was tremendous. Agricultural production surged. Grain output jumped 33 percent between 1978 and 1984. Because productivity increased even faster, a surplus labor force could itself invest in non-farm activities. Township and village enterprises (TVEs) are locally run factories that increased competition in manufacturing against established state-owned enterprises (SOEs).

In the urban economy, Chinese reformers also followed the dual track to ensure a gradual change aimed at fostering growth instead of disrupting it, as had occurred in Russia and Eastern Europe with the so-called institutional big bang. As explained in Chapter 3, the linchpin was the principle of economic responsibility of enterprises introduced in 1984. From that time on, firms had to fulfill their planned quotas fixed in absolute terms and to face market prices on the margin. In principle this clever reform permitted the smooth phasing out of central planning because the share of market output was constantly growing. Interrelationships developed and migration from the countryside was in full swing, notably fed by the return to cities of young people who had been forced to leave during the Cultural Revolution. Nonetheless, the reforms to break the Smithian high equilibrium trap were not complete as long as market expansion for industrial products was insufficient to trigger increasing returns in manufacturing. Foreign economic opening was to provide the impetus.

Foreign opening was thus conceived to enhance strong growth that the domestic market alone was not able to provide. In boosting industrial expansion in the eastern cities, foreign trade was mobilizing the rural population in the country-side. First, the high demand for labor in industry attracted young workers to the eastern cities. Second, high growth in industry raised the demand for agricultural products over the planned quotas and thus boosted marginal return for peasants. Therefore it contributed to the general acceptance of the reform. However, this win–win game was limited in the late 1980s, because productivity did not accelerate fast enough in industry, leading to inflationary production costs with higher wages.

Foreign opening has both virtues and pitfalls in sustaining development. Because of the earlier forced opening imposed by the Western powers, China had a long history of economic decline, as recalled in Chapter 2. Not only had the Socialist Revolution cut off political ties with the West and reduced economic relations considerably, but the Cultural Revolution had reinforced the country's isolation until the diplomatic thaw after the end of the Vietnam War. This is why the decision to open the country was not taken lightly. Reformers knew they would face strong opposition from conservatives inside the Party. They had to maneuver wisely in applying the dual track strategy to foreign opening.

In this chapter we show how Chinese reform has succeeded in transforming the country from a close economy to a global trade power in less than 30 years. Total foreign trade (exports + imports) reached a low of 5 percent GDP in 1970–1 and never passed 10 percent throughout the socialist era. It amounted to 64 percent in 2005, an amazing figure for a country of this size and much above the levels in other large continental countries. The joint domestic reform and opening to the world transformed the whole economic system. In Chapters 3 and 4 we studied the domestic side of the huge systemic change, showing that reform has gone through two stages under two different growth regimes. The two stages also encompass the process of opening. We first analyze the microeconomic side with trade and foreign investment policies and achievements. Then we examine the macroeconomic side with external monetary policy and the subsequent involvement of China in international debates on currency convertibility, exchange rates, and global imbalances.

Trade opening and foreign investment in China

The trade opening side of the reform has followed a dual track in setting two parallel regimes: an export-processing trade regime boosted by liberal rules and by the massive recourse to foreign direct investment (FDI) on the one hand, and an ordinary trade regime, relatively protected, on the other. As much as the dual track that transformed the domestic production system was designed to merge progressively in a single market economy with the shrinking then the disappearance of the planning system, the dual track in opening is designed to merge the trade regimes in a single open market economy. However, the transition from planned to market economy lasted until the launching of the second stage of reform in the mid-1990s.

Main features in trade policy before the mid-1990s

Chinese reformers were keen to expose the economy to foreign competition without dismantling the whole state-controlled trading system, a disruption that would not have been supported by SOEs and that would have engendered mass unemployment. Trade was expected to foster the growth of the domestic economy, not destroy it as it did later in Russia. The solution was to create special export zones (SEZs) within an export-processing system. This system was based upon contracts between Chinese firms and foreign companies. Imports in the zone were duty-free, as long as they were processed in the zone to produce exports. In this way, the domestic production system was not threatened, since Chinese industrial firms were not exposed to import competition.

TVEs in the Pearl River Delta were the first to benefit from trade opening as early as 1978 in contracting with Hong Kong businesses in the garment industry. The SEZs expanded rapidly in Guangdong and Fujian provinces. The right to grant contracts was decentralized, so that local authorities in the south-east, and then all over coastal regions, competed in attracting foreign businesses in SEZs. Local governments granted land plots and tax advantages to create jobs and export revenues. Export-oriented process trade channeled the most part of FDIs into manufacturing. After 1986 it was known as the Coastal Development Strategy. Most FDI inflows came from East Asian countries, predominantly Hong Kong and Taiwan.

The profitability of the export-processing system was assisted by setting a realistic currency value. In the socialist planning era, because industrialization was based on import substitution and foreign trade was monopolized, the currency was much overvalued. In 1980 the exchange rate was 1.5 Yuan to the US dollar. The government led the currency depreciation, so that in 1986 the exchange rate had been devalued to 3.5. Despite higher inflation in China in the 1980s, it was tantamount to 60 percent real depreciation. In 1986 the dual track was embodied into the exchange rate regime. Aside from the official exchange rate, foreign currency earned by exporters outside planned exchanges, mainly in the SEZs, could be traded on a secondary foreign exchange market at a much lower market exchange rate. Therefore the expansion of processing exports became highly profitable, while imports transmitted more and more the influence of world prices into the domestic economy. The higher cost of imports checked their growth.

In addition the government began to reform the main trading system from 1986 onwards. The foreign trade monopoly was replaced by foreign trade companies (FTCs). Not only national ministries but also local governments were allowed to set up FTCs. They were all state-owned but in 1988 they were independent and free from planned export procurements. They could contract with domestic enterprises as much as foreign firms did. The creation of FTCs radically changed the incentives. FTCs became promoters of labor-intensive goods in both light manufacturing and agricultural processing products. They contracted with TVEs in search of the cheapest producers. With the expansion of export markets at least in the coastal regions, producers in the rural economy were finally able to increase their real income. They mostly benefited from trade reform in a win–win game because the speed-up of overall growth had positive outcomes all over the country. The basic condition of the Smithian model to enhance sustainable growth was fulfilled.

The SEZs were the spur in process trade. They were enclaves in the domestic economy. Superficially one might say that they were like the old enclaves set up by the imperialist powers in the nineteenth century. Indeed, many officials in the Party were uneasy with the trend of the reform. However, there was a dramatic difference. This time the liberalization of trade and investment was entirely under China's sovereignty and was controlled by the state. Instead of being enclaves that had benefited only a handful of compradors, the new course of trade liberalization was one of the main mechanisms that released the enormous potential of the Chinese people. The regulation of foreign investment exacerbates the difference with earlier epochs, and also with other developing countries that were lured by the Washington Consensus to their own misfortune made blatant in the 1997–8 Asian crisis. Fortunately they drew lessons from that event and recovered their financial autonomy in accumulating foreign exchange reserves.

Foreign direct investment: the vector of Asian economic integration

The magnitude of inflows of FDI in China has been tremendous. Admittedly it started modestly at the beginning of the reform and increased slowly in the 1980s. But, in the transition from the first to the second stage, it surged between 1992 and 1998. The turmoil generated by the Asian and Russian crises provoked a retreat in financial globalization throughout the emerging-market world. Inflows of FDIs waned somewhat in 1999 and 2000, and then China's entry into the WTO triggered a second powerful wave up to 2005. However, growth was so fast that FDI inflows leveled off in 1994 as percent of GDP and then ebbed steadily (Table 5.1).

FDI inflows were distributed across the country very unequally. The regions with the largest number of SEZs received the most. On average, in 1993–2003, FDI inflows hovered at 13 percent provincial GDP in Guangdong, 11 percent in Fujian, 9 percent in Shanghai, and 7 percent in Beijing and Jiangsu (Naughton 2007: ch. 17). They were massive enough to transform the economies of those regions since they contributed a high proportion to fixed capital formation. The most important advantage brought by FDIs was technology transfer, linked with management expertise and trade channels. The reason is that FDIs were encouraged by China's rule unlike in the nineteenth and early twentieth centuries. In the first stage of reform foreign investors were intimately connected to TVEs

Table 5.1 FDI inflows

Years	In US$ billion	In % of GDP
1989	3.0	0.9
1990	3.2	1.0
1991	3.8	1.1
1992	11.2	2.4
1993	27.5	4.6
1994	33.1	6.0
1995	37.5	5.2
1996	42.0	4.9
1997	45.6	4.9
1998	45.5	4.6
1999	40.0	3.9
2000	40.2	3.5
2001	47.6	3.7
2002	52.8	3.8
2003	53.2	3.4
2004	60.1	3.2
2005	60.0	2.9

Source: Datastream and China Statistical Yearbook of various years

via joint ventures and subsidiaries using local suppliers. They made the most of low-cost labor and of preferential tax and land purchase advantages offered by the local governments wanting to create jobs. The magnitude of inflows began to surge in 1992 when larger and different SEZs were opened beyond the south-east. The Pudong development zone (East of Shanghai) was set up as a high-tech zone, sanctioned by local authorities and approved by central government, climbing up the international value ladder.

Intricate relationships were easily woven between foreign investors and local firms because investors were for the most part, at least in the early years, of Chinese origin: more than 60 percent of the total were from Hong Kong and Taiwan. In the latest wave after 2001 the Chinese diaspora used tax havens to channel investments, keeping the share including tax havens at 60 percent of cumulative investments in 1985–2005. Meanwhile the share of all developed countries together was 25 percent. The remainder came from Singapore and Korea whose investors prefer north-eastern provinces. It follows that FDIs are essentially a Chinese affair. They have created the basis for the Asian economic integration centered on mainland China as the industrial powerhouse.

Hong Kong and Taiwanese entrepreneurs had long specialized in labor-intensive consumer industries. They seized the opportunity now to delocalize in the SEZs created in the south-eastern provinces. Taiwan manufacturing industry moved to higher-technology products. Hong Kong specialized in business services (finance, marketing, and accounting). Their advantages over other foreign investors were grounded in their geographical proximity and in the commonality of customs and language. It was easy and cheap to create production and trade chains to export garment and footwear and to extend the process trade in the 1990s to consumer electronics. Since China's entry to the WTO, Asian integration has expanded with the diversification of export-process zones along the coast from south to north. Mainland China produces and exports a whole range of industrial products. It imports machinery from Japan and Korea, primary commodities from Australia and New Zealand, high-tech electronics from Taiwan and India, and business services from Hong Kong and Singapore. Economic integration makes Asia the largest trade area in the world, drawing national economic interests much closer despite political divisions.

From dual track to open market economy: the second stage of foreign trade reform

The export-processing regime fostered a momentum in exports after the dual exchange rate system was established in 1986. It had a major impact in the SEZs, keeping growth high in the newly created TVEs. Growth was financed by credit from state banks that were given as much freedom in decision-making as other enterprises. Banks operated at the time with a lack of supervision. Furthermore, the legal transformation in 1983 of the People's Bank of China to a central bank had not given any tool of macroeconomic policy. Therefore the lack of monetary management and supervisory control launched a credit spree. However, banks are not like other businesses. Without a risk culture brought about by tough supervision, competition cannot regulate the credit market. On the contrary, it nurtures a mimetic ballooning of credit supply in tandem with credit demand. The outcome is an inflationary drift with inflation speeding up markedly.

Inflation took root in 1988 and accelerated in 1989. It eroded real income and spread discontent within many strata of wage earners who had previously gained from the reform. Economic anger was a core ingredient in the political uprising that led to the Tian Anmen Square tragedy in June 1989. It merged with political dissent stemming from rising expectations of political loosening of one-party rule. The 1989 political crisis, together with a very sharp slowdown in growth in 1990–1, provoked a comeback of the conservatives. Reformers were convinced that the essence of reform was at stake. Reform had to undergo drastic changes leading to a new growth regime.

In Chapter 4 we discussed the reorientation of domestic reform and the ensuing economic achievements. Here we consider the foreign economic policy side that began in the spring of 1992. Deng Xiaoping undertook a southern tour and in a string of speeches reasserted the relevance of the reform concept as a vector of development. So senior was Deng's authority that it was enough to tilt the balance of power on the side of reformers. In October 1992 the 14th Congress of the Communist Party endorsed the principle of a socialist market economy: markets should be extended to all sectors and the dual track abandoned. While it led to huge institutional changes in the domestic economy, it also moved the country toward a full open market economy and the quest for WTO membership.

The first important decision was the unification of the exchange rate system on January 1, 1994. The exchange rate was depreciated to the lower rate in the secondary markets, entailing a huge devaluation of the official rate to the dollar. It appreciated again a little bit thereafter until mid-1995 and was fixed from that time for ten years at 8.3 Yuan to the dollar (Figure 5.1). In July 2005, the government decided to overhaul the exchange rate regime, resorting to steady appreciation, only temporarily interrupted at the height of the world financial crisis. With free access to foreign exchange upon presentation of documents attesting to trade flows, currency convertibility on current account was achieved de facto.

The stability, then the predictability of the nominal exchange rate regime in changing real economic circumstances had a dramatic impact on the real effective exchange rate meaning overall on China's price competitiveness. In early times after the unification of the exchange rate China's prices were still absorbing the remnants of the huge inflation in late 1980s and early 1990s. China's competitiveness deteriorated markedly, losing about 20 percent in two years. Then the Asian crisis erupted leading to deep exchange rate depreciation in the currencies of the East Asian countries directly involved in the Asian crisis. In deciding not to devalue the Yuan, the Chinese government accepted a surge in the real effective exchange rate for the sake of monetary stability, since the real effective exchange rate appreciated 10 percent more in just one year.

From the end of 1998 to China's entry in the WTO, competitiveness was the indirect outcome of fluctuations in nominal exchange rates of competitor countries against the dollar. Then two strongly opposite periods are observed that are closely related to the exchange rate regime adopted by the Chinese government. From the end of 2001 to the regime change in July 2005, China benefited the most from its increasing market share in world trade. With the rise in process trade, China became the so-called "manufacturer of the world." Since manufacturing is an increasing return sector, the expanding world market for Chinese products

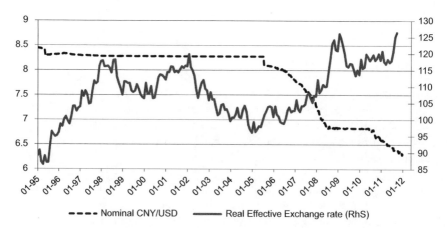

Figure 5.1 Nominal exchange rate to the dollar and real effective exchange rate.

Source: CEIC

triggered fast productivity increase. Because manufacturing firms enjoyed an infinite elasticity in the supply curve for labor, wages did not increase nearly as much as productivity. High profits accrued to finance capital accumulation, while prices could be kept stable. Therefore a round-about process fostered competitiveness that showed up in a larger trade surplus (Figure 5.2). Such was the origin on China's side of the so-called global imbalances that put pressure on the Chinese government to appreciate its currency. In July 2005 the government finally yielded to international pressure and adopted an informal creeping peg on the dollar.

As Figure 5.1 shows, the impact on price competitiveness was quite spectacular. From mid-2005 to the end of 2011, the effective real exchange rate appreciated 25 percent. If the trade balance kept widening to the peak of the financial crisis in the summer of 2008, it was because of the unsustainable surge in the US credit-induced demand spree. Putting the blame on China, as most Western economists did, was particularly ill-founded. Indeed, as soon as the credit boom receded leading to slowdown in world trade, China's trade surplus shrank, while the real effective exchange rate resumed its trend appreciation.

Exchange rate unification was part of a broader set of reforms that linked more closely domestic and foreign economic policies. With the transformation of SOEs into businesses in competitive markets, the state had lost its budgetary revenues that came straight from enterprises under central planning. A fiscal reform was enacted in 1994 to broaden the tax base with the establishment of value-added tax (VAT) and other business taxes. Because exporters are permitted to rebate VAT on exports, applying a VAT system uniformly to all actors in manufacturing suited China very well.

On the financial side things did not advance as much because domestic financial reform was a very lengthy task. Because the domestic financial system had remained underdeveloped and because the Asian crisis had demonstrated how much international capital flows were perilous for emerging-market countries, China kept capital controls for many types of flows other than FDIs.

The decisive move to open market economy was WTO membership. This was achieved after a lengthy and arduous negotiation that started first to join the GATT (General Agreements on Tariffs and Trade) and lasted 15 years from 1986 to 2001. Meanwhile, the GATT was transformed into the WTO by the Uruguay Round in 1996. WTO membership gave the opportunity of greater access to the markets of developed countries for light manufacturing and for products of agriculture. As a condition, China had to dismantle its dual track system because WTO membership required China to grant trade rights across the board. China shifted to a system of tariffs and quotas lowered progressively.

China's performance and shortcomings with export-led growth

Since the adoption of the strategy of a completely open market in 1993 and the currency and fiscal reforms in 1994, China has become the fulcrum of world industrial globalization. WTO membership has enhanced the evolution. From a

Table 5.2 Structure of Chinese foreign trade in 2004

Items	Exports (% of total)	Imports (% of total)
Electronics	24	19
Mechanical and electrical machinery	17	22
Plastics and organic chemicals	2	9
Optics	3	7
Garments and footwear	14	—
Furniture and toys	4	—
Fuel	—	9
Iron and steel	2	4
Others	32	30

Source: Global Trade Atlas database provided by Global Trade Information Services

specialization in garments, footwear, and toys, Chinese exports have made a startling breakthrough in electronics, machinery, and electric equipment (Table 5.2). It is the nature of process trade that the most exported items are also the most imported. More than two-thirds of microwave ovens, DVDs, TV sets, and computers are produced in China. They are made from imported components and software. Therefore the strategy of climbing up the technology ladder has been deceptive, contrary to India. Exports of technology products are at 80 percent in the hands of foreign subsidiaries. Within the technology sectors China exports standardized consumer products, remaining in the low and middle grades (Table 5.3). In the 1995–2007 period China did not much improve the value content of its exports compared with that of its imports, as reflected in the trend of its real effective exchange rate shown on Figure 5.1. Huge fluctuations occurred with the crisis of the early 1990s and the change of the growth regime thereafter. Nevertheless, all in all, the effective exchange rate did not change much in the end of the ten years from 1995 to 2005. This is quite an anomaly for a country that was able to grow so much.

Several forces should induce a trend appreciation in the real exchange rate. This trend means that an emerging country, converging with the real income of advanced countries, thanks to its participation in world trade, should improve

Table 5.3 Distribution of Chinese and Indian exports to EU by grades (%)

Technology grades	China		India	
	1995	2007	1995	2007
High	4	4	8	10
Average	27	30	27	37
Low	69	66	65	53
All	100	100	100	100

Source: Bensidoun *et al.* (2009)

its purchasing power on the value of its imports. In other words, the value of its labor should improve relatively to the value of foreign labor embodied in world prices.

First, sustained industrial growth raises total factor productivity in assimilating technological progress along a catching-up process. The productive base widens in scope and deepens in quality, which raises the value of domestic labor sold in world markets. The terms of trade improve and convey the rise in the real exchange rate. However, in China this process was shackled until recently. The process trade did not enhance domestic labor to the extent required to raise macroeconomically the real value of labor. Therefore China's growth regime inefficiently used its excess labor with highly capital-intensive techniques.

The growth regime in China was not typical of the catching-up process in other large countries. Its openness is far higher and the importance of the process trade is far larger. The participation in WTO dramatically reinforced these trends. It induced a reversal in the terms of trade and an evolution of relative prices inside the country, which was conducive to a decline in the equilibrium real exchange rate. Indeed, Figure 5.1 shows that the effective real exchange rate stopped its appreciation after the Asian crisis and more so after the entry into WTO until the decoupling from the dollar peg in July 2005.

The standard theoretical argument for an improved real effective exchange rate is the Balassa Samuelson effect. Insofar as technological progress impacts the value of domestic labor embodied in products sold in world markets, the domestic purchasing power of labor employed in the advanced sectors should increase. The reason is the low price of domestic products (notably services) in the dual structure typical of developing countries. The demand for these products should increase with the purchasing power generated in the export-led economy. Because productivity is laggard in that part of the economy, relative prices will rise and carry higher real wages if the labor market is not fragmented (Box 5.1). The overall catching-up in real wages over wages in developed countries induces a trend appreciation in the real exchange rate. The process has been hampered in China because the huge surplus of rural labor has fragmented the labor market. Millions of migrants into the cities suffered lawless conditions of exploitation. Differences in productivity showed up in wage disparities instead of a general rise in wages that could have percolated through in an increase in domestic prices. In that case, the formula for the real exchange rate in Box 5.1 shows that the Balassa effect is mitigated, eventually canceled altogether by disparities in real wages. This is why the socio-demographic change stemming from the end of surplus labor in the rural economy is a sea change for the future stage of development in the Chinese economy. We demonstrate in the next chapter that it will induce a profound change in the price system, which will provide incentives to move the production structure to higher technology, which in turn will increase real wages.

Box 5.1 Real exchange rate, relative prices, and double gap in productivity

1 Relative prices

Let us define p_T, p_N, and p as the consumer price index in the traded goods sector T, in the non-traded goods sector N, and in the overall economy (China) and the same indices in the benchmark country (the US quoted*). All indices are measured in logs. The consumer price index in both countries is

$$p = bp_T + (1 - b)p_N$$
$$p^* = b^* p_T^* + (1 - b)p_N^*$$

where b and $1 - b$ are weights of traded and non-traded goods respectively in the consumer basket. Posit e the nominal exchange rate of the Yuan against the dollar, e.g. the Yuan price of the dollar. The real exchange rate, defined on the consumer price index, is $q = p - e - p^*$.

The real exchange rate defined on T goods is similarly $q_T = p_T - e - p_T^*$.

The aggregate real exchange rate is compounded of two parts: the T sector real exchange rate and the so-called Balassa effect. The formula is augmented with a residual, stemming from the difference in the structure of consumption in the two countries:

$$q = q_T - (1 - b)[(p_T - p_N) - (p_T^* - p_N^*)] + (b - b^*)(p_T^* - p_N^*)$$

2 Productivity differentials

Posit w_T, w_N, π_T, π_N, wages, and labor productivity in T and N sectors in China.

Assuming that in the long run the margin rate over labor costs is constant,

$$p_T = w_T - \pi_T$$
$$p_N = w_N - \pi_N$$
$$p_T - p_N = (w_T - w_N) - (\pi_T - \pi_N)$$

In the US the labor market is supposedly unified (same average wage in sectors T and N).

The real exchange rate of the Yuan against the dollar is influenced by macroeconomic factors that impinge upon q_T and by relative wages and productivity:

$$q = q_T + (1 - b)[(\pi_T - \pi_N) - (w_T - w_N) - (\pi_T^* - \pi_N^*)] + (b - b^*)$$
$$(p_T^* - p_N^*)$$

The Balassa effect says that a higher productivity differential in China than in the US between sectors T and N must appreciate the real exchange rate of the Yuan. However, if the labor market is fragmented in China, wage differentials mitigate the effect and eventually cancel it if they meet the difference in productivity.

The second anomaly in the export-led growth regime in China is the ballooning surplus in the trade balance that has generated a lot of disagreement between the Chinese government, on the one hand, and the US Congress and government on the other. However, the widening of the surplus has been a late and transitory phenomenon not imputable to WTO entry (Figure 5.2). For three years after WTO entry exports and imports accelerated markedly in tandem, getting 8 percent more in percent of GDP. The trade balance surplus stayed at a low 2 percent of GDP. Then exports continued to accelerate, reaching a high 37 percent of GDP in 2007, while imports slowed down relatively, remaining at 29 percent of GDP. Thus the trade surplus widened immensely to reach an extraordinary 8 percent GDP. While overall growth had stood above 10 percent annually in 2005–7, net exports contributed to more than 2 percent.

Two factors were responsible for the drift in the trade surplus. The first factor was the runaway consumer demand in the US and other developed countries whose unsustainable domestic demand was driven by credit-financed real estate bubbles that were conducive to the financial crisis. The strong domestic demand in Western countries induced a big push in exports by the subsidiaries of foreign

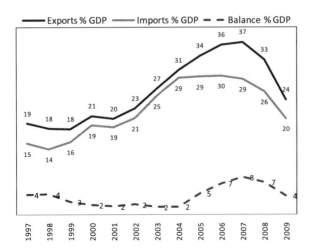

Figure 5.2 Foreign trade from 1997 to 2009.

Source: Aglietta and Lemoine (2011)

firms in China. Between 2004 and 2007 the balance between the value of their exports and of their imports in foreign trade jumped from US$ 50 billion to US$ 144 billion. The second factor was the success of import substitution by Chinese firms in ordinary trade. The government indulged in a deliberate policy of import substitution. Low wages, cheap credit, huge expansion in housing in the main coastal cities, and favorable tax rebates permitted SOEs to be highly profitable in capital-intensive industries. These firms invested massively and built production capacities large enough to substitute for imports in cement, iron and steel, and machinery equipment. From negative, the sectorial balance of trade turned positive. All in all, the ordinary trade of Chinese firms shifted from equilibrium in 2004 to US$100 billion surplus in 2007. During those years the Yuan appreciated against the dollar (20 percent from July 2005 to July 2008) and in real effective terms (Figures 5.3 and 5.4).

Between July 2008 and June 2010, the Chinese government re-pegged the Yuan to the dollar. But the sharp depreciation of a number of Asian currencies in the crisis produced a real effective appreciation of the Yuan by 11 percent. It decoupled again from the dollar in June 2010 and the Yuan began to appreciate substantially since September of that year. Finally, the period from 2004 to 2008 was exceptional for China because it was exceptional for the world. At the end of 2008 world demand plummeted, provoking a collapse in world exports. Chinese exports slumped from 37 percent of GDP in 2007 to 24 percent in 2009. At the same time GDP itself stalled from 13.8 percent (year-over-year) in the second quarter of 2007 to 6.1 percent in the first quarter of 2009.

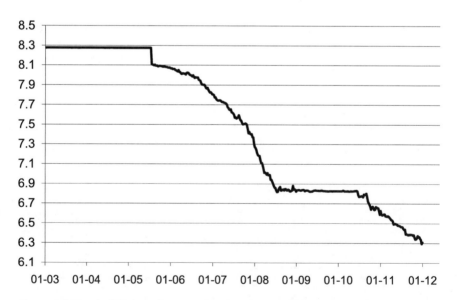

Figure 5.3 Nominal Yuan exchange rate against the US dollar.

Source: CEIC

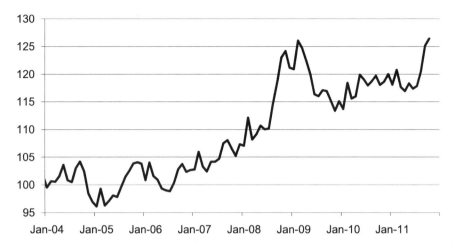

Figure 5.4 Effective real exchange rate.

Note: Basis 100 at January 2004

Source: CEIC

The much slower growth prospects in advanced economies will preclude China from counting on foreign markets as much as it did before the financial crisis. Beyond this major shock, the type of specialization pursued by China after WTO entry is too low in quality of exports and too dependent on foreign firms to be pursued the same way. As much as the distortions in the domestic economy disclosed in Chapter 4, the disequilibria in export-led growth call for a new stage of development.

China's foreign monetary policy and global imbalances

The persistence of US deficits is controversial among economists. However, viewed in the rest of the world, it has fed protectionist threats in Congress against China, political prejudices feeding the controversies. Nonetheless, there are multiple explanations for the phenomenon, some of them partially true, which is why a diversity of views can be upheld in good faith. Before focusing on China's exchange rate policy and foreign exchange reserve accumulation we examine these controversial views. We show that, starting in 2010, China has embarked on a decisive drive to decouple its currency from the dollar and to make it freely usable to non-residents from its offshore Hong Kong financial center. In the last chapter we argue that such a move is part of the larger goal of transforming the growth regime.

The debate about global imbalances

External accounts can be misleading. Because the trade balance makes the most of the current account balance for countries that are catching up, thanks to industrial development, a popular view makes the exchange rate the villain of the piece. The only thing to do to correct a trade surplus would be to appreciate the exchange rate. However, a current account imbalance reflects disequilibrium between domestic saving and domestic investment. The pattern of saving and investment in a country or region is structural and marginally sensitive to relative prices. Furthermore, investment depends on financing, not on saving. In the aggregate, saving is just the mirror of investment. Neither can be said to determine the other.

It is true that a discrete appreciation in the real exchange rate of a surplus country like China will increase the price of domestic goods relative to foreign goods. But it will lower the rate of returns in the traded goods sector and therefore impair domestic investment in this crucial sector for modernizing the process of production. On the consumer side, a country with protracted excess saving like China is supposed to be, thus with a huge stock of foreign currency (e.g. dollar) claims, will undergo a negative wealth effect with the fall of the dollar. If the jump in the exchange rate is in the order recommended to China by a few American scholars (20 percent instantaneously in real terms), it will weigh negatively on domestic demand, either private or public. Because imports will plummet with domestic expenditures, the income and wealth effect could offset the relative price effect, leaving the change in the trade balance ambiguous (Mac-Kinnon and Schnabl 2008). What is certain is that world growth would be abated, so that most countries will suffer.

Table 5.4 shows that negative net saving in the US was a well-entrenched pattern throughout periods of weak and strong dollar alike. So was the positive net saving of industrialized Asia, Japan included. The change from a deficit to a surplus balance in developing Asia except China was the aftermath of the Asian crisis that determined the governments to radically shift their growth policy for the purpose of getting rid of their foreign indebtedness and accumulating foreign exchange reserves.

In the course of accumulation of foreign assets, the contribution of China was modest up to and including 2004. With a US$43 billion rise from 1997 to 2004, China's current account surplus gained less than Japan, other emerging markets and other industrial countries. Then China's surplus increased briskly for reasons explained above. China generated excess saving while the US generated wider deficits from 2005 to 2008, exactly at the time when the dollar depreciated and the Yuan appreciated in real terms. Furthermore, Table 5.4 shows that the US indulged in deficits not only against China, but also against almost any region of the world except the CEECs. After the crisis, the US deficit shrank somewhat and China's surpluses more than halved in percent of GDP. In 2010 the country with the largest surplus by far was Germany.

There was no lack of interpretations for these global imbalances. Four views have been advanced: the new economy, the new Bretton Woods, the global saving glut, and the shortage of US saving (Eichengreen 2006). The new economy view can be

Table 5.4 Sources and uses of world saving: net financial saving (in % of national or regional GDP)

Countries or regions	1988–95 average	1996–2003	2005	2007	2008	2009	2010
Advanced economies	−0.7	−0.3	−1.0	−0.8	−1.3	−0.7	−0.3
US	−2.5	−2.7	−5.2	−5.2	−5.6	−4.0	−3.4
Euro Zone	n.d.	+0.5	+0.8	+0.8	+0.1	+0.1	+0.7
(Germany)	(−0.7)	(−0.1)	(+6.4)	(+10.4)	(+9.9)	(+6.8)	(+7.9)
Japan	+2.3	+2.5	+3.6	+4.8	+3.2	+2.7	+3.1
Asian industrial countries	+3.4	+4.1	+5.5	+6.4	+5.0	+8.6	+7.1
Developing and emerging economies	−2.0	0.0	+4.1	+4.0	+3.5	+2.0	+1.6
Sub-Saharan Africa	−0.9	−2.3	−0.3	+1.2	0.0	−1.4	−0.9
Latin America	−1.2	−2.5	+1.4	+0.1	−1.2	−0.6	−1.3
Emerging Asia	−2.4	+1.4	+4.1	+6.9	+5.8	+4.1	+3.0
(China)	(n.d)	(+2.6)	(+7.1)	(+10.6)	(+9.6)	(+6.0)	(+4.7)
CEECs	−1.4	−3.2	−5.1	−8.1	−7.8	−2.4	−3.7
Middle East	−4.1	+3.8	+17.4	+15.3	+15.4	+3.5	+5.0
Russia and CIS	−10.3	+4.7	+8.8	+4.0	+4.8	+2.8	+3.9

Source : IMF, World Economic Outlook, October 2010 and earlier issues, Appendices. Table A16

rejected straightway. It might have been relevant in the late 1990s, when IT technologies attracted capital into the US. It contends that US deficits reflect the attractiveness of the US territory for innovation. However, the structure of capital flows in the early 2000s has nothing to do with any "New Age" myth. In the years prior to the financial crisis, inflows were mainly invested in Treasury bonds and in mortgage-backed securities issued to finance the federal government and household indebtedness.

In the new Bretton Woods view surpluses in China and deficits in the US are the two sides of the same coin (Dooley *et al.* 2003). China pursues an export-led growth regime driven by an undervalued currency against the dollar. A surplus in China and a deficit in the US ensue. Both countries are pleased with this polarity that fits with their respective collective preferences. The dollar–Yuan exchange rate best adjusts the mutual interest of both countries. Because the US has a better-performing financial system, it imports Chinese saving invested in liquid securities and transforms part of it in direct investment exported to China. Chinese claims on the US are interpreted as collateral for the investment of US firms that transfer technology. However, the allusion to Bretton Woods is only partially correct. It is true that in the 1960s European countries accumulated dollar reserves because they respected fixed parities against an overvalued dollar. But the US current account balance was not in deficit. US debts offset massive direct investments of American firms in Europe no more. Furthermore, this view unilaterally focuses on China whose contribution to the US deficit was no more than 10 percent in 2005 and 8 percent of its worsening between 1997 and 2005. An argument specific to China cannot account for a widespread counterpart to the US deficit.

The world saving glut view is the interpretation broadcast all over the world after Ben Bernanke's infamous speech in March 2005. It was a clever move to ward off US responsibility in imbalances. Bernanke pointed out an array of independent factors that encouraged saving in the rest of the world. In East Asia except Japan the demographic structure has been moving toward high savers strata (40–65). In China the phenomenon has been reinforced by the weakness of retirement plans inducing a very high precautionary saving. Oil and gas price surges have fostered the saving of primary energy-exporting countries (the Middle East and Russia). Emerging-market countries have dramatically changed their policies in favor of export-led growth.

It follows from the flowing of excess saving that foreign investors have been busily looking for attract financial investments that the presumably (as it was thought at the time) efficient US financial system has been happy to provide. The inflow of foreign saving has driven down long-run interest rates, boosted real estate prices, and encouraged American households to spend. US deficits just mean that US households have acted as consumers as a last resort for the sake of world growth. However, it is not self-evident that there is a world saving glut. IMF statistics show that world saving barely increased for the 15 years prior to the financial crisis.

Finally, the US saving deficiency view stems from the indisputable observation that savings slumped much more in the US than in other developed countries, except the few (UK, Ireland, Iceland, and Spain) that underwent an enduring real estate bubble. After the stock market slump in 2001, the Federal Reserve was determined to avoid a Japanese-style recession due to painful debt deflation in the corporate sector. Monetary policy became proactive to boost credit-induced household expenditures. That was standard recession-fighting policy. But, after the resumption of growth in 2004, the American debt machine began to go astray in fostering a huge real estate bubble. As a consequence, the net rate of saving of US households slumped to −1.5 percent in the second quarter of 2006. Even more striking, the ratio of net cash flow collapsed to −7.3 percent. The lack of household savings drew the national saving rate downward despite the reduction of the fiscal deficit that had benefited from unexpected tax accruals.

To sum up, the primary cause of global imbalances stems from within the US economy. The key currency status of the dollar has been a permissive condition to the persistence of the financial polarization. It is nevertheless a threat to the global economy.

Meanwhile, it is not self-evident to determine what an imbalance is when one observes deficits and surpluses. In a financially integrated world economy there is no reason for all countries to be in current account balance even in the medium term. One can even say that financial integration should allocate saving and investment worldwide to countries with best risk-adjusted returns on capital. If the capital markets are able to assess risks and returns properly, they invest in countries with future flows of income produced by the investments they finance, so that the present deficits are sustainable in the very long run. Therefore the main cause of global imbalances must be looked for in the inefficiencies of the financial system. With the global financial system in the grip of Wall Street investment banks, which invented deliberately deleterious financial products in the single purpose of extracting extravagant rents on the real economy, it would have been surprising to expect finance to regulate imbalances so as to limit their size.

Now, even if one believes that excess saving has occurred in China, the reason might not be under-consumption, contrary to popular opinion in the West. Admittedly insufficient public health care services, a weak welfare safety net, and inadequate pensions for most citizens are causes of high precautionary saving. But that type of structural deficiency does not date from the years 2005–7 when China's surplus swelled. Besides, it cannot be cured by an appreciation of the exchange rate! Moreover, excess saving is much higher in the enterprise than in the household sector. As Dani Rodrik (2009) forcefully pointed out, most countries with excess saving suffer from a lack of profitable investment and from a vulnerable or inefficient financial system that hampers a dynamic credit supply to small and medium enterprises (SMEs). Profitable investment depends on good public infrastructures and on the dynamism of the modern traded goods sector that encapsulates technological progress. It means the best way to engineer a sustainable expansion in domestic demand is to start with a large program of public expenditures, both in infrastructures and health care. This is exactly what the Chinese government did in 2009 with its stimulating plan that diminished current account surplus markedly. Meanwhile, an undervalued exchange rate is a spur to channel resources in the modern sector and to upgrade the technology ladder. Of course, the output should benefit domestic consumers. It means that the real exchange rate should appreciate progressively with productivity gains and real wage increases. As Figures 5.1 and 5.4 show, this is exactly what has happened in China for the last seven years. And it will undoubtedly continue going forward. However, with the structural change in the labor market, the trend appreciation in the real exchange rate can rise more safely with higher inflation in the non-traded goods sector, boosted by higher real wages, than with wild fluctuations of the nominal exchange rate due to speculation. This line of reasoning leads to exchange rate policy and the problem of currency convertibility.

The management of the Yuan and the accumulation of foreign exchange reserves

We could call the present monetary system a semi-dollar standard. There is no strict dollar peg, with the exception of Hong Kong, Ecuador, and Panama, therefore it is not a pure dollar standard. But nowhere in Asia except Japan do governments let the exchange rate be determined solely and permanently by the market. There is no flexible exchange rate either. Even in Japan exchange rate policy alternates between stages of heavy interventions and stages of hands-off policy, on the provision that the fluctuations of the yen against the dollar are kept within tolerated limits. This is why we may safely say that the semi-dollar standard is a dollar-managed exchange rate system. Because the system is the vehicle of financing the rising flow of new dollar assets, since 2001 it has entailed a fast-increasing accumulation of foreign exchange reserves denominated in dollars (Table 5.5).

The phenomenon of reserve accumulation in dollars is not the outcome of imbalances in the world saving investment equilibrium. Rather, it is the outcome of malfunctioning in financial systems. It gives rise to a second imbalance in the world economy, which should not be confused with the imbalance due to saving and investment patterns. This is the explosion of liquidity depicted in Table 5.5. In principle, with well-integrated financial markets, imbalances stemming from saving investment patterns should be offset by capital inflows and outflows from private agents. Those capital flows denominated in the different currencies should be the outcome of portfolio optimization of institutional investors and other financial intermediaries. They should clear the markets for international assets denominated in the different currencies.

In the semi-dollar standard world, things do not go this way at all. Currencies of emerging-market countries are not traded freely in international money markets. As long as excess saving is growing fast, it is piling up in the domestic currencies, while the receipts of export contracts are dollar cash flows. It follows that financial intermediaries of these countries have liabilities exclusively in their domestic currency. If they were to offset the excess saving with capital outflows, they should invest a substantial portion of their liabilities in dollar assets. In this hypothetical scenario exchange rates would be flexible, since the whole purpose would be to avoid creating excess domestic liquidity as the consequence of the real imbalance. In doing so, financial intermediaries of emerging countries would face a gaping currency mismatch. The risk would be unbearable for institutions with social liabilities, like insurance companies and pension funds, and they would stop. With the exception of sovereign wealth funds that have no contractual liabilities, this is what they did from the beginning, especially in China. The central bank has had to take over in buying excess dollars over import payments and investing them in dollar bonds.

The conclusion of this analysis is the following. Financial globalization is far from deep integration. The latter is impossible with sovereign preferences and economic structures that are highly discordant, which is reflected in the twisted world saving–investment equilibrium. In the 2000s, the conflicting semi-dollar standard system had only one way to go: to let central banks absorb the currency mismatch. The People's Bank of China (PBoC) has done this to an impressive extent (Figure 5.5).

Table 5.5 Annual average variation of dollar official reserves (%)

	1987–92	1992–97	1997–2001	2001–05
All countries	6.9	11.4	7.7	14.5
East Asia and Japan	13.8	15.1	13.2	19.9

Source: IMF, Statistics on Official Reserves (selected years)

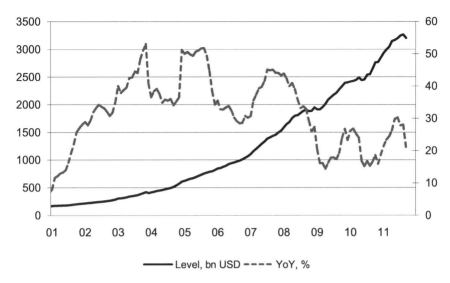

Figure 5.5 China: foreign reserves.

Source: Datastream. Computation Groupama AM

However, capital controls have been porous lately. Hot money can be approximated by the total of "other" capital flows and errors and omissions. The worsening of the crisis in H2 2008 with the subsequent slump in China's growth entailed a substantial outflow of hot money. After the launching of the stimulating plan and the fast recovery it brought about, however, capital inflows resumed and had to be absorbed with further reserve pile up. As a consequence, the accumulation of foreign exchange reserves has been partly disconnected from the trade balance and even the current account balance (Table 5.6).

The appreciation of the Yuan (about 25 percent between July 2005 and December 2011) did not stem the accumulation of foreign exchange reserves until lately for reasons explained here above. The predetermined steady appreciation was an incentive for foreigners to buy Chinese assets as much as capital controls allowed them. Furthermore, the capital inflow that the central bank had to absorb was magnified by the rapid decline in the Fed Funds rate, which fell from 5.25 percent in August 2007 to 2 percent in mid-2008 and about 0 percent after September of that year. The Fed indulged in quantitative easing, flooding the world with dollar liquidity. The accumulation of reserves continued unabated at a speed of yearly increase of 40 percent on average until the recovery led by the stimulating plan after May 2009. The pace of reserve accumulation has slowed down significantly and has never recovered its earlier pace because the current account surplus has substantially diminished. An analysis of China's balance of payments provides some insight into what happened (Table 5.6).

Table 5.6 China's balance of payments 2008–10 (in US$ billion)

Items	H1 2008	H2 2008	H1 2009	H2 2009	H1 2010	H2 2010
Current account balance	*191.7*	*244.4*	*134.5*	*162.6*	*124.2*	*179.7*
Of which:						
Trade balance	129.2	219.7	102.3	117.8	76.4	158
Capital income	38.3	3.1	16.9	26.4	28.3	−1.4
Current account transfers	24.2	21.6	15.2	18.5	19.4	23.1
Capital account balance	*70.3*	*−54.4*	*59.6*	*81.2*	*87.5*	*60.7*
Of which:						
Net FDI	40.8	53.6	15.6	18.7	37	63.5
Net portfolio	19.8	22.8	20.2	18.5	−7.3	31.3
Others	9.7	−130.8	23.9	44	57.8	35.9
Total balance	*262*	*190*	*194.1*	*243.9*	*211.7*	*310.4*
Errors and omission	−18.8	−8.8	8.2	31.4	33.7	−16.8
Foreign exchange reserves	*−280.8*	*−198.8*	*−185.9*	*−212.5*	*−178*	*−293.6*

Source: CEIC

Volatile capital flows ("others" and unrecorded flows) have an impact on the balance of payments that was very sensitive to the decoupling of the Chinese economy in 2009, reversing the outflow during the slump in Q4 2008. Those flows entered to take advantage of the buoyancy of asset markets under the stimulus plan, financing the stock market and the luxury real estate market. Comparing H2 2008 and H2 2009, a decline of about US$120 billion in the trade account was more than offset by a US$130 billion rise in inflow of hot money in the capital accounts, stemming primarily from "other" capital flows, e.g. essentially short-run loans and deposits from Hong Kong financial institutions.

Because China is becoming not only an economic but also a financial power, a regime change in the management of the exchange rate was warranted. In the short run the Chinese government has taken the wise decision to exit from the nominal dollar anchor. On June 19, 2010 the PBoC announced the removal of the dollar peg and the use of a basket of currencies as a reference in a more flexible exchange rate system. This decision was a milestone because, rather than a return to the post-July 2005 sliding peg to the dollar, it heralds a gradual change in the framework of monetary policy to domestic targets and a first step towards the convertibility of the Yuan. The decision to decouple from the dollar and re-establish an effective exchange rate benchmark has been supplemented by the far-reaching decision taken by China's monetary authorities to move gradually to Yuan convertibility for non-residents. The development of a new market for offshore Yuan assets and its prospect is described in the last section of this chapter.

The time is ripe because the financial crisis has brought dramatic changes in the world economy. Growth in advanced countries will be markedly slower than in the bubble decade, US households will increase their saving rate, and China will enter a stage of reform focused on domestic development. It follows that China's trade balance will shrink back to the 2 to 3 percent surplus seen before 2004. The forces pushing the exchange rate steadily upward will abate, but the impact of volatile capital flows on exchange rate instability will be stronger, requiring more flexible exchange rate management. This is the regime laid out by Chinese monetary authorities since mid-year 2010.

The new system has an intra-day trading band of + or –0.5 percent around the chosen daily rate, enlarged to + or – 1 percent in June 2012. Moreover, the rate and band of one day is not binding for the day after. The central bank has complete discretion in determining any rate it sees fit every day. Therefore it can imprint any flexibility against the US dollar to create suitable two-way risks for speculators. The formidable amount of reserves in the hands of the State Administration of Foreign Exchange (SAFE) makes it capable of breaking up any speculation. The SAFE can let the exchange rate drift either way, then mount a powerful intervention to trigger a mean-reverting move that would be devastating for the speculators. The policy can be reinforced by coordinated interventions with other ASEAN+3 central banks to keep up the coherence between cross-exchange rates. (ASEAN countries include Brunei, Cambodia, Indonesia, Laos, Malaysia, Myanmar, Philippines, Singapore, Thailand, and Vietnam. The "+3" refers to China, Japan, and South Korea.)

In the medium term the central bank can use the currency basket reference rate to drive a gradual appreciation of the real effective exchange rate to achieve three objectives: to enhance the purchasing power of households, to reduce the cost of imported primary commodities, and to provide incentives to firms to improve the value content of their exports. China needs both to preserve the value of its foreign assets and the stability of exchange rates in the East Asian region, where economic integration is deepening. Both objectives depend on the internationalization of the Yuan, e.g. full Yuan convertibility.

Yuan convertibility implies that the ongoing emergence of bond markets in China gains momentum, that large domestic institutional investors are able to channel household saving into portfolio diversification, including an array of foreign assets to substitute to central bank reserve accumulation, and that domestic bond markets are able to welcome foreign investors under manageable conditions of risk. It also implies a willingness among governments in East Asia to launch a political initiative, more ambitious than Chiang Maï, aiming at establishing a zone of monetary cooperation in East Asia as a foundation for safe internationalization of the domestic currencies in the region. Internationalization of currencies together with minimal regional cooperation to keep consistency in cross-exchange rates will substantially reduce the use of the dollar in the most dynamic region of the world. The reform in domestic capital markets and the opening of the capital account will be structural changes in finance, adjusted to the new stage of the whole economic reform.

China's drive to currency convertibility for non-residents

Chapter 4 has shown why full capital account opening is not yet in place. It must be preceded by the liberalization of financial services and therefore of the whole structure of interest rates. However, such a dramatic change cannot be accomplished overnight, all the more so since local governments (especially counties and municipalities) are overwhelmed with debts. Interest rates cannot become market-determined before those debts are cleared out and the solvency of local governments has been firmly consolidated. Meanwhile, monetary authorities have recourse to regulating bank-lending rates and subjecting bonds to bank rates, so that the cost of public finance is minimized. Of course, this inefficient financial regulation is costly for the nation. If the cost of capital is too low it distorts investment patterns and fosters overcapacities in heavy industries. Regulated interest rates channel all financing into a handful of state-owned banks, which get secured profit margins because household saving is poorly rewarded. They have no incentive for efficient risk management, without which the shock of capital liberalization would be hazardous and might entail devastating losses, as happened in the US, Japan, and several European countries in the 1980s and early 1990s.

As emphasized in Chapter 4, the main reason for this dismal state of affairs is fiscal. Because China has no political consensus for agreed-upon rules to transfer fiscal revenues among regional and local governments, the latter suffer huge discrepancies between their fiscal resources and their commitments to provide basic public services. They are forced to indulge in heavy indebtedness, collateralized by speculative real estate values. It ensues that fiscal reform is a prerequisite for domestic financial liberalization. This is a thorny problem of economic policy that impinges upon the political processes, which determine the sharing of fiscal revenues among province and sub-province levels of governments. Possible changes in the political system and its administrative impacts are discussed in Chapter 7.

However, the global financial crisis that struck the world in 2008 has accelerated deep changes in the world economy that are reordering the economic and financial relationships of China with the rest of the world. There has been a long-term structural change: an increase in the share of trade with emerging-market countries in developing Asia and in the rest of the world and, conversely, a decline in the share of trade with the West and with Japan. In the 2000s the share of the emerging world in China's foreign trade has doubled from 15 to 30 percent. For this type of trade, the dollar is a third-party currency. It is the chosen vehicle currency for invoicing and settling trade only if the transaction costs in using the dollar, involving two currency conversions between the partners in trade, are lower than those incurred in choosing the currency of one or the other partner. Transaction costs can be lower in using a vehicle currency because they depend essentially on the liquidity of the money market that the partners in trade have access to. The larger the volume of trade invoiced and settled in a vehicle currency, the lower the transaction costs and the broader the use of this currency in international commerce and finance. It means that dynamic increasing returns are path-dependent. Even when the share of the issuing country of the key currency has been shrinking for a considerable time in world trade, the key currency goes on being used as a vehicle currency unabated. While a currency has been accepted as a key currency in international payment, only a dramatic event that drastically reduces its liquidity can change the pattern of international payments. The global financial crisis brought about that event.

In the fall of 2008 dollar liquidity collapsed worldwide, while interbank lending had dried up. The dearth of international means of payments triggered an abrupt slump in world trade that induced a severe contraction in the economic activity of countries like China that were not intermeshed in Wall Street's financial turmoil. A shock of this magnitude was capable of upsetting the pattern of international payments. A Chinese importer and a Brazilian exporter, for instance, might find it advantageous to invoice and settle trade in Yuan, on the proviso that Yuan deposits generated by the payment of Chinese imports could get a competitive return before they were recycled in trade to pay for Brazilian imports of Chinese products. However, the domestic money market in China is closed to non-residents except a handful of qualified foreign investors (QFIs). This squander could only be resolved if Yuan-denominated financial assets were made readily available outside mainland China. Hong Kong was the ideal financial center to manage the financial services induced by the incipient offshore Yuan.

The Chinese monetary authorities lost no time. In 2009 they launched the pilot system of invoicing and settling foreign trade in Yuan. The system is located in the Hong Kong financial center, backed by a memorandum of understanding between the PBoC and the Hong Kong Monetary Authority (HKMA) to guarantee and regulate liquidity. Corporates and financials, even if not directly involved in trade with the mainland, have been authorized to open accounts in Yuan with accredited depository institutions in Hong Kong. It is the start of the CNH (offshore Chinese Yuan in Hong Kong) market, e.g. the market for offshore Yuan financial assets.

The main impetus for developing the CNH market is the settlement of Chinese imports invoiced in Yuan. The size of the market and therefore the share of the Yuan in global foreign exchange (FX) trade will depend primarily on the share of trade invoiced in Yuan in China's imports. Scenario 1 assumes that the share of Yuan invoicing in Chinese imports will increase from 1 percent in 2011 to 20 percent in 2015. Another source of liquidity in the CNH market might be a loosening of capital controls permitting funds from Chinese residents to flow out to Hong Kong. In scenario 2, 1 percent of resident bank deposits is supposed to be allowed to flow abroad. Table 5.7 sums up the results of the projections for both scenarios.

In scenario 1, a strictly limited number of banks with quotas, led by Bank of China HK, are allowed to invest and borrow liquid funds on the onshore money markets in China to facilitate the settlement of international payments in Yuan. Furthermore, willing foreign central banks can conclude swap agreements with the PBoC to diversify a share of their FX reserves in Yuan, in buying government

Table 5.7 Projections of Chinese imports invoiced in Yuan and Yuan deposits in Hong Kong (values in US$ billion)

	2011	*2012*	*2013*	*2014*	*2015*
Value of imports settled in Yuan	31	74	162	304	482
CNH deposits (scenario 1)	32	67	141	272	475
CNH deposits (scenario 2)	56	125	242	429	706

Source: CEIC; Standard Chartered Research calculation

bonds on the onshore interbank market. On this liquidity base, the CNH market creates diversified investment products (Dim Sum Bonds) and derivatives (CNH deliverable forwards and cross-currency swaps) to allow foreign enterprises to issue debts in Yuan and manage their foreign exchange risks. An impressive momentum is triggered by the rise of the CNH market. Investment banks move their FX trading desks from Singapore to Hong Kong and nurture their staff (BBVA, HSBC, Standard Chartered, and Deutsche Bank). A lucrative business of underwriting securities is opening.

Functioning and equilibrium of the CNH market

Because liquid funds offshore and onshore are imperfectly fungible, there are two spot and a forward FX markets in Hong Kong. The US$/CNY exchange rate for commercial transactions is benchmarked by the exchange rate on the onshore spot market since the Yuan is convertible in current accounts. The US$/CNH exchange rate for financial transactions unrelated with trade has a quotation and a liquidity of its own. Financial intermediaries in Hong Kong must hold separate accounts to manage their exposure. What are the relationships between these markets?

Figure 5.6 depicts the daily spot exchange rate in onshore and offshore markets, and Figure 5.7 exhibits the one-year forward in Hong Kong deliverable forward (i.e. the forward exchange rate one year ahead quoted on the CNH market in Hong Kong on contracts that will deliver Yuan one year from now at the exchange rate quoted today).

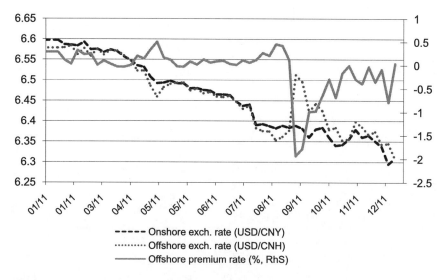

Figure 5.6 Spot exchange rate onshore and offshore.

Source: Bloomberg

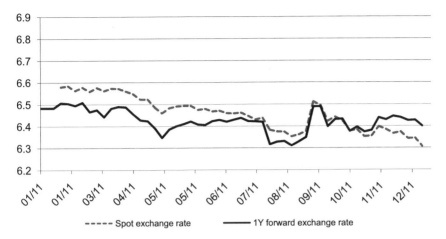

Figure 5.7 One-year offshore deliverable forward exchange rate.

Source: Bloomberg

Since capital controls hamper arbitrage between Yuan offshore and Yuan onshore, there are dual exchange rates. After the birth of the CNH market a huge demand arose for Yuan assets in Hong Kong. A lack of liquidity ensued that appreciated the offshore exchange rate compared to the onshore rate. The offshore risk premium culminated around 2 percent. However, the strength of the Yuan attracted foreign exporters in invoicing their exports to China in Yuan. Their deposits in HK banks built liquidity surprisingly quickly, so that the premium closed near year-end 2010. In November 2010 non-resident deposits in the CNH market had already quadrupled from August. This does not mean that the market is arbitraged once and for all. The liquidity premium can still be volatile, as happened in late April and early May 2011, because the depth of the CNH market is not yet well-entrenched. It means, however, that capital controls do not systematically distort the external value of the Yuan.

Nonetheless, more and more persistent and intringuing disturbances occurred in the summer of 2011. In August and September the euro zone crisis resumed with vigor. It upset the whole pattern of exchange rates worldwide. Until that time the CNH exchange rate premium, (onshore rate – offshore rate)/onshore rate, was roughly stable and slightly positive, meaning that the CNH Yuan was consistently and, admittedly, minimally more valued than the official rate against the dollar. In late September it depreciated abruptly and the premium slumped, before recovering progressively but remaining negative to year-end 2011. This event demonstrates that the CNH market is indeed an uncontrolled market, where liquidity can vary substantially. When interest rates spiked in September, international investors holding sovereign bonds of European countries except Germany made severe losses. US mutual funds withdrew funds from Europe and repatriated them in the US, triggering a rise in the dollar. As in every period of stress, international investors embarked on a portfolio reshuffling in favor of the most liquid market. They withdrew funds invested earlier on Dim Sum Bonds and the offshore Yuan plummeted. The European summit on October 27 calmed investors' fears of an immediate collapse of the euro zone and exchange rates reverted to a more normal pattern. However, the offshore premium remained positive.

The deliverable forward market confirms the finding. It points out a consistent but weak expectation of appreciation of the Yuan until mid-September and expectation of depreciation since October (Figure 5.7). The market expectation is at odds with that of the economists who are still forecasting a steady appreciation of the Yuan on the basis of their views on fundamentals. Is the market wrong or is it a better prediction of a change in regime? Is the Yuan approaching an equilibrium exchange rate due to basic economic changes transmitted to the shrinking of the current account surplus? With this alternative scenario the trend of appreciation in the Yuan/US$ exchange rate will abate markedly at best. In any case, the Chinese government is determined to go on expanding the use of the Yuan abroad, while making the onshore foreign exchange market more flexible.

To consolidate offshore Yuan convertibility, market participants want a range of assets covering maturities and risk ratings competitive with other convertible currencies. To accommodate this demand, Chinese monetary authorities have generated a benchmark government bond yield curve in the Dim Sum bond market. In early December the government issued Yuan 8 billion worth of fixed-income securities at two, three, five-, and ten-year maturities. In extending the yield curve to ten years, the Chinese leadership signals its will to incentivize international financial investors to invest in long-term financial assets. They have responded eagerly well ahead of issuers. Consequently two- to ten-year bond yields in Hong Kong are much lower than the corresponding yields on similar government bonds sold to domestic investors on the mainland (Table 5.8).

On December 26, 2011 the prime ministers of China and Japan jointly announced that the bilateral trade between the countries is to be settled in Yuan or Yen instead of dollar beforehand. Because this trade is large and because the shift in Japan's choice is highly relevant for stronger Asian integration, the political decision will strengthen China as the largest and most dynamic economy in the region. It will promote Hong Kong as the most prominent Yuan financial center for non-residents.

Correlatively the PBoC wants a more flexible exchange rate to make a two-way risk market where speculators who bet for appreciation of the Yuan can lose money. It also wants leeway to use the exchange rate as a tool of monetary policy. To achieve both goals, PBoC can loosen carefully the separation between

Table 5.8 Yields on two- to ten-year government bonds

In %	2 years	3 years	5 years	10 years
Offshore	1.6	1.0	1.8	2.5
Onshore	3.0	3.25	3.8	3.95

Source: Reuters Asian Markets News

the onshore and the offshore markets, use the information drawn from the CNH market and react within the conduct of monetary policy. It is in this controlled way that convertibility might progress.

Long-term significance of Yuan internationalization

Yuan internationalization has significance both for capital allocation in the domestic economy and for the evolution of financial relations of China with the rest of the world. The allocation of capital will be transformed because of the internationalization of the Yuan. The reason is that the market in HK includes domestic financial institutions. Those institutions have already issued corporate bonds in Hong Kong for domestic enterprises. This new opportunity of financing makes a link between domestic and foreign credit in Yuan. It is one of the reasons why, in 2011, the quantity of credit obtained by non-financial entities is higher than the planned credit aggregate determined by the central bank and than the aggregate of bank credit to non-financial sector. Therefore what is the motivation to emphasize the offshore market? There is an international motivation which is to use RMB as an invoicing and settling currency for trade. But there is also a domestic motivation which might be very important in the long run; that is, to use the HK market as an indirect way to reform the domestic financial market. Because the Chinese financial institutions will be confronted by international practices, for instance in risk management, they will change their behavior.

It is necessary to understand that the issue of Yuan convertibility is contentious among different power strongholds within the central government. On one side, the Ministry of Trade and the NDRC are growth-minded and much concerned about external competitiveness. They are allied with provincial officials alarmed at the slightest hint of rising unemployment and executives of SOEs, whose power is enhanced by high retained earnings ploughed back into fixed capital accumulation. They make a powerful and influential lobby while growth shows signs of weakening. On the other side, the PBoC and other financial regulatory institutions are well aware that the mechanism allocating saving in China and the excessive recourse to banks at the expense of capital markets entail a distorted allocation of saving and therefore widespread inefficiencies. Furthermore, the PBoC would appreciate being able to use the channel of interest rate more to run monetary policy if this channel could impinge upon the whole range of interest rates. The view of the PBoC has been strengthened by the threat of inflation. More flexible exchange rates allowing monetary policy to focus on domestic objectives would suit the PBoC very well. In launching the offshore program to internationalize the Yuan while getting rid of the de facto peg on the dollar, the State Council has struck a compromise. It allows SOEs to finance their expansion abroad in the cheapest way possible with the purpose of becoming global corporations before 2015. It creates a potentially large international market for the Yuan that enlarges its international use in trade and investment with other emerging-market countries. Meanwhile, it keeps the core of capital controls that preserves the dual market for interest rates.

As regards to practices and the efficiency of their business, Chinese financial institutions can learn during the process when operating in Hong Kong. But as regards financial asset prices, it is possible to keep two different systems running at the same time. A political decision has to be made to integrate the markets and move forward to full convertibility. Faithful to its gradualist method, the government will tighten the financial links abroad of the domestic economy step by step. Indeed, capital controls might not reduce the magnitude of capital flows overall, but it shapes its structure to discourage disruptive hot money and favors useful long-term flows.

In conformity with the principle of incremental change, the PBoC issued a new regulation in mid-June 2011 on cross-border FDIs. The rule allows all foreign companies (including subsidiaries of Chinese firms incorporated in Hong Kong) to remit on the mainland in the form of FDIs all funds raised on the offshore market. It is a big push for internationalizing the Yuan, which still protects the domestic market from many sources of speculative capital inflows. The new rule finds productive uses to increasing offshore Yuan deposits that had already reached Yuan 511 billion or about 8.5 percent of total deposits in Hong Kong.

The FDI regulation will give an impetus to the reform on share since remittances are conditional on investment projects consistent with the new directions of industrial policy. The rule will speed up and diversify the creation of Yuan assets offshore in bonds, loans, and equities.

Conclusion

China has entered a new stage of economic reform, which pursues twin long-term objectives: committing to sustainable growth in the domestic sphere and acceding to the status of world power in the foreign sphere. This dual objective can only be achieved by a joint transformation of economic structures and institutions. Exploring this formidable task will be the subject of Chapters 6 and 7, which are prospective in scope.

One of the most important institutions in the regulation of the whole economy is finance. The transformation of finance is being driven by the external side of the economy. It will not be confined there. The liberalization of financial services is badly needed to direct the cost of capital, so that the allocation of saving feeds a growth process grounded on the efficiency of all factors of production. This is what sustainable growth is all about. As we will see, such a financial reform is inextricably intertwined with fundamental fiscal reform that impinges upon the structure of power within the Party.

However, China cannot wait for the whole accomplishment of its political institutions to participate in world governance. Upcoming currency multilateralism is the inescapable consequence of the huge gap in growth between the large emerging powers and Western countries. The bold move to gradual Yuan convertibility starting with non-residents gives the tool that will permit China to influence the debate on the future of the international monetary system.

Part III

The new stage of reform toward sustainability

6 The making of sustainable growth

Nothing is more challenging for economists than understanding structural change while it is altering the core macroeconomic relationship of a growth regime. It is even more daunting while it is encompassing the world economy at large. However, this is what has been unleashed by the global financial crisis that erupted in 2007 and spread well beyond its origin in the US. The impact of the crisis has reverberated all over the world. Furthermore it has posed hard questions about the intellectual paradigm that has legitimated the dominance of financial capitalism since its rise in the 1980s and its expansion beyond the Western world in the 1990s. The collapse of financial markets in the fall of 2008 has not only demonstrated once more their incapacity for self-regulation, it has also raised doubts about the incentives provided by finance to economic agents according to the so-called Wall Street model.

What is at stake is nothing less than the most basic question of political economy since its early days in the eighteenth century: the question of wealth. In the conception of the world propagated by global finance, wealth is nothing but moneymaking money. Universal liquidity is all that matters to make all types of capital substitutes, transaction costs minimal, information symmetrical, and markets complete. This is the efficient market principle. This paradigm entails the famous Modigliani–Miller theorem according to which financing structures have no relevance whatsoever on investment opportunities and achievements. The allocation of capital is driven solely by risk-adjusted yields that efficient markets tend to equalize.

Financial globalization is viewed as the process by which market efficiency is realized worldwide. To get it the world should be flat because every part of the world should adopt the same institutions that support market efficiency as recommended by Wall Street, e.g. universal property rights, uniform laws protecting them, retreat of the state to a minimal social safety net and therefore full-fledged privatization. Elaborated since the 1970s, this doctrine has perverted political liberalism into a sectarian ideology that captured political power in Anglo-Saxon countries in the 1980s. The fall of the Berlin Wall was thought of as an opportunity to extend it worldwide under the so-called Washington Consensus label with the twin Bretton Woods institutions as missionaries.

Fortunately the world has not become flat. The 1997–8 Asian crisis showed what happened to the developing countries that listened to the sirens of Wall Street. The 2007–8 global crisis has dramatically shown how far finance is from the Modigliani–Miller world. Fragile financial structures were built quietly and hidden from the scrutiny of "market discipline." They interacted in ways that provoked devastating systemic losses. China's highly regulated financial system has been largely sheltered from the financial crisis. Nonetheless, as explained in Chapters 4 and 5, it is not without its own shortcomings in allocating capital. Therefore the dual experiences of Western and Chinese economic regulation raise the question: how best to finance future wealth creation?

But this question is superseded by more fundamental ones: which types of wealth are more welfare-enhancing than others for society in general? How should the categories of capital that produce wealth be invested and combined to implement development policy in the next two decades? These are the relevant questions for the new stage of reform in China. They pertain to sustainable growth. The reason is that wealth is not just moneymaking money. It has a real consistency. As we show in the present chapter, the 12th five-year plan is initiating many ways of reform that are transforming the economy in investing in types of capital that were formerly underdeveloped: human capital with structural changes in the labor market, social capital with improving governance of companies and institutions, natural capital with environmental concerns.

The advantages of broadening the concept of capital to frame development policies are considerable. The way forward thus lies in extending the concept of capital to all assets that contribute to the maintenance and expansion of social welfare for Chinese society as a whole over time. This is essentially a dynamic concept of *sustainability*. Sustainability is the new frontier of Chinese reform. The preceding stage of accumulation was based upon the assumption that the use of non-renewable resources was cheap, that the stock of non-used resources was free and that growth was unlimited. This crude growth model has become less and less relevant for the contradictions it has generated.

In our view of twenty-first century China, the concept of sustainable growth is being defined and developed with the purpose of being all-embracing, so as to bring about far-reaching reform in economic policy. Sustainable growth will lead to revolution in economic thinking, accounting, government policy, and the organization of finance. Broadly speaking, sustainable growth integrates into growth trajectories the long-term protection of the environment and hence the welfare of future generations. The countries able to monitor and integrate structural change according to the goal of sustainable growth will be the leaders in innovation. The Chinese leadership wants the country to move from being the manufacturer of the world to exploring modes of production and consumption that leapfrog the environment-destructive imitation of the present mode of consumption in affluent societies.

The first part of this chapter defines the concept of sustainable growth and shows how the goal of sustainability will impinge upon the political economy of reform in transforming the methods of strategic planning. The second and third parts of the chapter deal with the main structural changes that should be welfare-enhancing if monitored and incentivized so as to promote sustainability. The second part studies the consequences of the demographic transition and defines the framework of policies aiming at reversing the widening inequalities in income and wealth. The third part argues that the axis of the sustainable growth regime is the co-development of urbanization and environment protection. The next chapter focuses on the broad and ambitious land, fiscal, and social reforms to achieve these goals.

Sustainable growth: all-encompassing concept for China's new stage of reform

In its 2010 report on global development, the Organization for Economic Co-operation and Development (OECD) emphasized "shifting wealth" as the most important phenomenon in the world economy. Aggregate figures are striking. Expressed in PPP, the share of non-OECD members in world GDP has increased from 38 percent in 1990 to 50 percent in 2011. In conservative hypotheses it might reach 57 percent in 2030. Referring to Adam Smith, the report argues that wealth creation in the developing world has very deep social implications. Indeed, China has been the best performer for that matter, lifting more than 400 million people out of extreme poverty, while the poverty threshold has been defined in terms of money income. However, Amartya Sen has forcefully stressed that freedom is the ability of people to develop their human potential and that it improves with concrete life conditions that are far from being encapsulated in average money income. Wealth is the concept that can link concrete achievements to macro policy and performance.

However, even if the OECD report focuses on wealth, it reverts to GDP as early as the introduction: "due to the difficulty measuring nations' physical, human, and natural capital stock, this report refers solely to stock values that can easily be identified such as foreign reserves, sovereign wealth fund assets and the increased size of the global labour force." Significantly the report quotes only financial assets on top of undifferentiated labor force.

The theoretical problem of the link between the concrete structure of wealth in its specific items and the distribution of wealth ownership in the population of a country on the one hand, and the social welfare of the entire population as a measure of policy performance on the other, has lingered for decades among welfare economists. After years of research Sir John Hicks admitted that it was impossible to find out an objective index to aggregate individual income immune to ethical criteria, so that social welfare can be represented by a measure of national income. Amartya Sen showed that the marginal dollar possessed by a poorer person has a higher marginal value than the same dollar possessed by a richer one. Therefore it is necessary to account for the distribution of income, and the structure and the size of the population according to judgments that make ethical values explicit. The impact of externalities is also relevant. Besides, Kenneth Arrow (Arrow 1950) demonstrated long ago that it was impossible to assess and express social welfare with any procedure based only on individual preferences. Pure economics cannot exist.

The 2009 Report by the Commission on the Measurement of Economic Performance and Social Progress, chaired by Joseph Stiglitz, is the latest and most comprehensive contribution that attempts to link social welfare to wealth. Under the caveat that social welfare does not attempt to measure happiness, but is restricted to the satisfaction of needs that stem directly from the final objectives of economic activity, measuring problems can be overcome by developments in national accounting. It can be called economic social welfare. Therefore the way forward lies in widening the concept of capital to the whole domain of assets appropriate to the maintenance and expansion of economic welfare for the whole society over time. This is essentially a dynamic concept of *sustainability*. In such an all-encompassing conception of capital, public services are non-rival and non-exclusive public goods that are produced by tangible and intangible assets, which can be used by all economic agents. These collective assets are owned by society at large.

The advantages of enlarging the concept of capital for the study of development are considerable. One can analyze systematically the relationships between income and asset values. For instance, how much the capital invested in health impinges upon labor productivity and real income growth, feeding a sustained virtuous circle. Conversely, how much pollution depreciates human capital via health deterioration. While environment is degraded, one must distinguish between the initial impact, which creates losses affecting unequally the capital account of economic agents and the investments to repair the losses that are current expenditures appearing in flow accounts.

The change of perspective brought about by the sustainability approach raises questions about accounting reallocations. Items that had been traditionally treated as intermediary inputs should be reclassified as investments in capital. This is primarily the case of research and development (R&D) expenditures, formerly an intermediary input and lately reclassified as an investment in intangible capital in the 2008 UN system of national accounts. It is also the case of mining prospection, which generates new knowledge in sub-soil primary reserves.

The concept of sustainability fits with the ambition expressed by Chinese leaders to move the country toward a harmonious society. This ambition is surfacing in the 12th five-year plan. The concept will help the National Development and Reform Commission (NDRC) to deeply reform economic policies. Indeed, sustainable development will remain small talk without a macroeconomic framework embodying the concept to assure consistency in policies that impinge on many economic activities. But the task is gigantic. Sustainable growth will entail a revolution in economic thinking, in accounting, in government policies, and in the organization of finance. Broadly, sustainable growth takes the long-term protection of the environment and therefore the welfare of future generations within the growth regime. A flow accounting framework aiming at measuring and enhancing

GDP growth must be completed with a stock-flow accounting aiming at measuring total wealth (e.g. *genuine capital*), which is the resource base of producing future social welfare, and thus enhancing total wealth accumulation.

The World Bank is the institution that has plowed deeper into the task of measuring total wealth as a tool to assess the sustainability of growth paths in advanced and developing economies. It has drawn upon a pioneer work by Pearce and Atkinson, "Capital theory and the measurement of sustainable development: an indicator of weak sustainability" (1993). In its 2006 seminal report (*Where is the wealth of nations? Measuring capital for the 21st century*), the World Bank explored a methodology and empirical investigation aimed at changing development policies.

The advantage of China in using this methodology would be in its recourse to strategic planning. In order to elicit how strategic planning can be made a coordinating process in pursuing the goal of sustainability, we draw a formal framework from available research. This framework will embody a theoretical concept of sustainability, helping to explain how price incentives defined in this planning could guide policies to enhance total wealth.

Definition of total wealth and sustainability

Development depends on total wealth, e.g. produced, human, social, and natural capital. Sustaining total wealth is the key for viable growth regimes. The different forms of capital are defined in the following way:

Produced (tangible) capital = equipment + structures + urban land
Intangible capital = human capital + institutional infrastructures + social capital + net foreign financial assets
Natural capital = sub-soil assets + timber resources + non-timber forest resources + protected areas + crop land + pasture land

The sum of the three components is the real wealth of the nation. In the present state of our knowledge it is far from being comprehensively measured. Only a massive statistical effort, mobilizing government resources and international coordination, can make decisive progress. Future growth prospects are linked to changes in real wealth. Change in real wealth has been named adjusted net saving (or *genuine saving*).

Genuine saving is substantially different from saving in standardized national accounts:

Genuine (or net) saving = economic gross saving of the nation – fixed productive capital depreciation + change in value of human capital + change in value of social capital – depletion of mineral and energy fossil resources – net reduction of forests – damages due to pollution in $\approx CO_2$

Genuine or net saving is directly related to the change in real wealth adjusted from capital transfers and valuation changes:

Net saving = Δ (net real value of wealth) – net receipts in capital transfers other net changes in asset volumes – real gains or + real losses in holding wealth

These accounting relationships define the basis of wealth accounting as distinct from GDP accounting. Strategic planning requires the state to redirect its statistical apparatus to fill the accounting framework with as reliable data as possible on the components of real wealth, e.g. being as thorough as possible in measuring the relevant types of capital.

The theoretical problem is the modeling of the relationships between the types of capital compounding real wealth and social welfare. It is the well-known problem of growth theory that must be revisited. In standard growth theory, the Ramsey model derives optimal conditions from a welfare function whose argument is aggregate private consumption, the latter being produced by productive capital and labor according to production function à la Solow. In view of sustainability it has many shortcomings: welfare is assimilated to the utility of private marketable goods, social welfare to the sum of individual cardinal utilities, and capital is reduced to fixed productive assets.

The most crucial problem is the low substitutability between private consumption and the services of the environment, compounded by the social appropriation of these services, which are largely public goods. One cannot easily offset welfare degradation from higher concentration in greenhouse gases, from reduced biodiversity and from fresh water scarcity, with more private consumption. Therefore the social welfare function must introduce private consumption and the services of the environment as separate arguments. Correlatively, social welfare is farther away from the aggregation of individual preferences. It will depend decisively on political processes able to reveal collective preferences.

To make it harder, the time horizon of strategic planning will extend far into the future and radical uncertainty must be handled in a meaningful way. Climate change, depletion of forests, and oncoming scarcities in water and fossil resources are long-term challenges that carry the threat of extreme events decades ahead or in the next century. Therefore the threat involves future generations even more than present ones. This is so because the ecological system embodies a lot of inertia but may become vulnerable to uncontrollable diverging feedbacks if unknown thresholds are overstepped. Humankind faces a world of unknown unknowns that nonetheless depend on its own behavior in the next few decades.

Therefore we may understand why strategic planning is all-important. Will the Chinese government embark on a policy of massive investments in radical innovation at the expense of present and near-term consumption, in the hope that new renewable energy investments will make environmental and economic goods more substitutable in the longer term? Or will it wait in the hope of getting more information on climate change developments and natural capital depletion at the risk of letting irreversible damage occur? To better appreciate the dilemma, it must increase its knowledge on the processes that lead to sustainability or unsustainability of the economy; it has the duty to lead and regulate in highly alternative scenarios.

Box 6.1 sums up the derivation of the sustainability condition from a cardinal social welfare function. If the different types of capital that make the productive base of the economy in a general ecological and economic sense can be measured, the variation of total wealth per capita is the sum of the growth of total factor productivity and the growth in the aggregate volume of the different types of capital.

Box 6.1 From social welfare to economic sustainability

Definition of the welfare function

U is a social welfare function in continuous time. It is a function of two variables:

$C(\tau)$ an aggregate of extended private consumption embodying the value of social services that are directly allocated to households and consumed in the same period;

$E(\tau)$ the services of environment that flow from natural capital.

V is an inter temporal cardinal function:

$$V(t) = \frac{1}{1-\eta} \int_{t}^{\infty} U[C(\tau), E(\tau)]^{1-\eta} e^{-\delta(\tau - t)} d\tau$$

δ is the pure rate of time preference and η is the rate of relative risk aversion.

The imperfect substitutability between private consumption and the services of environment is described by a Constant Elasticity of Substitution function whose limited elasticity is σ:

$$U[C(t), E(t)] = [C(t)^{\frac{\sigma-1}{\sigma}} + E(t)^{\frac{\sigma-1}{\sigma}}]^{\frac{\sigma}{\sigma-1}}$$

Criterion of sustainability

The strong criterion of sustainability is that V is not decreasing:

$dV/dt \geq 0$

The final goods and services providing utility, either from consumption or from the environment, are produced by combinations of all types of capital according to the best available technology. The types of capital were defined above in describing the accounting framework. The different types of capital are depleted by their use in production and increased by investment (productive and human capital), by natural repletion if renewable (forests) or irreversibly reduced by extraction if non-renewable (sub-soil fossil resources). The output generated by the combination of all types of capital is compounded of consumption, services of environment, and investment in reproducible capital. The allocation of output depends on the adjusted rate of saving (genuine saving) and the public rule that makes environmental services available in specific quantities. One supposes that the allocation mechanism is such that *V is not an explicit function of time*. It follows that the stocks of the different kinds of capital in $t + 1$ are determined by the stocks in t and by the permanent allocation mechanism. This assumption is not so benign since it abstracts from uncertainty as far as the allocation mechanism is concerned.

Under this assumption strategic planning can proceed from period to period and determine in principle the entire future course of capital stocks, of different types and flows of consumption and environmental services. If there are n stocks of capital K_i at time t ($i = 1,\ldots, n$), the values of the macro variables in the economy are determined at all future times $\tau > t$. It follows that U is determined for $\tau \geq t$ and $V(t)$ is determined as well. One can write

$V(t) = V[K_1(t), K_2(t),\ldots, K_n(t)]$

The strong sustainability condition requires

$$\frac{dv}{dt} = \sum_{i=1}^{i=n} \left(\frac{\partial v}{\partial K_{it}} \right) \left(\frac{dK_{it}}{dt} \right) = \sum_{i=1}^{i=n} p_{it} I_{it}$$

where p_i is the contribution of the ith type of capital to inter temporal welfare, e.g. the shadow price of capital K_i, and I_i the net investment in that type of capital.

The strong sustainability condition means that, if capital is valued at its "fair price," the variation of social wealth in t is equal to the variation of inter temporal social welfare. *The criterion for sustainability is that real wealth is not decreasing, e.g. that genuine saving is ≥ 0.*

This condition is quite general. It does not require that the welfare function has the analytical form chosen above to show how environmental services can be treated separately from household consumption. The absolute value of V has not to be computed. *One has to compute the change in real wealth.* However, for strong sustainability to apply, *the prices with which the elements of wealth must be computed are shadow prices.* They are not prices one can observe. They are the prices that would prevail if all types of wealth were commodities traded in competitive markets under perfect foresight. Because many types of capital are not traded commodities at all, they are partly calculated as *discounted rents, e.g. the price that must be paid for the scarcity of the resource.* It is where the responsibility of strategic planning is paramount. Only it can price externalities that impede the measure of the services of environment.

Furthermore, in the above equation, shadow prices are measured in units of utility per unit of capital. This is not convenient for empirical use. One type of capital that has an observed market price can be taken as *numéraire*. Let us suppose it is $i = 1$. This price is posited 1. The prices of other types of capital, being expressed in this numéraire, become price indexes. Let us call W the total value of wealth expressed in this price system:

$$W_t = \sum_{i=1}^{n} p_{it} K_{it} \text{ and } \frac{dW}{dt} = \sum_{i=1}^{n} p_{it} I_{it}$$

The condition of sustainability is $dW/dt \geq 0$. It can be used to measure weak sustainability, where the range in the different types of capital is the most extensive that can be measured and where prices are the best possible approximations of shadow prices.

Technological progress and population growth

The condition of sustainability can be defined in a slightly different way. Dividing both terms of the equation by the value of the first type if capital, one gets:

$$\left(\frac{dV}{dt}\right)\left(\frac{1}{p_1 K_1}\right) = \left(\frac{1}{K_1}\right)\left(\frac{dK_1}{dt}\right) + \left(\frac{p_2 K_2}{p_1 K_1}\right)\left(\frac{1}{K_2}\right)\left(\frac{dK_2}{dt}\right) + \cdots + \left(\frac{p_n K_n}{p_1 K_1}\right)\left(\frac{1}{K_n}\right)\left(\frac{dK_n}{dt}\right)$$

The economy is sustainable if the sum of the growth in the volume of the different types of capital, weighted by their elasticity of substitution to the one type chosen as numéraire, is non-negative.

Now let us suppose that there is a Hicks-neutral technological progress. It can be interpreted as the rate of growth of "knowledge" taken as the numéraire.

Its rate of growth is the growth rate (γ) in total factor productivity (TFP). With neutral technological progress the elasticity of output to knowledge is 1. Therefore the rate of growth of real wealth becomes simply the sum of TFP growth and the growth rates of the other types of capital:

$$\frac{1}{W}\frac{dW}{dt} = \gamma + \sum_{i=2}^{n} \frac{1}{K_i}\frac{dK_i}{dt}$$

One must measure the growth in the volume of the different types of capital, including TFP growth, and add up.

The formula is valid if population is constant. If population is growing at rate g, the sustainability criterion must be applied in calculating the growth of real wealth per capita with the caveat of constant population growth and independence of the distribution of wealth on population change:

$$\frac{1}{W}\frac{dW}{dt} - g = \gamma + \sum_{i=2}^{n} \frac{1}{K_i}\frac{dK_i}{dt}$$

Since the variation of total net real wealth or *genuine wealth* is net investment of society, the condition of sustainability is that society does not destroy its wealth in mustering enough genuine saving (net adjusted saving) to match net investment. Therefore the sustainability condition becomes the following: *the development path of an economy is sustainable if, at every date, adjusted social saving (or genuine saving) is non-negative.* If it gets negative, society is destroying its wealth, meaning that the economic path is unsustainable.

We will study the new stage of Chinese reform with the guidance provided by this theoretical framework. Before proceeding into the content of strategic planning in the different ways of enhancing real wealth, let us first understand how the sustainability condition gives insight for the coordination of the whole plan.

The political economy of strategic planning for sustainable growth

There are three fundamental questions that are quite general and impinge upon the political regime of the country. How is social welfare revealed? How can the social value of carbon be determined? How is the future discounted under radical uncertainty?

Revealing social welfare

We raise the problem here, but in the concluding chapter we try to propose some ideas in the debate over the evolution of the political system relative to harmonious society. As already mentioned, Arrow's impossibility theorem demonstrated that social welfare cannot spring from individual preferences. It rules out the assertion that a market economy might be a self-sufficient system. Furthermore, GDP growth is no guide for sustainability even in a weak sense. It is true even in a perfect foresight world. It is all the more so under uncertainty, which erodes the ability of individuals to set time horizons and to keep risk aversion in check. Time horizons depend essentially on the social rate of time preference. We soon show that this rate cannot be determined by individual time preference, let alone by a market rate, but is a parameter determined by ethical considerations.

Social welfare is the outcome of political debate. Politics produce social goals in organizing debates between interacting coalitions of interests. The capacity of integrating conflicting preferences in striking formal or tacit compromises and producing a hierarchy of political goals depends on the dynamic of the debates. No existing political regime is suited to reveal inter temporal social welfare for the long run. Representative democracies are handicapped by their elective procedure that involves only living adults, while the consequences of their policies might impact unborn generations much more. The Chinese political regime has a major asset: its long-run view. It can be decisive while political choices about urbanization, infrastructures, energy sources, pollution abatement, and adaptation will shape people's lives for the remainder of the century. However, China is handicapped by the inclination of the regime to be captured by special interests. Only ethical imperatives, powerful enough to curb interest groups and to regulate the political process, might reveal social welfare better.

In the second stage of reform (1994–2010) described in Chapter 4, the forceful development of capitalism generated unsustainability in two basic respects: a widening income gap that threatens to divide the country into separate classes, and environmental degradation that threatens irreversible ecological damages. They are at odds with the philosophical underpinnings of Confucian precepts in politics: care for the needs of the less-endowed in resources and of the future generations, and unity of humankind and nature. The open question is: which evolution of the political regime will bring about those ethical norms in social welfare to be pursued in sustainable growth regimes?

Prices as instruments of sustainability: the social value of carbon

In an optimal dynamic that equates variation of social welfare to variation of real wealth, prices that should prevail are those that would exist if all types of wealth were traded on perfect markets. Obviously such dynamic equilibrium does not exist and will never be attainable, but the advantage of a government relying on strategic planning is that those prices are also instruments of policies, since they are the dual prices of the dynamic optimal programming that maximizes social welfare. Therefore it is possible to reform some key markets with an understanding of the price policies that are more likely to lead to sustainable growth paths.

For the time being the most important price distortion, which China shares with many developed countries, is the lack of a carbon price. It is so because there are negative environmental externalities whose costs are not recognized. One way to price at least partially the externalities engendered by the license to pollute without caring for the cost of the social damage inflicted is to institute a social value of carbon embodied in a carbon tax. This is tricky because it is plagued with huge uncertainty about irreversible future climate change and the magnitude of economic damages involved. How can those damages be priced? One way is to apply the precaution principle to define a real option value accounting for the irreversibility of climate change. Over time new information will be made available to structure a sequential decision-making process.

What is the meaning of fixing a social value for carbon emission? It is a notional price that defines a monetary value to a public good, which is improved service of the environment measured by an extra ton of CO_2 avoided. It is a price that must be embodied in long-term investment projects to reveal their true social yield. Most theoretical results are not practically useful because they are established under hypotheses of perfect foresight. They are useful nonetheless in identifying the variables that play a crucial role in the interaction between economy and environment. From this theoretical basis, strategic planning must balance two opposite complexities under uncertainty. On the one hand, environmental irreversibility stems from unknown thresholds and possible catastrophic feedbacks in the ecological system, while the concentration of greenhouse gases has overstepped those thresholds. This irreversibility recommends early actions to avoid fast-increasing costs of convex damages. On the other hand, technological irreversibility provides a positive option value of waiting for more performing techniques being available. It is an incentive for low initial investment.

Under perfect foresight, technological irreversibility should prevail. The optimal way to price carbon would be to fix a low initial value and to raise it overtime, because technological progress would abate pollution more and more effectively. But uncertainty on climate change dynamics and on the cost, the performance, and the availability of innovations changes the perspective substantially.

Uncertainty on the magnitude of climate warming weighs upon the speed of augmentation in greenhouse gases concentration, on the sensitiveness of temperature rise to higher concentration, on the thresholds that might trigger diverging feedbacks, on the magnitude, and variety of economic damages due to temperature rise and on their geographical distribution in so vast a country as China.

Uncertainty on technological progress is of two kinds. There is radical uncertainty on backstop clean technologies (zero emission) that are either not yet discovered or still far from being marketable. There is incremental uncertainty closer to quantifiable risk about the speed of diffusion of technologies that are already operational but costly. Their implementation depends on the right public incentives. Strategic planning must make upstream investments and organize R&D, learning, and competition to speed up diffusion. Models of endogenous growth under uncertainty lead to the conclusion that the best way is to start immediately low-carbon investment projects, upheld by an initially high value of carbon. According to simulations covering a large range of values for the unknown parameters, a price of carbon in the range of US$50 to 60 per ton of non-emitted CO_2 might be a proper guideline.

Discounting the future to allocate capital under uncertainty

In traditional cost–benefit analysis, the discount factor is the shadow price for discounting future costs and benefits. In the usual Ramsey optimal growth model, it is the amount of consumption an economic agent is willing to give up in the present to get one extra unit of consumption in the future. In a perfect foresight world the associated economic discount rate is the risk-free interest rate, equal to the rate of pure time preference plus the growth rate times the elasticity of substitution in marginal utilities. The latter parameter is equivalent to relative risk aversion under uncertainty.

Pro-market economists contend that indications drawn from the financial markets should be used to extract the risk-free interest rate. In his well-known 2007 review on the economics of climate change, Nicholas Stern disagreed strikingly. For his evaluation of future economic damage due to pollution and the subsequent simulations of widely alternative scenarios to make allowance of radical uncertainty, he used the value of the rate of pure time preference estimated at 0.1 percent for ethical reason. Justifying his choice later and responding to the controversy, Stern (2008) explained why referring to present market rates is quite wrong. The problem society faces is not a cost–benefit analysis along a given path of the economy, which would be regulated by market prices, but rather it is the choice between very different paths under radical uncertainty, which is a political choice that expresses the attitude of society toward its own future survival. Since society is dubbed immortal while individuals are mortal, the rate of social time preference has nothing to do with individual time preference. It should be taken to 0. The only reason why it might be taken slightly positively is the possibility of an ecological collapse that terminates life on earth as we know it.

There is another problem due to the environment that pleads for a low discount rate. Let us revert to the modeling of the social welfare function linked to the condition of sustainable growth paths displayed in Box 6.1. This function assumes that environmental services are not perfectly substitutable with consumption. The long-term protection of environment should be pursued *per se* for the path of the economy to be sustainable. It can be demonstrated that there is an ecological discount rate reflecting the relative price of the environment relative to consumption in the social welfare function. The lower the substitutability between private consumption and the services of the environment, the lower is the ecological discount rate relative to the risk-free interest rate drawn from financial markets.

What this means is that environmental issues become paramount in the long run in sustainable growth paths. The ecological discount rate is the one that matters more and it converges asymptotically toward the rate of pure time preference, which is close to 0, in the long run for natural capital to be preserved. Obviously the ecological discount rate is not a price that can be spontaneously determined on financial markets. Like the price of carbon, it is a policy-engineered price to allocate capital and promote innovative investment to achieve sustainability.

The paths of sustainable growth crucially depend on the substitutability between economic, human, and other types of intangible capital on the one hand and natural capital on the other. The lower the substitutability between economic goods and environmental goods, the more restricted is the range of sustainable growth paths. This teaching gives the rationale for strategic planning. *The government should acknowledge the complementarity between private consumption and the services of the environment in promoting innovative investments in renewable energy resources, infrastructures, urbanization, and abatement of carbon content in durable goods.* It amounts to deep change in economic policy whereby the goal of maximizing GDP growth gives way to the more general goal of real wealth sustainable expansion, leading to social welfare-enhancing growth regime. Strategic planning must rely on the measurement of all types of capital. It must improve the price system in view of rebalancing wealth towards intangible capital and natural capital that were either insufficiently developed or degraded in the previous growth regime.

In the following sections we apply the conceptual framework exposed above to the main topics that are becoming prominent in the new stage of reform: labor and services reform that will improve the contribution of intangible capital to social welfare on the one hand; urbanization and environment protection that will be the main drivers of sustainable growth in the upcoming decades, and climate change mitigation and adaptation on the other.

Reforming labor and service markets

The forces reshaping the fundamental conditions of growth stem from both the contradictions of the heavy accumulation cum export-led growth regime pursued by China since the mid-1990s and from the dramatic shifts in wealth and power in the world economy that have been magnified by the aftermath of the global financial crisis.

Forceful capital-intensive accumulation will meet rising obstacles that will affect its effectiveness and its profitability, because they impinge upon the markets at the core of its regulation: the labor market under socio demographic changes, the capital market that distorts capital allocation, the service sector that is retarded, and the mounting scarcity in primary resources and degradation of the environment.

The legacy of demography and widening inequalities in the labor market

The huge expansion of manufacturing, led by both foreign trade and urbanization, has attracted flows of young unskilled migrant workers at very low wage rates into eastern cities. Hence the productivity gains have accrued entirely to the large manufacturing firms and to the small businesses in foreign trade. From 2000 to 2007 research in the Academy of Social Sciences has shown that nominal wages of migrant workers have increased 5 percent a year (only around 2 percent in real terms) against 16 percent for permanent workers in SOEs. Average industrial wages have risen 14 percent and profits 28 percent. Consequently the share of industrial profits in GDP has climbed from 2 percent in 2000 to 10 percent in 2008. The correlative diminishing share of labor in national income explains the bulk of the reduction of household income from 55 to 48 percent of GDP in the same time span. Thus the shrinking of the wage share generated a spectacular decline of consumption/GDP despite the rise of an urban middle class, as documented in Chapter 4.

The fast-rising inequality within the labor force due to the so-called infinite elasticity of labor supply for young workers was a primary determinant of the adverse drift in wage share as percent of GDP. The unbalanced income distribution has stopped widening and is likely to reverse under the mix of structural changes in the labor market, of more bargaining power of workers in firms, and of income policy initiated by the central government using two main instruments: minimum wage catch-up and social transfers. Some inflexions have already been achieved. In 2010 the average wage in the eastern region was only 4 percent higher than the average wage in inner regions, against 15 percent in 2004.

Leaving the study of social policy for the next chapter, we focus now on structural changes and on the regulation of labor market that might emerge.

Structural changes in the labor market

The structural change in the labor market is conceptualized along the lines of the Lewis turning point. The British development economist, Arthur Lewis, Nobel laureate, published in 1954 an influential article "Economic development with unlimited supplies of labor" (Lewis 1954). This article was about what has been labeled the "Lewis turning point" (LTP). It is the configuration that arises in the labor market when the surplus of cheap labor runs dry. Lewis argued that developing nations do not have a homogeneous labor market because their economies exhibit a dual structure, e.g. a rural–urban divide. As long as the rural sector provides surplus labor, the excess supply can match the demand for low-skilled labor in the cities and sustain fast industrial growth without increase in the factor price. Theoretically the labor market presents *an infinitely elastic labor supply curve*. It ensures that surplus value in the industrial sector, stemming from productivity increase, accrues to profit and fosters capital accumulation.

This was the model at work in the second stage of Chinese reform studied in Chapter 4, while corporate law, fiscal reform, and attraction of foreign investment had finally broken Adam Smith's high equilibrium and released capital-intensive accumulation. The LTP is depicted in Figure 6.1. The horizontal portion of the labor supply curve is the infinitely elastic supply curve of labor. As long as the demand for labor is low enough, the labor market balances at the constant subsistence wage. While demographic processes slow down the growth of the labor force and industrialization pushes the demand of labor rightward, the time arrives where the supply of labor gets upward-sloping. The labor market normalizes: with labor demand shifting rightward with rising income, the equilibrium real wage increases. The LTP is the point of transition where the regime changes.

In reality, there are two turning points in the long-run dynamic of the economy. The first one has been reached in China. It is the point where the demand for unskilled labor in the manufacturing sector exceeds labor supply at the given fixed wage. Urban real wage for low-skilled workers begins to rise with labor demand. Wage increases reduce profit and subsequently slow down the pace of capital

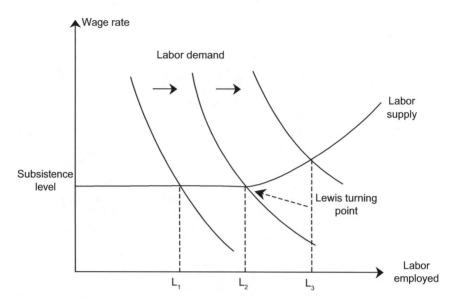

Figure 6.1 Lewis turning point in the labor market.

accumulation. The second point occurs when the transfer of labor from the rural sector to industry no longer reflects an excess supply, but is engineered by the price mechanism, e.g. the marginal productivity differential between urban and rural activities. The first LTP inaugurates a phase in development whereby less labor supply and increasing demand for food in the cities are driving food prices up. However, the subsequent higher profit in agriculture will induce investment in seeds, fertilizer, and machinery that will raise marginal productivity, reducing the gap with urban activity. Therefore the combination of demographic factors leading to zero, then negative growth of the overall labor force on the one hand and rising marginal productivity of labor in agriculture on the other hand, will lead to the integration of the labor market.

Nonetheless, the process has a long way to go because the gap between productivity in the primary sector and the rest of the economy is still large. The former is six times lower than the latter, while in developed countries they are roughly similar. The narrowing of the gap will need a marked fall in agricultural employment with correlative urbanization. It will also need a lot of investment in agriculture steered by concentration in land plots. It is why policies to regulate the flow of migrants must be carefully designed. Social policies and rural land reforms are needed to increase rural income, so that farmers and their families who move to cities have enough wealth to integrate with a reasonable chance of upward social mobility. But these policies should not subsidize the preservation of farmers on their land plots.

In China demography is changing fast (Figure 6.2). The age groups that have migrated to eastern cities for employment in industry (*mingong*) were young workers age 15–24. This population reached its peak in 2008–10 and started to decline at the time when the stimulating plan gave a powerful boost to growth. Therefore the first LTP was attained before the start of the 12th plan. From 2015 onwards aging will take its toll. The dependency ratio (age > 65/total population) will rise markedly from 27 percent in 2015 to 37 percent in 2040. The size of the labor force will level off from 2015 to 2025 and then decline. Therefore the second LTP will occur in the second half of the present decade.

As a consequence, the urban average wage will be determined by an augmented Phillips curve-like relation: the nominal wage indexed on CPI an increasing function of excess demand of labor by firms. As long as growth remains high and firms compete for labor demand, workers will acquire bargaining power. Because of aging of the labor force, firm managers will face mature, family-conscious workers with much higher claims than the young migrant workers of the past. They will demand some productivity sharing. Because of the second turning point in 2020, China must elevate the overall real income of the population before the population starts shrinking, when growth will come only from technological progress and intergenerational transfers will become an overriding social problem. It will raise problems of labor regulation in the current decade.

Meanwhile, according to the Chinese Academy of Social Science, the rural labor force age < 25 is already 10 percent of total rural labor force, making only 17 million people, and under 30 it is 19 percent, making 33 million. It is much less than the demand for rural workers in urban areas. According to the 2009 migrant workers survey issued by the National Bureau of Statistics (NBS), migrant workers declined 8.9 percent in 2009 in the whole eastern region and 22.5 percent in the Pearl River delta, just at the time of the sharp recovery from the aftermath of the global financial crisis. Moreover, the rebalancing of growth to central and western regions, helped by government initiative has meant that the young migrants, who had returned to their original regions during the 2008 sharp slowdown, have found jobs there and have not returned to whence they came.

In a nutshell the transfer of migrant workers has shifted from a situation of excess supply to shortage. The immediate outcome is the shift in bargaining power and subsequent wage rise, all the more so since the government is backing the move with an incentive given to local government for a huge increase in minimum wage (20 percent a year expected until 2015). Several consequences will arise. On the supply side, manufacturers facing rising labor costs in eastern regions will either upgrade their production lines to higher value added products if possible, or relocate to regions where labor costs are lower. The first option implies investing in intangibles, human and organizational capital, therefore developing the service sector. The second involves rebalancing the structure of production on the territory, namely manufacturing in central China (the six provinces around Wuhan) and natural resource exploitation in the west with ecological concern and low-carbon efficient transportation systems. On the demand side, with a general rise in wages pushed by the shortage in the lower strata of income distribution and pulled by the demand for higher skills, the purchasing power of the middle class will increase steadily and foster a robust expansion of private consumption.

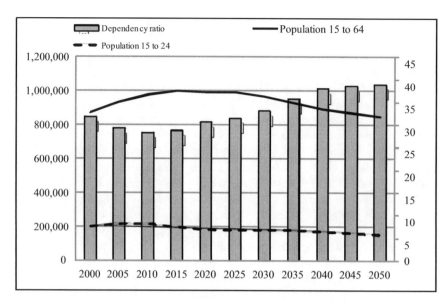

Figure 6.2 Demographic trends (2000–50).

Source: UN, demographic trends to 2050

However, labor tensions must be regulated for wage growth to become a central price in the oncoming growth regime.

Regulation of the labor market, corporate governance and civil society

The labor relation between workers and firm managers, which specifies in concrete situations the more general relation between labor and capital, is rife with potential conflicts. Furthermore, at the stage of development when the growth regime depends primarily on the steady increase in the real income of the population at large and on the development and diversification of the mode of consumption, overall demand fluctuations must be smoothed by inbuilt stabilizers in income determination. Historical experience in developed countries has shown that regulation of labor stemmed from institution building: union power, collective bargaining at the firm or industry level, labor law and labor jurisdiction, and social welfare in multiple dimensions (unemployment insurance, minimum wage, social assistance, social housing, tax policy, health care, and education).

In China labor relations raise specific theoretical and political problems. They compel researchers, who understand the reform as an interactive process of economic development and socio-political transformation, to make assumptions on the type of society the country is leading to. The cultural heritage, the decisive importance of social networks, and the basic understanding of the nature of the state in China, as we have defined in Chapter 1, will be accounted for. Most assumptions on plausible evolution in social institutions and political regime are addressed in the following last two chapters. However, in this chapter we assume that sustainable growth is the economic concept that makes intelligible the direction of reform from now on. This concept embodies the regulation of labor in economic terms and involves institution building. In a broader setting sustainable growth involves more participation of civil society in the provision of public goods and in social choices – what Amartya Sen calls real democracy.

In mitigating social tensions and endemic unrest, the questions are: how will labor conflicts be mediated at the firm level? In what respect will the capacity of the state to intervene in the economy influence the rebalancing of income distribution? How will the state be able to redirect the factors of production from fixed capital to human capital, from tangible to intangible assets? Will it be able to rebalance the structure of the economy away from the priority to export-led growth in avoiding transient mass unemployment and uncontrollable migrations? Sweeping reforms in governance are consubstantial to the transformation of the growth regime, which is jointly a mutation in the social model rooted in labor relationships.

The institutional setting to regulate the labor market is based upon the labor law of 1995. In principle it covered all employers and employees. It required written labor contracts, adherence to social security and payment of wages on time. As often in China, the legislation was not enforced. In 2005 only 50 percent of urban employees overall had contracts and no more than 10 percent of migrant workers in private companies.

In 2008 three new labor laws were introduced. The first is the *labor contract law*. This makes it mandatory to use written contracts, either fixed-term or open-ended. The Labor Inspectorate at county or higher administrative level has a duty to oversee labor contracts and to respond to complaints of workers and labor unions. The law also refines and specifies in more detail the employment protection rules. The second is the *law on arbitration and mediation in labor disputes*. This describes the procedures workers and trade unions can use to file complaints against employers in the arbitration tribunals. The third is the *employment promotion law*. It makes the government responsible for providing employment services, employment insurance, vocational training, and active labor market programs.

The new laws provide a comprehensive regulatory apparatus to empower workers so that they are actually paid for the work they have done. Specifically forced overtime and retention by employers of employees' property or money as security are forbidden. Employees must be consulted in the event of changes in work conditions relative to what is stipulated in contracts.

The problem is essentially enforcement in the private sector. Up until now employment protection has been applicable to SOEs and to some extent foreign companies. Enforcement depends crucially on how employee interests are represented and what effectiveness they have to strike compromises in labor conflicts. The conflicts have multiplied lately, mainly in the south-east, where many firms dedicated to exports were hurt by the slowdown in Western economies.

The new generation of workers is both older and more educated. They have aspirations of better working and living conditions and they are no longer afraid of directly confronting local management in the workshops. The organization of independent unions is likely to be a dead end since the Party will not tolerate independent associations of interests that can become the basis of a pluralistic political society. Employers cannot organize either. This is why clashes can erupt in different places in the open and multiply, but they stay scattered, having no legal way to connect and unify into class conflicts. However, news can be conveyed much faster throughout the nation via the Internet and can trigger debates the Party leadership would prefer to keep concealed. Indeed, the institutional building process that occurred with the New Deal in the US and post-World War II in Europe, a labor society based upon collective bargaining between social partners, has no political background in China. Nonetheless, social mediations must be built to deal with the aspirations of a civil society being transformed by the rise of a large middle class, by the much higher level of education, and by the demographic aging of the population.

In Western countries, financial capital has taken over the governance of corporations. Social compromises on income sharing that had regulated post-war growth have been destroyed and replaced by the overwhelming dominance of shareholder value in the objectives of the firms. Firms are ruled according to the interests of all potential shareholders, meaning that their strategic decisions are wrapped up in the tyranny of the stock market. The dominant power of finance has destroyed the former social compromises, weakening dramatically the share of labor in real national income of the main countries, chiefly the US, hampering upward social mobility and tying up people to the constraints of debt.

In China a similar deterioration in labor share of national income and deprivation of social rights has occurred in the second stage of reform under enforced capital-intensive accumulation described in Chapter 4. The power relationship has drifted to the benefit of SOE managers and local Party officials. The grabbing and giveaway of land has been the main driver of the distortions in social balance.

In both social universes the global crisis has revealed the unsustainability of pursuing the same social model. However, the process of change will not be generated by the same forces because the nature of sovereignty is quite different. In China the state is not infiltrated by capitalist interests as Western governments are. Even if the weight of private activities is ever growing and covers the largest share of GDP, the centrality of the state is paramount and provides political levers on the economy non-existent elsewhere. Labor laws were not enforced because the priority of the government was maximum growth via intensive capital accumulation. The change in priorities provides ethical justification to establishing law-based economic relations. Local governments in some major cities are running pilot programs, making local registration available to newcomers, education available to all on the same footing and allowing migrant access to subsidized rental social housing and medical insurance. At the firm level government can instruct official unions in big companies to take care of labor interests in the monitoring of the implementation of the labor laws. In the realm of wage determination, the state also has the capacity to set up wage guidelines on top of setting minimum wage. Already introduced to regulate the pay of employees in SOEs and differentiated among territorial administrative levels, they give benchmarks to firms on the pay levels practiced in a large array of occupations in many districts.

As we explain in the next chapter, the land market is pivotal in changing a nexus of power relationships that make corruption prosper. The struggle of the people in towns and villages to maintain or recover the right to allocate the use of the collective ownership of the land is citizen democracy. It is recognized by the constitution, politically legitimated by election, but largely confiscated by local bureaucrats, in collusion with corporate managers and urban developers. Most recently the news of an emblematic struggle of the residents of the village of Wukan in Guangdong was instantly spread on the Weibo (a Chinese version of Twitter). In a ten-day standoff with the police the residents took over the village. They elected their leader as the new Party chief of the village and forced the inter-vention of the Guangdong province political leader, who committed himself to look into their complaint about the illegal seizure of rural land. Even if they have not all succeeded, many incidents have arisen lately, which point to the increase in democratic consciousness that can be fostered from one place to another through the Internet. As long as the sovereignty of the unitary state remains legitimate – and all opinion polls show it is by far – an original mix of grassroots democracy in civil society and imperial leadership of the Party can work if the central govern-ment is responsive to social demands and can align the interests of the bureaucrats with the needs of the people.

Within corporations, labor must be able to organize either in appointing their delegates or in taking over official unions. Investing in the sense of reciprocity deep in Chinese culture, it might be possible to create a firm culture whereby loyalty of the workforce is traded against security of jobs and some sharing of productivity gains. Autonomous work teams might be encouraged and coordi-nation enhanced through strategic planning. Instead of achieving outward labor flexibility via the open labor market, an alternative corporate governance model can achieve inward flexibility in cooperation within corporations. It will have the advantage of reducing uncertainty in wage setting and limiting inequalities according to a stakeholder model of corporate governance.

Therefore a viable way to mediate social conflicts in industrial relations impinges upon corporate governance according to Asian style and models. The upgrading of firm efficiency in implementing strategic planning at the micro level, informed by the broad directions of the national plan, will be the most effec-tive means of adjusting to changes in the labor market and of acquiring more value added in production. To make the most of their planning, and to capture large pools of productivity, industrial companies must be able to benefit from much improved business services.

Upgrading industry and developing the service economy

Responding to price changes in labor and land

Two relative prices that have increased substantially lately can be critical for the location of manufacturing: labor costs and rental land costs. On average they amount roughly to 70 percent of total operating costs in manufacturing. The coastal cities have been the most hurt by their recent dramatic increase. Their rise impact both domestic and foreign companies. Referring to the latter, the Ministry of Commerce in 2009 launched its "Go Inland" campaign, focusing on six central provinces whose core city is Wuhan (capital of Hubei). The six provinces are Anhui, Jiangxi, Henan, Hubei, Hunan, and Shanxi. Together they account for 28 percent of population and 20 percent of GDP. The objective is to concentrate the bulk of manufacturing in central China and to invest in high-tech, R&D, technopoles, and high-grade business services in the large eastern cities and surrounding provinces.

Do government intentions meet the incentives of manufacturers? Depending on the destination of the output and the efficacy of transportation, the cost saving can outweigh (or not) the higher transportation costs. For that matter, the construction of high-speed railway tracks able to transport goods swiftly is a wise policy, contrary to what some prominent Western economists, who know nothing of China, peremptorily say. The problem resides with local government policies. To attract firms they are eager to distort prices, providing factory rentals at uneconomic discounts to offset land costs. Nonetheless, the rental costs differential between major south-east cities (Guangzhou, Shanghai, Shenzhen) and central cities including Wuhan is about two to one.

What about labor costs? Minimal wages have increased across the board without any trend in regional differences. But the scale of wages is not homothetic between regions and mandatory welfare payments can vary. All in all the Ministry of Commerce estimates that total labor costs are 60 percent less in central regions than in eastern regions. Therefore the total rental plus labor costs gives a serious cost advantage to the central regions. It is unlikely that transportation costs offset so large a cost advantage after the huge railway investment in the last few years.

However, the strategic decisions of companies go beyond cost advantages. The contribution of human capital in the production functions of different industries can be a prominent factor of choice, as long as recruiting high-skilled professionals is difficult in some regions. Some other industries are heavily determined by the proximity of key input suppliers (electricity and water) or marketing facilities. Therefore we should move beyond cost analysis and show how China, as well as other emerging-market countries, is revolutionizing industrial technology for the new world where consumer demand growth will come from a large population of low- and middle-income consumers.

Creating entrepreneurship and promoting indigenous frugal innovation

We have been accustomed to a division of labor where marketable creativity stems from Western multi-nationals and their vast network of sub-contractors and where other countries manufacture the goods in importing technology. This differentiation has been exploited to its utmost in China, which has become the "manufacturer of the world" through the well-known process trade.

According to standard growth theory, this is what catching up is all about. There is a technology frontier determined by the state of knowledge produced by investment in new technologies undertaken in the most developed countries. The technology is diffused according to different channels: buying property rights, welcoming technology-linked FDI, stealing, and imitating. The farther a developing country is from the frontier, the wider are the opportunities to assimilate the imported technology and the faster is its total factor productivity growth (TFP).

However, the ability to assimilate is limited by institutional impediments in developing countries. The distribution of economic power between the social strata that compound the domestic economy may hamper the development of a class of entrepreneurs. Corruption may hinder the political will and ability of the state to undertake basic investment in education, public health, and infrastructures. The political elite may fail to create the market institutions necessary to benefit from the opening to foreign influence. These considerations mean that there is no single best way from technological diffusion to social change. The process is interactive and mediated by politics. The lack of political leadership dedicated to modernization in embracing capitalism has often thwarted opportunities to start or thereafter to gain momentum in economic development. Adam Smith's high equilibrium trap, studied in Chapters 2 and 3, is a powerful brake to development in countries affected by a sharp rural–urban divide.

Box 6.2 Innovation and catching up in Schumpeterian growth theory

TFP growth and catching up

In Schumpeterian growth theory, the most recent technologies replace the old ones that have become obsolete (see Box 2.2). The process triggers growth dynamic in the leading countries. For the rest of the world there will be a region-specific catching-up process in TFP. The differential speed of catching up reflects the distance in TFP of the developing country to the frontier, modulated by the ability of the developing country to assimilate new technologies. The level of TFP in the country at the technological frontier (the US) is $A_{1,t}$. It is supposed to grow at the exogenous rate $\bar{g}$ a year: $A_{1,t} = (1 + \bar{g}) A_{1,t-1}$. The diffusion of technological progress to a country (i) is given by the following equation:

$$\frac{A_{i,t}}{A_{i,t-1}} = (1 + g_{it}) = [1 + \lambda^i] \frac{A_{1,t}}{A_{1,t-1}} \left[\mu_i' + (1 - \mu_i') \frac{A_{1,t-1}}{A_{i,t-1}} \right]$$

The first bracket captures the speed-up in the rate of diffusion of the technological progress of the leader, due to shortening the time of diffusion in technological innovations. It means that λ is an accelerator to the convergence in the growth rates. The second bracket embodies the catching-up effect due to the lag in the level of TFP relative to the leader A_1/A_i, the catching up being modulated by the brake μ, due to the difficulties to create the proper social conditions to assure a speedy diffusion.

Indigenous technological progress and mix of both sources of growth

A catching-up country is not condemned to solely import and assimilate foreign technology. It can develop its own brands of technological progress. There can be a second factor of TFP growth, function of home-grown intangible capital (h), both human and organizational, and tangible capital (k) required for innovation.

$$\frac{A_{it}}{A_{i,t-1}} = [1 + \gamma_i(h_{i,t}, k_{i,t})]$$

China can benefit from both sources of growth in proportion θ and $1 - \theta$, so that the rate of growth of TFP becomes:

$$\frac{A_{it}}{A_{i,t-1}} = \theta(1 + g_{it}) + (1 - \theta)(1 + \gamma_{it})$$

Nonetheless, China has largely overcome those impediments in the course of its reform since the late 1970s, as documented in Chapters 3 and 4. However, the growth in TFP has been attributed to the standard process of technological diffusion (Box 6.2, first paragraph) via intensive capital accumulation. But pursuing the same growth trajectory leads to violation of sustainability conditions defined in Box 6.1.

Why has indigenous technological development become an overriding goal in the present stage of reform? The answer is because the mode of consumption of developed countries can no longer be held as a model. The whole world is under the threat of unsustainability of the credit-induced, natural resource-wasting, and runaway pollution-emitting "American way of life." Catching-up countries must leapfrog the historical era of unlimited suburban housing cum universal car ownership and accelerated obsolescence of consumer goods. Indigenous technologies must be frugal.

Frugal technologies are not second-hand technologies. They are drawn from the most advanced pool of knowledge to create new lines of products. They give access to modernity to low-income populations and they are friendly to environmental constraints. Therefore they transform the technology frontier.

Frugal technologies are innovations that are adapted to low- and middle-income countries and that will be adopted by developed countries under the constraints of sustainability. Therefore they are reverse innovations. They combine low costs and creativity. They save the use of non-renewable resources and they have a low ecological footprint. Firms in emerging-market countries are best placed to undertake them because they are in the vicinity of large pools of demand for low-cost simple goods that allow only very thin unit margins. In China it might be the realm of private businesses.

Technological breakthroughs embodied in radically new products, bought first by Western elites and eventually trickling down, are far from being the bread and butter of innovations. Far more important economically are incremental innovations improving products and processes for hundreds of millions of people that will enter the middle class in the next two decades. Frugal innovation can stem from reconfiguring existing technology to spare the use of raw materials and to reduce the impact on the environment. China and India will compete in this incremental cost-cutting and environment-friendly innovation. Their firms can compete successfully against Western multi-nationals.

A few examples are provided in a special report by *The Economist* (April 17, 2010). A low-tech device with huge social use value is a water filter developed in India by Tata Chemicals. It uses rice husks to purify water. It is robust, relatively cheap (US$24 for initial investment and US$4 every four to six months depending on use to change the filter), portable, and can give an abundant supply of clean water for large families. Another improving health device is the hand-held portable electrocardiogram (ECG). It simplifies the handling, compresses the hardware, and can be packed in a small bag for transport. The price is divided by 2.5 compared with conventional ECG and the cost of the test is reduced to US$1 per patient. In China too Mindray is a company that specializes in cheap and easy-to-manipulate medical equipment. Similarly, Weigao is a Chinese firm that has built a research and manufacturing center for medical technology north-east of Beijing, which has entered a joint venture with the well-established American firm, Meltronics, to design and launch inexpensive novel products that Meltronics would not have made on its own. Weigao is just one of the firms that will allow China to become a major world force in medical technology in the present decade because sales of medical technology are exploding in China and because the Chinese government is planning to spend the equivalent of US$125 billion over three years to expand health care outside the big cities.

Medium-sized private companies can work in flexible networks of associated suppliers organized along mutual solidarity lines structured by their *guanxi*. It makes it easier to adjust to volatile demand with low spare capacities and short waiting lines. Consumer research centers in prominent cities can handle cultural complexities and fuzziness in taste to help in transforming new products brought by companies to suit local tastes in cosmetics, tooth paste, herbal tea, and the like. The most successful innovations are the ones which can create markets for people that had never consumed industrial products before. They rely on specific marketing able to approach poor people's day-to-day habits. To penetrate the countryside, local governments also have an important role to play in investing heavily in on-the-run education. For instance, teaching people basic hygiene is a prerequisite without which markets for soaps and detergents have no chance of taking root.

Western macroeconomists are used to providing complacent advice on shifting to a consumer model of growth without the slightest idea of what it means concretely. Frugal production inclusive of masses of poor people as customers requires new concepts of management and an entrepreneurship that China does not lack. The new management paradigm is based on conventional ideas: the consumer is king and economies of scale entail dramatic reductions in unit costs. However, these ideas are applied to an entirely new market environment. Potential demand stems from hundreds of millions of customers that have been excluded from the market economy up to now. What is happening is reminiscent of former paradigm changes that have extended consumer markets far beyond what was known beforehand. Such was the staff-and-line concept introduced by US companies in the 1920s to handle mass consumption in durable goods. It was also the case of the lean production concept implemented by Japanese companies in the 1960s. Just-in-time production returned a disadvantage (lack of storage space) into a strength. What is now at stake is turning the poverty of consumers into strength.

Because the private sector is so overwhelmingly important in China, frugal innovation will be a paramount driver of sustainable growth in the present decade. Indeed, in 2010 there were roughly 43 million companies in China, 93 percent of them were private and they employed 92 percent of the labor force. These companies need efficient services and capital to prosper. Transforming the service sector will be a most important piece in the new stage of reform.

Associating city development and environment protection

In a high-flying report published in March 2011 (*Urban World: Mapping the Economic Power of Cities*), the McKinsey Global Institute (MGI) heralded the incoming triumph of urban life in the developing world. A powerful database, Cityscope, covering 2,000 cities and gathering demographic and economic data in 2007, makes it possible to project city development paths to 2025. By that time, 600 of the largest cities around the world will have 20 percent of population and account for 60 percent of world GDP. The composition and ranking of the top 600 cities will be dramatically overhauled. As many as 136 new cities of the developing world will enter the top 600, with an overwhelming domination by China (100 cities out of 136).

Megacities are cities with population over the threshold of 10 million inhabitants. However, the type of cities that will contribute most to the growth of urban population through inward migrations, and also to the growth of income per capita, are not currently megacities but middleweight cities. In China, 216 middleweights are expected to contribute to 30 percent of global city growth between 2007 and 2025.

City development will be the driver of China's comeback to global prominence. From 2007 to 2025, the MGI expects Greater China (encompassing mainland China, Hong Kong, Macau, and Taiwan) to add 325 million inhabitants in the largest cities and generate 20 percent of world GDP, against 5 percent in 2007.

However, for these expectations to come true, long-horizon careful planning and high managerial skill are required. Indeed, large cities enjoy huge cost benefits and innovative demand, thanks to agglomeration forces. But cities generate countervailing dispersion forces due to diseconomies of scale through high land prices, congestion in transport, and pollution. To strike a better balance in overcoming dispersion forces, multi-level and multi-function strategic planning must combine strong infrastructure building, incentives to high-skilled jobs in the private sector and clever coordination of activities and interactions, so as to manage pollution.

Not all cities are alike by any means. Since China will have the opportunity to create and develop entirely new cities, the choice of models under the responsibility of urban planners must encapsulate preferences of people living in the cities, but also encompass environment constraints since structural choices will imprint city life for many decades, thus shaping modes of consumption of unborn people. Therefore we must first learn from the teachings of up-to-date economic theories of cities, and then draw lessons to get insights on the type of city planning that could be conducive to sustainable growth.

The dynamics of city agglomeration and dispersion

What makes cities so important? They are basically loci of increasing returns via processes of agglomeration of human interactions. Agglomeration stems from communication and information-intensive activities. They foster pure externalities, which are spatial if they are due to proximity. Those activities are characteristic of urban functions. Cities provide institutional architecture to marketplaces and shelter institutions of political coordination. They also produce superior business services: R&D, finance, marketing, management, and consulting, all functions that are sources of economic power. Cities are also places of symbolic power through cultural activities, conservatorship of historical memory, esthetical architecture, and providers of amenities. Power is concentrated in the centers of cities where direct human interactions are crucial.

Being essentially centers of coordination and knowledge, cities connect their talented inhabitants with one another by face-to-face interactions due to geographical proximity. Cities also weave distance interactions with the countryside and with other cities by information and communication technology (ICT), which offers virtual proximity. Both types of interactions are complementary and hierarchical, not substitutes. It is why the use of ICTs in almost every social activity has reinforced the leading role of centers, not weakened it. With the rise of global finance, a few megacities have become or are becoming global cities, as already perceived by Saskia Sassen in 1991 (*The Global City*).

Urban functions and processes of agglomeration

Post-industrial urbanization has two characteristics: inflows of migrants are growing faster the more populated the cities are; the share of services in employment and value added increases in cities with more complex activities. Knowledge and information processing are intensive upstream of material production in the conception and development of new products, and downstream in marketing and distribution. Production processes of those dematerialized activities involve intangible capital, chiefly human capital. They bear high fixed costs and fast-decreasing marginal costs with production size, e.g. strong increasing returns to scale. As long as the externalities at the origin of increasing returns are spatial in nature, they foster agglomeration conducive to face-to-face human interactions. This type of interaction combines increasing returns due to size and flexibility in coordinating conception, production, and distribution of differentiated goods.

Superior services are hubs of concentration in global city centers because intense cooperation of high-skilled human capital in top research laboratories is at the root of the production of new knowledge and because proximity to clients is necessary to provide complex and customized business services. These drivers of agglomeration are reinforced by information technologies. Being a non-rival good, information generates spatial externalities, the reason being that codified information and tacit information are complementary. The former requires heavy fixed costs for efficient distant transmission. The latter is face-to-face, human capital-intensive, and it deploys social connectivity in the spatial proximity of city centers.

Increasing returns trigger path-dependent processes. Cities can spring and develop endogenously and self-organize from an initial accidental impulse or from political will. Because space is naturally heterogeneous, some places have comparative advantages in natural resources or transport facilities. Agglomeration forces can start on small accidental spatial differences and launch irreversible, self-reinforcing concentration of people and activities with spatial externalities. However, if agglomeration forces get stronger with the concentration of activities they muster, why does the population of an entire country not gather in a single city? To understand why human space is organized in systems of cities interspersed with rural countryside, one must account for dispersion forces and the dialectic of agglomeration and dispersion.

Dispersion forces and urban sprawl

The main endogenous force of dispersion is generated by land and real estate values. Competition for the use of land due to the demand for proximity creates a rent of localization that determines the distribution of prices linked to land uses. There is an arbitrage between the price of land for residential and professional location on the one hand and transport costs on the other. It is easily observable that the share of land value in the price of real estate has been increasing in big cities.

Land generates rents because it is a non-produced commodity in fixed supply that is tradable because it has been made an object of private ownership. Land value is very badly regulated by market mechanisms because of the externalities that feed the demand for land use. Land is a localized and multifunctional commodity. Economically it is demanded for production, consumption, wealth accumulation, and pure speculation. Symbolically it is a means of power and social identity. It is why land prices exhibit a very wide spatial range of values among cities and within each city, together with a high dynamic volatility.

Transport costs impinge upon the distribution of goods and the daily two-way moves of people between house and work places. The equilibrium between dispersion and agglomeration is much affected by changes in transport costs because they affect the choices of mobile workers. Lower transport costs enhance agglomeration in city centers. However, it triggers a rise in land prices and wages in the centers. The latter rise in production costs induces delocalization of standardized services that can still be connected to the center and coordinated by formal information transmission. Therefore a city can sprawl, either homogeneously around the center, or more likely in creating multipolar cities when sprawl is itself structured by space heterogeneity.

Sprawl can be measured in many ways. A most useful one is density gradient. A generally accepted relation (Clark law) makes population density a decreasing exponential function of the distance to the center (Box 6.3). When expressed in logarithm the relationship becomes linear (Figure 6.3(a)). The density gradient is the slope of the straight downward sloping line. The lower the gradient, the higher the density at any given distance to the center. Looking at the relationship over time, a decrease in the gradient means an increase in density at any distance from the center. Therefore population increases faster at the periphery than in the center. This is urban sprawl. It is also shown on Figure 6.3(b) as a concave function of cumulative population as function of distance to the center. Sprawl is measured by the rate of increase of population at any distance to the center.

What determines the interaction between agglomeration and dispersion? On the consumption side, preferences for amenities attract people to the center if they have sufficient discretionary income. They depend on preference functions embodying environment and proximity of health care facilities. On the production side, the division of labor outsourcing services intensive in intangible capital, whose productivity depends on tacit knowledge, is a powerful factor of agglomeration.

Box 6.3 Measures of sprawl

Density gradient

Density of population (number of people by unit of space) d is an exponentially decreasing function of distance x to the center:

$$d(x) = d_0 e^{-\gamma x}$$

$$\log(d(x)) = \log d_0 - \gamma x$$

γ is the density gradient, e.g. the rate of decrease of population density with distance.

There is urban sprawl if $|\gamma|$ diminishes over time.

Index of sprawl of Lopez and Hynes

Density is computed in every elementary unit of census track. Density numbers are ranked in high and low density; h is the percent of units of high density and l the percent of low density. An index of sprawl is defined, which varies from 0 to 100.

$$IE = \left(\frac{l-h}{100} + 1\right)50$$

Index of sprawl of Burchfield

The decrease of the gradient is neither uniform with distance nor isotropic. Urbanized zones are interspersed with non-urbanized zones within cities. They are scattered in the agglomeration. This leapfrogging is measured by the following procedure. Space is carved in elementary units and the percent of non-urbanized space per km^2 is measured in each unit. The index is the average of percent for all units in the metropolitan area.

Index of compacity

The minimal circle containing the urban surface of the city is drawn. The index of compacity is the proportion of land effectively built within the circle.

The rise of average income can be a factor of sprawl if the consumption of space increases with real income and if cities develop under the endogenous forces of self-organization without any intervention of urban planners. On top of income

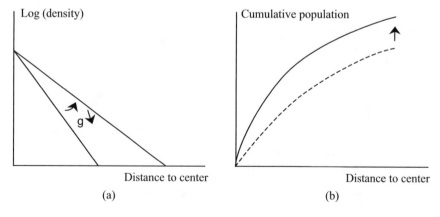

(a)   (b)

Figure 6.3 Urban sprawl.

growth, the technology of intra-urban transports is critical to determine if a city is compact or sprawled. When demand for space increases with income, land prices rise, entailing a shift of residential housing to the periphery. Density increases at the periphery and the gradient diminishes. The intra-urban migration to the periphery is magnified if the region around the city has plenty of free land and if individual cars are preferred because a dense road network is built. The network of road reduces the time of pendular commuting in and out the city center, augmenting the attraction of the periphery. It is the model of sprawled cities like Atlanta, Houston, and Los Angeles (Alain Bertaud 2004). Those cities, with one car for every adult, large houses, and air conditioning in every house, foster maximum pollution and energy consumption. The extension of such cities is only limited by higher prices of rural land with the ever expanding demand for space. The opportunity cost of rural land increases the purchase price of space at the periphery and limits the extension of the city. There is even worse. In Johannesburg, Brazilia, and Moscow the population density increases with the distance to the center up to 20 to 30 km! The positively sloped gradient lengthens the average distance to the center and raises the transport cost. Such an aberrant pattern reveals a completely broken land market. Conversely, Asian cities (Beijing, Hong Kong, and Bangkok) showed a well-behaved pattern of fast-decreasing density, indicating high gradient conducive to compact cities at least until the early 2000s (Figure 6.4).

What determines the interaction between agglomeration and dispersion? On the consumption side, preferences for amenities attract people to the center if they have sufficient discretionary income. They depend on preference functions embodying environment and proximity of health care facilities. On the production side, the division of labor outsourcing services intensive in intangible capital, whose productivity depends on tacit knowledge, is a powerful factor of agglomeration.

Compact cities shorten daily transports in distance and time. If there is an efficient public network of subways and buses to get to the center, local trips can be walked and cycled. Furthermore, a monocentric city reduces the number of trips because they are all convergent to the center. The sum of distance weighted by population is minimized if the city is both monocentric and compact, e.g. with a high density gradient. Furthermore, reducing the use of cars to a minimum in trips to the center releases space there for meaningful activities, because cars must park and compete in the use of scarce space, even though they are subsidized since it is impossible to charge parking the true value of rent, with the exception of Singapore. Therefore without city planning strictly limiting car parking via administrative rules, cars are sure to destroy the amenities of downtown areas. The proliferation of car parking in city centers is a gross misallocation of land at the expense of shops, offices, housing, and cultural buildings.

Moreover, the magnitude of air pollution is strongly related to the shape of cities. Low density, sprawled cities magnify air pollution generated by transport. Low density has a double harmful effect: it increases trip length and raises the proportion of car trips compared with public means of transport and local walking and cycling trips.

Nonetheless, the pressure of population migrating to megacities makes sprawl unavoidable. To regulate the expansion of big cities, long-term planning

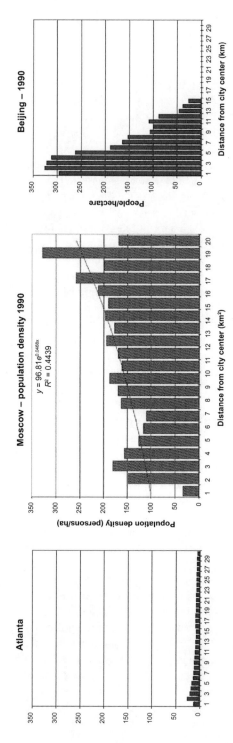

Figure 6.4 Sample of density profiles.

Source: Bertaud (2004)

legitimized by strong political will is essential. Strategic planning must coordinate the expertise of urban designers, transport engineers, and financiers. What does theory tell us about relevant models of large cities?

Multipolar cities and systems of cities

Let us spell out the challenge of city development. Cities exert a force of agglomeration like magnets. The pressure of inward population migration boosts land prices. Without any public regulation of the use of space, the land market is unable to allocate space efficiently because cities generate powerful externalities. The land market provokes anarchical sprawl and triggers a strong demand for individual modes of transport and the necessary web of roads. The result is a severe deterioration of the environment that is not conducive, to say the least, to sustainable growth. Strategic planning is essential to achieve three interconnected objectives: controlling urban sprawl, investing in collective transport infrastructures, forestalling the waste of natural resources, and preserving agricultural lands. What are the models of urban development best suited to guide strategic planning?

Multipolar cities make a late trend in urban growth. They are the outcome of complex interactions between the forces of agglomeration and dispersion and are hierarchical in the sense that the business historical center is predominant. The center houses the most acclaimed activities: higher education and research, finance and assurance, law services, media and marketing, historical and social amenities. Therefore such cities are still monocentric. However, instead of isotropic sprawl, there is an urban division of labor that shapes poles of differentiated activities. Each pole gathers consistent economic activities. Poles are localized along lines of communication, which are rivers, highways or railways. Because residential housing is more sprawled than employment, there are pendular trips from pole to pole on top of concentric trips.

Multipolar megacities are systems of cities. How are they organized? Agglomeration forces exist within specialized activities. When firms located in different places perform the same activities, their profit decreases with the distance between them (Box 6.4). When firms are agglomerated, workers must move to follow the labor market. They undergo a transport cost by unit of distance that is reflected in the wage. It is the force of dispersion. The concentration of firms doing business in the same activity is all the greater than the profit drawn from the gradient of density in the bundle of firms is higher relative to the transport cost of workers by unit of distance. Different spatial organizations arise depending on the value of this ratio. Practically one can observe three types of urban configurations: a complete dispersed structure, a center surrounded by multipoles and residential dispersed locations, and a single center location of the firms with sprawled residential housing. Polycentric structures are more likely if firm profit is not a linear but convex decreasing function of distance, meaning that the speed in the diminution of profit is slower the farther from the center of agglomeration. It follows that low transport costs favor compact cities, if the positive externalities of agglomeration are strong enough.

Considering now many sectors of production or different functions in production processes that can be outsourced, the organization of the firms in networks of production units generate spatial differentiations of urban poles with coordination separated from execution. It ensues that a system of cities depends on decentralized decisions driven by the forces of agglomeration and dispersion. Firms are looking for the proximity of markets for their products and the proximity of diversified labor market. Workers have more opportunities of jobs if they are close to diversified demand for labor. These are the forces of agglomeration. The forces of dispersion are the intensity of competition between firms, which is higher the closer the firms are to one another, and transport costs, which increase with the size of population. It follows that the gains from agglomeration rise with the size of the population up to an optimal size N*. However, because private agents take their decisions without being able to interiorize the externalities due to their interactions, the process of self-organization is inefficient. Cities become oversized. Only strategic planning can induce people to migrate to a new city in *investing preliminarily in infrastructures generating positive externalities*. It is what Chinese planners do, bewildering Western media unable to understand why they would wish to build empty cities. In so doing, strategic planning can build systems of cities in controlling the land market, so that externalities are internalized.

Box 6.4 Agglomeration of firms in a single sector of production

Let us consider a firm located in x and interacting with other firms located in a set of places $y \subset Y$. The impact of the distance d_{xy} on the profit of x is $\pi_{xy} = \beta - \alpha d_{xy}$, where α measures the intensity of the force of agglomeration. If $m(y)$ is the density of the firms located in y, the profit of x is: $\Pi(x) = \int_Y (\beta - \alpha d_{xy}) m(y) dy$

The intensity in the force of dispersion is measured by the cost of transport t by unit of distance. Therefore the concentration of the firms in x is the higher, the larger the ratio α/t.

If the function of profit is non-linear with the distance, $\pi_{xy} = \beta e^{-\alpha d_{xy}}$, and $\frac{d\pi}{d_{xy}} = -\alpha \pi$. The speed in the decrease of profit with distance diminishes as long as the distance increases.

The optimal size of cities depends on the types of activities that are gathered inside, because the forces of agglomeration are specific to the activities, while the forces of dispersion from land prices, transport costs, and congestion are the same whatever the sectors of production or the economic functions. It follows that cities have advantage to specialize. Because coordination functions, higher business services, and amenities generate stronger agglomeration forces than industry, the optimal size of a global city N_S* is higher than the optimal size of an industrial city N_I*. Nonetheless, relative prices of land and labor can adjust so that the net advantages from agglomeration are equalized in every city (Figure 6.5).

A nation can develop a hierarchical system of cities whereby the services of coordination in megacities satisfy the demand of industrial cities. Transport infrastructures, price of land, and relative wages in different locations determine an endogenous process of deconcentration and relocation of industrial activities that can move across regions. This is what the Chinese goal "Go West" will achieve.

Urbanization: the driver of sustainable growth in China

In his recent best seller, *Triumph of the City*, Edward Glaeser (2011) concludes:

> China's leaders seem to understand that high densities will enable their once poor country to become rich. They seem to get the fact that tall towers enhance productivity and reduce environmental costs. If China embraced height rather than sprawl, the world's carbon emissions will be lower, the planet will be safer from global warming, and China will be less dependent on the oil-producing nations of the Middle East.

Indeed, the Chinese leadership views sustainable growth and urbanization as two sides of the same coin. Four hundred million people will migrate from the countryside to cities and will become permanent dwellers in the next 20 years. The

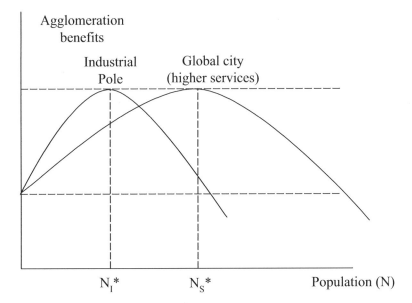

Figure 6.5 Diversity of cities by size and specialization.

choice of urban pattern to avoid sprawl and the subsequent strategic planning will be the linchpin of the growth model.

Theoretical teaching described in this chapter provides guidelines to the planning process of city development. To use resources most efficiently, multipolar cities must build on strong compact urban cores. To regulate the price of land urban developers should build taller to get more housing space per square meter of land. Denser development at and close to the urban core is the only way to guarantee environmental sustainability. Strong core cities depend crucially on human capital. Massive education investment enables business centers to produce the services that hugely enhance productivity per capita. Migration from the countryside is the best way to eradicate poverty. With the subsequent overhauling of agricultural land that will become more concentrated, productivity will increase substantially in the farms too. Strengthening complementarity between dynamic cities and their hinterland will overcome the urban–rural divide decisively.

However, harmonious development will not happen spontaneously. Cities can create huge inequalities because high density has costs. To combat those costs and deliver basic public services to everyone, the government must engineer massive investment in clean water and sanitation, health care services, and good public schools. Contrary to what is being done at present in China, combining both equity and efficiency in social services is better achieved by funding at the national rather than the local level. Going this way would require drastic changes in the fiscal system that is discussed in the next chapter.

Affluent cities are consumer cities. However, the prerequisite for innovative consumption are the basic public services: security, fast and reliable public transport to commute to the center, good schools, and affordable social services. Without the huge investment able to provide such social infrastructure, the routine call to redeploy the share of domestic demand to consumption is just small talk. To link infrastructure investment to sustainable growth, we must dig deeper into city development.

China's growth potential in city development

For the time being, China has two mega cities (more than 10 million inhabitants): Beijing and Shanghai. According to MGI projections, in 2025 it will get six new more: Tianjin, Guangzhou, Shenzhen, Wuhan, Chongqing, and Chengdu. Together they will make up 25 percent of national GDP. They will attract the most talented people and a lot of FDI. They will be centers of clusters of smaller poles, according to the multipolar systems of global cities. Those poles will be middleweight cities of population less than 5 millions. Network effects within those clusters will spur economic growth.

The urbanization drive in China, and to a lesser extent in India, will decisively shift the center of gravity of the world economy from West to East. Greater China is expected to get half of the new 250 million city households that will accrue worldwide between 2007 and 2025 – obviously a huge consumer potential if the right urban policies are consistently pursued. In doing so, a tight complementarity will be maintained between infrastructure investment and consumer demand in goods and services. Therefore consumption per capita can rise steadily without any augmentation of the share of consumption in GDP. To repeat again for people who want to see the share of investment diminish in China, transportation and affordable housing in compact cities are two of the most capital-intensive sectors in the economy. China may need to construct 800 to 1,500 new metro railways and subways and build 1.6 to 1.9 billion square meters per year to 2025.

Investment in education and correlated high-skilled services are essential for the fast growth of households with sufficient income to support discretionary spending. In the new mega and middleweight cities, China will be able to get 75 million more middle-income households (income >US$20,000) and 30 million higher income households (income >US$70,000) between 2007 and 2025. If urbanization can proceed at this speed, it can be expected that mega and middleweight city GDP growth could be 9 percent per capita and 2.5 percent population growth mainly via migration, making total city economic growth of 11.5 percent in the 2007–25 period. It will be enough to get the nation's overall growth at or over 8 percent.

Strategic planning is the key

At this point the question arises: can China live up to the expectations of its future? Absorbing 400 million people into cities in 20 years is a huge task. If successful it will project China into the realm of developed countries. To succeed the most efficient models of city growth must be implemented. We know that this model is made up of a few megacities and systems of multipolar monocentric megacities. A substantial part of city development will be inland. Wuhan in the central part of the country will be the hub for the migration of industries. Chongqing and Chengdu will be the base camps for the Go West strategy.

In the March 2009 *China Quarterly Review*, Tom Miller takes the case of Wuhan (Miller 2009). The geographical position of Wuhan in central China is ideal. Striding the Yangtze River at the confluence with the Han River, Wuhan is at the junction of the fast-track railways linking the main megacities: north–south from Beijing to Guangzhou, and east–west from Shanghai to Chongqing and Chengdu. Wuhan is a major education center, which makes it a magnet for migrations. The pressure of population growth makes it imperative to adopt a multipolar system, which will absorb from five to 12 million people. The poles of development will be diversified enough to create employment opportunities so that daily pendular transit to and from the city center will be minimized. The transport plan foresees express ways and railways to link all satellite cities to the core. Strict regulation will be enacted to prevent urban sprawl and keep the core urban area compact. Enormous infrastructure investments (bridges and tunnels across the Yangtze) are being made prior to the city development in order to relieve traffic bottlenecks. At odds with other developing countries that allow sprawling suburb to contaminate their megacities, Chinese planners think that investing in infrastructures comes first. Public services, like treatment of waste water and a massive house-building program, is underway.

The biggest problem, not handled yet either in Wuhan or elsewhere, is the problem of social services that would equalize social benefits for migrants and the local population of the city. This fundamental problem links the pattern of urbanization to income distribution and to social equity. Full social security is necessary for social stability within global cities. But the present fiscal system in China, whereby local governments have grossly insufficient revenues to meet their commitments, precludes large developing cities from achieving their social goals. As already noticed, a substantial overhaul of fiscal responsibilities, increasing substantially the responsibility of central government in providing social services, is inescapable. Migrants must have access to these services to be able to settle with their families in the cities and become urban consumer households. Raising the role of central government will also have the added advantage of improving the consistency of strategic planning over the whole territory of mainland China.

Furthermore, the potential for consumer growth in large cities can only be enhanced if the distribution of goods is improved and the costs of logistics are drastically lowered, together with the development of frugal technology able to make industrial goods affordable to income groups in the US$5,000 to US$10,000 annual income range, as mentioned in the preceding section of this chapter.

Finally, despite the massive urban drive, the rural population will still be enormous. In 1950 the Chinese population was almost entirely rural. In 2007 rural population still made 55 percent of the total according to the National Bureau of Statistics. The rural–urban divide was somewhat crystallized by the *hukou* (household registration) system. Each individual was bound to an urban or rural location depending on the place of his (or her) birth. It was a means of spatial control to avoid the disorderly flow of migrants swelling slums in the uncontrollable sprawling suburbs of Mumbai, São Paulo, Lagos, and the like. Alleviating the *hukou* system has become a major headache. Experimentation is being done in Chongqing and Chengdu to allow peasants to sell their rights on land use if they are in constructible expanding urban areas and still keep their rights on other parts of rural land. The objective is to incentivize them to migrate to cities with enough resources to hope for social housing and schools for children so that they have good opportunities for social upward mobility in expanding cities.

Urban development and energy saving

Energy saving is a key link between urban development and sustainable growth. Multipolar cities must be green cities. Energy saving must be found in the pattern of cities. Compact urbanization is more energy efficient than sprawl. But much more can be done. As analyzed in the modeling of sustainable growth in the first section, energy saving can chiefly be improved with price policies undertaken by the government to provide guidance to the behavior of economic agents so that they rationally act for the sake of higher energy efficiency and lower carbon emissions.

Energy saving depends on major innovation in energy production, either in investing in renewable low-carbon energy resources and in using primary energy sources in producing electricity with lower carbon emissions. China's government has prioritized strategic industries where it wants the country to upgrade to the technological edge. The policies to reach leadership in new environmental technologies are addressed in the last section of this chapter.

However, there is much more to do. Choices in means of transport and in everyday consumption are sources of diffuse pollution and environmental degradation. According to GlobalStat, by Enerdata, the share of urban energy consumption in the total energy consumption of the countries in 2008 was 27 percent in China and 30 percent in India, against 70 percent in France and UK and 76 percent in the US. What this means is the impossibility of imitating Western modes of consumption, as long as China urbanizes and income levels rise. An energy-efficient mode of development cannot depend on technology alone. Inventing new modes of consumption is the quest of our times. This is possible because the relationship between energy consumption and GDP is very loose for countries at roughly the same level of income per capita. The comparison between Japan and the US is striking for population density and the use of cars, with radical consequences for energy consumption (Table 6.1). Compact cities instead of sprawl and much higher taxes on energy consumption have led to energy efficiency in transport three times higher in Japan than in the US. The lesson is that China should eschew the American way of life and follow the Asian method of organization of space and modes of consumption. With strategic planning it is even possible to leapfrog what have been trends in developed countries and invent twenty-first-century modes of consumption. In order to explore low-energy consumption urban policies, the Chinese Council for International Cooperation on Environment and Development summoned a task force in 2009 to make recommendations on policies that should be embodied into urban planning.

The main result of country comparisons is not surprising: the lower the price of energy, the larger the consumption of space for urban sprawl, the more intensive the use of cars, and the higher the consumption of energy and the emission of greenhouse gases. Therefore city planning in China must decouple urban energy consumption and rise in income. Furthermore, CO_2 emission abatement can be directly achieved by a carbon tax sufficiently high ($\sim$ US\$50 the ton of non-emitted CO_2) to be dissuasive in shaping the mode of private consumption. The Chinese government has already embarked in a stepwise rise in energy prices. A carbon tax would complete the change in relative prices to trigger thermic isolation of housing, if supported by subsidies for lower-income households. Moreover, in compact cities with rapid and reasonable frequent public transportation to and from the center, walking and cycling to move within the center would combine an environment-friendly and health-enhancing way of life. Electric cycling might be an effective way to combine low-energy transportation and mobility in cities with undeveloped public transportation. However, the support to the automotive industry in the 2009-stimulating plan was contradictory to the long-run goal of sustainable growth. More generally the coordination between urban

Table 6.1 Use of cars and energy consumption in the US and Japan in 2008

	US	Japan
GDP per capita	US$43,000	US$37,000
Average density	31 pers./km^2	350 pers./km^2
Cars per household	2.4	1.2
Energy consumption due to transports/pers/year	1.82	0.6

Source: GlobalStat, by Enerdata, 2008

planning, infrastructure construction, and public transport management is less than satisfactory. Only with stronger involvement of central government might it improve substantially.

For the time being, no uniform rule exists to prioritize public transportation nationwide. Therefore land pre-emption, financing of infrastructures, and legal rights to operate transportation networks have no common legal framework for planning. Central government does not subsidize enough of the financing of public transport to have its say in the management of the system. Too low tariffs push public transport firms into deficits and downgrade the quality of the service. Consequently higher income people, especially in eastern provinces, make the choice of individual cars and poorer people are deprived of the proper organization of space that would allow them to improve their quality of life.

Imitating Western modes of consumption is the most serious threat for China's development. It would go on exacerbating social inequalities and degrading the environment. Controlling urban energy consumption is the only way to satisfy the needs and the aspirations of the majority of the population in the cities. We are back to our analysis of social welfare and real wealth at the beginning of this chapter. GDP per capita is no longer the proper indicator of development. Reducing energy consumption, while planning multipolar compact cities with the right investments in infrastructures and education, will enhance real wealth in its human and environmental components. To firmly stick to sustainable growth policy, strategic planning should set standards and objectives of energy consumption at the municipal level and use price incentives. The NDRC should monitor the achievement of objectives at the national and municipal levels. It is possible only if the rhythm and pattern of urbanization, the modes of transportation, and the environmental impact are integrated into national strategic planning.

Economic development and climate change

Let us revert to the modeling of the social welfare function linked to the condition of sustainable growth paths displayed in Box 6.1. This function assumes that environmental services are not perfectly substitutable with consumption. The long-term protection of environment should be pursued *per se* for the path of the economy to be sustainable. It is the paramount long-term goal that strategic planning should convert into environmental long-term investment, the social return of which must be calculated using the ecological discount rate. This rate should be lower the higher the price is of environmental services relative to private consumption, so that the long-run return of investments for a low-carbon future is revealed.

Furthermore, there are radical uncertainties in the chain of interactions between the chosen target (limiting the rise in global temperature) and the policies worked out to meet the target. The reason is that the complex chain of interactions encapsulates non-linear feedbacks that can deliver catastrophic outcomes. It means that under present knowledge the aggregate discounted welfare function has a fat-tail probability distribution of catastrophic climate change. The very nature of the systemic risk involved by climate change stands out. In financial systemic crisis not all asset classes are struck by losses. High-powered money stands out as pure liquidity against all other assets and polarizes the behavior of people in search of a refuge. In systemic climate crisis there is a possibility that overall damages strike all asset classes. All the components of real wealth might suffer disastrous losses worldwide.

The threat of those dire scenarios vindicates the precautious approach required to undertake the shift to sustainable growth as early as possible. Keeping risks at an acceptable level (no more than a 2°C rise in average world temperature) means checking the rise of, then reversing greenhouse gases (GHGs) concentration as early as possible. Postponing action is not an option because there is a danger of lock-in to high emission paths due to the long lifetime of carbon-intensive energy infrastructures.

The challenge humankind faces is worldwide. It is true that the capital-intensive growth regime pursued after the mid-1990s has made China the most energy and carbon-intensive economy. China's economic structure is highly dependent on coal for power generation and on heavy high-polluting industries (iron and steel, cement, aluminum, and the like). Transforming the economic structure into a low-carbon knowledge-based economy is a daunting task. It implies a massive transformation of the energy mix and the energy-intensive use in the transport and building sectors. China must achieve deep carbon reduction, which is no less than decoupling emissions from growth. There is an inertia that makes emissions go on climbing because of the lack of available new large-scale technologies. To respect the 2°C cap on temperature rise, a viable scenario was studied by the Stockholm Environment Institute and the Chinese Economists 50 Forum in 2009 (*Going Clean: The economics of China's low-carbon development*). It shows that emission intensities have been growing from 3.6 tons CO_2 per capita in 2005 and will go on growing but at declining speed to top 5.3 in 2017 and then will decline precipitously to 1.3 in 2050.

Structural transformation of this magnitude at such a speed for the peak of emissions to arise at the shortest time entails high transition risks. Intense innovations must occur in almost every corner of the economy. There will be massive depreciation of existing capital with early retirement. Disruptive destruction of capital can induce disturbing job losses. For the process to be politically feasible and socially acceptable, social and labor market policies are needed on a large scale. Labor market policies should be pursued actively to increase labor mobility across industries and regions and to invest massively in education and retraining. Those policies are addressed in the next chapter.

We have dealt with the problem of transport, housing, and appliances pollution in the preceding section in showing that improvements depend on the model of urbanization. We now look at China's government priorities in energy saving and raising energy efficiency in industrial sectors on the one hand, and in investing in renewable energy primary sources and capturing carbon in power generation on the other. We conclude with government policy actions on the pricing of energy and of carbon on regulation and financing.

Energy saving in industry and environmental protection

In 2008 the Chinese government published its *White Paper on China's Policies and Actions for Addressing Climate Change*. In 2009 the NDRC issued a progress report as part of the follow-up of the clean energy policy enacted by the State Council in the 11th five-year plan. The objectives were multifold. The first was to upgrade the productive structure in ten major industries (real estate, automobile, non-ferrous metals, iron and steel, equipment manufacturing, IT, textiles, ship-building, petrochemicals, and light manufacturing). For automotive and heavy transformation industries, the objective was establishing more rigorous standards on energy consumption per unit of product. In these industries and in shipbuilding it was also to phase out outdated production capacities. Moreover, pilot projects were launched to promote circular economy, e.g. to recycle waste in resource utilization. In light manufacturing, the objectives were raising energy efficiency in appliances and reinforcing economic incentives for energy-saving products. Lighting (energy-saving lamps) and ten categories of appliances were targeted. Investment in low-carbon renewable energy was scaled up, including photovoltaic solar energy, wind power, biomass, and bio ethanol fuel. Finally, efforts were made to mitigate GHG emissions in agriculture and to promote afforestation to increase carbon sequestration.

In October 2010 the State Council decided to target seven strategic industries with objectives at the horizon of 2015. Among those industries, three directly concern energy: energy saving and environmental protection, new energy, and new energy cars. The other four are: new generation IT, bio-technology, high-end equipment, and new materials. Although the objectives are at the horizon of 2015, their development will last much longer. In 2020 four of them (energy saving and environmental protection, new generation IT, bio-technology, and high-end equip-ment) are programmed to achieve a technological edge. In 2030 they all should be the pillars of China's sustainable growth. This is significant because right now manufacturing makes 55 percent of final energy consumption. By 2009 China consumed seven times as much energy per unit of output as Japan and six times as much as the US. Therefore improving energy efficiency is the primary goal. Ambitious objectives are the reduction by 17.3 percent of energy consumption by

GDP unit in the 12th five-year plan (2011–15) and 16.6 percent during the 13th plan (2016–20). Correlatively oil consumption is expected to be cut by 10 percent in 2015 and CO_2 emissions by 40 to 45 percent per GDP unit in 2020.

Investing in high efficiency energy-saving equipment will contribute to the objectives. In iron and steel there will be a switch to electric arc furnaces. In cement improvement will come from a lesser content in concrete. In paper and pulps and in wood and wood products there will be greater use of biomass and agricultural residues. In lighting that absorbs 12 percent of power consumption, compact fluorescent lamps (CFL) can save 80 percent of power compared with incandescent bulbs.

Electric power generation is the most important production process that emits CO_2 since it is heavily coal-dependent. Coal accounts for 70 percent of China's energy consumption, much more than in the rest of the world. In 2015 the government hopes for a decline of the share of coal to 64 percent and non-fossil energy including nuclear power to reach 10 percent, the rest being produced with oil and natural gas. The best way to reduce emissions is early retirement of inefficient coal-fired electricity generation and large-scale deployment of efficient coal-fired power with carbon capture and storage. The new power plants will capture 90 percent of CO_2 emitted. However, the technology is still far from commercialization. The new power plants will be available after 2020. For the time being, costs are high and storage capacity uncertain.

Meanwhile, China is investing massively in new renewable energy to shift energy mix from coal to other sources. Non-fossil primary energy includes wind power, solar panels and solar photovoltaic, bio mass and hydropower plants, plus significant increase in nuclear power. The latter raises great hope in China, driven by technology transfer of third-generation reactors and investment in equipment and components. Wind power is a very promising source of primary energy in the long term. China has already surpassed the US and become the world's largest wind turbine market in 2009. In the short term the power grid is a bottleneck because wind turbine capacity increases much faster than grid network construction. The NDRC makes expanding grid network construction a priority to mobilize idle capacity. It favors a "go offshore" strategy because coastal areas are well grid-connected, at the expense of Inner Mongolia and the north-east where grid congestion may last a few more years. Solar power has less potential because the solar cell-producing industry is itself very energy intensive. The cost of solar power is high relative to other new energy sources, which is why although China is the world's largest solar power equipment maker, it lags behind in solar power installation. The retardation is aggravated by the low grid connection of solar power plants. It is most useful for solar farms in the western, non-connected part of the country.

It follows that building smart grids is one of the most useful investments in developing new energy. The NDRC is planning a smart grid capable of long distance and high voltage transmission. The smart grid will enhance safety, improve energy efficiency, and eliminate bottlenecks to release the large energy capacity that is being built. The smart grid will be developed through stages to 2020.

New energy cars are also very strategic. The government aims to make China the world leader in high energy efficiency and low emission cars. This is consistent with the development of high density cities. The State Council has announced investments in hybrid cars, in electric cars, and in part associated industries: fuel cell, battery, motor, and electric control systems. Electric cars are the radical solution to drastically abate GHG emissions in transportation. Not only do they cut emissions but they are much more energy efficient than traditional cars. The inconvenience now is the slow charging speed and the lack of charging stations. However, the 12th five-year plan is focusing on improving quality. The government is subsidizing new energy car purchases in five pilot cities (Shanghai, Shenzhen, Changchun, Hangzhou, and Hefei). The role of the government is critical in a nascent industry because cash flow is negative throughout the value chain. The government will finance the infrastructure of charging stations and will tax ordinary cars to help the purchase of electric cars. The goal is for electric cars to account for at least 17 percent of market share by 2020.

Environmental protection does not only stress policies to mitigate climate change. It also relies on policies to adapt to climate change. They are dedicated to agriculture, forests, and other natural resources. Because China has many dry regions, water conservation and irrigation must be improved to increase grain production capacity. Agro research is being pursued strenuously to improve varieties of seeds and to optimize the structure of breeds. Massive investment in forests and other natural ecological systems is being undertaken. Forests are carbon pits. A nationwide campaign for afforestation has been launched to arouse the initiative of collective owners of forests. Local governments have an obligation to prevent and control desertification. Infrastructures are built to increase the water supply capacity of the water conservancy system. Because the price of water is too low in China, despite the scarcity of the resource, raising the price will provide the incentive to reduce water consumption in industrial use. To reverse the degradation in biodiversity the government has established 18 areas for marine ecology monitoring in the coastal zones where the waters are protected. To enhance marine ecological systems, mangrove woods are planted and coral reefs are protected. Finally, contingency plans are laid out to deal with the health consequences of natural disaster, such as contagious diseases involving the climate factor.

Pricing carbon and financing innovation

In exposing the drawbacks of the capital-intensive growth regime in Chapter 4, we have repeatedly underlined the distorted price system that makes capital allocation inefficient and consumption inimical to the environment. Energy and water resources have been grossly underpriced to maximize the growth of heavy industry and to make China the world's manufacturing base for cheap consumer goods and equipment. Interest rates are too low and many services are priced too high to induce both attractive capital returns and shifts in consumption toward a service-pioneered economy. This is the structure of domestic prices and not the exchange rate that raises problems. The transition to sustainable growth makes comprehensive price reform imperative.

Here we focus on the price of carbon, the importance of which for sustainable growth we have already demonstrated theoretically in the first part of this chapter. A relevant carbon price is at the core of any strategy to cut emissions and increase energy efficiency. A country capable of strategic planning has a decisive comparative advantage because climate change is an utter market failure. No carbon price will ever appear spontaneously. Government policy must create the market in interiorizing environmental externalities. However, introducing a high enough carbon price (we suggested above a minimum of US$50 per ton of CO_2 abated) is a political challenge, because it makes goods and services more expensive. It is a regressive wealth distribution, making a uniform across-the-board tax socially unacceptable and therefore politically unfeasible. The first move should be to phase out all subsidies on fossil fuel as part of an overall price reform aimed at overhauling the allocation of capital. Then implementing a carbon price raises the following questions. Which mechanism to choose? Which price range and how to alleviate the distributional effects on the poor? *The Stockholm Environment Institute and the Chinese Economists 50 Forum* has made suggestions. There are two mechanisms, a carbon tax or a cap-and-trade market. They can be made equivalent in principle. Theory does not say anything decisive on the choice. Neither the one nor the other can be said to be welfare-superior. The choice is entirely political. It involves institutional feasibility, acceptability, and simplicity.

Carbon taxes are environmental taxes on carbon dioxide. They reduce emissions through the lower demand of high-carbon products. One regime is a direct fuel tax, e.g. an input tax on primary fuel. Another is an indirect tax, e.g. an output tax on output products. With the second mechanism the key for acceptability is the ability to measure the carbon content of goods, thus the volume of emissions, reliably. If the carbon tax is a means in the manifold policy for energy saving and environmental protection described above, the carbon content of fossil fuel inputs should be taxed to exploit all cost-efficient abatement options. Because China is so dependent on coal, the level of the carbon price should be calculated so that the price of coal increases 10 then 20 percent. In any case, part of the revenues from the carbon tax must be redistributed to alleviate its negative social impact.

A cap-and-trade system sets up a carbon price through the trading of emission rights. Those rights are made explicit and transferable. The market values them and, in a global market, emissions could be reduced wherever it is cheapest to do so. The national system could be linked to the global one on condition there is a single universal carbon price. However, no such harmonization would exist for long. If China decides to pilot a system to learn trading on small volumes, it must do it for its own sake. Indeed, there are pitfalls in implementing such systems. One is the measuring. Emissions will be measured and monitored on an individual basis and individual emitters will be identified and charged adequately. It requires a sophisticated administration.

Another is the distribution of permits. If they are freely distributed, incentives to reduce emissions are distorted. Polluters who expect that allocations of permits will be updated will invest more in dirty technologies to increase their emissions in order to get more free permits in the future. The system will be locked in the bad technologies because existing plants will stay in operation to get free permits. Then giving for free permits that have a monetary value encourages intense lobbying from private interests who act to influence the government. Therefore only the auctioning of permits should be chosen. Polluters are made aware of their carbon costs, which is the purpose of the mechanism. The revenues of the auction accrue to government, which can redistribute to low-income groups and invest in the development of new technologies. Therefore auctioning provides stronger incentives for technological innovation.

What should be China's choice? Since urbanization is the backbone of the new growth regime, a carbon tax is better suited to cut urban emissions. It can be integrated in the broader reform of the tax system in the existing structure of government without requiring any institutional change. A cap-and-trade system might be created later when an international agreement on a world carbon price will make it possible in a global carbon market.

A carbon tax system on top of subsidy removing on fossil fuel will provide financial resources for urban infrastructure and innovative investment in new energy and new energy cars. Electric cars and carbon capture and storage will absorb hundreds of billions of dollars to develop the technologies to the commercial stage. Other self-generating resources will be the cost saving from lower energy use. Social costs will also be cut from less risk of natural disasters, from improving public health and revenues accruing from labor-intensive jobs if the right model of urbanization is developed.

Apart from current profit in the public sector, the main source of finance for investments in renewable energy will still be credit from the banks to state-owned utilities. Nonetheless, other sources of finance will have to play an increasing role over time. China is not able on its own to bear the burden of generating the financing and technological resources needed to achieve the common objective of limiting temperature rise to 2°C. This is why at some time a global cap-and-trade system will become essential to regulate the effort shared among nations. Developed countries should buy emission rights from China, so that China can receive financial resources to follow a more ambitious emission reduction trajectory. A hybrid system will be developed in China, mixing a tax and cap-and-trade system with price floor and ceiling and linked to the global system.

Conclusion

In the next 20 years or so world capitalism will undergo a transition to a new regime of growth. Like other times in history since the beginning of industrial revolution the dynamic of capital accumulation has been hampered by a financial crisis that revealed the inability of the incumbent institutions to tame the multiple contradictions generated by the existing growth pattern. In every transition the driver of structural change is a wave of generic innovation capable of overhauling the whole production structure and spreading over all sectors of the economy.

In early twenty-first-century China, the insuperable contradictions stem from the huge waste of human, social, and natural capital due to deep distortions in the price system that have engulfed powerful vested interests within the state bureaucracy. Those contradictions make the present path of capital accumulation unsustainable.

The generic innovation to redirect capital accumulation is both social and environmental. Optimizing total real wealth of the nation should replace maximizing GDP growth as goal of strategic planning. This means revaluing all types of resources that have been massively underpriced: labor, savings, energy, rural land, and environment. Price reform should be the linchpin of the new mode of regulation. It cannot be accomplished without big changes at all levels of administration and corporate establishment to give more say to the people. Environment-friendly urbanization backed by universal social welfare should be the driver to achieve a less unequal social structure and postmodern mode of consumption. Such a common goal, if promoted by strong political leadership and steadily pursued in strategic planning, involves a huge investment in education and R&D aimed at lifting global factor productivity in China to the technological edge.

The next chapter researches how the all-important reform in the price system and associated change in the bureaucratic governance could be made.

7 A road map for the transformation of China's economic structure

Chapter 6 elaborated the concept of sustainable development and laid down the theoretical framework for its pursuit. It accentuated the indispensability of strategic planning in revealing integrated social welfare for the long run, and setting prices for externalities and discount rate that reflect real intergenerational risks. As China is facing ever-stronger challenges from demographic transformation, rapid urbanization, climate change, and environmental deterioration, maintaining the current capital-intensive, export-led growth regime would only destroy total wealth and deepen social conflicts. Yet if China's strategic planning could succeed in synchronizing macro trends with welfare-enhancing structural changes under the framework of sustainability, challenges could well be translated into chances. Such is the dialectic Chinese concept of "danger-chance" ("wei ji"). In this chapter our main task is to demonstrate how such a transition is attainable, and how China's road map to sustainability could deploy.

In the past ten years Chinese political leaders and economists have repeatedly expressed their concerns over the imbalances and unsustainability of the Chinese economy. It has been widely acknowledged that the Chinese saving rate has been disproportionately high and there has been considerable over-investment and overcapacity in many industries. As domestic consumption has been sluggish, export-dependency of the economy deepened and since 1994 China consistently has run a current account surplus (widened markedly between 2004 and 2008). Meanwhile, such an investment-heavy growth model exacerbated domestic social and regional inequalities, as well as accelerated natural resource depletion and environmental deterioration.

All these structural problems urged the Wen Jiabao administration to launch multiple rebalancing measures immediately after they took office in 2003. Structural adjustments under this administration were usually intertwined with macroeconomic policies. Restructuring endeavors were the most intense when Chinese economy experienced overheating (e.g. 2004 and 2006), while the enforcement of those restructuring measures would often relax when economic growth slowed down. Although monetary policies were also integrated, the main restructuring mechanisms involved administrative regulations directly on investment processes, such as: raising capital requirements for capital-intensive industries; restricting the construction of development zones; controlling the supply of land,

and tightening NDRC's sanctions for new projects. Preferential industrial policies were also exercised to curb the growth of energy-intensive, pollution-heavy, and natural resource-based productive activities. Tax rebates for such industries were eliminated in 2006. Inefficient and surplus production capacities in industries, such as coal mining, thermoelectricity generation, and iron production, were shut down on a large scale. In order to alleviate trade imbalance, in July 2005 the PBoC also declared the start of exchange rate reform. In the following three years, RMB appreciated 22 percent against US dollars.

Briefly the Chinese government demonstrated strong interest in rebalancing the economy and in leading development onto a more sustainable and welfare-enhancing path. In both the 11th and 12th five-year plans, Chinese government envisioned beautiful pictures of a harmonious society. The problems of all facets of Chinese society are accurately identified in those plans and directions for correcting those problems are also given. However, all endeavors seem to have been in vain. Not only has the economy not shown any signs of rebalancing, but all the imbalances discussed above have increased at an accelerated pace.

Table 7.1 breaks down GDP by categories of expenditure from 1978 to 2010. We can clearly observe that China's investment rate has remained above 40 percent ever since 2003, while consumption's share of GDP has continued to drop from 56.9 percent in 2003 to 47.4 percent in 2010. Most surprising is the performance of trade. After the start of exchange rate reform, China's external imbalance actually enlarged. Net export peaked at 8.8 percent of GDP in 2007 while it was 2.6 percent in 2004. The reasons for the surge in net trade were explained in Chapter 5. Here, we just emphasize again that this sharp rise was mainly due to the leveling off of import share, while manufacturing firms built the capacity to recover the domestic market.

Table 7.2 illustrates the dominant role the secondary sector played in the Chinese economy. In 2006 the secondary sector made up 48 percent of Chinese GDP. Such a percentage was significantly higher than that of any other countries in a similar phase of development. Although the service sector has been growing steadily, its share of GDP still lingered around 40 percent in the first decade of the twenty-first century. Compared with other countries at a similar development level, this share is about 10–20 percent too low. Clearly, the true vigor of the service sector in China is yet to be released. Worse still, albeit massive, China's industries are still weak in their ability of value adding. The share of value added in total industrial output in years 1995, 2000, and 2005 are 38.26, 35.8, and 34.07 percent respectively. Not only was this share in decline, but it was also about 20 percent lower when compared with OECD countries.

As regards national income distribution, households' share of national income was on a declining trend in the first several years of the new century (Table 7.3). The redistributing mechanisms solely transferred a proportion of enterprise income to governments. The household income experienced a slight decrease rather than an increase after income redistribution. The impoverishment of households weakened the purchasing power of Chinese population, thus making "encouraging domestic consumption" an empty slogan. What is more, the inequality of family income had also deepened. In 2006 the GINI coefficient was estimated to

Table 7.1 Chinese structure of GDP by categories of expenditure (% of GDP) from 1978 to 2010

Year	Consumption (%)	Investment (%)	Net export (%)
1978	62.1	38.2	−0.3
1979	64.4	36.1	−0.5
1980	65.5	34.8	−0.3
1981	67.1	32.5	0.3
1982	66.5	31.9	1.6
1983	66.4	32.8	0.8
1984	65.8	34.2	0.0
1985	66.0	38.1	−4.0
1986	64.9	37.5	−2.4
1987	63.6	36.3	0.1
1988	63.9	37.0	−1.0
1989	64.5	36.6	−1.1
1990	62.5	34.9	2.6
1991	62.4	34.8	2.7
1992	62.4	36.6	1.0
1993	59.3	42.6	−1.8
1994	58.2	40.5	1.3
1995	58.1	40.3	1.6
1996	59.2	38.8	2.0
1997	59.0	36.7	4.3
1998	59.6	36.2	4.2
1999	61.1	36.2	2.8
2000	62.3	35.3	2.4
2001	61.4	36.5	2.1
2002	59.6	37.8	2.6
2003	56.9	40.9	2.2
2004	54.4	43.0	2.5
2005	52.9	41.6	5.5
2006	50.7	41.8	7.5
2007	49.5	41.7	8.8
2008	48.4	43.9	7.7
2009	48.2	47.5	4.3
2010	47.4	48.6	4.0

Source: China Statistical Yearbook of various years

be 0.41192 in urban China and 0.3918 in rural China. (GINI is a measure of the degree of inequality in income distribution varying between 0 (perfect equality) and 1 (one person gets all income). It is admitted that a coefficient above 0.5 flashes a dangerously high degree of inequality.) Both figures were considerably higher than in the first stage of reform (and hardly comparable to the equalitarian society before 1978). Combining the fact that income gap between urban and rural China had also widened (urban average income was 3.33 times rural one in 2009), China's overall GINI coefficient was approaching the dangerous threshold of 0.5. In 2006 it was estimated to be 0.4691 (Zhou and Tan 2008). Increasing family income inequality further decreased China's total domestic consumption capacity

Table 7.2 GDP composition by sector (% of GDP) from 1978 to 2010

Year	Primary sector (%)	Secondary sector (%)	Tertiary sector (%)
1978	28.2	47.9	23.9
1979	31.3	47.1	21.6
1980	30.2	48.2	21.6
1981	31.9	46.1	22.0
1982	33.4	44.8	21.8
1983	33.2	44.4	22.4
1984	32.1	43.1	24.8
1985	28.4	42.9	28.7
1986	27.2	43.7	29.1
1987	26.8	43.6	29.6
1988	25.7	43.8	30.5
1989	25.1	42.8	32.1
1990	27.1	41.3	31.6
1991	24.5	41.8	33.7
1992	21.8	43.4	34.8
1993	19.7	46.6	33.7
1994	19.8	46.6	33.6
1995	19.9	47.2	32.9
1996	19.7	47.5	32.8
1997	18.3	47.5	34.2
1998	17.6	46.2	36.2
1999	16.5	45.8	37.7
2000	15.1	45.9	39.0
2001	14.4	45.1	40.5
2002	13.7	44.8	41.5
2003	12.8	46.0	41.2
2004	13.4	46.2	40.4
2005	12.1	47.4	40.5
2006	11.1	48.0	40.9
2007	10.8	47.3	41.9
2008	10.7	47.5	41.8
2009	10.3	46.3	43.4
2010	10.1	46.8	43.1

Source: China Statistical Yearbook of various years

as the wealthiest families demonstrate lower propensity to consume relative to their income.

To conclude, it is safe to say that, by 2008, China's rebalancing policies still had a lot to be desired. In order to develop more efficient restructuring mechanisms, Chinese leaders should stop entangling themselves with the multitudinous problems emerging every day, but tackle directly the core contradiction of the previous regime. As it was forcefully pointed out in the previous chapter, what China needs is a holistic strategic planning that integrates price, monetary, fiscal, administrative, social, and political instruments to reverse the root imbalances of the previous growth regime and guide China on to an endogenous path of development leading to sustainability and welfare-enhancement. In the following part of the chapter,

Table 7.3 National income distribution from 1992 to 2008

Year	Compositions after primary distribution			Compositions after redistribution		
	Households (%)	Enterprises (%)	Governments (%)	Households (%)	Enterprises (%)	Governments (%)
1992	66	17	17	68	12	20
1993	63	20	17	65	16	20
1994	65	18	17	67	15	19
1995	65	20	15	67	16	17
1996	66	17	17	68	14	18
1997	66	17	17	69	13	18
1998	66	16	18	68	13	18
1999	66	18	17	67	15	18
2000	63	19	18	64	17	19
2001	61	20	19	62	18	21
2002	61	20	19	61	18	21
2003	60	21	19	60	18	22
2004	58	26	16	58	23	19
2005	60	23	17	59	20	21
2006	59	22	19	59	19	23
2007	58	23	20	58	18	24
2008	57	25	18	57	21	22

Source: CEIC

we share our views on how China's strategic planning for the next ten to 20 years should deploy, by identifying the core contradiction of the second growth regime after reform (1994–2008) and suggesting the tools that would be the most powerful in correcting this.

Tackling the core contradiction of the second phase of reform (1994–2008)

The reasons for China's current imbalances are manifold. Some of the reasons are endogenous and some are related to the larger environment China is situated in. In the past few years, numerous economists have provided their interpretations for China's structural problems and most of these interpretations have their validity. However, in order to construct a holistic policy set that could alter core macroeconomic relationships and systemically lead the country into a new growth regime, it is crucial for us to identify what is the core contradiction of the 1994–2008 growth regime that serves as the root of China's major problems today.

The 1994–2008 Chinese growth regime took shape around a ruling crisis of central government. Attempting to achieve universal welfare improvement for the whole population in the first phase of reform, the central government in 1994 suffered from serious deterioration of fiscal balance and waning power of regulation over the economy. Hence reforming measures applied in 1994 and onward focused on strengthening the fiscal position of central government and consolidating its political power over the national economy. During this process, the once carefully protected benefits of the Chinese working class (especially the urban SOE employees) had been sacrificed, considerable public assets were privatized, and certain vested interests of local bureaucrats in the old political patronage system were also eliminated (see Chapter 4).

In order to maintain the CCP's political legitimacy, those losses had to be compensated in other forms. Under the circumstances, rapid economic growth, powered by strong investment and exportation, became the most immediate and universal remedy. Robust growth and buoyant economic activities provided abundant employment opportunities that absorbed the laid-off workers, new accrual of labor force and millions of migrant workers. Myriad infrastructure projects, real estate development programs, and industrial development zones provided local bureaucrats vast space for seeking new political patronage and economic rents. Vibrant economy saturated Chinese society with optimistic and somewhat feverish sentiments. All contributed to the stability and sustainability of the CCP's political regime, at the time.

Consequently, in the second phase of Chinese reform, the rapidity of economic growth became an objective in itself. For the purpose of encouraging and protecting this rapidity of growth, the pricing of key capitals (tangible and intangible alike) had been distorted towards the lower end, through monetary, fiscal, and regulative policies. Such a price system defined a specific relationship among key capitals, which gradually carved the economic structure of China into the one we observe today. The overly low price of tangible capitals enticed capital-intensive investments, which crowded out labor's contribution to GDP. As a result, households, especially salary-making households' income diminished as a share of GDP and so did domestic consumption. Large profits of these more and more capital-intensive enterprises drove up the saving rate. Accordingly, the momentum for capital-intensive investments rose even higher. Obviously, the distorted system of factor prices is a root tension of China's previous growth regime and the economy would not rebalance, nor go onto a sustainable path of development, unless a new price system, which can correctly reflect externalities and intergenerational risks and promote welfare-enhancement instead of GDP growth, could be established. For the next 10 to 20 years, the task is very clear, i.e. to improve the price system in view of rebalancing wealth towards labor, other intangible capital and natural capital that were either insufficiently developed or degraded in the previous growth regime.

Factor prices have been distorted throughout the 1994–2008 growth regime

Costs of factor price distortions: an overview

Professor Huang Yiping (2010) argues convincingly that the skewed and incomplete price reform has been an important reason for both outstanding growth in the first decade of the twenty-first century and serious distortions making such a growth process unsustainable further ahead. Price distortions are part of an unfinished reform. Product markets have been almost entirely liberalized. As we showed in Chapters 4 and 5, this has led to a competitive economy both domestically and internationally. It was a policy adopted as early as 1994, which inaugurated the second stage of reform under the overall objective of maximum growth. However, factor markets (labor, capital, energy, land, and environment) were left under heavy administrative control. The twin outcomes of high growth and structural imbalances stem from this biased approach. Indeed, undervaluing production costs is like subsidies to the users of factor resources and taxes on their owners. Users not paying the marginal cost of the resources they employ enjoy rents that are not justified by innovation or superior efficiency. This skewed income distribution has occurred on the basis of almost every factor of production.

Very low wages and denial of social welfare for migrant workers reduced the share of wages in national income, prevented household income to rise as much as it should have done, and depressed consumer spending. Artificially low prices for the plots of land, grabbed from farmers for industrial development and sold to suburban developers or to foreign firms to develop industrial parks, contributed to the real estate bubble in many cities and led to over accumulation of capacities in heavy industries. Too low a price of credit in relation to the growth rate drove huge amounts of capital to big SOEs, earning extra rates of return. Energy prices much below world prices and lack of carbon price have led to distortions pointed out in Chapter 6. Natural capital has been wasted and pollution has become alarming in several industrial regions.

The theoretical sustainable growth model in Chapter 6 (Box 6.1) has shown that the "right" factor prices are the dual prices of sustainable paths of the economy that value all factors of production. Therefore it is not enough to say, as Professor Huang Yiping argues, that the purpose should be to liberalize prices in the sense of letting markets work freely. Some key factors, such as pollution or many types of intangible capital, do not have any market or very poor-functioning markets like the market for land. Besides, when markets do exist, as in finance, we have observed with the global financial crisis how much they can get endogenously distorted. Therefore improving economic efficiency is a mix of liberalizing and regulating the use of resources to provide proper incentives to economic agents in order to reach an overall policy goal. We forcefully argued in Chapter 6 that this goal should no longer be maximum growth but sustainable growth carefully defined.

Nonetheless, Professor Huang Yiping has made a good start in computing rough estimates of distortions in some factor markets. The main problem in quantifying the income transfers due to price distortions is obviously the benchmarks against which actual factor costs should be compared. He gave estimates of implicit subsidies for labor, capital, land, energy, and environment.

For labor market he does not use any competitive wage as a benchmark. He notices that the main cause for distortion is the underpayment of welfare contributions to migrant workers. The benchmark is the payroll that should be paid if employers follow strictly government regulations. It amounts to 30 percent of total payroll. Concerning interest rates that are heavily administered, debtor subsidies accrue from lending rates that are so-called "repressed." A capital cost lower than the theoretical level equal to the user cost of capital is supposed to facilitate leverage, boost investment, and raise growth. But no one knows what the true cost of capital is, since financial markets have been shown to be highly imperfect under uncertainty. The author uses a guess saying that interest rate can increase by 2 percent upon the total outstanding of bank loans. If the price of urban land sold to developers is taken as the benchmark, land sold for industrial use is supposed to be 30 percent below. International oil prices are widely volatile, so taking them as the benchmark year after year is unreasonable. It is assumed that the international market for oil, which is quite cartelized and highly volatile, is a competitive price that helps compute subsidy equivalents. An average price gap of US$20 is found. Because the environment is still an externality whose destruction is not internalized, the official estimation of a cost of 3 percent GDP is a pure guess. Summing the five categories of cost distortion, Huang Yiping arrives at 7 percent GDP. What can be done with such a result? It can help in setting policy priorities in the areas of reform. Let us dig a little deeper in the different areas of suspected distortions.

Credit price

Entering into the second phase of reform, the central bank had been assigned the responsibility of monetary policy (see Chapter 4). Although the PBoC adjusted the benchmark rate often according to macroeconomic situations, this rate had been kept excessively low compared with GDP growth and CPI. The PBoC one-year deposit rate fluctuated in a range of 2–4 percent. The highest rate was observed in the fourth quarter of year 2007 when the one-year deposit rate jumped 1.62 percent higher to 4.14 percent to curb overheating in the economy. Considering that, in the same year, Chinese CPI was 4.8 percent (food price rose 12.3 percent) and GDP growth was 13 percent, this rate was still considerably favorable to the debtors that had access to bank credit, while detrimental to depositors. With the outbreak of the global financial crisis in 2008, the benchmark rate dropped rapidly again to around 2 percent.

Undoubtedly, low bank interest rate stimulates investment. However, it does not stimulate all types of investments equally. When bank interest rate is too low compared with GDP growth and CPI, it no longer poses a reasonable hurdle rate for the future return of investment projects. In the absence of sophisticated risk management skills, state-owned Chinese banks naturally favor large-scale capital-intensive projects, which offer land and other fixed assets as collateral, such as investment programs of large SOEs, local government infrastructure constructions and real estate developing projects, instead of labor-intensive SMEs. Among all the outstanding loans in 2010, about half the total amount was in the hands of SOEs (Huang 2011) and 20–30 percent in the hands of controversial local government investment vehicles (PBoC 2011). In the meantime, labor-intensive

SMEs had great difficulties in seeking financing at low cost. In Wenzhou region, an experimental site where private lending was legalized in 2003, the market one-year return for lenders fluctuated in the range of 13–17 percent from 2003 to 2010. The one-year credit rate of private lending agencies fluctuated around 20 percent. Both rates were about 10 to 15 percentage points higher than the PBoC rates during the same period. Such significant differences cannot be assigned to risk premium only. They indicate serious distortion of official bank credit prices and a large amount of rent seeking for whoever has access to bank credit. This distorted financing system not only promoted the high share of investment in GDP in the 1994–2008 growth regime by taxing Chinese depositors, but also heavily bent the structure of investment to the capital-intensive side. That is to say, low interest rates exploit Chinese households through two mechanisms: one, capital-intensive economic structure skews returns to entities and individuals who have access to tangible capitals, while it decreases the importance of labor in economic activities, thus decreasing the share of household income in national income distribution; the other, average households with no access to diversified investment channels but bank deposits, are denied any reasonable return.

Charges on using natural resources and environmental services

The history of China charging any fees or rents over the extraction of natural resources is very short. In the socialist period China did not charge any royalty for the extraction of natural resources, as both the resources and the enterprises that extracted them were state-owned. Partially because of this "tradition," even today the charges China puts on the usage of natural resources and environmental services is still very limited. According to incomplete statistics, out of 150,000 mining companies, only about 20,000 obtained their mining right through market-based mechanisms. The rest gained their mining rights through allocation, the cost of which was virtually zero (Fan *et al.* 2010: 146). Royalty is only applicable to the extraction of mineral resources on the basis of quantity.[1] Differentiated by the quality of mineral resources extracted, China charges 8–30 Yuan per ton for crude oil, 2–15 Yuan per ton for natural gas, and 0.3–5 Yuan per ton for coal. Charges and fees other than royalty also exist in China, but their scale is even more limited. Such a low level of charges is significantly below international common practice and hardly reveals the true social value of those resources, thus detrimental to the sustainability of the Chinese economy. Take royalty on crude oil extraction, for example: in research carried out by Fan Gang and his research team (2010), it is estimated that Chinese petro companies pay about 660 Yuan (about US$83[2]) less than their international counterparts for the extraction of each ton of crude oil. This means that, in 2007 alone, China charged 117.81 billion RMB less for crude oil and 380 billion RMB less on total mineral resource usages.

Similar to the situation in most other countries, Chinese enterprises have not been paying enough for environmental services either. In both the 11th and 12th five-year plans, China set up hard targets for the reduction of carbon emission and the emission of other pollutants. However, supervising the fulfillment of those targets is a tricky task. The 11th five-year plans required that, by the end of 2010, energy intensity per unit of GDP be reduced by 20 percent from the 2005 level. In April 2011 China was still 8 percentage points away from this target. However, under strong pressure from the State Council, at year-end, China abruptly reduced unit energy intensity by 19.1 percent compared with the 2005 level. We cannot help but worry about the quality of such a reduction. In order to achieve a more lasting effect of environmental protection, China must integrate environmental services into the price system of all factors, so as to guide the behaviors of all economic agents. This requires an institutionalized price scheme that poses correct prices for environmental services by fiscal and administrative mechanisms, such as carbon tax and price regulation. We discuss these schemes in more detail later in the chapter.

A fragmented land market

While the skyrocketing real estate price in China was hitting the headlines every day, it might have sounded confusing to discuss the undervaluation of China's land. Indeed, any generalization of Chinese land price would be flawed as the market is extremely fragmented and under-regulated. Except for national authorities, local land authorities from provincial level down to collectives all possess certain powers of transferring land in their jurisdiction for residential, commercial, and industrial purposes. The 1994 Tax Reform centralized most of fiscal income. However, land-transferring fees stayed out of budget and were at the complete disposal of the local administrations. Without central supervision, such fees became a major source of income for local governments and facilitated strong incentives for rent seeking and corruption. Farmland was often seized by local officials without sufficient compensation to the farmers, and then either transferred at high prices for residential and commercial real estate development or at cut-rate prices for industrial purposes in expectation of lucrative future tax revenue that was ten times higher than farm taxes (*China Hand* 2009). Obviously such practice encouraged excessive expansion of suburban dwellings and industrial parks. It harmed the benefits of both the former landholders (mainly the farmers) and the new home purchasers in the cities. In the 2000s central government realized the gravity of China's land problem and strengthened its supervision of the market. In 2002 the Ministry of Land and Resources issued "Regulations on Granting State-owned Land Rights by Invitation for Tenders, Auction, or Listing." Since then, market-based schemes were better applied for the transfer of land for residential and commercial uses. However, bringing land transfers for industrial uses (80–5 percent of total land transfers) under a unifying market scheme encountered greater resistance. Local authorities were so anxious to attract investments to their jurisdiction that even after Beijing issued national standards of minimum transferring fees of land for industrial purposes in January 2007, the price of industrial land was still far under market value and, in some cases, the local government would refund the land-transferring fees in the form of tax rebate or other types of subsidies to avoid the minimum standards.

To sum up, China's land market is a messy one. Current land-transferring practices created incentives for local officials to abuse the powers they possess. Industrial land has been priced at a cut-rate level and has stimulated waste, rent-seeking, and extensive growth patterns. Most importantly, all these practices have greatly damaged the interests of Chinese households. Farmers lost their land for compensations that would not enable them to settle down in the urban areas. And urban dwellers sank their life-long savings into apartments to live in. Social wealth has been transferred on a large scale from average households to local officials, developers, enterprises, and affluent investors through these operations over land, which poses tremendous negative effects on the rebalancing of the Chinese economy.

Chinese labor market and the price of human capital

In a speech delivered on January 23, 2010 in Tsinghua University, Zhou Qiren, a PBoC advisor and Peking University professor, believed that in 2010 Chinese average labor price was still only about 10 percent of the level in industrial countries. Such a low price level of labor should be examined from different aspects. On the one hand, China's low labor price was partially due to China's demographic structure and development level. At the beginning of reform, China retained a large pool of surplus labor in the countryside. The marginal labor productivity of this surplus labor force was next to zero. Thus almost any labor price higher than subsistence level was acceptable by Chinese workers. In recent years, as China has been approaching the "Lewis turning point," the labor price has been on the rise (see Chapter 6 for a more detailed discussion about China's current and future demographic structure). However, according to the 2010 census, 70.14 percent of the Chinese population is still aged 15–59. This means that China still possesses a relatively abundant supply of labor. If China had lower labor costs by international standards solely because of this large supply, it would not necessarily create any problems or imbalances. This comparative advantage can make Chinese companies more competitive in labor-intensive industries. If so, over time the population could enjoy fuller employment and wider education. Gradually, labor productivity would increase together with the inflow of technology and accumulation of human capital, thus enhancing salaries and improving social welfare. This is roughly what happened in the first phase of Chinese reform.

However, this is only one aspect of the story. In reality, with serious distortions of the costs of tangible assets, the Chinese economy became more and more capital-intensive, instead of labor-intensive, in the 1994–2008 growth period. Thus from a macro perspective, the dependency of the economy on human capital declined vis-à-vis tangible ones. The labor force further lost its bargaining power against capital and salaries could not increase at the same rate as labor productivity gains. This trend was fully reflected in the declining share of household income in national income distribution (see Table 7.3). Moreover, after drastic reforms of SOEs took place in the 1990s, Chinese workers completely lost their bargaining tools with the management inherited from the socialist era. However, new efficient counter-balancing mechanisms have not yet been developed. Hence individualized workers have extremely weak bargaining power. They could not be sufficiently organized to speak up for their own rights. Even after the new labor law was issued, its enforcement was at the mercy of local governments. What is more, Chinese enterprises took advantage of the relatively young demographic structure. Workers were not adequately compensated for their seniority. According to research by Park and Cai (2011), in 2005 about 46 percent of China's labor force was informally employed. That is to say, nearly half of China's total workforce was excluded from the social security system. This situation was even more serious and complicated for migrant workers.

Now is the key time for these distortions in China's labor market to be abrogated. As we argued in the previous chapter, China has already reached the first Lewis turning point and is approaching the second. The active population will cease to grow around year 2015. This means that salary increases will eventually outpace productivity gains, or at least the differential between these two would narrow. The slightly increased share of household income in national income distribution in 2009 and 2010 proved that this trend is already occurring. Moreover, the behavior of China's new generation of migrant workers has drastically changed from the behavior of their fathers. In the first 30 years of reform, rural China served as a reservoir of labor for industrial activities. Farmers migrated between their homes in the country and their work posts in the factories according to business cycles. When economic activities shrank, these migrant workers could be dismissed and sent back to their home towns with almost zero compensation. This situation will change. A new generation of migrant workers will want to settle in the cities where, even if facing unemployment, many of them would still choose to stay. This is what happened to Japan in the 1960s. If channels for collective bargaining still do not exist, and if workers' salaries are still not high enough to afford a normal and decent life in the cities (including housing, public services, care for their family members, etc.), there will be harsh labor conflicts in the years to come.

To sum up, China's price system for capital has been distorted and these distortions must be diligently adjusted. They are directly responsible for most macro-imbalances of the Chinese economy. Excessively low prices of tangible capital encourage wasteful investment, especially over-investment in capital-intensive, energy-intensive, and resource-based industries. Such growth patterns diminish the bargaining power of labor and the importance of intangible capital (human, institutional, etc.). National income distribution skews to enterprises, governments, and individuals who possess access to cheap capital. Wealth accumulates into the hands of the few and this accentuates social inequality. With the real income growth of average households slower than that of GDP growth, domestic consumption cannot sufficiently absorb the output of the economy. Fortunately or unfortunately, feeble domestic purchasing power was complemented by over-consumption in the US for most of the 2000s. Thus a fragile international "equilibrium" formed with China's accumulation of FX reserves and the deterioration of the US debt structure. The financial crisis has destroyed it and necessitated structural adjustment.

What is more, pervasive distortions of energy and environment costs provided negative incentives for efficient usage of resources, and posed direct obstacles to sustainable growth. On top of creating serious health problems and inflicting economic damage, environmental degradation provoked recurrent extreme events such as droughts in northern China and floods in southern China. Subsequently policy objectives for renewable energy substitution to fossil fuel and environment conversation will make a major contribution in reshaping the next growth regime.

Hence price incentives must play a larger role for a better allocation of capital. Without comprehensive correction in the price system, it is impossible to talk about rebalancing the Chinese economy, or the rise of domestic consumption, or the development of services and green economy in China. The core of China's next growth regime relies on a net transfer of social wealth to households and adequate compensation to environmental services.

Obstacles for the upward adjustment of capital prices

We have to admit that, in recent years, progress has been made in adjusting cost distortions. Labor protection has been repeatedly emphasized in governmental directives. Regulations on land market have been strengthened. Energy prices have been brought closer to international levels. The price of coal is the closest to market price. Electricity tariffs are set by the authorities and account for public consultation. Oil product prices are set according to a formula linking domestic to world prices with a twist to raise domestic prices closer to world level and a sweetener to smooth market price spikes. Concerning environmental protection, the government has already set a comprehensive package of regulations. Carbon tax is also under extensive discussion. However, implementation of a great many measures has not been effective, as long as local governments still prioritize GDP growth over total real wealth increase. Moreover, the most distorted credit price has not seen sufficient adjustment to guide investment and promote capital return for average households. Why is a revolutionary price adjustment so arduous?

First of all, a comprehensive adjustment of capital prices is a tricky game. Forcefully pushing up certain prices is suicidal, especially in an open economy. Raising interest rates too sharply would inflict universal financial stresses on the economy. A sudden tightening of liquidity and financial cost would push many enterprises into bankruptcy and lead to massive unemployment. Although hopefully these laid-off workers would be absorbed gradually by the rise of SMEs, the process is nevertheless painful and dangerous. Raising salaries is also an extremely tricky measure. If labor costs increase – or rather, if the gap between labor costs and labor productivity narrows – someone would have to compensate for that increase, creating income distribution issues. The pivotal question in policy-making is thus: who will lose? Would the government make an earnest commitment to social-welfare enhancement and make a substantial transfer to the people? Or should SOEs finally start to pay genuine dividends? Or would the government just go on raising the minimum wage? In the latter case the labor-intensive SMEs would be the first ones to suffer losses. Some of them may have to quit the market and the economy would be even more capital intensive. Such effects would be the exact opposite of rebalancing. Obviously, the adjustment of capital prices must be a slow process and other institutional tools should be applied to guide the change of capital prices.

Another weighty obstacle for the adjustment of capital prices in China is related to China's political regime. A salient feature of the political system is that the decision-making process is collective among top bureaucrats. Capital-price manipulation and resource allocation were two cornerstones of the political patronage system in the previous growth regime. Thus vested interests of a large number of bureaucrats impinge upon capital prices. They resort to the collusion between SOE managers and administrative bureaucrats, and they disturb the political bargaining among ministries. Consequentially, capital-price reform requires steadfast determination from the central government, together with an iron yet subtle hand.

A more immediate obstacle for significant upward adjustment of credit price is the fact that a majority of Chinese loans were issued to SOEs and local governments. The 4-trillion RMB Stimulus Plan substantially fueled the growth of local investment vehicles, such as the urban development investment corporations (UDIC; see Chapter 4 for more information about UDICs). At the end of 2010, the total size of local investment vehicle loans ranged from 9 trillion to 14 trillion RMB.[3] Thus a sharp increase of credit price would significantly increase financial costs of these investment vehicles and trigger a string of corporate defaults, which in turn would hinder China's infrastructure constructions and provoke local government bankruptcy, which is prohibited by law. As a result, central government would be the last resort for banks, SOEs, and local governments. If that situation occurred, central government's fiscal health would be destroyed. Thus to adjust the price of credit, the local shadow-banking system has to be completely cleaned up. A rebalancing of the fiscal relationship between central and local governments is a prerequisite also. Local governments must be endowed with steady revenues commensurate with their financial obligations and with formal tools to borrow safely in order to fund investments approved by the NDRC in the implementation of strategic planning along the direction outlined in Chapter 6.

Should these obstacles eliminate our hope for Chinese economic rebalancing? Yes and no. If we were looking for an immediate solution that could solve all the problems once and for all, our chances of success would be slim. However, the rebalancing process is a co-evolution integrating all social and economic factors. As far as future planning can pilot the price of capital assets as dual prices of economic trajectories fulfilling the criterion of non-decreasing social real wealth, it will be possible to channel wealth from capital holders to labor and upgrade the evaluation of environmental services. Then, the economy will realize its large potential for sustainable future development. The strong tide of urbanization and the immense domestic demand yet to be unleashed serve as perfect opportunities for China in the years to come. What Chinese leaders will do in the next 20 years will be decisive for China's future and quite possibly for the world as well.

The rebalancing of the Chinese economic structure will be lengthy. Nevertheless, the experience of the past 30 years and the earlier two-thousand-year history of empire has proved that the ultimate value top Chinese bureaucrats tend to protect is the sustainability of the political regime. Chapter 6 demonstrated that the previous growth regime is no longer suitable for China today or in the future. Political patronage over land and tangible assets has undermined the credibility and authority of central government. Increasing social inequality has aroused widespread discontent, while overwhelming capital accumulation has jeopardized human values and creativity. Meanwhile, social awareness is surging rapidly in civil society and forceful online discussions directly attack the legitimacy of the CCP. Once again, Chinese leaders are facing a critical phase in that only radical reforms can save the political regime and bring China to the next stage of progress. The question is not about whether it is possible or necessary to push Chinese reforms further or not, but how to do it.

In the remainder of the chapter we present the three mechanisms we identify as the most promising in effecting the rebalancing of China. These are: the development of the service sector, further reforms in the fiscal system, and the institution of a social welfare system. Combined, these mechanisms point to a plausible roadmap for China's future reforms.

The linchpin for rebalancing the Chinese economy is the development of the service sector

Rebalancing the economy requires rebalancing the price relationship between tangible and intangible capitals, especially the relationship between labor and fixed assets. In order to foster domestic consumption, the price of human capital has to be upgraded so that households take an advantageous position in national income distribution. As suggested in Chapter 6, the institutionalization of workers' representation and the transformation of the corporate management paradigm are vital mechanisms to protect the benefits of labor. Another equally important, if not more fundamental, determinant of wages is the supply and demand relationship in the labor market. As Kalecki (1943) and many other researchers have pointed out, full employment is one of the strongest weapons in increasing the bargaining power of workers. Thus a more labor-intensive instead of capital-intensive economic structure would favor the welfare of labor. What is more, environmental sustainability requires China to leapfrog into post-industrial society, where immaterial services will outweigh material consumption. The accelerating aging and urbanization processes also call for better supply of social services. To conclude, the expansion of a labor-intensive service sector lies not only at the nexus of the labor–capital relationship, but also the nexus of China's next growth regime. Enhancing total factor productivity (TFP), absorbing labor, realizing the value of human capital, and decreasing the resource-dependency of the economy are all ways for China's rebalancing towards sustainable development.

Admittedly, the under-development of China's tertiary sector is itself a consequence of the imbalances of the previous growth regime. Excessively low tangible capital prices suppressed the growth of the service sector in attracting investments into capital-intensive industries and in diminishing households' capability for purchasing services. However, capital-price distortion is not the only reason contributing to the under-development of services in China. Empirical evidence from other countries shows that government policy has great impact on the deployment of the service sector. The type of welfare state developed over 80 years in Scandinavian countries, for example, greatly promoted the expansion of social services, and created enormous employment and social values. Future progress in China's service sector, we believe, also asks for the decent political commitment of Chinese leaders. While directly correcting the price relationship of key capital assets may encounter severe political and macroeconomic difficulties (we examined the negative consequences above about raising interest rate or wage single-handedly), advocating the surge of a Chinese service sector could encounter less political friction, but still have strong rebalancing effects upon the economy.

In 2010 Chinese annual per capita income in urban regions reached 21,033 RMB (about US$3,093). According to international experience, when per capita income surpasses US$2,000, the tertiary sector often enters a phase of rapid expansion. China is certainly ready for the takeoff of the service sector. If the development of services can be orchestrated with the reform of the financial system, this would be the smoothest way for China to transform an extensive growth regime into a sustainable one. Beijing must make a wholehearted commitment to nurture the development of services, especially producer services and social services.

The significance of developing the service sector

The significance of developing the service sector for pushing up returns on human capital

The trajectory of development in all industrialized countries has indubitably shown that, over a certain level of wealth, the share of primary and secondary sectors dramatically diminish in employment. Society needs high-end services embodying upgraded skills, such as managers, researchers, health professionals, artistic designers, and the like. They are drivers of the knowledge economy. In the US, for instance, the fast growth in employment mainly occurred in education, distribution, and government administration in the 1960s and producer services, health, and entertainment in the 1970s (Esping-Andersen 1990: 199–200). The rise of services, especially services with high human capital content, is also often accompanied by the expansion of middle-class families and the maturation of a welfare state. Both these two trends will be tremendously beneficial in transforming the growth regime in China.

Table 7.4 depicts the structure of China's employment by sector. Undeniably, the service sector in China has been built up gradually over the past 30 years of reform. However, when compared with Table 7.2, a striking difference between capital intensities for Chinese secondary and tertiary sectors appears. In 2006, for example, the secondary sector generated 48 percent of national GDP, while

Table 7.4 China's employment by sector (% of total employment)

Year	Primary sector	Secondary sector	Tertiary sector
1978	70.5	17.3	12.2
1979	69.8	17.6	12.6
1980	68.7	18.2	13.1
1981	68.1	18.3	13.6
1982	68.1	18.4	13.5
1983	67.1	18.7	14.2
1984	64.0	19.9	16.1
1985	62.4	20.8	16.8
1986	60.9	21.9	17.2
1987	60.0	22.2	17.8
1988	59.3	22.4	18.3
1989	60.1	21.6	18.3
1990	60.1	21.4	18.5
1991	59.7	21.4	18.9
1992	58.5	21.7	19.8
1993	56.4	22.4	21.2
1994	54.3	22.7	23.0
1995	52.2	23.0	24.8
1996	50.5	23.5	26.0
1997	49.9	23.7	26.4
1998	49.8	23.5	26.7
1999	50.1	23.0	26.9
2000	50.0	22.5	27.5
2001	50.0	22.3	27.7
2002	50.0	21.4	28.6
2003	49.1	21.6	29.3
2004	46.9	22.5	30.6
2005	44.8	23.8	31.4
2006	42.6	25.2	32.2
2007	40.8	26.8	32.4
2008	39.6	27.2	33.2
2009	38.1	27.8	34.1
2010	36.7	28.7	34.6

Source: China Statistical Yearbook (2011)

only absorbing 25.2 percent of labor. In contrast, the tertiary sector absorbed 32.2 percent of the working force, while producing only 40.9 percent of GDP. Considering that the share of the tertiary sector in Chinese GDP is exceedingly low compared with countries of similar levels of development, the above ratios indicate immeasurable potential for the service sector to absorb Chinese labor, and even more importantly, to absorb a highly educated, highly skilled labor force, while improving labor productivity.

If the obstacles for the development of these high-end services could be identified and relieved, human capital in the whole economy would be enhanced accordingly. Thus household income of high-skilled professionals would be steadily raised. These people will compose the main body of China's future middle class and they will have a strong propensity and capacity to consume. Additionally, the expected need and higher price for high-skilled human capital will provide both incentive and capability for families to further invest in their children's education. A virtuous circle between accumulation of human capital and total real wealth of the country will be set in motion, making a beneficial contribution to the sustainable development of China.

Increasing TFP by enhancing producer services

The development of producer services (such as logistics, financial services, R&D) also directly enhances the efficiency of industries and thus helps China to climb up the value chain. For example, one of the largest domains in services, where a significant improvement in efficiency can boost TFP, is supply chain management. Inefficient goods distribution impairs productivity severely. High transaction costs, combining transport and logistics, eat up to 18 percent of GDP compared to 10 percent in the US, according to the research institute Dragonomics (Mooney 2009). Reducing these costs impinges upon both the service sector and goods distribution. It will lower goods prices and make them more affordable to low-income consumers. It will also make a wider variety of consumer goods available, making the most of frugal innovation.

China's inefficient distribution system divides territorially the market for consumer goods, which is not a single national market yet. The reason can be found in the extreme fragmentation of the wholesale distribution sector made up of local trading intermediaries, which cannot afford investing in efficient logistics, do not research demand fluctuations and subsequently do not optimize inventories. The retail sector is itself fragmented, unable to exploit economies of scale in distribution in standardizing supply chain operations.

The inefficient structure of facilities is enshrined in a mosaic of provincial regulations, making interprovincial shipments costly. Consequently there is no pan-China network of transportation, but 760,000 logistics companies whose size

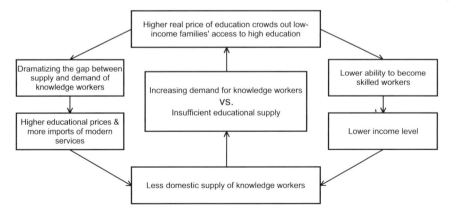

Figure 7.1 Vicious circles formed because of under-development of education.

varies from one to three trucks. The resulting lack of scale economies increases costs and lowers productivity. Foreign logistic companies are entirely focused on exports. They do nothing for the national distribution of goods. However, in the 2000s world retailers (Carrefour, Wall Mart, and McDonalds) set up chain stores in the big cities. For their own businesses they established efficient distribution networks. They have collaborated with foreign logistic providers eventually in partnership with Chinese logistic firms to provide high-quality cold chain in food distribution and scheduled delivery for all items.

The government has started to tackle the problem. The Rural Retailing Network Project was established in 2005 by the Ministry of Commerce. It aims at incentivizing retailers to set up outlets in total areas. Involving the juice company Huiyuan Group, the dairy company Yili Group, and Procter & Gamble, the project has achieved coverage of 75 percent of rural counties. According to the Hong Kong logistic company, Li & Fung Research, it generated RMB 100 billion of new rural retail sales in 2008. Another project aims to invest in information systems on demand, warehouses, and cold storage facilities in rural counties. Nevertheless, capital invested in refrigerated trucks and food security devices to massively reduce waste from farms to retailers remains woefully inadequate. It will improve because logistics is one of the ten sectors selected as strategic industries for restructuring and revitalization. The Asian Development Bank is commissioned to make a detailed plan with targets to lower logistic costs nationwide by 2015.

Reforming the distribution of goods is central to reorienting the growth regime to domestic consumption, while stimulating indigenous frugal innovation in industry. To achieve it the strong support of central government is crucial. Cross-provincial networks are the ways to efficiency. They meet jurisdictional obstacles and vested interests at the provincial and municipal level. The NDRC should be empowered by the State Council to break the parochial resistance of local governments. The ultimate incentive for central government is to sustain high-productivity growth and support dynamic consumer demand. Linking this side of the growth regime to environment conservation and rehabilitation is the road to sustainability. The mix of high-skilled labor, high-productivity growth, superior services, and environment protection, together with robust consumer demand, can only be found in city development, as we demonstrated in Chapter 6.

Private services are indispensable for China's urbanization and aging process

As we estimate in Chapter 6, in the next 20 years, 400 million Chinese will migrate from the countryside to cities and will become permanent urban dwellers. And from 2015 onwards, aging of the Chinese population will accelerate. The dependency ratio (age over 65/ total population) will rise from 27 percent in 2015 to 37 percent in 2040. Both of these two trends could represent tremendous challenges, or chances. The defining factor is the deployment of Chinese services, especially social services.

To avoid rapid urbanization turning into an agglomeration of slums, it has to be accompanied by the corresponding creation of urban employment and the sufficient supply of proficient and affordable public services, most notably education and medical care. Similarly, to avoid the high dependency ratio crushing Chinese families, the increasing supply of health care services should also be in line with China's aging process. Since 1949 China has accumulated considerable human capital through the improvement of both basic and advanced education. In 2010 the number of China's new university graduates increased to 6.31 million. If China could release its service sector from unnecessary impediments, this sizeable supply of educated labor would promote the expansion and maturation of China's tertiary sector, rebalance China's industrial structure, and harmonize the drastic transformation of China's social and demographic structure.

Measures to release the service sector from shackles and distortions

Without proper measures to increase the real income of households, especially the salary makers, "promoting China's domestic consumption" would be nothing more than an empty slogan. Similarly, without measures to eliminate shackles and distortions, "encouraging the growth of service sector" would be a futile wish as well. When factor prices, especially tangible capital prices, are bent to the extreme low end, and while salary levels are on the rise, the labor-intensive service sector is suppressed rather than encouraged. Chinese authorities have to take more active measures in protecting and nurturing the growth of the service sector.

Liberating the service sector from myriad administrative obstacles

The under-development of some of China's producer services and most of the public services has one single cause. It stems from myriad administrative obstacles.

First of all, a majority of these services are still highly monopolized by SOEs and strictly controlled by various supervising governmental bodies. Private actors face extraordinarily high entry barriers into these markets and even if they succeeded in entering them, unstable regulations and even direct interferences from governmental bodies could create further difficulties for management. In 2005 the State Council issued 36 clauses to protect and encourage private actors to enter domains that were traditionally occupied mainly by SOEs. A majority of those domains mentioned in those 36 clauses were services, especially high-end services, such as financial, distributive, and social services. However, five years later, those 36 clauses did not seem to liberate private activities from discriminative treatments in those domains. In 2010 the State Council had to issue the so-called "New 36 Clauses," which again emphasized the importance of releasing shackles over private activities. The effectiveness of these new 36 clauses is yet to be observed, but most Chinese researchers are pessimistic. Indeed, to sincerely promote private participation in the provision of high-end services, the measures applied had to be more concrete. To release private service providers from administrative shackles, for example, would require redefining the functions of the regulatory authorities concerned, especially the Ministry of

Education and the Ministry of Health. Currently, these two ministries and their local branches directly own a majority of medical and educational institutions. Large monopolistic interests make sure that these regulative bodies are hostile to private participation. As Table 7.5 shows, in 2010 private participation in public services and some producer services was still minimal. For health- and culture-related services, 88.9 percent of the related personnel were employed by SOEs. The provision of education was an extreme case: 95.9 percent of educators and other school employees belonged to public entities. The scarcity of private educational activities was out of line with China's development level. The reason for such degree of distortion is associated with the regulations of the educational system in China.

In order to better understand the relationship between the under-development of China's potentially high-flying services and governmental behavior, let us take the health care system as an example. Generally speaking, health care provision in China has been in relative shortage, especially the provision of primary care. During the second phase of reform, investments in medical facilities expanded rapidly, especially for the construction and renovation of large hospitals in the cities. However, investments into primary care were left out. What is more, as the increase in the number of doctors and nurses did not catch up with the growth of hardware, the demand for health care, especially the demand for outpatient consultations, was not adequately met (OECD 2010). The density of doctors with at least college education is only 0.1 per thousand of the population. The limited

Table 7.5 Provision of services in China by ownership types in 2010

	Total employment (10,000)	Employed by SOEs (10,000)	% Employed by SOEs
Traffic, transport, storage, and post	631.1	403.3	63.9
Information transmission, computer services, and software	85.8	62.5	33.6
Wholesale and retail trades	535.1	137.3	25.7
Hotels and catering services	209.2	54.6	26.1
Financial intermediation	470.1	144.3	30.7
Real estate	211.6	45.4	21.4
Leasing and business services	310.1	131.5	42.4
Scientific research, technical service, and geologic prospecting	292.3	219.6	75.1
Management of water conservancy and environment	218.9	189.9	86.7
Services to households and other services	60.2	28.9	47.9
Education	1,581.8	1,517.4	95.9
Health, social security, and social welfare	632.5	562.6	88.9
Culture, sports, and entertainment	131.4	113.1	86.1
Public management and social organization	1,428.5	1,415.6	99.1

Source: China Statistical Yearbook (2011)

human resources in medical care were unevenly distributed to favor urban areas, where the density of doctors was 0.9 per thousand (Anand *et al.* 2008).

The curious thing is that, meanwhile, China had an over-supply of newly trained medical students. According to an OECD report, in 2005, there were 0.4 million medical students in bachelor and associate programs. In the meantime, the total stock of doctors with similar qualifications in 2005 was only 0.8 million. The supply of medical students with postgraduate degrees was also abundant. In 2005, about 40,000 postgraduate students were in medical schools, forming a sharp contrast with a total stock of 42,000 doctors with such qualifications in the same year. With fierce competition, only students in the top percentile of grades could obtain a job position as doctor. From 2004 to 2006, of the graduates of Peking University's prestigious five-year clinical medicine program, only 28 percent were working as doctors in 2007 (Anand *et al.* 2008). For the trained-to-be nurses, the situation was quite similar.

One of the main reasons for the mysterious phenomenon described above is the structure of Chinese health care provision. In China, the dominant providers of health care, including primary care, are hospitals. They produce nearly 80 percent of the value of all first-level medical consultations (OECD 2010). And a majority of these hospitals and other medical care establishments are state-owned and under strict supervision of health departments at various governmental levels. The entry barrier for opening a private clinic to provide primary care is excessively high, thus the number of private clinics and family doctors is extremely low in China. The sole opportunity for medical graduates to carry out medical practices is through state-owned medical institutions. Undoubtedly this rigid structure of health care provision impedes the momentum of job creation in the health care sector. Due to constraints in infrastructure and administrative capacity, large state-owned hospitals cannot expand limitlessly in order to fully satisfy market demands and to absorb newly graduated medical students. As a result, not only is there a waste of precious human resources, concentration of medical care provision to urban hospitals also increases the difficulty of accessing primary care, especially for patients in rural areas. One survey found that 20 percent of outpatient visits in hospitals were for colds or gastroenteritis (Lim *et al.* 2002). This rate could be significantly decreased by the development of a net of private clinics and family doctors. Moreover, the monopoly of public hospitals also impedes the efficiency of China's health care provision system. As medical facilities are subject to a wide range of inadequately coordinated supervisory authorities, at the moment they are accountable neither to public sector mandates nor to the market, and are often operated for the benefit of their staff and management (Hougaard *et al.* 2011).

Obviously, liberating the entry into the health care market and releasing the health care system from myriad administrative interferences are two key solutions for the takeoff of the Chinese health care industry. Unfortunately, the current debates about China's future medical reform seem to focus on whether or not China should privatize the current hospitals. We are afraid this is the wrong question to tackle. Public hospitals have their own indispensable role in a national health care system. The key question is not about whether it should be the state or certain individuals to monopolize the health care market. Rather, the question is how to liberate this market and level the playing field for both public and private players. A unified national standard should be established to regulate the behavior of public institutions, private non-profit institutions, and private profit-making institutions on an equal basis. Liberating the health care market would significantly increase the supply of primary care and absorb newly trained practitioners. What is more, it would bring in competition and thus urge the public hospitals to improve their services. The health regulatory bodies must retreat from direct management of hospitals but focus only on the regulation of this market. Amelioration of management is immediately needed in public hospitals.

The structural problem of health care services is a typical example. Similar situations could be found in China's education, transportation, and several other service markets. Fierce political resistance from the ministries concerned seriously impeded the reforming process in the above-mentioned domains. However, at this critical moment of bifurcation in the growth regime, letting the vested interests of these ministries continue to have their say would impinge negatively upon the economic and social progress of China as a whole and resultantly the sustainability of the political regime. Considering the dire consequences, resolute reforms in these domains should not be delayed any longer, no matter how bitter the political confrontation, in order to make the public interest prevail.

Except for administrative obstacles and interferences, the Chinese service sector also faces an unfavorable tax regime. Unlike industrial enterprises, Chinese service enterprises do not pay VAT but business tax. Business tax is charged on sales, and the tax rate ranges from 3 percent to 20 percent depending on the type of services provided. Compared with VAT, business tax has a larger tax base and has the problem of double taxation. Take airplane leasing for example. High prices of airplanes push up revenues in the airplane leasing industry. As this industry is a service industry, all revenues are subject to business tax. Even if we take the lowest tax rate, which is 3 percent, the volume of tax paid would still be gigantic. Heavy tax burdens become one of the major factors that impede the healthy development of the airplane leasing industry and many other service industries as well. After the VAT reform in 2009 industrial enterprises further decreased their tax burden as fixed-asset investment became deductible from VAT tax base. This reform further decreased the competitive advantage of tertiary sector to secondary sector in China. Similar structural tax reduction reforms should be expanded to services as well.

Last but not least, as China still has a rigid *hukou* system (a household registration system), and the social welfare provision for people from different geographical areas is still uneven, and the geographical mobility of the Chinese population is hindered. This limited mobility of labor poses an unnecessary restraint over the development of service sector both on the supply side and demand side. As migrant workers face difficulties in seeking social services, especially education for their children, many children were left behind in the countryside to live with their grandparents. However, we have shown in Chapter 6 that carefully planned urbanization will be the spear of development for the next two decades. It will spread and raise social welfare, if upward mobility is generated by migration from the countryside to the cities. Cities are the loci of knowledge externalities, inherent to communication and information-intensive activities in both business and public services, due to the agglomeration of human activities. To take full advantage of the process, however, migrants and their families should be able to benefit from a massive investment in education and be entitled to the same social protection as city residents. They should become unrestricted citizens in their new homes and places of work. This requirement involves a deep reform of the *hukou* system, which was introduced to avoid unfettered flight of millions of people from the countryside, swelling huge unmanageable slums in suburban areas of megacities that can be observed from Mumbai to São Paulo and from Lagos to Mexico. Therefore the reform of this *hukou* system, as well as the reform of rural land ownership to assure farmers that they will get a fair price for the land-use right they sell, should be part of the parcel of strategic planning to achieve successful urbanization.

Dealing with debts generated in financing local governments

The first immediate task before introducing new incentives in finance is cleaning up the debts generated in financing local governments that took advantage of the stimulating plan in 2009 to finance lots of unapproved projects.

The government has had recourse to rigorous and thorough evaluation of the magnitude of the debt. In June 2011 the State Audit Bureau released the report on local government debt. It covers the outstanding debt of local governments and local government financing vehicles (LGFVs). It discloses the breakdown of the outstanding amount by borrower, region, sector, maturity, and government responsibility. Several features are highlighted. At the end of 2010 the total outstanding debt of local governments and all LGFVs amounted to Yuan 10.71 trillion, of which 4.97 trillion for LGFVs. Of total debt, 79 percent (Yuan 8.47 trillion) were bank loans. Of the outstanding 8.47 trillion bank loans, local governments have responsibility to repay 59 percent and they have guaranteed 23 percent. The sector breakdown of the outstanding debt is 36.7 percent in urban construction, 24.9 percent in transportation, 10.6 percent in land reserves, 9.5 percent in education and public housing, and 4.8 percent in agriculture. The repayment schedule is given in Table 7.6.

The report provides clarity to define a resolution strategy. However, the asset quality of the bank loans has not been revealed. The 18 percent of bank loans that escape responsibility or guarantee of the local governments from land sale might well be a source of future NPLs. Furthermore, if some local governments do not have the means to fulfill their responsibility or honor their guarantee, more potential NPLs could appear. This is more likely to occur in smaller cities. The report shows that debt is more than 100 percent of annual revenue for 78 city-level and 99 county-level financing vehicles. All in all, as much as 20 percent of total outstanding loans, amounting to Yuan 3 trillion might be potential NPLs because their repayment might not be covered by sufficient cash flows.

Table 7.6 Repayment schedule of the outstanding local government and LGFV debt

Years	% of total per year
2011	24.5
2012	17.2
2013	11.4
2014	9.3
2015	7.5
2016 and after	30.2

Source: State Audit Bureau (2011)

Even if the NPL ratio reached 20 percent of total local government debt and LGFVs debt, e.g. an amount of Yuan 2,000 billion, it would be manageable. Part of it would be transferred to central government funding; another part would be absorbed by local government revenue and asset sales or converted into long-term government bonds. The last portion left to banks to write off would amount to 20 percent of total NPLs. Given previous efforts of the China Banking Regulatory Commission (CBRC) to strengthen bank balance sheets, the banks, which have enjoyed fat profits in the last few years and which had a very low NPL ratio in 2008, can afford to write off the remainder. Suppose the remainder is 20 percent of total NPLs and loss given defaults is 50 percent, this amounts to no more than Yuan 200 billion to write off.

Deepening the reforms of the financial system

The development of a vibrant financial system in China has peculiar importance for the growth of the service sector. Not only is finance itself a pivotal service industry, it also plays a vital role in supporting the growth of other service providers, especially in providing financing to SMEs with reasonable cost and encouraging innovations.

Since Asia including China is, like Europe (but unlike the US) a bank-centered financial system, the core problem is making banks more competitive and more efficient. The first thing to do is to strengthen their balance sheets further.

To strengthen bank balance sheets, the CBRC has announced the new prudential regulation to be implemented from 2012 onwards. They are stricter and the schedule is much tighter than Basel 3. The CAR (Capital Adequacy Ratio) imposed on banks as a minimum equity ratio to risk-weighted assets is 11.5 percent for large banks and 10.5 percent for other banks against 7 percent in Basel 3. The simple leverage ratio is 4 percent of non-weighted assets against 3 percent in Basel 3. The CBRC has retained the same constraints for the counter-cyclical surcharge and the two liquidity ratios. The implementation of the whole paraphernalia is following a faster schedule: 2013 for systemic banks and 2016 for other banks against an adjustment period that is running to 2019 in Basel 3. Capital requirement is one aspect of achieving a more robust banking system. Two others are more demanding supervision and better risk management. They are closely related to properly valuing bank assets, thus to prices that reveal risk more adequately.

In the first section of the present chapter we remarked that credit prices are still among the most distorted. Before the global financial crisis, the international organizations (World Bank and OECD) advocated unashamedly wholesale financial liberalization cum full opening as the only single way to get rid of price distortions. Since the demise of the Wall Street model based upon initiating credit, pooling, securitizing, and distributing under the pretence of disseminating risk, it is hard to advocate this as the most efficient panacea. The European banking system, built under the principle of mammoth universal financial conglomerates, is not attractive either, since it has been trapped into the sovereign debt crisis, and has suffered from poor supervision and under-capitalization. Therefore the problem of reforming the financial system in China is no menial task. It is haunted by the following question: what is the proper role of banks in an emerging market country at the present stage of development?

The role of finance to implement the strategic planning that will guide the transition to sustainable development is critical. We have shown in Chapter 6 that sustainable economic paths into the future are plagued with huge uncertainty. Because finance is the trade of promises over time, it is the institution that structures economic time. It does so in setting possible time horizons for decentralized economic agents and transforming undifferentiated uncertainty into a differentiated structure of risks that can be managed and transferred. Financial prices are so important because they make possible the expression and comparison in money terms of future promises embodied in any venture that uses social resources in the hope of producing higher future social values. These expressions are the net present values of investment projects, e.g. the discounted expected future streams of cash flows from money invested today adjusted to estimated risk. This is why administrative rules fostering vested interests from positions of power can provoke persistent biases in financial prices that seriously distort the allocation of social resources.

Important progress in financial liberalization can be a byproduct of fiscal reform. Local governments should be allocated fiscal resources to adequately fulfill their social responsibilities in providing public goods to citizens. Then public investment plans must be made compatible with objectives and criteria of strategic planning. Specific projects of spending over a minimum amount to be determined by central government should be scrutinized by planning agencies with the proper expertise under the authority of the NDRC. Medium-term investment budgets made of approved projects under central oversight and some guarantee of central government can be financed by municipal and provincial bonds. Primary issues would appeal to institutional investors, chiefly domestic but also open to some extent to foreign investors in search of diversification. Banks can be regulators of secondary markets. Because urbanization is a long-term direction of development, the bond market has a large potential of growth.

What does financing the process of urbanization mean for banks? On the one hand, with the huge investments involved they will need more capital than they can generate from retained profits, all the more so since fiscal reform (depicted in the next section) advocates that big banks like other SOEs pay dividends to the state. Because urbanization implies enlarging the consumer base in broadening the population that can afford urban modes of consumption, the banks must build up consumer banking and offer diversified banking services to low-income people without losing money. Banks, if they are adequately capitalized and tightly supervised by CBRC that is pushing them to invest in modern risk management systems, can afford higher costs on deposits. This is the right way to increase the cost of capital in forcing the banks to make the financial system more competitive to keep their deposit base. Correlatively the authorities should encourage the developments of institutional investors able to bring equity capital to banks and to non-financial corporations, on the one hand, to buy bonds issued by corporations and local governments on the other. Institutional investors are key actors to finance long-term investments if they operate in a non-volatile environment. Domestic institutional investors can be long-run shareholders of banks, allowing the state to withdraw partly without jeopardizing the stability of ownership. Even if the state wants to keep majority control there is much room for strengthening capital with institutional investors' participation. This is one more reason to keep the financial system sufficiently protected from international capital flows while promoting competition domestically. China is a large enough country to improve competition substantially without full opening to foreign capital. Instead of hazardous speculation in stock or real estate markets to avoid negative real yields on their deposits, households will be able to build up their financial wealth in diversifying their saving between bank deposits, life insurance contracts, and pension funds. A competitive banking system should be able to avoid the proliferation of insecure mutual funds.

Aside the five big retail networked banks, which collect together about 80 percent of total deposits, city banks should play a much more important role in providing basic banking services to the poor and supplying mortgage and consumer credit to the expanding middle class. City banks and rural cooperatives in the countryside are the ones that can reach the "unbanked." As far as ownership is concerned, state banks, private banks, and mutual banks can coexist. Such a mixture can be more robust macroeconomically to hold credit in a downturn. Over time the share of state banks will decline gently to 50–60 percent of deposits.

Tax incentives can be granted to expand banking in backward regions as part of the "Go West" objective of the 12th five-year plan. With tax incentives and more leeway to adjust interest rates on their credit, rural cooperatives can become profitable, as long as a credit culture can spread in the depth of the countryside.

Increase investment to producer and public services

Although the Chinese economy is investment heavy, investments in the tertiary sector, especially some key public services, are still limited. According to a calculation by Li and Yuan (2010), in 2007 the share of education investment in China's total investment diminished to a mere 1.7 percent from 3 percent in 2003. China's public services were still in serious lack of funding.

The reasons for such low investment rate in social services are manifold. The administrative impediments mentioned above blocked private investments into those domains. Thus the current investment in social services is single-handedly dependent on governmental investments. This further leads to two questions. What are the fiscal resources available for social service expenditure? What are the incentives for the relevant governmental bodies to invest in these services? Currently in China expenditure for social service provision is mainly the responsibility of local governments and their appetite for investment in social services is not strong. Central government is trying to adjust local officials' investment preference by setting up evaluation schemes on social service provision and injecting fiscal funding for such provision by ad hoc specialized transfers. Although these measures are helpful, they are not fundamental and institutionalized solutions to the problem. In order to boost investments into social services, the markets must be open to private actors and stable fiscal resources must be dedicated to such uses.

Continuing China's unfinished fiscal reform

Fiscal reform is one of the most direct and powerful tools in adjusting the distorted factor prices and redistributing national income. It influences the behavior of all economic actors: individuals, enterprises, and governments alike. Through tax-sharing schemes, it also defines the national administrative structure, both vertically (central and local government relationship) and horizontally (the relationship among regions).

The framework of China's current fiscal regime was established in 1994. Facing a severe administrative crisis, the immediate purpose of the 1994 fiscal reform was to strengthen the financial position of central government. Thus the design of the 1994 fiscal regime focused on enlarging the tax base, simplifying tax administration, recentralizing fiscal power and facilitating economic growth, whereas certain nuances of a modern fiscal regime were not fully addressed. In other words, the 1994 fiscal system was inchoate. The policy-makers at the time envisioned a continuous process of fiscal reforms which could accommodate the rapidly changing economic situation in China. Yet since its institution in 1994, the core of the fiscal regime has been left intact for nearly two decades.

Meanwhile, China had been through dramatic structural changes. The 1994–2008 growth regime had been through its full cycle of birth, growth, triumph and decline. As a cornerstone of this growth regime, the 1994 fiscal system had also been losing its positive effects over economic and social developments. The emergence of a new growth regime calls for uncompleted fiscal reform to resume. In this section, we discuss the detailed measures to pursue China's next fiscal regime that would facilitate the rebalancing process of the Chinese economy and promote the smooth transition to the next sustainable growth regime.

The incompleteness of the 1994 tax reform can be analyzed from three aspects. First, as explained in Chapter 4, the 1994 tax regime was the first modernized tax regime in China. Before 1994 governments relied on profit remittances from SOEs as their major source of income. However, with the rise of the market economy, such socialist fiscal doctrine was no longer relevant. The tax base of central government was severely eroded due to the lack of effective taxation measures over private activities. In order to quickly strengthen the financial position of central government, the 1994 tax design emphasized the effective extraction of large-ticket tax items, especially the ones that could be easily administrated. This is partially the reason why the current Chinese tax regime is so heavily dependent on turnover taxes. This strategy successfully reversed the down-trend of central fiscal revenue, and leveled the playing field for enterprises with different ownership types and geographical locations. As turnover taxes were heavily levied upon consumption, such a tax structure also encouraged capital accumulation and fixed-asset investments, which were still badly needed at the time. However, since 1994, hyper growth has utterly altered the exposition of China's economic and social structure. The biggest challenges China faces today are how to upgrade domestic consumption and redistribute wealth from capital owners to wage earners, as well as how to induce the transition of the growth regime onto a more sustainable path. As a result, a consumption-heavy tax regime is no longer suitable for China's present and future. The tax regime must be reformed in order to overhaul the economic structure and to redistribute wealth.

Second, the 1994 tax-sharing system has redefined the tax revenue-sharing scheme between central and local governments, yet has failed to prudently re-examine the corresponding expenditure sharing on public goods and services provision. Important questions, such as what an optimal intergovernmental fiscal relationship should be in China and how social functions should be allocated to different level of governments, have not been addressed. In order to narrow the gap between local government income and expenditure, ad hoc transfers have been made from central government to the provinces with constant political bargaining. Such an uninstitutionalized transfer system has at least two main drawbacks. First, the adhoc nature of these transfers disturbs the long-term planning of local areas and creates political frictions in the bargaining process. Second, transfers from the central government are normally granted to provincial governments who then fully control the disposition of these financial resources among subordinate areas. Such a top-down distributive channel is directly responsible for the widespread financial difficulties at the lowest levels of Chinese jurisdictions. Unfortunately key social services, such as primary medical care and elementary education, are carried out at these lower administrative levels. The scarcity of financial resources seriously hampered the provision of basic social goods and services, especially in rural areas. For the healthy deployment of China's next growth regime and the establishment of an effective national strategic planning system, Beijing must advance the unfinished reform in tax sharing by distinctively redefining the division of social responsibilities among different administrative levels and by matching each social function with corresponding financial resources in an institutionalized manner.

Last but not least, the 1994 fiscal reform has diminished but not eliminated extra- and off-budgetary items in China. One of the largest extra-budgetary items was the income gained through transfer of land. From 1994 to 2008 competitions among provinces and municipals for tax bases urged local governments to allocate land for industrial uses at low cost. Such behavior played a positive role in promoting industrialization and urbanization in China when capital accumulation was badly needed. However, for the purpose of achieving balanced and sustainable development with social welfare enhancement, the contradictions caused by such unregulated land transfers are dramatic. Predatory land seizure deprived former landholders – especially farmers – the fair compensation they deserve, which in turn aroused bitter social discontent and impeded healthy urbanization. If the landless farmers cannot obtain enough resources to settle down in urban regions, they will pose tremendous threats to China's social stability, because they and their families will not bear silently the deterioration of their quality of life. Another issue China has to tackle seriously in the next phase of fiscal reform is the collection and distribution of SOEs' profits. To sustain heavy capital accumulation, SOEs have benefited from sizable allocated resources from the state; yet the dividends they paid to the state and Chinese people were minimal. Regulations of those extra- and off-budget items must be strengthened and institutionalized.

In the following we offer our thoughts on how China can resume its unfinished fiscal reform in the three aspects highlighted above. The purpose is to foster a modern tax regime that can help rebalance China's national income distribution, erase the distortion in factor prices, and guide the transition to the sustainable growth regime depicted in Chapter 6.

Restructuring the tax system for the next growth regime

When talking about a tax regime, the first question many might raise would be: is the overall tax burden too high? Similarly, when discussing the future tax regime in China, many ask: should China decrease or increase its overall tax level? However, isolated from a country's economic growth, societal structure, governmental functions, and social welfare systems, such questions do not have much meaning. More intriguing inquiries should be not about the level of total tax, but about what structure of tax sources and fiscal expenditures is most suitable for today's China and its transition to next growth regime embodying social welfare enhancement and sustainability.

The current tax structure stifles consumption and SME industrial upgrading

China's current tax regime is heavily dependent on turnover taxes. In 2009 65 percent of national tax revenue was generated by turnover taxes,[4] among which domestic VAT contributed 28 percent of total tax income. As turnover taxes are regressive, the current tax structure provides adverse incentives for promoting social equity and encouraging domestic consumption.

In China's current tax system, the so-called domestic consumption tax is better understood as a luxury, or excise tax. It is charged over the consumption of certain goods, which are considered as luxury or harmful to public health. These tax items composed only 8 percent of total tax revenue in 2010. However, although Chinese VAT is collected from the production side, the ultimate bearers of this tax have always been Chinese consumers. Heavy VAT thus increases the real prices for consumer goods and services, and decreases the real purchasing power of Chinese consumers. Moreover, China's VAT has a nationally unified tax rate of 17 percent (a 13 percent preferential rate also exists). This undifferentiated tax rate implies that poor regions, small enterprises, and low- and middle-income households retain a large proportion of the VAT burden. This is exactly the opposite of what is desired for rebalancing domestic economic structure.

The second biggest item of China's tax revenue is corporate income tax. It constituted 18 percent of China's total tax revenue in 2010. Combined with VAT, the tax cost for Chinese enterprises mounted to 80 percent of corporate profit (Fan *et al.* 2010: 126). This ratio is lower only than Argentina. Domestic small and medium enterprises carried the greatest of this tax burden. Before 2008 foreign enterprises enjoyed preferential rates for corporate income tax. Large enterprises, foreign and domestic alike, often benefited from tax rebates from national or local governments, in expectation of their further investment. However, small private companies were usually left out of both these schemes, despite the fact that private SMEs are the most vibrant component of China's future economy and that they are by far the largest providers of jobs. Such an unfavorable tax environment considerably dampens private SMEs' vigor and weakens their competitiveness in the market.

Hence, in the next tax regime, the tax base has to be further widened and tax items further diversified so that Chinese tax will not be single-handedly levied

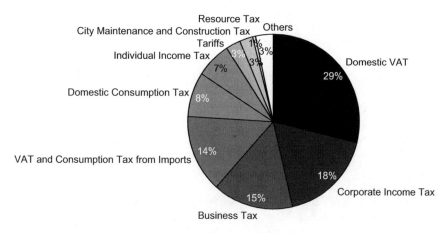

Figure 7.2 Composition of Chinese tax revenue in 2010.

Source: China Statistical Yearbook (2011)

over general consumption and production. The weight of turnover taxes in the tax system must be diminished in order to create a more progressive tax structure and higher incentives for domestic consumption and industrial upgrading. Introducing new tax items and expanding the tax items that have strong impact on income redistribution and sustainable development, such as asset taxes and resource taxes, would be a good solution.

Strengthening the role of the fiscal system in income redistribution

The tax items that possess the most direct and significant impact on wealth redistribution are income taxes and asset taxes. However, both of these two tax types are not sufficiently developed in China.

The concept of taxation of personal assets was quasi-non-existent in the 1994 tax regime. There were at least two major reasons for this. First, in 1994, Chinese individuals had hardly any personal assets, not to mention large concentration of personal wealth. Second, asset taxes are direct taxes and the cost of collecting these would have been much higher than turnover taxes, especially when China lacked a comprehensive personal credit system. Although endeavors have been made to fill this void in recent years, progress has been slow. China still does not have a complete system of property taxes. Important tax items, such as taxation on residential real estate properties, inheritance taxes and donation taxes, are either entirely missing, or charged only on an extremely limited scale and at minimal rates. Collection of these taxes also leaves much to be desired. The lack of imposition on property taxes not only is a loss of an important source of fiscal income,[5] but also of a powerful tool to rebalance wealth distribution and regulate the inflationary trend in real estate markets. Developing these types of taxes is one of the weightiest measures China should apply to establish a new tax structure that provides positive incentives for the deployment of China's sustainable growth.

Unlike property tax, China had already developed a complete range of personal income taxes. However, systemic reforms of the structure of personal income tax are still essential in order to rebalance the relationship between human capital and tangible capital. Such structural adjustments should focus on two major aspects.

The first aspect concerns the relationship between taxing salary income and taxing capital gains. China's personal income tax system differentiates carefully tax categories according to the varied sources of income, and all these categories of tax are levied independently. Among these categories, tax on salary income accounts for more than half of total personal income tax and its share has been rising over the years. In 2008 it composed 60.4 percent of total personal income tax revenue. In contrast, taxes on operation income and capital gains were rather limited. The imposition on capital gains has especially lagged behind. Not only is the base for capital gains tax not broad enough, the rate for capital gains taxes is fixed at 20 percent. Compared with the 45 percent tax rate for high salary income, this rate on capital gains is moderate. For the next growth regime, China needs to increase the weight of human capital over tangible capital. With this logic, the structure of Chinese personable income tax should be adjusted in favor of skilled wage earners instead of capital owners. Moreover, the widening wealth inequality among Chinese families is highly attributed to their disparate access to income other than salaries. For the purpose of strengthening income redistribution and reducing the wealth gap, the relationship between personal income tax on salary and other types of income taxes should be modified.

The other aspect of future reform concerns the structure of income taxes on salary. Decisions about the threshold for personal income exemption, the range of tax rates and the progressiveness of the scheme are all crucially influencing the behavior of employees and employers.

Generally speaking, China's personal income tax regime has not been friendly with the growth of middle classes, despite the fact that Chinese policy-makers accentuated on several occasions the importance of developing a normal distribution of income. In Table 7.7 we can observe that both before and after the reform of personal income tax in 2011, taxation on China's middle-income earners is quite substantial. Tax rates jump extremely rapidly from a low rate of 5 percent to 20 percent in the old scheme and from 3 percent to 25 percent in the new scheme. The upper limit tax rates in both of these two schemes are 45 percent, charged

Table 7.7 The regimes of personal income tax on salary (before and after 2011)

Before September 1, 2011

Taxable monthly income (Yuan)	Tax rate %
0–500	5
500–2,000	10
2,000–5,000	15
5,000–20,000	20
20,000–40,000	25
40,000–60,000	30
60,000–80,000	35
80,000–100,000	40
100,000 and above	45

After September 1, 2011

Taxable monthly income (Yuan)	Tax rate %
0–1,500	3
1,500–4,500	10
4,500–9,000	20
9,000–35,000	25
35,000–55,000	30
55,000–80,000	35
80,000 and above	45

Source: Chinese State Administration of Taxation (http://www.gov.cn/flfg/2011-07/01/content_1897307.htm, accessed September 2011).

for employees with monthly salaries higher than 100,000 RMB (before 2011) or 80,000 RMB (after 2011). This is an extremely elevated rate by international standards.

The recent reform in personal income tax has indeed benefited China's low-middle salary earners. By raising the threshold of personal income tax exemption from 2,000 Yuan per month to 3,500 Yuan per month, the new scheme has released 60 million Chinese employees from income tax payment. The ranges applicable to the lowest tax rates have also been enlarged. Those changes are appreciably positive in increasing the real income of low-middle class families and strengthening their purchasing power. This reform in personal income tax is an encouraging step towards the right direction in enhancing the redistributive function of the Chinese tax regime.

However, the tax burden on the middle-high class in China has, in fact, been increased with the new personal income tax regime. Under the old tax regime, the 20 percent marginal tax rate covered a large monthly income range from 5,000 Yuan to 20,000 Yuan. In the new regime the marginal tax rate quickly rises to 25 percent once salaries exceed 9,000 Yuan. The middle-high class is made up of China's best-educated professionals. They are the mainstay in China's transition to the next stage of growth. Taxing these people heavily impedes the upgrading of the economy and puts China in a disadvantageous position in the international competition for skills. Further tax cuts on the salary income of China's middle-high class should be considered.

To sum up, the current Chinese tax regime is inadequate or even counterproductive in rebalancing income distribution. In order to narrow wealth inequality, China must increase the weight of direct taxes against turnover taxes, especially raising the imposition of property taxes and taxes on capital gains. A prerequisite for achieving this purpose is to improve the country's tax administration ability. A comprehensive database of each Chinese family's financial information has to be created as soon as possible. This is the basis for correctly and effectively collecting income taxes and property taxes. Such a database is also a crucial tool for the fine-tuning of income redistribution when combined with information about a family's financial burden.

Setting the correct prices for natural resources and environmental services by tax

Energy efficiency and environmental protection are two essential components for sustainable development. The most effective mechanism to promote energy efficiency and environmental protection, as argued in Chapter 6, is to set up correct prices for natural resources and environmental services. However, today in China the pricing mechanisms for both natural resources and environmental services are in their infancy. There are two major reasons for such immaturity. First, property rights for the uses of these resources and services are ambiguous. Second, China has not yet established a tax regime able to price these resources and services in relation to their social value. In the following, we focus on strengthening the role of tax policy in setting correct prices for natural resources and environmental services.

China first began to tax natural resources in 1984. At the time this tax item was mostly designed to redistribute income. As long as the profit margin obtained from natural resource usages did not exceed 12 percent, the extraction of natural resources was still free of charge. Current resource tax in China is charged on the volume of natural resources extracted. As explained earlier in the chapter, such tax charges were minimal compared with international standards. In 2005 tax rates on the extraction of mineral resources were slightly adjusted to the upper end. However, the widely expected radical reform in resource taxes was abandoned in 2008 because of the global financial crisis.

As shown in Figure 7.2, in 2010 the proportion of resource tax in total tax revenue was a mere fraction (less than 1 percent). Taxes over environmental services were quasi-non-existent. Even for resource-rich north-western provinces, the proportion of resource tax revenue in total tax revenue was still very limited (see Table 7.8). This situation not only hampered environmental protection and clean energy investments, but also ingrained social inequality. With the sharp rise in energy prices, the profit of mineral resources-related enterprises swelled, while the energy cost for consumers increased. Poor western provinces, which were not adequately compensated for their resources, faced enormous environmental costs and ecological deterioration caused by natural resources extraction. A comprehensive reform on resource tax and environmental tax, including carbon tax, has to be brought into China's political agenda as soon as possible.

In June 2010 a pilot reform on resource taxes was enforced in Xinjiang province, a resource-rich province in north-western China. Resource taxes on crude oil and natural gas were charged at 5 percent on sales instead of a fixed amount on volume.[6] This reform showed immediate results. Resource tax revenue in Xinjiang province increased sharply from 1.2 billion Yuan to 3.2 billion Yuan. In September 2011 China amended its law on resource taxes to charge resource tax on value instead of volume. At the time of writing, no specific tax rates are announced yet. These are positive signs.

However, stronger political resolution is required to further resource tax reform. The coverage of resource tax has to be expanded and tax rates have to be adjusted upwards in order to fully compensate losses created in the extraction process to local environment, ecological systems, and the lives of local residents. Tax rates of natural resources are prices of these resources for extractors and thus should be integrated into the strategic planning of the nation. Similarly, for environmental services, it is critical to establish a clear tax regime so that the price system for environmental services can guide the behavior of economic actors to a greener path.

At the moment the political debates about resource and environment tax reform, including the implementation of carbon tax, focus on the potential impact of these taxes over China's economic growth. One popular view is that China must go through a polluting and extensive phase of growth before it can tackle the environmental problems, just like the industrialized countries of

Table 7.8 Proportion of resource tax in total tax revenue for China and five north-western provinces in 2010

	National total	Shaanxi	Gansu	Qinghai	Ningxia	Xinjiang
Total tax revenue (RMB bn)	7,321.1	71.1	22.0	8.9	12.7	41.6
Resource tax revenue (RMB bn)	41.8	2.2	0.6	1.0	0.2	3.2
Ratio of resource tax in total tax revenue (%)	0.6	3.1	2.8	10.8	1.5	7.8

Source: China Statistical Yearbook (2011)

Europe in the past. This view cannot be more wrong. China is not nineteenth-century Britain and must not be. As a giant latecomer in the industrialization process, our one and only earth cannot afford for China to go through the same extensive development process as Britain, nor embrace the wasteful American consumption style. This is a road doomed to ecological catastrophe. What China should be doing is to leapfrog into a post-industrial society empowered by environmentally friendly technologies. Taxes charged from resource extraction and pollution can be used to compensate environmental losses and invest in green innovations. This is the only way for China to take the lead in shaping a new global order as Arrighi expected.

On the expenditure side of tax regime

Discussions about a tax regime often single-handedly focus on the revenue side. However, in order to judge whether a tax regime is reasonable or not, it is critical to understand the story on the expenditure side as well. What is the size of public spending in China? Is it coherent with revenue? How is public spending allocated? Is the structure of this allocation welfare-enhancing? Is the process of allocating spending efficient? Some of these questions will be dealt with in the following section about furthering tax-sharing reform. Here we focus on the overall size and composition of public spending in China. The analysis below uses data on Chinese fiscal expenditures. Orchestrated with the expansion of fiscal revenue, the year-on-year growth of fiscal expenditure consistently outpaced GDP growth in the second stage of reform. In 2006 China's fiscal expenditure was 19.2 percent of GDP. This ratio was not exceptionally high by international standards. Even if taking extra- and off-budgetary expenditures into consideration, the size of China's fiscal spending was still nothing extraordinary.

Table 7.9 shows the complete trajectory of China's fiscal expenditure since the beginning of reform in 1978. Generally speaking, the size and growth of China's fiscal expenditure had been coherent with the evolution of fiscal revenue and the characteristics of each growth regime. With 1994 as a turning point, the weight of fiscal expenditure as a share of GDP experienced a lengthy decline in the first stage of reform and bounced back steadily in the second, thus evolved into a V-shaped trajectory. This is consistent with our discussions in Chapters 3 and 4 about the logic and deployment of Chinese reform.

However, controversies emerge when attention is shifted to the structure of China's fiscal expenditures. Most debated is capital spending, especially spending on infrastructure investment. In the influential 2006 OECD report, "Challenges for China's Public Spending," an international comparison was made about capital expenditure's share in total fiscal expenditure and in GDP (as shown in Figure 7.4). The figure distinctly indicates that in 2002 China invested a larger share of its fiscal resources on fixed assets than most of the OECD countries except for South Korea. When evaluated as a percentage of GDP, Chinese governmental capital spending was the largest, about double the highest OECD country, Korea. A conclusion was

Table 7.9 The evolution of China's fiscal expenditure from 1978 to 2010

Year	National fiscal expenditure (bn RMB)	Growth of national fiscal expenditure (%, YoY)	Fiscal expenditure/ GDP (%)	Growth of fiscal expenditure/GDP growth	Fiscal expenditure per capita (Yuan)
1978	112.20	33.0	30.8	2.4	116.60
1979	128.10	14.2	31.5	1.2	131.30
1980	122.80	-4.1	27.0	-0.3	124.40
1981	113.80	-7.4	23.3	-1.0	113.70
1982	123.00	8.0	23.1	0.9	121.00
1983	141.00	14.6	23.6	1.2	136.90
1984	170.10	20.7	23.6	1.0	163.00
1985	200.40	17.8	22.2	0.7	189.30
1986	220.50	10.0	21.5	0.7	205.10
1987	226.20	2.6	18.8	0.1	207.00
1988	249.10	10.1	16.6	0.4	224.40
1989	282.40	13.3	16.6	1.0	250.60
1990	308.40	9.2	16.5	0.9	269.70
1991	338.70	9.8	15.5	0.6	292.40
1992	374.20	10.5	13.9	0.4	319.40
1993	464.20	24.1	13.1	0.8	391.70
1994	579.30	24.8	12.0	0.7	483.40
1995	682.40	17.8	11.2	0.7	563.40
1996	793.80	16.3	11.2	1.0	648.60
1997	923.40	16.3	11.7	1.5	746.90
1998	1,079.80	16.9	12.8	2.5	865.50
1999	1,318.80	22.1	14.7	3.5	1,048.40
2000	1,588.70	20.5	16.0	1.9	1,253.50

continued

Table 7.9 continued

Year	National fiscal expenditure (bn RMB)	Growth of national fiscal expenditure (%, YoY)	Fiscal expenditure/ GDP (%)	Growth of fiscal expenditure/GDP growth	Fiscal expenditure per capita (Yuan)
2001	1,890.30	19.0	17.2	1.8	1,481.10
2002	2,205.30	16.7	18.3	1.7	1,716.80
2003	2,465.00	11.8	18.1	0.9	1,907.50
2004	2,848.70	15.6	17.8	0.9	2,191.50
2005	3,393.00	19.1	18.3	1.2	2,594.90
2006	4,042.20	19.1	18.7	1.1	3,075.10
2007	4,978.14	23.2	18.7	1.0	3,767.60
2008	6,259.27	25.7	19.9	1.4	4,713.20
2009	7,629.99	21.9	22.4	2.6	5,717.50
2010	8,987.42	17.8	22.4	1.0	6,702.50

Source: China Statistical Yearbook of various years

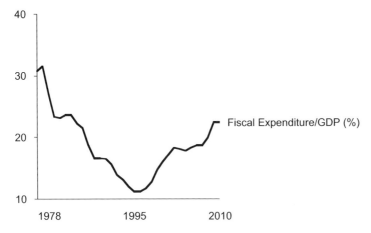

Figure 7.3 The V-shaped trajectory of fiscal expenditure to GDP.

Source: China Statistical Yearbook of various years

thus drawn that Chinese fiscal expenditure on physical investment was too high (OECD 2006).

We call for some caution before reaching this conclusion. First of all, as argued in previous chapters, China's current development stage and the rapid movement of urbanization require high investment in infrastructure. However, where China should draw the fine line between "too much" infrastructure investment and a fair amount is still an unsettled question. The inefficiencies and low qualities of a large number of public infrastructure projects were indeed worrisome. These problems suggest that the process of project planning and implementation needs earnest improvement and reform. Yet they do not necessarily mean that, because of these operational problems, China should scale down fiscal supports for infrastructure investment projects.

In fact, if we look into the sources of financing for China's fixed-asset investments, it is striking how little was financed by state budget (see Table 7.10). Ever since the beginning of reform, budgetary spending declined as a share of total social fixed-asset investment. In 1994 the state budget constituted only 3 percent of total fixed-asset investment. During the second phase of the reform this ratio experienced fluctuations in accordance with countercyclical macroeconomic policies. Especially after the Asian Crisis, state-led infrastructure investments were often resorted to for the stimulation of economic growth. Yet, even so, the average state budgetary share in total fixed-asset investment was a mere 4.5 percent from 1994 to 2009. This ratio was out of line with that of most developing and industrialized countries.

Some may argue that the Chinese government relied heavily on banks and local governments' extra- or off-budgetary funds to finance government-led projects. Although those funds were not fiscal, they should still be considered governmental.

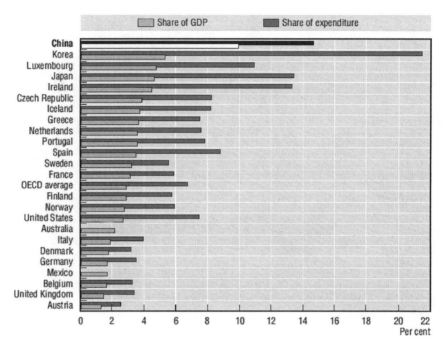

Figure 7.4 Government capital spending as a percentage of GDP and total
expenditure (2002).

Source: OECD (2006)

This argument is right, and such a phenomenon has had profound implications
for the development of the economy. However, government-encouraged expenditure and fiscal expenditure are two entirely disparate concepts. For our discussion
here about China's tax regime and whether China has been making fair and efficient use of its tax resources or not, it is only fiscal expenditure that should be
considered. Hence, contrary to common impression that the Chinese government
had been investing too much, it was actually that it had not been shouldering its
fair share in public investments. Consequently we have reasons to ask: did the
government succeed in providing the social goods that its people paid taxes for?
Has China been making efficient uses of its tax resources? If a large part of infrastructure construction was financed by cheap bank credit, does that mean Chinese
people were implicitly taxed again? If most of the projects were financed by bank
credits and self-raised funds, wouldn't this financing structure put the provision
of non-profitable public goods in great danger?

Another salient feature of the evolution of China's public spending composition
was the sharp increase in administrative expenditures. The share of administrative cost in total fiscal expenditure increased from 4.7 percent in 1978 to 18.7
percent in 2006. The growth rate of administrative cost averaged 21.2 percent
in the 1994–2006 period, which was more than double the GDP growth rate in

Table 7.10 Composition of China's financial sources for fixed-asset investment (%)

	State budget	*Domestic loans*	*Foreign investment*	*Self-raising fund and others*
1981	28.1	12.7	3.8	55.4
1982	22.7	14.3	4.9	58.1
1983	23.8	12.3	4.7	59.2
1984	23.0	14.1	3.9	59.0
1985	16.0	20.1	3.6	60.3
1986	14.6	21.1	4.4	59.9
1987	13.1	23.0	4.8	59.1
1988	9.3	21.0	5.9	63.8
1989	8.3	17.3	6.6	67.8
1990	8.7	19.6	6.3	65.4
1991	6.8	23.5	5.7	64.0
1992	4.3	27.4	5.8	62.5
1993	3.7	23.5	7.3	65.5
1994	3.0	22.4	9.9	64.7
1995	3.0	20.5	11.2	65.3
1996	2.7	19.6	11.8	66.0
1997	2.8	18.9	10.6	67.7
1998	4.2	19.3	9.1	67.4
1999	6.2	19.2	6.7	67.8
2000	6.4	20.3	5.1	68.2
2001	6.7	19.1	4.6	69.6
2002	7.0	19.7	4.6	68.7
2003	4.6	20.5	4.4	70.5
2004	4.4	18.5	4.4	72.7
2005	4.4	17.3	4.2	74.1
2006	3.9	16.5	3.6	76.0
2007	3.9	15.3	3.4	77.4
2008	4.3	14.5	2.9	78.3
2009	5.1	15.7	1.8	77.4
2010	4.7	15.2	1.6	78.5

Source: China Statistical Yearbook (2011)

the same period. Such a disproportionate hike in administrative cost indicated a terrible inefficiency of the Chinese bureaucratic system in public management. It encroached on fiscal funds for social goods and services provision. Overly sophisticated governmental bodies and myriad administrative regulations also interfered in microeconomic activities and aroused extensive social discontent. Wasteful and incompetent public administration also directly undermined the political credibility of the CCP. Consequentially, a drastic restructuring of China's bureaucratic system is urgently needed. Responsibilities of different ministries must be further clarified and sub-national administrations simplified. Political reforms do not only refer to whether China will have representative democracy and general elections or not. Ameliorating governmental structure and functions has crucial importance for administrative effectiveness and efficiency. We will illustrate our views on such reforms in the later part of this chapter and in Chapter 8.

Table 7.11 Evolution of Chinese administrative costs from 1978 to 2006

Year	National public administrative costs (bn RMB)	Growth of administrative costs (%, YoY)	Share of administrative costs in total fiscal expenditure (%)	Administrative costs per capita (RMB)
1978	5.3		4.7	5.5
1979	6.3	19.2	4.9	6.5
1980	7.6	19.8	6.1	7.7
1981	8.3	9.4	7.3	8.3
1982	9.1	9.9	7.4	8.9
1983	10.3	13.5	7.3	10.0
1984	14.0	35.6	8.2	13.4
1985	17.1	22.4	8.5	16.2
1986	22.0	28.6	10.0	20.5
1987	22.8	3.7	10.1	20.9
1988	27.2	19.0	10.9	24.5
1989	38.6	42.2	13.7	34.3
1990	41.5	7.3	13.4	36.3
1991	41.4	-0.1	12.2	35.7
1992	46.3	11.9	12.4	39.5
1993	63.4	36.9	13.7	53.5
1994	84.8	33.6	14.6	70.7
1995	99.7	17.6	14.6	82.3
1996	118.5	18.9	14.9	96.8
1997	135.9	14.6	14.7	109.9
1998	160.0	17.8	14.8	128.3
1999	202.1	26.3	15.3	160.6
2000	276.8	37.0	17.4	218.4

continued

Table 7.11 continued

Year	National public administrative costs (bn RMB)	Growth of administrative costs (%, YoY)	Share of administrative costs in total fiscal expenditure (%)	Administrative costs per capita (RMB)
2001	351.2	26.9	18.6	275.2
2002	410.1	16.8	18.6	319.3
2003	469.1	14.4	19.0	363.0
2004	552.2	17.7	19.4	424.8
2005	651.2	17.9	19.2	498.1
2006	757.1	16.3	18.7	576.0

Source: CEIC

Given the discussions above, it is not surprising to observe that China allocated an exceedingly small share of its fiscal expenditure on culture, education, public health, and R&D. In 2002, China spent slightly more than 5 percent GDP worth of fiscal funds on social services. That was lower than any OECD countries (Figure 7.5). Earlier in the chapter we pointed out that because of arduous entry barriers, private investment could hardly enter those markets either. As a result, Chinese social services face severe under-funding.

To conclude about China's current tax regime, here are our findings. Although the overall weight of tax burden in China was not high according to international comparisons, the structure of fiscal expenditure manifested excessive inefficiencies in public management and misallocation of tax resources. Fiscal spending on public goods and services must be boosted while wasteful administrative costs must be strictly constrained. In order to better match tax resources with productive usages, administrative organizations have to be restructured and governmental functions reoriented. Such reforms require strong political commitment but the provision of welfare-enhancing social goods and services are essential for China's urbanization process and transition to a sustainable development path.

Furthering the reforms in a tax-sharing scheme

China is a unitary country. Its administrative structure is strictly hierarchical, especially with regard to the personnel system. Central government delegates power to 34 provincial governments and names their governors. Similar delegations of

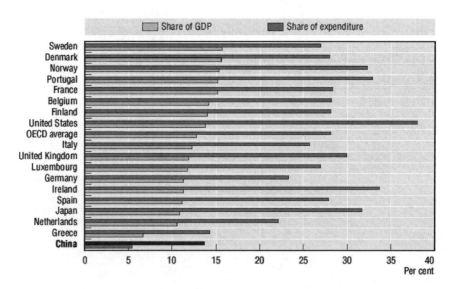

Figure 7.5 Ratio of fiscal expenditure on culture, education, public health, and science to GDP and to total expenditure: an international comparison (2002).

Source: OECD (2006)

power from superior level to subordinate level then extend down to prefectures, counties, and townships (Figure 7.6 illustrates the administrative hierarchy in China). Below township level there are still villages, which are not included in the formal administrative hierarchy. This hierarchical administrative structure and personnel system often gives the impression that the Chinese political system is extremely centralized. However, when evaluated from the angle of intergovernmental fiscal relationship, this judgment becomes rather obscure.

As explained in Chapter 4, one of the main purposes of 1994 tax-sharing scheme was to enhance the share of central fiscal revenue in the total national fiscal revenue. To realize this goal, clear allocation of fiscal resources between central government and sub-national governments was designed and institutionalized. As demonstrated in Table 7.12, the biggest tax item, VAT, was divided between central and local governments at a 75/25 ratio, i.e. the central government retains 75 percent of VAT and local governments 25 percent. The second biggest, income taxes, were divided at a ratio of 60/40 (central/local). Plus the central tax items, such as the consumption tax, the share of central government's revenue stabilized to slightly over 50 percent of total on-budget national revenue after the 1994 tax reform. Thus, as regards tax revenue allocation, the Chinese fiscal system had become more centralized under the 1994 tax-sharing scheme.

However, even after the 1994 tax reform, the degree of fiscal decentralization remained astonishingly high on the expenditure side. The centralization of fiscal revenue had not been correlated with similar centralization of budgetary expenditure responsibilities. After 1994, local governments still had to carry out more

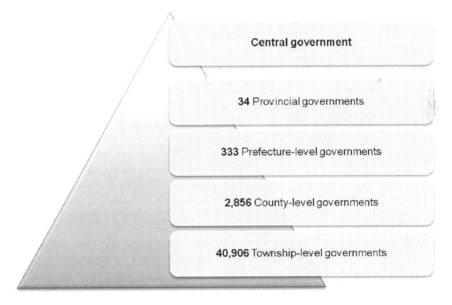

Figure 7.6 The administrative hierarchy of China.

Source: China Statistical Yearbook (2011)

Table 7.12 Sharing of major tax items between central and local governments (%)

Tax items	Weight in total tax revenue in 2010	Central share	Local share
VAT	29	75	25
Business tax	15	0	100
Consumption tax	8	100	0
Corporate income tax	18	60	40
Personal income tax	7	60	40
Others	23	n/a	n/a

Source: China Statistical Yearbook (2011) and Chinese State Administration of Taxation

than 70 percent of total budgetary expenditures. Down the years, this percentage has been growing instead of declining. In 2010 local governments undertook 82.2 percent of total on-budget expenditures. Table 7.13 gives us a snapshot of how major expenditure responsibilities were partitioned in 2006 between central and local governments. Except for national defense and interest expense, local governments were responsible for the majority of current expenditure, especially for social services and welfare provision.

The structural mismatch between fiscal resource distribution and fiscal responsibility sharing was even graver when we take into consideration the partition of fiscal responsibilities among sub-national governments (provinces, prefecture, county, and township). Local governments, especially prefecture- and county-level governments, had to take full responsibility for pension and social relief expenditures. Townships, the lowest level of formal administration, bore the entire cost of compulsory education provision in rural areas and 55–60 percent of public medical care subsidies[7] (Yang *et al.* 2006: 20). In other words, it was the lower levels of administrations that carried out the majority of responsibilities in primary social services provision.

In sharp contrast with the bottom-heavy allocation of fiscal expenditure responsibilities, fiscal transfer system, the major mechanism to narrow down the gap between local governments' revenue and expenditure, is a top-down system. Each year, central government transferred large amounts of central resources to provincial governments, which then had the power to allocate these resources to lower administrations. Although the detailed mechanisms of how such transferred funds were handled varied from province to province, such a top-down resource distribution scheme favored the higher levels of the hierarchy and created universal financial difficulties in the lower levels of administrations, especially in the poor regions. To conclude, China's bottom administrations had rather worrying financial positions and resultantly the provision of social goods and services for the most needy in China was jeopardized.

Why was there such a delay in reforming the expenditure-sharing system to match up with the centralization of tax revenue in China? The main reason is related to the political will of the national leaders. The resolute implementation of

Table 7.13 Expenditure sharing between central and local governments (2006)

Year	Amount (bn RBM)	Central share (%)	Local share (%)
Capital construction	439.0	33.8	66.2
Innovation funds and science & technology promotion fund	174.5	24.8	75.2
National defense	297.9	98.9	1.1
Government administration	335.6	13.7	86.3
Culture, education, science, and health care	742.6	9.7	90.3
Social security subsidiary	212.4	11.4	88.6
Pensions and relief funds for social welfare	90.8	0.6	99.4
Urban maintenance and construction	169.9	0.0	100.0
Industry, transportation, and commerce	58.1	23.2	76.8
Supporting agriculture production	216.1	9.0	91.0
Geological prospecting	14.2	26.8	73.2
Public security, procuratorial, court, and judical agency	217.4	4.5	95.5
Armed police troops	38.8	86.4	13.6
Foreign affairs	10.9	87.5	12.5
External assistance	8.2	100.0	0.0
Supporting undeveloped areas	22.0	1.9	98.1
Price subsidies	138.8	39.7	60.3
Other departments	146.2	7.6	92.4
Other expenditures	372.2	13.7	86.3
Interest payment	97.5	100.0	0.0

Source: National Bureau of Statistics of China (2008)

the 1994 tax reform stemmed from a severe ruling crisis of the central government (see Chapter 4). Naturally, the priority of the reform was for the centralization of fiscal resources, rather than the centralization of expenditures. Centralized fiscal power guaranteed the mandate of central government in directing economic development and reinforced the ultimate authority of central government in a unitary hierarchical political system. Once these goals were achieved, the momentum for continuing the reform of intergovernmental fiscal relationship on the expenditure side rapidly receded. What is more, even after the 1994 tax reform, a significant amount of extra- and off-budgetary revenues were still available to local governments. While at that time central government could not, or did not want to, incorporate all of these items into national budget, leaving a gap between the budgetary revenue and expenditure of local governments was the most efficient strategy in forcing local administrations to channel their extra- and off-budgetary income for fiscal uses. It is also worth noticing that the actual degree of fiscal revenue centralization after 1994 was not as deep as was generally perceived. For one thing, when the fiscal reform was designed, in order to gain acceptances

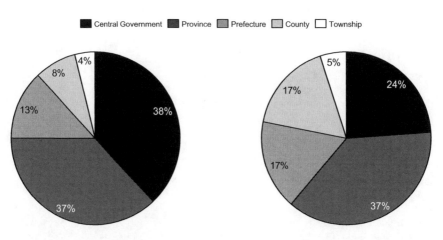

Figure 7.7 The distribution of revenue and expenditure across government levels (2002).

Source: China Statistical Yearbook (2011)

from the local areas, intensive political bargaining was carried out between the State Council and the heads of most provinces. Because of their better bargaining positions, the richer provinces were promised larger transfers in exchange for their acquiescence in reform. Resultantly, fiscal resources truly at the disposal of central government were thwarted, and the ability for central government to balance regional fiscal inequalities was handicapped too. Besides, the practices of tax collection also had the potential to undermine central fiscal resources. Although new tax bureaus under the direct supervision of the State Administration of Taxation were set up in 1994 to collect central and shared taxes, their daily operations still relied heavily on the local areas they resided in. Their personnel needed social goods and services that only local governments could offer. Thus when conflicts occurred between central and local interests, oftentimes it was local ones that prevailed.

Over time several of the above-mentioned impediments to further reforms in intergovernmental fiscal relationships have since disappeared, whereas the problems resulting from this unfinished reform deepened. The impoverishment of low-level governments had greatly impaired the provision of primary social goods and services, hence suppressed the accumulation of human resources, damaged social welfare, and posed a threat to the long-term health of Chinese society and economy. Meanwhile regional inequalities also intensified. The current intergovernmental fiscal relationship lacked institutionalized mechanisms to transfer resources horizontally. Although in recent years central government strengthened earmarked transfers to the poorer central and western provinces, these measures remained ad hoc. A more systemic solution is needed to alleviate regional inequalities. A more immediate danger catalyzed by the troubled intergovernmental expenditure-sharing system concerns extra- and off-budgetary resources seizure by the local governments. The large gap existing between local fiscal revenue and expenditure served as a carte blanche for local governments to obtain large extra- and off-budgetary resources. If in the 1990s the seeking of those resources still, arguably, played a positive role in promoting interregional competition and stimulating industrial growth, such extra- and off-budgetary revenue seizure is no longer compatible with China's goal of building a harmonious society. (We explain the problems of extra- and off-budgetary items in more detail later in the chapter.) Relentless land seizures intruded on the interests of farmers and aroused sharp social discontent and conflict. With considerable personal interests at stake, local governmental officials were enticed into risky and radical behavior, and if this trend cannot be efficiently curbed in the near future, it will not only undermine the country's public financial stability, but also damage the legitimacy of the whole political system.

Excessive fiscal decentralization is detrimental to social wealth

Thus a critical decision Chinese leaders must make in the near future is how to redesign intergovernmental fiscal relationships so that public finance and function can match. There are two possible directions of reform: one, central government should give local governments more tax power and a larger share of national fiscal income to match their expenditure responsibilities; the other, China should centralize certain fiscal responsibilities that are currently carried out by local governments. Such centralization could, at the same time, relieve local governments, especially at the lower levels, from overly heavy financial burdens, and strengthen central government's capacity for strategic planning and guarantee a relatively equal provision of primary social goods and services for the entire population. In the following, we discuss these arrangements of fiscal decentralization and suggest which one would be more suitable and possible for today's China.

It is not the purpose of this chapter to get involved in the extensive theoretical debate about the pros and cons of fiscal decentralization or centralization. Thus we focus directly on the Chinese case. As argued earlier, the 1994 tax reform only altered the partition of national fiscal revenue in China but left fiscal responsibility sharing intact. In Table 7.14, we can clearly observe a jump of central share of national fiscal revenue from 22 percent in year 1993 to 55.7 percent in year 1994. Although in following years this percentage was never as high as it was in 1994, it stayed stable and fluctuated in a relatively small range of 49–55 percent. In sharp contrast, the evolution of fiscal expenditure sharing did not experience any drastic change in 1994. From 1993 to 1994 the local share of expenditure diminished by a mere 2 percent, nothing comparable with the more than 30 percent loss in revenue partition. Since 2003 the degree of fiscal expenditure decentralization has even rapidly increased. In 2010 the part of expenditure responsibilities undertaken by local governments reached an astonishing 82.2 percent. Such a level of fiscal decentralization exceeded that of most other nations, developed and developing alike.

The usual arguments that support fiscal expenditure decentralization include the following. First, as local governments have better access to local information

Table 7.14 The evolution of the central–local fiscal relationship since 1993

Year	Fiscal revenue (%)		Fiscal expenditure (%)	
	Central share	Local share	Central share	Local share
1993	22.0	78.0	28.3	71.7
1994	55.7	44.3	30.3	69.7
1995	52.2	47.8	29.2	70.8
1996	49.4	50.6	27.1	72.9
1997	48.9	51.1	27.4	72.6
1998	49.5	50.5	28.9	71.1
1999	51.1	48.9	31.5	68.5
2000	52.2	47.8	34.7	65.3
2001	52.4	47.6	30.5	69.5
2002	55.0	45.0	30.7	69.3
2003	54.6	45.4	30.1	69.9
2004	54.9	45.1	27.7	72.3
2005	52.3	47.7	25.9	74.1
2006	52.8	47.2	24.7	75.3
2007	54.1	45.9	23.0	77.0
2008	53.3	46.7	21.3	78.7
2009	52.4	47.6	20.0	80.0
2010	51.1	48.9	17.8	82.2

Source: China Statistical Yearbook of various years

than central government, they are more efficient in providing social goods and services for the local population. Second, fiscal decentralization can constrain the Leviathan State, and curb the "grabbing hand" of government. Third, competitions among local governments can provide the citizens with different sets of social goods and services to choose from, hence motivate local governments to provide better social support in order to win a larger tax base.

The validity of the above-mentioned arguments depends heavily on certain assumptions. As Roy Bahl points out, decentralized governments are more efficient only when they are truly "accountable and responsive to citizens' needs and preferences" (Bahl and Martinez-Vazquez 2007); and are more accountable only "when sub-national governments have an adequate level of autonomy and discretion in raising their own revenues" (Bahl and Martinez-Vazquez 2007). Whether these two assumptions can be fulfilled or not depends on the idiosyncratic political system of the focal country. Thus the benefits of fiscal decentralization should not be taken for granted, but be treated with caution. An empirical study (Davoodi and Zou 1998) using a panel data set of 46 countries actually finds a negative relationship between fiscal decentralization and growth in developing countries. Other China-specific research (Zhang and Zou 1998; Qiao 2002) also showed that over-decentralization had a negative impact on China's local economic growth and was detrimental to regional equity.

Those empirical results were hardly surprising. The strictly hierarchical personnel system dictated that Chinese local officials were more sensitive to the intentions of their superiors than to the wills of local population. Thus their accountability and responsiveness to local needs were greatly obstructed. The current taxation law and budget law also constrained Chinese sub-national governments' autonomy in raising their own tax revenues. They cannot decide which tax items to charge, or to adjust tax rates, or to borrow from capital markets. Hence they can hardly be held accountable for their financial moves either.

Meanwhile, extreme fiscal expenditure decentralization provoked what Zhang Yongsheng called vertical and horizontal opportunistic behavior of local governments (Zhang 2009). Vertical opportunistic behavior means that higher-level governments would retain as many fiscal resources as possible while pushing fiscal responsibilities to the lower-level administrations. Horizontal opportunistic behavior means that as sub-national governments, especially low-level governments, face extensive financial difficulties, they would be enticed and pressured to seek rents from the market using administrative powers they possess. Additionally, extreme fiscal expenditure decentralization also makes coordination in social goods and service provision among local governments more expensive and thus creates repetitive construction and negative externalities. Such behavior indeed occurred in China and posed great threats to social welfare and political stability.

Integrating tax-sharing reform with sustainable development

For fiscal decentralization to function positively in China, we have to at least satisfy the two assumptions mentioned above. That is to say, the Chinese political system has to transform from its unitary form to a federal form. Not only do we not believe this is possible in any near future, nor do we regard such radical transformation as necessary. The previous chapters have comprehensively demonstrated that China, both in its glorious imperial era and in its recent reforming period, retains its unique political logic and societal texture. Hoping to transform this nation without regard to its peculiar trajectory would, quite likely, be doomed to fail, or at least require an extremely long time and considerable economic and political upheavals.

Obviously we have to look for alternative solutions to balance China's intergovernmental fiscal relations. Our suggestion has four main components: shrinking the size and diminishing the levels of local authorities; centralizing fiscal responsibilities for primary social services to national level; institutionalizing a more redistributive fiscal transfer system; and developing a well-regulated and diversified bond market for local governmental debts. Let us elaborate these points one by one.

In Figure 7.6, which illustrates the layers of China's administrative hierarchies, we see that China has five official administrative levels. But if we include villages this enormous hierarchical system would again expand. Either compared with China's own history, or compared with other countries, six layers of administration are excessive. Such an all-encompassing hierarchy was a heritage of the socialist era. When the economy was under central planning, the state needed a comprehensive network to mobilize resources and supervise the enforcement of central orders. After 30 years of market reform such an extensive bureaucratic system is no longer needed and is impeding the healthy development of China. While it is impossible for each level of hefty government to have its own stable tax incomes, local governments became "grabbing hands" in the market and administered resource allocation for their own best interests. The lack of accountability undermined local governments' incentives to provide sufficient and high-quality social goods and services. Moreover, the very existence of those official governmental bodies impedes the development of grassroots self-government also. As a result, the provision of primary social goods and services in China is under great threat, especially in interior rural regions. It is high time to revise the deployment of the current administrative hierarchy.

As the five levels of administrative hierarchy are set up by the Constitution, complete elimination of certain levels requires a long political process. Nevertheless, even without amending the Constitution, it is possible to weaken the fiscal functions of certain governmental levels and constrain their administrative powers as well. The fiscal functions of two administrative levels, the prefecture level and township level, for instance, can be revised to enhance the efficiency of the state. Prefecture level is immediately below provincial level and its role in the administrative hierarchy is rather obscure. Usually several major cities in a province would be chosen as prefecture-level cities and their administrations would supervise the governments of several adjacent smaller cities (county-level). This hierarchical relationship between prefecture-level cities and county-level cities does not serve irreplaceable functions; however, it gives prefecture-level governments opportunities of retaining more central transfers for themselves and thus diminishing central transfers to the lower county level. Pilot projects have been installed in several provinces, such as Zhejiang, Hainan, and Hubei, to reduce the fiscal functions of prefecture level. The former functions carried out by prefectures were partially delegated to counties and partially centralized to provinces. Those measures are called "qiang xian kuo quan" (expansion of power for strong counties) and "sheng zhi guan xian" (direct supervision of counties by the province). The other administrative level that should be liberated from fiscal functions is the township level, the bottom level of Chinese hierarchy. Townships have the most disadvantageous financial position in the current fiscal system of China. Especially after the elimination of the Agriculture Tax, townships lost any direct source of financing. Yet they still had to carry out myriad fiscal responsibilities in primary social goods and services provision. Even if the amount of earmarked central transfers has been increasing in recent years, they are not sufficient to make up the deficits faced by the counties. Starting in 2003, pilot projects were launched in An Hui province to move the fiscal functions of townships up to the county level. In 2006 this measure, called "xiang cai xian guan" was encouraged nationwide. However, as the county level also faced widespread financial difficulties, such measures simply mitigated the problems instead of solving them.

A possibly better solution is the centralization of fiscal responsibilities, especially the responsibilities of primary social goods and services provision. Central government can set up national standards for the minimal provision of social goods and services (Yang *et al.* 2006: 21), and provide direct financing for a majority of these minimal primary goods and services provisions, while leaving local governments liberty to make any marginal amelioration according to local needs. Examples of these responsibilities are obligatory education provision, basic medical care provision and other social benefits. In recent years public teachers' salaries, for instance, have already experienced a certain degree of centralization. However, we believe such centralization can be deepened, generalized, and most importantly institutionalized. Centralization of certain fiscal expenditure responsibility is not only essential for rebalancing revenue distribution and expenditure sharing in China's intergovernmental fiscal relationship, but also beneficial to China's transition to a sustainable development path. It better guarantees the equalized provision of social goods and services across the nation, and strengthens Beijing's capacity in nationwide strategic planning. With the development of information technology (cloud technology, for example) and a modernized banking system, central government can and should take more direct responsibilities of fiscal expenditures without adding significant transaction costs.

The centralization of fiscal responsibilities for primary social goods and services provision would not eliminate the necessity of central transfers to different levels of local governments. A gap between sub-national fiscal revenue and expenditure would very possibly persist. Moreover, China is a country with extreme diversity. Different regions deviate greatly as regards to their ability to raise fiscal funds. Resultantly, it is unlikely that all sub-provincial governments could meet their expenditure needs under a standardized revenue sharing scheme (OECD 2006). A redistributive transfer system is essential to aid financially troubled regions and reduce inequalities. However, the current transfer system has to be improved and, to start with, it must be institutionalized. Ad hoc transfers impinge upon local governments' ability to make long-term plans and encourage local officials to highlight their financial problems with the purpose of obtaining more central finance. Second, the size of transfers to different regions should be better matched with the real disparity between fiscal revenue and expenditure of focal region. The allocation of transfers should play a larger role in rebalancing regional differences. Third, the channels of transferring should be more direct, i.e. central funds should be injected directly into the accounts of the level of governments in charge of the usage of the funds, instead of trickling through all levels of administration in the hierarchy.

Once local governments have expenditures corresponding with revenues, bond markets can be developed for local governments to finance their infrastructure projects. The benefits of well-functioning bond markets are fivefold. First, debt-issuing capital markets help to smooth investment cycles in avoiding credit crunches and creditors' runs while the banking sector has been loaded with problem loans. Second, as opposed to bank credit, which involves private risk assessment and monitoring by bank management, bond markets improve the efficiency of resource allocation in laying out a mechanism of public risk assessment and dissemination by the whole investing community. Deep and liquid government bond markets will provide a yield curve relieved from tightly regulated bank interest rates. Those market rates will in turn help pricing credit risk at each maturity, making room for the development of corporate bonds. A well-defined yield curve, extending to long-term bonds, opens a new source of finance for long-run investment projects. Third, bonds make a basic asset class in the strategic allocation of long-run institutional investors. For long-run investors the riskless security in strategic asset allocation is not a short-term bill but a long-term bond. The reason is that long-term bond yields exhibit mean-reverting processes, while rollover short-term bills do not in an uncertain interest rate environment. Therefore enriching capital markets has the subsequent advantage of enhancing institutional asset management in China where the population is aging and the government is establishing compulsory retirement plans. Fourth, the more public information is gathered in financial markets, the sooner the central bank will be able to shift from direct credit control to the price channel of monetary policy. By being able to communicate to the financial markets a forward view of the future path of the economy, the central bank will be able to smooth out fluctuations in real variables and make the growth path steadier. Fifth, an efficient domestic market is a precondition for safely phasing out capital controls in the future. This is a step forward toward linking the domestic capital market to global markets. With a broader and more diversified capital account it will become possible to move smoothly to a more flexible exchange rate regime.

The local government bond market has the potential to expand dramatically in the years ahead as the financing through shadow finance linked to the big banks (trust funds, credit platforms, and the like) is phased out with the will of central government to clean up the shaky pyramid of debts assembled by local governments in the aftermath of the Stimulus Plan announced in 2008.

As is usual in China, an experimental plan has been announced by the Ministry of Finance to be launched before the end of 2011. The plan covers two cities (Shanghai and Shenzhen) and two provinces (Zhejiang and Guandong). These will be authorized to issue bonds to alleviate their financial constraints and reduce the risks stemming from their ballooning debts. However, the new financing facility comes with strings attached. For the time being it is a quota of issuance but in the future, while the bond issue is generalized nationwide and becomes the normal instrument to finance public investments, bond issuance will come with central control on the budget by the NDRC to establish a hard budget constraint, audit of the projects to be financed and rating of the bonds on the secondary market for the institutional investors who will hold the bulk of the debt. Therefore this side of financial reform is quite consistent with the centralization of fiscal responsibilities we advocate to overhaul government budget.

Regulating extra- and off-budgetary revenue seizure is crucial for sustainability

So far our discussion about China's fiscal system has been confined to the on-budget items. However, China's extra- and off-budgetary governmental revenue is not only sizable but also problematic. The 1994 fiscal reform diminished but did not eliminate extra- and off-budgetary items in the country. Nowadays local governments' revenue seizure through these items, especially through land transfer, has become one of the biggest threats to stability and social welfare. In this part, we focus on the issue of land transfer and SOE profit to illustrate how reforms in these domains can be critical for the deployment of China's sustainable development.

Land transfers

Who owns land in China? This seemingly simple question has a rather perplexing answer. According to the Constitution, China has two types of land ownerships. In rural China land is collectively owned. However, the Constitution did not specify whether it should be the townships, the villages, or the village groups (autonomous groups in villages) that exert ownership rights. In urban China, land is state-owned. The Ministry of Land and Resources supervises the use of land on behalf of the state. Most sub-national urban governments also have local land bureaus that administer local operations over land. Apparently, private freehold ownership does not exist in China legally. However, after 1978, rural land was contracted to farmers. They are the actual holders of land-use rights in rural areas. Nevertheless, they cannot transfer,[8] sell, or mortgage the land they use, nor change its status from agricultural land to land for construction. In the cities land-use rights were granted or sold to private entities, at first by central government, starting from 1988, and then by municipal governments, starting in year 1992 (*China Hand* 2009). Similar to the situation in rural areas, these private entities only have land-use rights for a fixed term (usually 50–70 years), but potentially the lease can be renewed upon expiration (*China Hand* 2009). Only provincial governments have the right to change the status of a piece of land from "agricultural land" to "land for construction." According to the 2004 amendment to the Constitution and Land Administration Law, the state even possesses the power to compel holders to surrender land with compensation if the land seized were to be used for "public interests" (*China Hand* 2009).

Such a peculiar land ownership structure and land policies contributed significantly to the formation of China's growth regime of 1994–2008. Since only governments have the right of changing the status of land uses, governments at various levels became the monopolistic suppliers of land in China. By changing land status from agricultural land to land for construction, local governments may obtain revenue through at least two main mechanisms. One is through the collection of land-transferring fees. The 1994 reform in real estate greatly stimulated the land market. Demand for residential buildings skyrocketed and so did the real estate price. Thus local governments could charge high prices for the land transferred for residential and commercial developments. Meanwhile, agricultural lands were often seized at extremely low costs because compensations to rural collectives were calculated according to the annual agricultural yield of the focal land instead of the future market value of it. When lands were seized on the ground of "public interest," the compensation would be even lower. Thus a large margin existed between the two prices and this margin became an important source of income for local governments. Before 2006 land-transferring fees were mostly retained by local governments and were not regulated under the national budget at all. After 2006 land-transferring fees were integrated into the national budget and central government took 70 percent of these fees. However, land transferring remained a lucrative income source, which enticed local governments to engage in large-scale land-transferring activities. In 2010 total land-transferring fees in China was as high as 2.7 trillion RMB, which is 33.75 percent of total fiscal income of the same year. As most land transferred was former agricultural land, such behavior of local governments accelerated the urbanization process in China. From 1998 to 2005 urban areas expanded from 21.4 thousand square km to 32.5 square km. The annual growth rate was 6.18 percent (Jiang *et al.* 2010: 4).

Land transfers are also conducive to local tax base expansion. If the transferred land were to be developed for residential purposes, the real estate developing activities would generate business and corporate income taxes. If the land were transferred for commercial and industrial uses, the expected commercial and industrial activities would then provide the local governments with a stable base for business tax and VAT revenues. In order to compete for such tax base, local governments were willing to provide industrial land at cut-throat prices. Myriads of so-called "science parks" and "development zones" were constructed by local governments to attract enterprises to settle in their areas. Such competition among local governments was often a race to the bottom. It suppressed the price of industrial land and stimulated China's extensive mode of industrialization in the second stage of reform.

Land also played a crucial role in sustaining the extremely high investment rate throughout the 1994–2008 period. Real estate investment made up a staggering 12 percent of GDP in 2010 (see Figure 7.8). Land-transferring fees and land collateral loans are the major sources of financing for infrastructural projects. In Chapter 4, we analyzed in detail the mechanisms that urban development investment corporations (UDICs) applied to obtain financing through land. According to a national investigation conducted by the National Audit Office of China, up to the end of year 2010 Chinese local governments held 10.7 trillion RMB worth of debts, of which 2.5 trillion was promised to be paid back by land-transferring fees (National Audit Office of China 2011). A report released by the Ministry of Land and Resources showed that 258.2 thousand ha of land were collateralized for a total of 3.53 trillion RMB bank credits in 84 major cities of China. In coastal regions, fiscal funds only financed about 10 percent of total

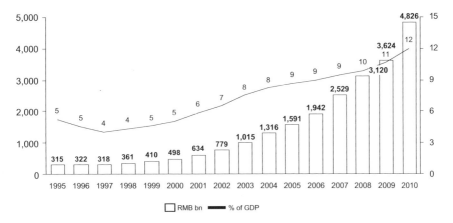

Figure 7.8 The evolution of real estate investment in China.

Source: CEIC

infrastructure investments. The rest of financing was all land-related. Typically, land-transferring fees would compose 30 percent of total investments and the remaining 60 percent are all land collateral loans (Jiang *et al.* 2010: 6). Land became the magic wand that supported China's rapid constructions and high investments.

During the growth regime of 1994–2008, local government operations over land made positive contributions to China's brisk processes of urbanization, industrialization, and capitalization. However, as the emphasis of the new growth regime had shifted to sustainability and harmony, the tensions caused by such land policies sharpened. Exceedingly low prices for industrial land encouraged wasteful uses and provided negative incentives for industrial upgrading. Over-reliance on land-related financing escalated financial risks for local governments and China's financial system, especially the banking system. Once the demand and price of real estate and land began to drop, many local governments faced increased difficulties in paying back the loans they backed; and banks faced possible defaults. Moreover, land-seizing behavior of local governments had aroused acute social discontent. On the one hand, residential prices skyrocketed and impeded many Chinese families from purchasing an apartment for self-use; and, on the other, former landholders, especially farmers, were not sufficiently compensated. According to the current laws and regulations on land transfers, farmers are compensated by less than 30 times the value of the annual yield of the land in question, instead of by the market price of that land's commercial value. If the land were seized in the name of "public interest," the price would be again lower. Taking advantage of the ambiguous definition of "public interests," local governments relentlessly abused this term to dress up their commercial projects. Such deeds, in fact, robbed land from the hands of the farmers and exacerbated widespread public anger. Worse still, even the limited compensation promised would seldom go to the pockets of farmers as expected. Local governments often failed to pay what they had promised, and as rural land is collectively owned, it is not unusual for the collectives to retain land compensations for their own interests. This government-controlled land-transferring process encourages corruption at each step. The credibility of Chinese governments, including central government, has been greatly undermined because of this. Indeed, it is high time China went through profound reforms in its land policies.

The most critical issue about future land policy-making is the protection of former landholders', especially farmers', interests. Compensation for land losses were usually the main financial resource farmers could attain to facilitate their settlement in urban areas. Thus guaranteeing that farmers indeed received enough compensation for their land is a prerequisite for China's smooth urbanization process. In order to better protect farmers' interests in the land-transferring process, China needs to work on the following aspects. First, farmers' ownership rights over the land they work on or live on must be better defined and protected. In rural China, there are two types of land: rural collective construction land (i.e. land used for collective members' lodging) and agricultural land. Rural collective members were entitled to free access to both types of land, but most farmers did not have any legal documents to testify to their user rights, thus are vulnerable to the misbehavior of local governments. Hence issuing each rural family with proper written documents to clarify their long-term user rights over the land they lodge on and farm is the first step towards the protection of farmers' rights over land. This step is also a prerequisite to solve the lingering problem of *hukou* (the household registration system), which has been widely acknowledged as a major cause of China's widening rural–urban divide. However, most analyses have focused on the fact that migrant workers could not have equal access to urban social goods and services as the urban *hukou* holders, and suggested that eliminating the *hukou* system would boost the interests of rural *hukou* holders. Such a conclusion is both wrong and dangerous. Rural *hukou* is the only official paper that can verify an individual's membership to a rural collective, thus is also the only official paper to entitle rural households with free access to rural land uses. As China's social welfare system is only at its early stage of development, actual benefits an urban *hukou* can provide is no match with the value of land lost, nor can it ensure the proper settlement of a rural family in urban areas. Hence granting farmers with the long-term land-use rights of both rural construction land and agricultural land in the form of written leases and licenses is an essential step before eliminating the *hukou* system. If this step is missing or inappropriately handled, elimination of the household registration system would further impoverish Chinese rural households and aggravate the wealth gap between China's former urban dwellers and rural dwellers.

Once the written long-term leases are established, they should enjoy full legal protection and must not be altered or abolished with any excuse. Even if the farmers changed their status of household registration from rural to urban, their user rights over land must not be retrieved. In order to promote the efficient use of land and allow the rural population to benefit from the true value of their lands, farmers should be allowed to trade, transfer, rent, and mortgage their land as long as the operations are legal and compatible with government planning. A market should be established for the free trading of these user rights independent from government operations. Direct trading of land-use rights between farmers and future land users cut the "grabbing hands" of rural collectives and urban local authorities out of land operations. Government role in land should be confined to functions such as planning, supervising, and administrating. In Sichuan province experiments of such free land markets were proven to have significantly raised the transferring prices of land. A three-year fieldwork study conducted by the National Development Center of Peking University showed that farmers could obtain an average of 32,000 Yuan for each mu (666.67 square meters) of agricultural land they rented out for a period of 30–50 years. That was twice the gain compared with when land was seized permanently by local governments. For rural construction land, compensation attained from a free market could be 10–40 times higher than what local governments would pay. Obviously if farmers' land-user rights could be legally protected and traded, they can bring enormous benefits to rural households. Those benefits ensure the integration of former rural households into China's urbanization and industrialization processes.

Another consequential issue of Chinese land policies is how to improve land-use efficiencies and enhance the national strategic planning of land. The establishment of the above-mentioned free land market would enable farmers to merge the formerly fragmented agricultural lands and exploit economies of scale in agricultural production, thus contributing positively to the efficient uses of land. Moreover, China needs a national scheme of strategic planning for land uses. Currently local land bureaus at different levels all possess certain powers of city planning. Consequently the deployment of China's development lacks the big picture. Successive projects and constructions were launched in each local area with the purpose of attracting a larger tax base, yet the local governments often ignored the reality of local situations. Blind industrialization attempts in ecologically fragile provinces, such as Guizhou, Qinghai, and Gansu, caused irreversible damage to China's environment. National government should play a stronger role in the strategic planning of land uses and centralize certain planning rights from localities so as to diminish externalities and repetitions of urban constructions, and to ensure the sustainability of China's development. At the end of 2010 China finally released a Grand National Plan, which divided the country into four major functional regions, each with a specific focus for future development. This plan was a major step toward more efficient and sustainable uses of land. However, such strategic planning has to be implemented properly to exert its true power. Some regions were designed to focus on ecological protection or agricultural production; thus they would face more financial difficulties than the industrialized regions. Central government has to integrate fiscal-sharing reform with national land-use planning. A horizontal transfer system must be established to coordinate different regional functions and diminish regional inequality.

To sum up, China's current land policies are intertwined with fiscal policies. Since 1994 Chinese local governments had been increasingly dependent on off-budgetary land-related revenues. Such a trend has to be curbed. Land-use planning must be put under a national or large regional scheme. Off-budgetary income through land transferring has to be entirely regulated under the national budget. The imbalance between local government revenue and fiscal responsibility should be addressed by simplifying local bureaucratic structures, centralizing certain fiscal responsibilities and the establishment of an institutionalized transfer system. Nevertheless, deepening land reforms can potentially offer local governments more stable and reasonable incomes. If a free land market could be opened, land transactions would be more active and local governments could obtain substantial land-transferring taxes thanks to these transferring activities. Moreover, if property tax could be installed, it would provide a stable and substantial source for local tax revenue as well. These land-related tax resources are progressive and encourage sustainability. They also provide positive incentive for local governments to strengthen their responsibility for land management, instead of land seizure. Such are the land policies needed for China's next growth regime.

SOEs' profit

The size of SOEs in China is significant. Although Chinese SOEs had diminished substantially in number after 1995, they still held more than 40 percent of China's assets and made more than 60 percent of all enterprise profits in 2010. In the 2011 ranking of China's 500 strongest enterprises, 316 of them were SOEs. Chinese SOEs' operations are concentrated in several industries. Typically, they are industries with high monopolistic profits (e.g. telecommunication, electricity grids, tobacco), or industries heavily related with resources and energy (e.g. mining, petro refining). Although SOEs are independent corporations, they enjoy widespread preferential treatments. Most notably, land, credit, and other critical factors were often channeled to SOEs at extremely low prices.

However, from the mid-1980s to 2007, these SOEs had never paid a penny's dividend to their major shareholder – the State, or rather, the Chinese population. In other words, SOEs had been using public assets free of charge for more than 20 years. Such behavior was neither reasonable nor acceptable. Beginning in 2008, the State-owned Assets Supervision and Administration Commission of the State Council (SASAC) started to charge a proportion of SOEs' profits as dividend. However, such requirement was only applicable to the 128 SOEs under direct control of SASAC. SOEs in the finance sector (including state-owned banks), the railway industry, media, publishing, education, and local SOEs were not under SASAC and thus were exempt from dividend paying even after 2008. For the ones that did pay, the rate of this dividend charge was just 0–10 percent of their net profits, varying according to the industries they operate in. In 2008, 2009, and 2010 SOEs paid 54.8 billion, 87 billion, and 44 billion RMB respectively to SASAC as dividend. Such amounts were only a tiny fraction of SOEs' total profits. In 2009, for example, SOEs under direct supervision of SASAC made a net profit of 702.3 billion RMB. The dividend paid in 2010 (based on the profit of 2009) was 44 billion RMB. That is to say, only 6 percent of these SOEs' net profits was paid as dividend. If we take into consideration all SOEs in China, this rate would be at least halved. In 2011 China expanded the scope and rate of SOEs' dividend charges: 1,631 SOEs were subject to dividend charges and the rates of charge were from 5–15 percent. The total amount of dividend expected was 63 billion RMB. Apparently, even with the increase, the dividend paid by Chinese SOEs is still excessively low. What is worth noticing is that the limited dividend paid by SOEs was not injected into the general budget of China, but retained in a special fund managed by SASAC. And the main responsibility of this fund was to support the growth of SOEs. Thus the dividend paid by SOEs was, in fact, re-injected back to SOEs. The whole mechanism merely redistributed funds among SOEs, instead of redistributing funds in the whole of society.

A major *raison d'être* of state ownership is its ability to rebalance income distribution in a nation. While it is difficult to introduce full competition or eliminate externalities in natural monopolistic industries and natural resource-dependent industries, SOEs can potentially assist in channeling the massive profits obtained in those industries to the state or to the whole population, instead of to the hands of few. In order to achieve this goal SOEs ought to contribute a large share of their profits to the general budget, or to social security funds, or directly to the population. Obviously Chinese SOEs have not been carrying out their redistributive function properly yet. In the past decades, as China placed economic growth as its over-arching aim, SOEs justified their large retention of profits by their needs for high investments. However, in recent years, those retained profits had been increasingly wasted on excessive administrative costs and repetitive investments. For a country at the transitional moment to sustainability, it is high time to strengthen SOEs' role in redistributing national income from capital holders to households. As Chinese SOEs' profits were really sizable, altering the uses of this fund from investments to households' welfare would have an immediate impact on the whole economic structure. This is one of the most direct and plausible measures to stimulate China's domestic consumption, cool down investments, diminish current account imbalance, and enhance social welfare level in the short term. China should not and could not ignore this magic bullet in rebalancing its economy and facilitating its transition to the "harmonious" growth regime.

To sum up, China must integrate a larger share of SOEs' profits into its general budget. SOEs' dividend payment is an indispensable component of China's fiscal income. Not only do SOEs have full obligation to pay dividends to their ultimate owners – the Chinese people – their dividend payment, when significant and transferred to households, would also be a systematic promoter for China's current transition from an extensive growth regime to a more sustainable and welfare-enhancing regime. China cannot ignore such an immediately effective tool in rebalancing its distribution of national income and economic structure in general.

Social welfare: strengthening social membership

Growth is not a social end in and of itself. It is a general phenomenon that makes it possible to reconcile the requirements of profit and capital accumulation with the need for cohesion and progress in labor societies. This reconciliation does not occur spontaneously. The dynamics of capital, which is a gigantic productive force, are such that it can also be a raging and unfocused power. Capitalism of whatever brand carries within itself a capacity for mobilizing human energies, and for transforming them into economic growth. However, it is unable to build social cohesiveness out of the collision between vested interests. The result is that societies that are quite different from one another may achieve similar economic growth rates. However, some societies are veritable nightmares, and others are havens of human happiness. There are societies that cause inequality and social marginalization and others that protect employees from economic risks; societies devoured by greed in their unfettered pursuit of personal riches or societies that deploy collective systems of solidarity. Thanks to the institutions that are born out of the conflicts unleashed by capitalism, the mode of regulation can orient economic growth, so that it improves employees' living conditions. The feasibility of a mode of regulation geared towards social progress depends above all on the political system.

Political intervention allows institutions that were born out of capitalism's development to turn into a system themselves. It lends substance to the mode of regulation. The pre-eminent role of the political relationship can be witnessed in the very nature of sociality. Contrary to what a number of neo-liberal economists believe, or pretend to believe, society is not an association of individual contractors. The social contract is not just an exchange between equal and free individuals, each of whom is pursuing an egotistical interest. In the very logic that underlies capital accumulation, the principle of individuals' equality to transact market exchanges mutates into its reverse, i.e. the image of an unopposed oppression of the have-nots by the haves. This is why solidarity cannot be guaranteed by market-driven insurance contracts. Solidarity requires a whole set of rules and institutions that allow a nation to confront the risks that constitute a threat to life in society. The problem of social cohesion is that it is ultimately impossible for an individualistic society to exist. Democracy so often advocated cannot work well if respect for the public good is not integrated into citizens' aspirations. Even so, we must still try to understand the origins of the higher principles that legitimate social rules and that enhance the quality of the mode of regulation.

Politics is as vulnerable to the myth of the social contract as economics is to the myth of the pure market. This is a representation giving birth to state power placed above particular interests. Nonetheless, state power that imposes itself as the final resort will corrupt a society whose inequalities have been exacerbated by entrenched bureaucracy and by bitter conflicts of interests, unless such power is legitimated by strong ethics, as Confucian thinking has forcefully emphasized. State power cannot be trusted if it is imposed without any other legitimacy than its own affirmation that it represents the will of the people. It is no less under threat when it is denigrated by interests masquerading under the colors of Libertarianism. When the state is a battlefield between unfettered party cliques, each one pretending to represent the will of the people, it is unable to make people recognize the common values of social membership.

Between the economy and the state, there is civil society. The rules, behaviors, routines, and institutions that are embedded therein are not the result of the contracts that have been drawn up by its members. They stem from a collective heritage, a system of relationships that each generation receives as a social inheritance and which perpetuates the temporal continuity of societies. Political mediation represents this system of relations through the collective values that the members of a given society recognize as being the principles of membership in their social body. *These collective values are embedded and make society a totality that is distinct from the individuals of which it is comprised.* Political endeavors are the instruments that extract these values from a society's historical heritage. They shape the identity of nation and are expressed in symbols, common beliefs, and the fundamental norms of the law. As long as it is a depository for these values, the state is invested with an authority that legitimates its power above all other powers.

By focusing on civil society, we can exorcise the specter of globalization as a steamroller homogenizing the entire planet. Because regulation is not a mechanical toy, and because instrumentalist conceptions of reform are a dead end in reality, there is no use in castigating the state, its alleged economic inefficiency, or the fact that one country is not acting the same way as another.

In post-World War II Europe social progress became the core value of social membership. This value was written into welfare, educational, and housing programs. It established a system of social benefits that was an active part of the regulation of Europe's regime of growth. The reproductive capability of this mode of regulation was such that most political parties adhered to it. Even when not claimed in political slogans, social democracy was the key concept of a stakeholder regime of growth, whereby growth benefited every member of society. In the last 30 years Western democracies have been undermined by financialization that has promoted a politico-financial elite whose aim at capturing a huge rent on society has succeeded in eroding most social achievements built in the previous 30 years. Meanwhile, the outreach of globalization has shaped in China a growth regime that has entailed huge social costs. Those costs have shown in exacerbating the rural–urban divide and in creating a large layer of workers deprived of the rights of social membership. Such a trend fragments society and jeopardizes the legitimacy of state power. It is why implementing a social welfare system adapted to Chinese society is a linchpin in the transition to a sustainable growth regime.

Social welfare and macroeconomic regulation

The principle of social welfare has been justified from a political point of view, that of citizenship. No member of society should be left aside. All should be treated equal. The models of social welfare to be institutionalized and the specific mechanisms to be implemented depend on the status of labor in capitalist societies. The large extent of state ownership in China will give *sui generis* characteristics to the model to be chosen.

Social reproduction of labor in capitalist societies

Capitalism is based on social separation within market economies, which creates a power relationship in generating social classes. Capitalists are those who have access to money in order to fund the acquisition of means of production; workers are those who have access to money in selling their working capacities. It is why the desire to accumulate money for its own sake, e.g. to transform money into capital as the aim of economic activity, entails power over others. The wage is the money price for letting one's capacity of work for a definite period of time.

It follows that the labor contract is not an exchange contract, contrary to appearance. In an exchange contract, the co-contractants are on the same footing. They bare symmetric risks due to the uncertainty in supply conditions and in the demand for the product or service sold. In a labor contract the worker is subordinated to the management and ultimately to the objective of the firm in executing the contract. The economic risk borne by the worker is not related to the execution of the contract, but to the financial condition of the firm and to the macroeconomic situation. These are economic risks of being deprived of his or her job upon which he or she has no means of protection individually. Furthermore, work compensation is based on working time eventually modulated by incentive to work, called efficiency wage, defined by normal standard set up by competition in the different sectors of production. The intensity of work is not part of the contract. It accrues to the firm whose management has all interest to push it to the utmost. It is why very often technological innovation is not in the direct interest of the workers. It deepens subordination in getting labor productivity gains that are due to hidden higher work intensity not converted into higher wages. For that matter state ownership is no more civilized than private ownership. Only labor laws, strong unions to oversee working rules within firms, and independent jurisdictions to arbitrate litigations can mitigate abuses due to the power relationship inherent to the status of labor.

Therefore social welfare starts with improvements in the status of labor within firms. To achieve these improvements, workers must be able to organize collectively to negotiate profit-sharing contracts. It means that labor compensations should be indexed on productivity gains of the whole firm on top of normal wage that compensates for working time. In a country like China, where the political leadership likes to view it as a socialist economy with capitalist characteristics, such profit-sharing mechanisms should be developed in full. Multi-year collective bargaining should be the linchpin of a stakeholder economy with the following attributes: price indexation of nominal wages, real wages linked to productivity gains, a stable wage ladder with skill and seniority, upward mobility, and job security.

The institution of collective bargaining is so important because it is the mediation between the firm and the macroeconomic level in the social reproduction of labor. Marx defines the latter as the double process of reproduction through the flow of money whereby the social classes reproduce their positions (Figure 7.9). Workers reproduce their working capacities in spending their income on consumption goods both fungible and durable and in investing in housing. Capitalists reproduce their purchase of the services of workers' capacities on a larger scale in reinvesting the money accruing from profits and the proceeds of new debt.

Social welfare and macroeconomic stabilization

This economic reproduction is not immune to unemployment. If labor compensation is disconnected from productivity gains, as it has been in the second stage of reform, the latter accrue entirely to profits. The purchasing power of labor is not increasing fast enough to foster consumer expectations of the firms at the level necessary to employ all the working population. It is why full employment has been sustained by the massive export drive and by the housing boom for the affluent, launched after the privatization of urban land use in 1994.

If the transition to a sustainable growth regime is the objective of the present decade, the social reproduction of labor should be the primary vector of the steady growth in consumption able to deliver full employment without forceful capital accumulation (Figure 7.10). The value created by labor in processing capital cum technological progress shows in labor productivity that is shared between profits and wages with the mediation of collective bargaining. Spending labor income and reinvesting profit are the main components of domestic demand modulated by bank credit. The resulting level of aggregate production is compatible with the level of employment that feeds the wage fund necessary to sustain consumption.

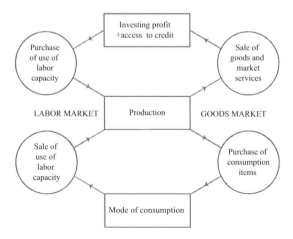

Figure 7.9 The double reproduction of capital and labor.

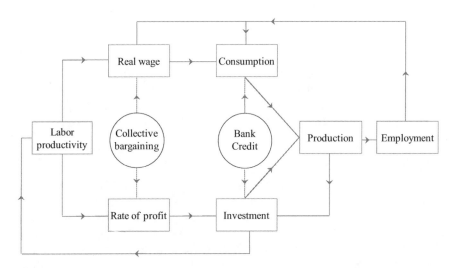

Figure 7.10 The macroeconomic relationships in a consumption-led growth regime.

The institution of collective bargaining is the primary mechanism to regulate labor income so as to match potential supply and effective aggregate demand. Implementing it on so large a labor force is a daunting task. It cannot be done without a dedicated will of the central government and a change in corporate governance to allow for the collective claims of the workers to be embodied in income formation. Regulating primary income is not sufficient, however.

China already benefits from regulated financial institutions. They are being discouraged to finance speculation in residential housing and reassigned to the financing of welfare housing. The latter establishes social standards in the mode of consumption because it triggers demand in a host of durable mass consumption goods (furniture, household appliances, communication, and leisure equipment). Another and most important pillar of the oncoming mode of consumption is the system of social transfers.

Institutions of social transfers are social security, unemployment benefits, minimum wage, progressive income tax, and assistance to low-income families. Their macroeconomic impact proceeds from smoothing fluctuations in aggregate domestic demand, in partly decoupling household disposable income from any temporary weakness in primary income. The bulk of the social apparatus is made up of institutions of social insurance (social security, retirement income, and unemployment benefits) compounding replacement income. They provide income to people who are temporarily (for unemployment or sickness) or permanently (for retirement) out of the labor market. Progressive income tax transfers income from low to high propensity to consume. Those transfers have inbuilt stabilizers and are therefore countercyclical. Whenever aggregate demand is flagging, leading to slowdown in primary income due to declining output to capacity ratio, tax revenues diminish and unemployment benefits increase. An endogenous temporary budget deficit generates a positive demand multiplier, which dampens the negative shock in demand. Assistance to low-income families for housing, education, and health has primarily an equity purpose for the sake of social cohesion. However, it also contributes to supporting domestic demand.

The lack or the dearth of social welfare compounded with regressive tax system is the most important cause of uneven and unstable growth in many developing countries. It is also the main reason why catching up stalled in middle-income countries of Latin America that were much richer than Japan after World War II. It is high time China takes a decisive drive for the better in redirecting its powerful financial resources towards its people.

In the following, we examine the current social welfare system in China and its role in redistributing national wealth. As the political legitimacy of the Chinese state has always been based on the concept of amelioration of primary social wellbeing, building a welfare society in China should be an integrated constituent of its political system. However, ever since the collapse of the socialist social welfare system in the 1990s, China is still struggling to find the kind of welfare state it desires and is able to install. Although the void of a wholesome social welfare system had been covered, to a degree, by the rapid growth in the second stage of reform, the need for the establishment of a welfare state is more and more pressing every day. Which types of welfare state should appear in China? We probably cannot give a singular answer in this chapter. Nevertheless, we expect to point out the possible bases for China's future reforms in the social welfare system by linking China's past, present, and future.

A brief review of China's current social welfare system

Chinese economists and governmental officials have long realized that the creation of a welfare state is a principal remedy for upgrading Chinese households' position in national income distribution and for boosting China's domestic consumption. A social welfare system tends to stimulate domestic consumption through the increase of households' real revenue (income effect) and through the lessening of precautionary savings (security effect). However, for those two effects to take place, at least two conditions have to be fulfilled first. On the one hand, there has to be a net financial transfer favoring the households; on the other hand, credible institutions have to be installed to guarantee the variability of financing for social schemes. After 1978, especially after the large-scale SOE reform in 1995, the socialist welfare system completely collapsed in China. For most of the second stage of reform, China did not have any systemic approach for rebuilding a welfare state. Since 2008, though, a series of consequential reforms in the social welfare system has been announced. In the following, we give a brief review of the current welfare system in China with special focus on the reforms in labor protection, medical care, and pensions.

Labor protection

As most social welfare benefits in China are associated with employment relationships, understanding the labor market and labor protections should be the first step in evaluating the current social welfare system in China.

In February 2010 the China Federation of Trade Unions claimed that almost all SOEs' employees and more than 90 percent of the employees in private enterprises (with annual revenue 5 million RMB or above) had written contracts. That was a great leap forward thanks to the so-called "new labor laws." This is a set of laws that came into force in January 2008 concerning the regulation of the labor market. Except for the most mentioned Labor Contract Law, there were also the Law on Arbitration and Mediation in Labor Disputes, which specifies the procedures to file complaints against employers; and the Employment Promotion Law, which makes governments responsible for employment and for providing employment services. This new set of laws was introduced in order to create a more equal basis for employment relationships and provides stronger and more detailed employment protection to the employees, especially the unskilled ones, who worked in small and medium-sized private enterprises. Under the Labor Contract Law written contracts are mandatory and social security should be provided to every employee. Procedural requirements in the event of changes of working conditions are much stricter and broad obligations are imposed on employers to pay on time and in full (especially for work overtime).

If those official data were true and if all clauses of the "new labor laws" could have been implemented faithfully, China's labor market would be a market that offered strong labor protection and the social welfare system would already have a solid basis. However, reality is far less rosy. The problem is not that the government was lying. Rather, the problem is that the official survey only covered large and medium-sized enterprises. The situation in smaller enterprises was much more problematic and the enforcement of "new labor laws" for socially less powerful populations such as the migrant workers progressed much slower. A survey of 300 workers in Shenzhen suggested that, although large employers with over 1,000 workers were signing contracts with nearly all of their employees, only half of the employees of smaller domestically owned companies had written contracts (Dagongzhe Migrant Workers Center 2009). In the first half of 2009 Zhicheng, a non-governmental organization (NGO) providing legal assistance to migrant workers, carried out a survey of 581 migrant workers in 15 provinces. Among the workers surveyed only 27.5 percent of them had a valid written contract. Although this ratio had doubled from the mere 12.5 percent in 2008, the proportion of migrant workers without any labor protection was still alarming. Even in large enterprises, including SOEs, tactics were developed to avoid and lessen the impact of the "new labor laws," especially for job positions where only unskilled workers were needed.

Hardly anyone argues against the necessity of improving the working conditions and payment of workers in China. However, whether the best solution is imposing laws arouses much debate. Most of the social researchers and activists we interviewed affirmed the positive role of the new laws, arguing that having a more protective legal reference was better than nothing. Yet the opponents, notably some economists, point out that the law could not alter the fundamentals, i.e. the balance of power between labor and capital. In their opinion, weakly enforced laws would hardly change the disadvantaged position of Chinese workers in an employment relationship. With an abundant supply of labor, no freedom of association for workers (all unions are under the All-China Federation of Trade Unions which was, effectively, controlled by the Communist Party), employees' bargaining powers remained weak. The situation was further worsened by the extensive mode of economic growth featuring high dependency on capital input and low profit margin. Thus effective labor protection should rely on enhancing TFP, and increasing the workers' capacity of collective bargaining by allowing free association of unions. Legal protection was indeed necessary. However, its effectiveness depended greatly on governments' inclination for strict enforcement and the cost workers had to bear by bringing disputes to court. Local governments had never been fans of strong labor protection. The outbreak of the economic crisis gave them good excuses for relaxing their supervision over the new labor laws' enforcement. When the Labor Inspectorate and trade unions were inactive, employees could only turn to arbitration and litigation courts, where the legal processes were often too time-consuming and too costly for the employees to bear. At the time of writing, no significant improvement had been reported concerning the implementation of "new labor laws."

Social security system (medical care and pensions)

In January 2009 the government announced an ambitious reforming plan for China's medical care system. One of the key elements in the plan was to achieve 90 percent medical insurance coverage in 2011 and a universal medical insurance coverage by 2020. We are optimistic about the realization of these goals. Urban residents who had formal employment had always been covered by certain medical insurance schemes. Medical insurance coverage in rural China was traditionally weak. However, after the implementation of the "New Rural Cooperative Medical System" (NRCMS) in 2003, the number of rural residents covered by medical issuance scheme multiplied. In 2009 more than 90 percent of the rural population was already covered by NRCMS. In 2011 the State Council declared that more than 95 percent of the population (1.27 billion people) was covered by certain medical insurance schemes. The first step of the medical insurance target was indeed well accomplished.

As regards pension schemes, the improvements in recent years have also been notable. About 40–5 percent of the population was covered by certain pension schemes. However, there existed a sharp inequality between urban and rural China. While 90 percent of urban dwellers were covered, in 2010 only less than a quarter of rural residents were covered. Similar to medical insurance, the goal of the government was also to achieve universal coverage of pensions by 2020. However, unlike the general optimism felt for medical insurance, most analysts deem such a target for pension coverage unrealistic. Woetzel *et al.* (2009) estimate Chinese pension coverage in 2025 to be 60 percent and Sin from World Bank (2005) predicts 90 percent coverage in 2055.

In order to create a variable pension system, China still must conquer two major problems. First, the official age for retirement must be adjusted. Currently, the average age of retirement in China is just 56. Legal limits were set at 60 for men and 55 for women. Both were too low compared with the limits set by other countries. Early retirement will increase the burden of pension payment in the years to come, especially now that China is entering into a fast track of population aging. Second, the current fragmented pension schemes should be united under a national system. Chinese pensions schemes vary greatly according to types of employment (e.g. public servants or private employees), the "household registration status" (rural or urban), and the location of residence. Such fragmentation prevents central government from efficiently supervising the pension schemes, and impedes the free movement of labor within the country.

Although advances made in medical insurance and pension coverage were great steps towards the establishment of welfare state in China, only a positive net transfer to households can have a real impact on the real disposable income of families and increase their propensity of consumption. How generous were the social security schemes in China? Where did social security funds come from? Was there a net transfer from government enterprises to households? In the following, we examine the financing of China's social security system.

So far reimbursement rates for medical care and the replacement rate[9] for pension provision are still fairly low. Although the reimbursement rate promised for hospitalized treatments is set at 70 percent, the real reimbursement rate for such treatments averages only 23 percent (OECD 2010). As for pensions, the current replacement rate is just 33 percent on average. In the socialist era, the replacement rate was 77 percent (OECD 2010). Those limited compensations offered by China's social security schemes are not distributed to the population progressively either. Urban residents typically receive higher compensation than rural residents, and wealthier families actually benefit more than the poorer ones. Such regressive phenomena are mainly due to the fact that both social contribution and compensation are based solely on individuals' salaries. That is to say, the more one contributes, the more one benefits. The current arrangements of the Chinese social security system carry little redistributive function in rebalancing income among the population.

The primary source of social security funds is the social contributions paid by individuals and enterprises based on individuals' salaries. This salary-based social contribution mechanism means that labor-intensive enterprises bear heavier social burdens than capital-intensive enterprises. According to our calculation, the social contribution paid by employees and employers in China represents 40–50 percent of total salaries. By contrast, central government carries little financial responsibility for social functions. So far we have not found significant evidence for net transfer from government to households.

Ironically, reverse transfers from households to governments, especially to local governments through social contributions, can be seen extensively in China. The social contributions paid for pensions, for example, have been collected at the provincial level since 1993. Theoretically, those funds should be managed as two separate accounts. One is the "individual account." This account should be tied up directly to a specific individual, who contributes 8 percent of his/her salary each month into this account and his/her employer also injects 20 percent worth of his/her salary each month. The other account is the "social account," which collects budgetary funds injected for social uses. However, local governments have widely abused "individual accounts" to finance current social expenditures. Hence, in reality, China's social security system has become a "pay-as-you-go system." Up to 2005, 800 billion RMB was missing from those "individual accounts." In other words, households had been financing the social responsibilities that should have been carried out by government! At the same time, those "empty" accounts indicated great risks for the individuals concerned. Once they retired, they would face the great danger of not receiving the pensions they had been promised.

A social welfare system with Chinese characteristics

In the seminal book, *The Three Worlds of Welfare Capitalism*, Esping-Andersen (1990) identified three welfare state regimes: conservative, liberal, and social democratic. Typical examples of a conservative welfare state regime are Austria, France, and Germany. In these countries, provision of social welfare is universal and indiscriminate. However, status differences among social classes are preserved. This social welfare system carries little redistributive function. The state is ready to displace the market as the provider of welfare. However, it will not interfere in affairs that are traditionally considered as family responsibilities, unless the family's capacity to serve its members is exhausted. The liberal social welfare regime prevails in the US, Canada, and Australia. The most salient features of this regime are the constrained social rights, minimal benefits, and market-based welfare provision. Discriminative social insurance is provided to the poorest after strict tests. The liberal welfare regime does not believe in the necessity of de-commodification of labor, nor does it diminish social stratifications. The society forms a class–political dualism between the poor who receive state assistance on an equal basis, and the majority of people who obtain their social security through market mechanisms. The Scandinavian countries feature the "social democratic" welfare state regime. The reason why this regime is called "social democratic" is due to its special mix of "socialism" and "democracy." In this regime, social welfare provision is carried out by the state and covers the whole population equally without discrimination of social status, employment status, or income level. The degree of labor de-commodification is extremely high and inequalities in society are reduced to a minimum. The provision of social welfare is integrated with the goal of full employment and costs of family-hood are pre-emptively socialized (Esping-Andersen 1990: 26–9).

Can China neatly fit into one of these three distinctive welfare state regimes? At first glance, the answer seems to be "no." China's universal coverage ambition for medical insurance and pension provision resembles the conservative and social democratic regime. However, the minimal compensation seems to be a liberal feature. As social security schemes are still highly tied up with employment relationships, the de-commodification effects of the Chinese social welfare system are low. This is also similar to the liberal regime; nevertheless, the state is the dominant provider of social welfare services in China. Public servants and SOE employees enjoy a special social welfare scheme in China, and families' provision of social welfare is often exploited. Both features can be found in conservative regime-dominated countries, such as France. If China is not copying any existing welfare state regime, what form of welfare state should China aim at constructing? In the following we try to give a preliminary conjecture of China's future path for welfare state development based on the interactive effects of China's historical, societal, and political factors.

Although China's welfare state regime is still inchoate, several anchoring strategic decisions can already be observed. The first choice is about social rights. The government has plainly demonstrated its preference for universal coverage with minimal benefits, over limited coverage with high social benefits. The main purpose of universal coverage is not about de-commodification, but about providing primary social security to guarantee people's minimal needs. This preference is coherent with China's long-lasting political tradition. Since the imperial era, the Chinese state has based its legitimacy upon the provision of minimal stability, security, and welfare for the population. Failing to provide basic security and welfare would jeopardize the political regime yet, without supervision from pluralistic interest groups the government has no incentive to provide social rights better than the minimal requirements either.

The second choice is about the role of welfare system in social stratification. The design of China's social welfare system shows a strong tendency to reinforce the existing differences in income level and status. The reinforcing effects can be mainly substantiated by two mechanisms. One, the design of China's welfare system has been heavily centered on employment relationships. The calculation of both contribution and compensation (especially pension) has been based on an individual's salary in his/her active years, instead of toward an average earning of the society. Thus it fortifies the social differences already existing and exhibits weak redistributive and equalizing effects. The other mechanism, worse still, directly forms dualism in Chinese society. Public servants and SOE employees enjoy particularly favorable welfare schemes compared with employees in the private sector. In 2004 the annual pension of a retiree from a private enterprise was, on average, 6,830 Yuan less than that of a retired SOE employee and 8,451 Yuan less than that of a retired public servant. All central government's employees, and a majority of local governments' and SOEs' employees, also benefit from free medical care either explicitly or implicitly. The former vice Minister of Health, Mr Yin Dakui, revealed at a conference that of the total fiscal expenditure invested in medical care, 85 percent was spent on governmental officials. Whereas for common people medical insurance compensation is rather limited and there is a ceiling for annual compensation no matter how catastrophic the diseases are. Such sharp contrast between general welfare schemes and the special schemes for state employees incited strong dualism in China. Although a number of measures have been applied to reduce and eventually eliminate such dualism since 2009, the differentiated treatments to public and private employees are still widespread. The difficulty in eliminating this dual system is directly related to China's political structure. Chinese authorities depend on its bureaucratic team to realize their political goals. As long as China is still heavily reliant upon state capitalism, dualism between public and private employees is unlikely to disappear.

The third essential choice concerns the relationship among state, market, and family in social welfare provision. As argued in Chapter 1, family and other lineage groups had been the most flexible and resilient providers for the needs of the Chinese population for thousands of years. The functioning of Chinese society had been heavily dependent on informal social networks rather than formalized organization. Although industrialization has broken the coherence of the traditional family-based society, family and other family-induced social connections are still assets for China and deserve to be integrated into its pursuit for welfare and sustainable development. The recent policies in social welfare have clearly indicated that China would not give up the fundamental role of family connections as an ultimate safety net for its population. In the design of a welfare state, the government is consciously exploiting family capabilities. Nevertheless, it also has to be conscious that China is no longer a family-based agrarian country. In an industrialized society, a state-backed social welfare system is not only a complementary part of a family system, it also carries macro-functions that individual families can never accomplish. In the one or two decades to come, China has to motivate strong social transfer to its average households in order to promote domestic consumption and motivate the transition of economic growth mode. Families need more active assistance from professional service providers; and the state is indispensable in providing equalized social welfare for its population.

To sum up, there is some consensus in China about the relationship between state and family in social welfare provision, even though some fine-tuning is still needed. The relationship between state and market in social welfare provision, however, is still an issue of hot debate. So far, the state is the primary provider of most social services, yet such state-led social service provision is frequently questioned for its inefficiency and rigidness. Bringing private actors into the market of social service provision, we believe, can indeed enable the social welfare system to be more flexible in meeting people's needs. However, we remind our readers to be extremely cautious about the calls to privatize existing public medical care facilities. In order to enhance the efficiency of China's social welfare provision, the key is about breaking the monopoly over the market, not about whether it should be the state or private actors to run such a monopoly. All things being equal, it is in fact easier to align the payment system of a welfare state with provision if the bulk of welfare is provided by the state. What the government has to do is stop suppressing private actors from entering the market of welfare offering, and reorientate governmental functions from mediating daily management of social service providers to regulating and supervising the healthy operation of the markets, with both public and private players in it.

The above-mentioned strategic choices open to China have the potential of evolving into a holistic regime of a welfare state with Chinese characteristics. The first pillar of this welfare state regime is universal insurance. In Chinese tradition (see Chapter 1), the state is the protector and regulator of macro stability. In order to guard the legitimacy of its sovereignty, it is in Beijing's interest to establish a national social security system that guarantees minimal universal insurance. This preference, as we have pointed out, has already been clearly demonstrated by central government's ambitions in enlarging social security coverage. The second pillar is the maximization of social capital. Chinese institutions, especially those developed in the imperial era, stressed sustainability of social order over material growth. The government has long been conscious of the importance of social, especially human, capital accumulation for obtaining such sustainability. For more than 2,000 years China was a meritocratic society and the importance of education widely acknowledged. Whereas Confucius accords different levels of wealth and social status to people with different levels of intelligence and merits, vertical mobility and equality of opportunity, especially equal opportunity for education, are always encouraged. Consequently the society behaved redistributively when it came to social and human capital protection. Whenever social inequality reached a degree that it hindered the collective accumulation of the social and human capital of the nation, sharp social sentiments for redistribution arose. Social norms compelled the rich to help when there were large groups of people struggling for survival (e.g. in the case of natural catastrophes) and to donate for education-related purposes. Although Chinese society has been through drastic transformation in the past century, such behavior can still be observed in today's China, and we believe it is high time to encourage the revival of such tradition.

The third pillar of China's welfare state is the indispensible role of civil society in social welfare provision. The essence of Confucianism is to understand human beings and human society in relational terms. China has a long and strong tradition as a self-organized civil society based on complex and overlapping human relationships. While the state was responsible for macro stability and social wellbeing, micro organization of society had been largely spontaneous. Although the organic family has reduced its economic function in an industrial society, vibrant and widespread social networks still prevail in China and they are precious assets in complementing state-led provision of social welfare. The CCP has to learn how to actively integrate civil society into the current welfare system and guide its development, instead of allowing local governments to interfere in its functioning.

The most worrying obstruction for the welfare state described above to take shape is the reverse transfer from households to governments. In reforming the welfare system it is most important to ensure fairness. The way to do this is to distinguish carefully which benefits are contributive and which are not. Contributive benefits are the ones that finance risks directly related to work (injury at work) and economic risk (essentially unemployment). They should be financed by social contributions of employees and employers. Wage income is their basis. Rates of contribution should be determined at industry level and negotiated and re-examined according to a specified schedule between labor unions and industry associations of employers. The flows of contributions and benefits should be managed by special agencies. Rates of contributions should be adjusted periodically, so that the budget of the agencies remains balanced over the cycle.

Non-contributive benefits cover universal risks. There is no rational reason for their financing to bear on wages alone. The bulk of those benefits are made of health insurance and assistance for low-income families under conditions of limited resources (aid for housing, child rearing and old age assistance). Their financing should be universal, including both labor and capital income, rents and imputed rents enjoyed by households who own their housing. The broader the tax base, the lower the rate for a total given amount of benefits.

If China intends to build up a welfare state featuring universal insurance and social capital accumulation, non-contributive benefits will constitute the main body of the system. Thus the social funds cannot alone be collected through salary-based social contributions. A social tax based on all household income and levied directly by the economic entity that generates the income of the individual is both fair and simple: levied on payrolls by employers, on pensions by retirement funds, and on interests and dividends by fiduciary institutions. Similar tax can be charged on corporate income as well, regardless of the salary cost of the enterprises. China should also take advantage of its large state-owned assets and enterprises to enrich its social welfare funds. SOEs' dividends should be a major and stable financial source of the social welfare system. Briefly, the social tax can be made as progressive as social policy deems it economically efficient and socially fair. Once social tax can be made the principal source of social welfare funds, a positive social transfer can be expected.

What is more, a universal social tax will bring unification to the current fragmented social welfare system of China. Indeed, China's social welfare system lacks national unification, as most of the operations, including social contribution collection, fund management, and benefits payment are all handled locally. Many provinces lack the necessary skills in fund management and thus cannot obtain a reasonable return for the funds they hold. What is worse, scattered funds make it difficult for central government to supervise the fund uses, hence incite local officials to reallocate the funds for other uses, while leaving the social welfare accounts empty. If the social welfare funds could be centralized it will not only make fund management more efficient and accountable but also lower the transaction cost in the entire social welfare system. With current information technology it is easy to support a nationwide social security database, which stores and calculates all information about Chinese social welfare, and injects payments directly into the bank accounts of the beneficiaries. Moreover, a united national fund, and better still, a united national welfare scheme, will significantly promote the free movement of labor in China. Because of the difficulty of shifting one's personal social security accounts from one province to another, or from urban to rural, China's migrant workers have lost much of the benefit they ought to enjoy. A national unification of social welfare and social welfare fund management can increase the credentials of China's social welfare system. Opponents of a nationally unified welfare scheme often point out the regional differences in living expenditures. This argument hardly stands up. As China's social welfare scheme stresses only the satisfaction of minimal needs, regional differences in that is shrinking. In fact, the differences in living expenditure can potentially entice some people to migrate to cheaper regions. Such flow can contribute positively to the balanced development among regions. In 2001 the Central Committee of

CCP and the State Council established the National Social Security Fund (NSSF). This is the first national fund dedicated to social welfare. However, it does not centralize the funds managed by the provinces. Most of its funding comes from fiscal injection from the general budget, profits from the Welfare Lottery Fund, and shares contributed by listed SOEs. At the end of 2010 the fund had grown to 856.8 billion.

Once the flow of transfer can come from the governments and capital holders to the households, and the management of funds strengthened, China should consider reasonably raising the benefits of its social welfare scheme. At the current time, any alleviation of social burdens from the shoulders of Chinese families would have substantial effects in stimulating China's domestic consumption and rebalancing China's economy.

Conclusion

This is the longest chapter in the whole book and it has a good reason to be so. In this chapter, we pinpointed a relatively detailed road map for China to transit from the current extensive growth regime to a sustainable and welfare-enhancing one.

The whole chapter deployed around the key contradiction of the 1994–2008 growth regime, i.e. the disadvantageous position of intangible capitals compared with tangible ones. For a variety of reasons, the prices of key factors in China had been distorted to the lower end during the 1994–2008 period. Such distortion encouraged extensive investment for capital-intensive projects and thus diminished the role of labor in production input. Salaries remained at a low level thus impeding the purchasing power of households. Vast production could not be absorbed by domestic demand and flew into the international market, causing the widely discussed disequilibrium in the current account. Meanwhile, domestic consumption was sluggish and social inequity widened.

In order to correct this key contradiction, China needs national strategic planning that upgrades intangible, especially human capital prices, to that of tangible ones. There are three major mechanisms to enable such adjustment. One, the services sector has to be liberated from the myriad administrative obstacles. High-end services, especially producer and social services, are the linchpin for rebalancing the economy because they enable TFP gains, absorb highly educated professionals, increase the importance of human capital in the economy, and provide badly needed support for China's upcoming urbanization and aging. Another powerful mechanism is through deepening fiscal reform. In this part we discussed the amelioration of the current tax structure, adjustment of intergovernmental fiscal relationship, and regulations over extra- and off-budgetary items. The fiscal system carries essential redistributive functions. Each and every aspect of fiscal reform has systemic importance for the trajectory of the economy and society in the years to come. Last but not least, the establishment of a welfare state, Chinese style, is not only a key element in strengthening Chinese households' wealth position, but also the key to building the harmonious society Beijing envisions. The cohesiveness of Chinese society and the legitimacy of

Chinese sovereignty are dependent on China's ability to level wealth distribution and improve the wellbeing of the lower-income populace in the years to come.

Whether China is about to rebalance its economy and transit smoothly to the next growth phase featuring sustainability and social welfare enhancement depends heavily on its policy choices in the following decade. The implementation of the policies we suggest above would require strong political determination and the resolute commitment of Chinese leadership. In the last chapter of our book, we examine the tradition and current state of Chinese politics in relation to those policies.

8 From policies to politics

Times are changing. It has been 20 years since the USSR was dismantled. This extraordinary event heralded the triumph of liberal capitalism, which was in full swing in the wake of Reagan's and Thatcher's ultra-conservative counter-revolution. The US philosopher Francis Fukuyama proclaimed the end of history. The whole world was exhorted to adopt the political structures of Anglo-Saxon capitalism. Since the US was supposed to uphold the universal value of human rights, its global extension was expected to bring about what ancient Chinese thinkers called "all under heaven," e.g. universal harmony.

The same Francis Fukuyama 20 years on wrote an article in the *Financial Times* (January 18, 2011) entitled "Democracy in America has less than ever to teach China." What motivated this 180 degree turnaround? In the meantime, war had raged in Iraq, Afghanistan, and lately Libya. Promoting democracy by means of military invasion is not the best way to get acquiescence to the idea! Africa had become a land of confrontation and Arabic "revolutions" were turning to anything but Western democracy. The Washington Consensus, which had encapsulated the idea of the end of history, produced a string of financial crises, not less the Asian crisis that convinced Asian countries to recover their economic sovereignty with export-led growth and foreign reserve accumulation. Last but not least, financial liberalization, which enslaved US regulatory policy to Wall Street interests, had run its course and produced a devastating financial crisis with long-lasting consequences on Western economies.

The powerlessness of US democracy in the face of vested interests has bewildered the world in the tragi-comic episode of the US debt ceiling. The ability to make hard decisions has been paralyzed by political partisanship, after Wall Street was bailed out without any counterpart. Meanwhile, social inequalities have been left widening extravagantly. US public infrastructures are crumbling, reform of the health care system has been watered down, and national decisions on the challenge of climate change are at a standstill.

Therefore it gets difficult to persuade the world that Western democracy is the model to follow. But the events of the first decade of this century raise deeper questions on the foundation of political systems for the twenty-first century. These questions lead us to the problem of addressing social welfare. Are eighteenth-century principles that still underpin representative political systems well-suited to expressing the long-run social needs embedded in sustainable growth? How should democracy be expressed in legitimate political decisions leading to changes in the mode of consumption necessary for environmental protection? How can it express the will of unborn generations that will be the most exposed to the long-term consequences of present decisions or lack of decisions?

We will discuss the problems of evolution between formal representative democracy on the one hand, and grassroots, participative, and interactive democracy on the other. Then we highlight the views of ancient Chinese philosophers on good government that may be useful in overcoming present-day political shortcomings in measuring and becoming accountable for social welfare. Finally we will suggest possible directions of change in China's politics in both domestic and foreign affairs.

Democracy and social welfare

Even if we set aside the question of happiness that is out of the realm of social sciences, revealing economic welfare of society as a whole is beyond the scope of economics, because social welfare cannot be measured and interpreted within the framework of utility theory. The utility approach tries to use prices to integrate measures provided by national accounting in welfare. But the relationship between market prices and marginal utility is highly problematic, especially if one wants a cardinal measure of utility to aggregate personal preferences, not least because the search for comparison of interpersonal utilities is rife with insuperable difficulties. Already Alfred Marshall, in his *Principles of Economics*, doubted that it was possible to apprehend utility value beyond the vicinity of market prices (Marshall 1920). The alternative approach of considering the final objectives pursued by economic activity is not that much promising either for the purpose of an aggregate measure of economic welfare. It has to spell out what the final objectives are and to look for multiple "objective" standards of physical measure, whose integration in a single aggregate is either impossible or quite arbitrary.

The problem becomes more inextricable if policies are aiming at changing economic structure in the long run, which is what sustainable growth is all about. As demonstrated in Chapter 7, one must consider social policies aimed at reducing inequalities and improving the wellbeing of lower-income citizens as a condition for a better social cohesiveness of the nation. Such policy orientation is legitimized by ethical criteria, which are out of the realm of utility theory. It is essentially Amartya Sen's approach. In his 1976 article ("Real national income") he used an ordinal framework (Sen 1976). He showed that the marginal dollar possessed by a poorer person has a higher marginal value than the same dollar possessed by a richer one. Therefore it is necessary to account for the distribution of income, and the structure and the size of the population according to judgments that explicit ethical values. For ancient Chinese thinkers those values are the foundation of political principles.

Democracy stipulates that the only legitimate source of political power is the People. It is the indivisible expression of sovereignty. However, this principle means unanimity. In a recent book Pierre Rosanvallon (2008) asks the question: how can it be that the general will of the people is assimilated to majority vote, which implies division? The principle that the part is worth the whole has no substantial, only procedural justification. The latter gives rise to party politics, with their manipulation of opinions, clientèles, and financial subjugation to private economic interests. Furthermore, the people are consulted once every *n* years. It is postulated that the punctual electoral event is worth the people's will for the period of the mandate. With those shortcomings, the election of representatives is trapped in a double bind: it is an unsurpassable procedure, but it is no longer a credible expression of social welfare.

As contemporary societies get more and more complex and open, the legitimacy of representative democracy has been undermined by the advent of privatization of former state prerogatives in finance, transport, and communication regulation, by the establishment of non-elected independent authorities like central banks, and by bureaucratic international organizations like the European Commission. Moreover, neo-liberal rhetoric pretends that the market is the agent of collective welfare, while it has been demonstrated that this is false. Civil servants feel no longer invested in the public mission of realizing the general interest. They are ashamedly connected to private interests. Last but not least, the fiction of homogeneous majority expressing a collective willpower has become an empty shell, as much as society is getting more differentiated and the public interest is declined in more specific objectives. This is why defiance of electoral procedure is getting stronger, election after election, in most countries. It has become obvious that democratic legitimacy should be reconstructed. On what basis? How can citizenship express itself politically? How can political power act in taking responsibility of the needs of all citizens?

Instead of considering society through the prism of the law, an abstract juridical principle of formal equality, legitimacy should be built on the political awareness and treatment of all concrete situations. Rosanvallon calls it common interest through the attention to peculiarities. This type of democracy weakens the importance of electoral procedure. This is democracy in flux in everyday life, democracy of continuous interaction, and participation of the citizens. It is an open question to surmise whether Western countries or China are better-equipped to create this type of democracy, which for the time being exists nowhere. However, it is the legitimacy that can support the policies expounded in Chapters 6 and 7 for sustainability of society and environment.

Citizens are preoccupied by decisions that impact directly on their lives. However, in comparing decisions and judging the actions of institutions, they refer to their perception of *equity*, which in turn depends on the sentiment that those who have decided have been aware of the peculiarities of the situation. Many researches based on surveys have highlighted this inclination. The feeling of equity of the institution fosters self-esteem of the individuals. It can be called *procedural equity*. Because equity comes with attention to peculiarities, it is closely related with care, which is an ethical conception of the relation to others. Rosanvallon points out a duality in ethics: a general principle of social justice on the one hand, a behavioral attitude to peculiarities on the other. *The main problem in redefining democracy is to build up political legitimacy on an ethical basis.*

Interactive democracy means political power close to the people. It should be bottom-up in continuous time as well as top-down. It requires civil society to self-organize in an array of social structures with political purpose: local committees of districts, villages, and townships; think tanks and conferences of citizens taking hold of the problems raised by city development; consumer associations; academies and NGOs; Internet blogs. All those structures of political governance are part and parcel of participatory democracy. The move in this direction started in the US as early as the 1960s. However, it has never been able to impinge upon the decay of party politics, or been able to rejuvenate national politics. What could be the institutional linkages by which local participatory democracy feeds national democratic debates? It cannot happen if national politics is solely based upon the "State of Law" and on abstract "Human Rights." It should be based on ethics in all matters of practical policy action. Let us consider what ancient Chinese thinkers say about this.

Ethics and good government

The philosophy of Chinese politics was shaped amid hot and contentious debates in the long epoch of history covering the "Spring and Autumn" period (770–476 BC) and the Warring States period (476–221 BC), terminating with the unification of the Empire. Confucius, who lived in the late "Spring and Autumn" (551–479 BC), stands out in universal culture, though he did not create any grand religion like Buddha or Christ, or any ideal philosophy of human behavior like Socrates and Plato. Confucius's thinking was practical and much involved in politics. However, his teaching constitutes an ethical conception of humankind that has shaped Chinese culture ever since, as we show in Chapter 1. Indeed, China has never conceived any religion of its own, any transcendence dictating norms of conduct from dogmatic belief in revealed and immutable truth. The Chinese conception of "Heaven" is that of cosmologic harmony between nature and humankind.

The teaching of ancient thinkers on China's politics

Confucius was essentially concerned with political questioning. How can it be that dynasties decay, that political order unravels, that the harmony of "all under heaven" disintegrates? Confucius's thinking is in his teaching. Education is everything and it should not be mainly theoretical, but concerned with practical achievement. Being educated is becoming a man of Good in serving the community. It means that Confucius has a relational conception of what is a human being. He calls his conception the *ren*, the sense or quality of humanity. One becomes human in relation to others. As Anne Cheng (1997) stresses, the *ren* is the moral glue that constitutes the nature of all human beings. However, the *ren* is not a divine source. It is the process by which one should strive to act with equity and wisdom in relation to others. It ensues that networks of relationships that

290 The new stage of reform toward sustainability

conform to the *ren* are reciprocal and solidary like in a family. Confucius thought that the sense of humanity is expressed in acts if relationships are ritualized, e.g. if they respect social norms. The *ren* and the ritual (*li*) are intertwined. The *li* entails respect for others and therefore guarantees harmony in social and political relationships. To sum up, becoming human is the process through which one is learning ritual relationships with others.

The Confucian conception of good government stems from the unity of the *ren* and the *li*. Governing is not exerting power but showing capability of harmonizing human relationships. Men of political responsibilities should be the most learned and the wisest in society, the ones best able to accomplish ritualized relationships. The good sovereign is not the one who imposes norms and metes out punishments. He is the one who educates people by exemplarity in the pursuit of social harmony. When rituals are undermined, individuals are captured by selfish desires and contempt for others. Society becomes the prey of disorders and violence. Whatever his sheer power, the sovereign is no longer respected. Confucius says: "governing is being in rightness."

The Chinese way in politics was shaped during the Warring States period amid controversies dividing contenders and followers of Confucius. One of the most prominent contenders was Mozi, who lived in between the death of Confucius in 479 and the birth of Mencius in 372 BC, Confucius's most famous follower.

Mozi was the founder of the Moïst School, a brand of knowledge comprehensively articulated and thoroughly written, at odds with Confucius's teaching. The core of Mozi is made up of rationally argued theses. Criticizing Confucius's *ren*, which he considers to be too dependent on sentiments for close people and declining as one gets away from the vicinity of the family, Mozi asserts that care for others is justified by the *common interest*. Contrasting with the subjective and ritualistic reciprocity advocated by the Confucians, the Moïsts defend the idea of a *social contract* between the sovereign and the people. Mozi is more pessimistic than Confucius on human nature. He stresses the transformation of conflicting individual interests into the common interest by virtue of the political order. Therefore good government has the task of applying universal moral principles. The generation of this principle in government depends crucially on a dual mechanism in selecting and applying competencies: bottom-up in the democratic recruitment of political personnel, top-down in the conformity to the conduct of superiors. The sense of equity at the higher level of social hierarchy is the common denominator to realize the common interest.

What is fascinating is that the concept of authoritarian power drawn from Moïst theory of the political order still informs present-day China. It has pervaded the millennia of imperial political institutions with the institutionalization of the system of exams to recruit servants of the state from the broadest social basis according to the criterion of competences. The ban on inheritance or purchase of official charges has permitted social mobility both upwards and downwards.

Mencius is the most prominent defender of Confucius's teaching in the fourth century BC against the Moïsts and other anti-Confucian intellectual schools. In his effort to convince, Mencius is led to develop considerably Confucius's aphorisms into logical discourse. He aims at teaching the principles of good government to the sovereigns, e.g. how to govern in implementing the *ren*. He did so in a very hostile political climate when the kings and feudal lords pursuing of their own strategic goals did not want to listen.

Mencius claims that caring for the people is the only way to get a unifying consensus that guarantees cohesion and stability in society. The people legitimize the sovereign if they can see the sign of his sense for human conformity with "all under Heaven." If the sovereign is not faithful to the mandate given by the people, the latter are justified in ousting him. Therefore Mencius pushes to its ultimate consequences the Confucian conception: *ethics is the foundation of politics*. Political hierarchy is legitimate on condition it rests on the *ren*. The most important division of labor is between political functions on one side, other social functions on the other. It fosters reciprocity that nurtures social cohesion.

Beyond his ethico-political theory of the social order, Mencius can be described as modern and non-religious in his rejection of any belief in an ontological evil. Morality is intrinsic to human nature. It allows the possibility of harmony between nature and humankind. This is a permanent theme of Chinese philosophy. It is in actualizing virtual disposition to morality through education, not because of a divine origin, that one becomes human. It is a self-generating process. Good and bad people are just different in the degree of moral humanizing. For there is no dichotomy between body and soul, no struggle between good and evil as ontological entities. The human being is a whole in relation to others.

Chinese thinking, which has developed the theory of politics from the praxis of ordering society, emphasizes the ways and means of preserving and strengthening the state in the late Warring States era with Xunzi and Han Feizi who represent two opposite poles in organizing society: the Confucian ritualists on the one hand, the Legalists on the other hand.

Xunzi rehabilitates Confucian rituals in introducing a new theoretical idea: *the structure of rituals reproduces the harmony of nature* (the *Dao*). Learning the *Dao* in practicing the rituals gives access to culture that makes our humanity.

The Legalists, whose primary theoretician is Han Feizi, are modern in their historical analysis, which replaces the reference to the Sages of Antiquity. Contrary to Mencius and Xunzi, who consider that the law needs an ethical foundation, the Legalists think that the law is self-fulfilling. They proclaim that equity is contained in objective, written, and publicized laws. Everyone should be subject to the rigor of the law irrespective of one's ranking in the social hierarchy. The problem the Legalists want to solve is assuring the working of the state irrespective of the moral status of the sovereign. They view state power in the efficiency of political institutions capable of imposing the respect of the law whatever the personal value of the sovereign.

The contradiction in the two streams of Chinese thinking has been displayed by Mao Zedong. Both are incompatible. If the law is in a position of strength it does not depend on moral value. What is needed is a bureaucratic mediation between the sovereign and the people. Bureaucrats get the delegation of power and must simultaneously be subject to strict control. However, competences and capabilities are required to align the interests of the bureaucrats on the common interest embodied in the law by means of rewards and punishments. In imperial China the system of examinations was established to check the real competences of the civil servants to be recruited.

Han Feizi tries to build a philosophical foundation to the practical preoccupations of the Legalists for the techniques of power. In his endeavor he has recourse to the common presupposition well-anchored in ancient Chinese thought: *the contiguity between natural order and human order*. Objective law is amoral, but it is efficient in expressing and realizing the common interest because it conforms to the order of the universe. For Han Feizi the State of Law and the authoritarian state are the same concept. There is nothing in the concept of law that relates it to democracy.

Relevance of neo-Confucian ethics for contemporary China

What conclusions can be drawn from this bird's eye view of ancient Chinese political thinking for the problem of adapting political institutions to policies conducive to sustainable growth? There are promises in the neo-Confucian ethic that it can help answer the questions on political proximity with the people and interactions with civil society that emerge with the disruption of the existing growth regime.

In 2007 the Chinese scholar Lily Tsai published the results of a most valuable field study: *Accountability without Democracy: Solidary groups and public goods provision in rural China*. When she writes "without democracy," she means "formal" democracy. In her detailed inquiry with a team of students that conducted in-depth interviews with local officials and with villagers, she found that villages with a similar level of economic resources had very different provisions of public goods and services. What makes villages so different, even though they are all subject to scarce financial resources?

In some villages but not in others, government officials are subject to informal rules and unwritten norms, which are beyond the state system. These norms spring from civil society, established by social groups and enforced by the communities of which the officials are members. Officials embedded in such social networks feel obliged to provide public goods because they can be punished if they fail according to the moral norms of the group.

In present-day China there is a vacuum of accountability in local governments, due to the difficulty of central government in supervising local officials, and alternatively to weak or non-existent formal democratic mechanisms of accountability. They can be substituted by solidary groups based on shared moral obligations beyond shared interests. Those solidary relationships stem from neo-Confucian doctrine teaching that care for others is constituent of our own humanity.

Social norms and obligations are informal institutions of accountability, which can reinforce or substitute the public obligations that the state system is supposed to establish but that is deficient. In many counties local officials squander resources and dispense private goods to their clients. In others local governments lack the financial resources because direct transfers by central government are too low or because there is no effective mechanism of redistribution. It is no better in the US where fiscal dumping results in declining public goods provision and unfunded mandates for social services.

The obligation to provide public goods is not an attribute of formal democracy. It is a requirement of sustainable development whatever the political system. The first answer can be, indeed, the responsibility of public institutions driven by real democracy, where citizens intervene in everyday life management of local governments via their interactions with elected local assemblies. An alternative mechanism is provided by bureaucratic institutions where competent higher-level officials, trained in the importance of ethics in politics, closely supervise lower-level officials in top-down processes and prevent them effectively from abusing their power. It is the Singaporean way of public management. The right type of recruitment, training, and career opportunities encourage bureaucratic norms emphasizing the sense of duty and loyalty to the common good. The combination of competitive salaries for higher-level officials and harsh punishment for failure deter public servants from indulging in corruption and in the theft of public property.

Both real democracy and the bureaucratic model of accountability can apply to China. In the late 1980s, village, county, and municipal elections were instituted with the standard rationale of formal democracy. However, without the will in central government to closely monitor the locals, there has been no major impact in the provision of public goods in the countryside. This is why the third way, solidary groups and informal accountability well-embedded in Chinese culture, can have significant impact. According to Confucian philosophy, higher moral standing is an important source of soft power. They do not work like civil society associations, which make counter-powers. They are embedding and encompassing groups that incorporate local officials as members. They work in sharing a common set of ethical standards and moral obligations that help judge the behavior of members. One fundamental solidary obligation is doing one's fair share to contribute to the group. This informal accountability is effective in political systems that are fragmented, with weak law enforcement and litigation mechanisms.

We understand now why Fukuyama says that the US has not much to teach China in the way of politics in the twenty-first century. China is not any authoritarian political regime: it is a *sui generis* model. It is authoritarian because the authority of the Communist Party does not proceed from majority rule. But Chinese politics is embedded in a very long-standing culture, with a strong ethical underpinning of the basic view of harmony between nature and humankind. It ensues that the government is in many ways accountable to the people. The issue now is that those twin mechanisms of informal and bureaucratic accountability have been weakened by the capitalist growth regime of the 1995–2008 period of economic reform. What are the main characteristics of the contemporary political regime and how might it be improved in mobilizing the Chinese conception of humanity to promote social welfare?

Politics in China

Politics in China still bears much resemblance to what it was in the imperial era. First and foremost, it must be asserted that the Communist Party faces no direct challenge to its authority from any other entities. Chinese society, although much more diverse than its agrarian past, is still not pluralistic. The two-layered societal structure that we described in Chapter 1 lingers in present-day China. The CCP, with its over 80 million members, is deeply embedded in society. The power of finance has been kept in check. The Party, as much as the empire used to, has been able to eschew the capture of the common interest by concentrated financial interests.

In order to maintain the legitimacy of its authority, the Party has two-way relationships with the people. On the one hand, the government has to know how to cater for the aspirations of its populace. The economic reform has delivered rising real income and consumption growth to middle and working classes in urban areas. Discontent in rural areas is admittedly widespread, but dispersed and expressed against local officials. It is mitigated by solidary networks, as explained above. Moreover, the government has begun to handle the problem in the 12th five-year plan. It responds with its priority for education. A free program of education in the poorer inland provinces has been launched with the objective of providing nine years of free public education all over the country by 2015 and 85 percent of the younger population with at least a high school degree by 2020.

On the other hand, the Party is quite conscious of the need to renew its membership to carry out the new phase of reform to economic sustainability. Bottom-up the Party has been capable of profound renewal in co-opting the urban elite. The massive effort in education feeds a bureaucracy capable of dealing with objective information, analyzing tensions as they arise, and shifting policies in a very professional way. From the mid-2000s onwards there has been a renewal in municipal, county and township government, and Party committees. The number of local Party officials has been reduced and their qualifications improved. The new provincial elite is younger and better educated. As a consequence, the government is competent in experimenting and resorting to objective criteria in a gradual manner. The reshuffle is meant to counter the power of business interests.

Such a specific Chinese political system has two major assets compared with representative politics. One, the focus of representative politics is the legitimacy of state power, often generated through procedural democracy. Whichever faction of society wins the election will have the legitimacy to exercise state power on behalf of its own beliefs and interests, but at the same time subject to the checks of other social and political groups. Although periodic election has held it accountable for its misuse of power, the state is not responsible for problems that arise from civil society, such as sustainable development. In contrast, Chinese authority does not gain its legitimacy from procedural democracy. Its legitimacy stems directly from the acquiescence of civil society, based on its administrative performance. Thus Chinese government is held directly responsible for any problems emerging in civil society, especially when the problems concern the security, sustainability, and wellbeing of the general population. The other asset of China's government is its long-run view and associated strategic planning. Independent from money power, Chinese government has the potential to behave in the long-term interest of its populace, instead of in the interests of particular groups. Our optimism in achieving the objectives of the new growth regime outlined in Chapter 6 and the policies to achieve them analyzed in Chapter 7 is based on our acknowledgment of these two advantages of China's political system. With city development and environmental issues linked together and prioritized, China can develop an original brand of capitalism.

The drawbacks of the Chinese political system, nevertheless, are equally prominent. The absence of countervailing institutions to state power endangers the accountability and responsiveness of the ruling bureaucracy. "Power corrupts and absolute power corrupts absolutely." In order to enhance the accountability and responsiveness of its administration, China has to strengthen the two mechanisms we pointed out earlier: real democracy and the bureaucratic model of accountability.

As opposed to formal democracy, real democracy emphasizes continual participation of citizens in the concrete situations of everyday life. Democracy, in this case, should no longer be treated as a state of being but an infinite process of becoming. The means of obtaining such democracy is not confined to election. It is embodied in the self-organizing of civil society in diverse forms. Unlike political parties, spontaneous organizations in civil society do not have exclusive membership. One individual can belong to a variety of organizations concerning different aspects of his/her life, or according to different relationships he/she has in the community. Resultantly, society will be built upon densely woven nets of human relationships, instead of fragmentations and divisions. Luckily, China has a long tradition of self-organized civil society (see Chapter 1). In recent years, the rapid prosperity of NGOs, rural communities, and online social networks further proved the potential of such self-organizing civil entities in mediating social conflicts, complementing social service provisions, and supervising the performance of governmental bodies.

However, for Chinese civil society to develop into a brand of real democracy, there are still at least two conditions to be fulfilled. One condition is recognition from the central government. The status of civil society in China's political system nowadays is rather ambiguous. Instead of treating spontaneous civil organizations as potential political threats, it is time for Beijing to acknowledge the indispensable role of these organizations in promoting harmonious society. Without a vibrant civil society, China will lack efficient mechanisms to manage situational problems in people's everyday life, to channel opinions from grassroots to bureaucracy, and to supervise the behavior of bureaucrats, especially local bureaucrats. Such lack can lead to serious consequences, such as class stratifications, sharpening discontents toward governments, or both. Violent frictions are almost inevitable in any of these consequences. The other condition to be fulfilled is shrinking local governments and re-orientating their functions. In the imperial era, Chinese local governments were "one-man governments." Small formal political structure on the sub-national level gave civil society sufficient room to develop.

Yet in the socialist period, extensive local governments with excessively complete functions were established to carry out economic and political fiats. With the Chinese economy shifting from planning to market, such extensive local governmental branches are no longer needed. Not only are they wasting precious fiscal resources, they are becoming grabbing hands and hinder the healthy growth of civil entities. In Chapter 7 we made concrete suggestions about how to downsize local governments and re-orientate their functions. There is no need to repeat our arguments here. Curbing local officials' interference in civil society is prerequisite for the institution of interactive and participatory democracy in China.

The bureaucratic model of accountability is also an effective mechanism in enhancing administrative responsiveness to the people. Skeptics of this model may laugh this mechanism off as "asking the fox to guard the chicken." While we admit human beings are selfish animals, we have to also acknowledge the social side of us. When compensation for their diligent service is decent and juridical risks and moral condemnations are significant, it is possible to select a group of competent and disciplined bureaucrats. What is more, corruption in China should be understood in political terms. When properly managed, corruption is a key mechanism in calibrating the relationship between economic and political power under Party rule; and the relationship between central direction and local behavior. The Party wants to increase the economic resources at its disposal to achieve its strategic objectives domestically and abroad without renouncing its monopoly on political power. Corruption is the way to solve the dilemma. It arises as an acceptable price for getting things done. Political power is the ability to command people to do things: it needs resources to act. Economic power is the ownership of resources to do things: it needs rules to protect its resources. In the West the mediation is the law and the jurisprudence apparatus with lawyers, courts of justice, and counselors of all kinds that draw an enormous amount of resources on society that becomes overly juridical. In China, the Party does not want a legal system and enforcement mechanisms that might help holders of economic power to exercise political power through the judges. In this way, corruption has been the mediation between interests of the state and of business in an intertwined hierarchy. Corruption is also the cost of political patronage. It is the price paid for aligning the behavior of local officials with central will. When confined under a certain threshold, corruption in China does not weaken the legitimacy that accrues to the central government. Quite contrarily, as corruption is often attributed to individual officials rather than to the system in public opinion, and central government has the role of arbitraging official morality, corruption is a key component in managing the rules of the game set by the Party. Economic agents and bureaucrat officials must accept the rules. When the rules are transgressed, it means that some actors are trying to grab political power for themselves. Then the Party strikes back harshly to deter the multiplication of such events, as it did in Shanghai and Chongqing. That said, managing corruption is an extremely tricky task. As corruption in the bureaucratic system deepens and spreads, public opinion will eventually blame the central administration and the system. In this situation the whole political regime is jeopardized and risks losing its legitimacy.

How will corruption evolve in China? Considering that the process is fostered by the mutual rise of economic and political power with growth, and that growth consolidates the legitimacy of the Party, corruption can go on. Nevertheless, with the amelioration of economic conditions, the people's call for social justice is increasing sharply. In a recent online survey (CLSA 2011), "cracking down on corruption" was rated as the top priority of Beijing, surpassing "curbing property prices," "controlling inflation," and "improving employment." China is reaching a point where economic gains can no longer compensate for the loss of social justice.

The transition to sustainable growth will widen the scope of economic activities in developing cities and promoting services. There can be less corruption if the role of solidary networks based upon strong ethic becomes more widespread in making bureaucrats accountable. Conversely, there can be more corruption if business interests capture the political system. None of these outcomes is inevitable. In order to manage corruption while improving the responsiveness of the political system to citizens' desires without undermining Party rule and legitimacy, it is crucial to re-establish a national system of moral values and select bureaucrats accordingly; and to allow administrative transparency to enable supervision by civil society. The major challenges China faces in its transition to the next growth regime – accelerating market reforms, redistributing wealth to poorer areas, and establishing a universal safety net – have been discussed in Chapter 7. The philosophical legitimacy for such undertaking can be found in a renewed interpretation of Confucian *ren* as a way to express social equity in concrete terms. The broadening of the power base of the Party must go on in integrating entrepreneurs, without being captive to the rich elite that might emerge from the necessary reordering of financial prices with the liberalization of services. The government is likely to tackle this problem by reforming the tax system and establishing strong financial supervision.

China and the world

China's ascent creates great concern in the US, where politicians and political scientists alike cannot think of international relationships except in terms of hegemony. In the post-World War II era the concept worked. The Cold War was interpreted as a low profile struggle for hegemony against two universal ideologies: liberal capitalism and socialism. After the collapse of the USSR, the US felt justified in asserting its ideology in a triumphant way and to perceive its hegemony as natural.

With China's rise something disturbing is happening in international relations. Ideas not understood, because they are not framed in Western theories of international relations, come to the fore with the declarations of Chinese leaders: "soft" versus "hard" power; equitable international norms binding a hierarchy of countries in global harmony versus equal countries whose security is dependent on a single hegemon.

Clarifying those misunderstandings is a precondition for gaining insight on how China will impinge upon international relations in future decades. To start with, the distinction between hard and soft power is crucial. In Chinese political philosophy, hard power refers to economic and military power. Soft power means cultural and political power. According to Yan Xuetong (2011), hard power plus cultural power stand for the resources of power. Only political power is operating power. It means that, without the wisdom of strong political power, hard power is either of no use or destructive. An evil use of political power was the military-industrial complexes in the 1950s, denounced by President Eisenhower for their excessive influence on government. For ancient political philosophers, politics will have the upper hand; it will dominate economics and the military and follow principles that foster trust and reliability in international politics.

Following the distinction we sum up the successes of China in hard power as far as international relations are concerned, as discussed in Chapter 5, which has shown how the opening to the world has been an intrinsic component of economic reform. Then we introduce the security issue, heavily related to military power. Finally we discuss the concept of soft power in revisiting the viewpoints of the ancient thinkers we have already introduced in this chapter.

Economic integration and global expansion

In the last 20 years, China has largely diversified its trading partners and accelerated its integration in the world economy (Table 8.1). East Asia has been integrated around China, so has Australia, the first supplier of primary commodities. Integration of the rest of Asia is progressing fast. On other continents China

Table 8.1 China's share of countries' total foreign trade*

Countries	1992	2010
East Asian countries:		
Japan	5.0	20.4
South Korea	4.0	22.8
Taiwan	0.5	22.1
Other Asian countries:		
India	0.4	10.5
Indonesia	3.5	12.7
Malaysia	2.2	16.3
Thailand	2.2	12.0
Countries outside Asia:		
Australia	3.7	20.6
Brazil	0.9	14.0
Saudi Arabia	0.9	12.8
South Africa	1.8**	13.1
US	3.5	14.3

* % of total exports + imports for countries (where China's share is over 10%). ** 1998
Source: IMF

has expanded its trade mainly with primary resource exporting countries: Brazil, South Africa, and Saudi Arabia. Among developed countries, its trade links with the US stand out. Because European countries are themselves integrated, the share of China in their foreign trade is modest.

For the most part the pre-financial crisis expansion of China's trade was induced by the growth regime which propelled China as the manufacturer of the world, chiefly after its WTO entry. The pattern has changed with the much lower potential growth in Western countries due to the lingering impact of the financial crisis. China has redeployed its trade links toward developing countries, while upgrading the product content of its exports. This is just the beginning of a structural change. In its pursuit of sustainable growth China is planning to become one of the world leaders in the strategic industries it has prioritized (see Chapter 6, last section). China wants to forge a new phase of globalization where its enterprises go global and where it is able to set world standards. As long as it replaces the US in the position of dominant partner for many countries in the world, China gets the economic clout, which is the underpinning to shaping international rules and institutions. Financial power is a potent means of reaching this goal.

China's banks are financing infrastructures and energy supply in developing countries, boosting their growth rate and expanding the two-way trade that binds them to China. In East Asia the purpose is closer integration excluding the US as much as possible. The firepower for this strategy is the Chinese Development Bank (CDB) and the Chinese Exim Bank. In 2009–10 the two banks made together US$110 billion in long-term loans to developing countries, more than the World Bank and without any political condition attached. Furthermore, CDB, which granted US$65 billion alone, is well-managed and very profitable. CDB is a policy bank dedicated to assisting the policy line of the nation. It participated in the financing of the oil pipeline from Russia, Kazakhstan, and Burma, and also of the railway line from Burma to south-west China via Laos and Vietnam. It contributes to the "Go West" strategy that aims at developing the western regions on resource exploitation. Beyond Asia, CDB has agencies in 141 countries, its latest hunting ground being South America.

Policy loans are not the only spears in China's global reach. The ambition of making the Yuan a leading international currency by 2020 is an indication of how China has been drawing lessons from the financial crisis. The drawbacks of US monetary hegemony was self-evident in the fall of 2008 when dollar liquidity dried up in the international money market. Then in August 2011 the position of China as the main foreign creditor of the US was jeopardized by the downgrading of the rating of treasury bonds, the linchpin of the world financial markets. These events have persuaded Chinese leaders that it is high time to curtail US dominance in the international monetary system.

We highlighted in Chapter 5 the early move to promote Yuan internationalization in the Hong Kong offshore market as the first step of the strategy. As long as the Chinese currency is not fully convertible, the government will use Hong Kong, a city of high finance, to allow international corporations and financial investors to hold, borrow, and trade Yuan-denominated financial products. Since mid-2009, Hong Kong has become a kind of special zone to test the impact of progressive liberalization of the Yuan. Then the decoupling to the dollar in June 2010 accelerated markedly the use of the Yuan in trade finance and corporate bond issues. The reliance on US dollars is reduced at the bottom, in settling import and export deals with counterparts in Asian and other emerging-market countries where foreign trade is growing the fastest. Yuan-denominated bond sales have been arranged for Chinese and multinational companies after the Chinese government created a yield curve in issuing an array of public bonds of different maturities in Hong Kong. Finally, investing in the mainland Yuan deposits in Hong Kong is being released progressively, which increases capital inflows. The pressure strengthens the position of the People's Bank, which seeks to speed up the reordering of domestic financial prices to foster competitive domestic markets. It would allow Chinese institutional investors to manage diversified portfolios, thus being able to export capital to foreign countries and subsequently alleviate the pressure on official reserve accumulation. At that point, toward the end of the 12th five-year plan, China's demand for international monetary rules to manage a multipolar monetary system will become credible.

Security issues

US critics on China's modernizing its defense system, especially the navy, have become voluble. They accuse China of acting to drive the US out of the Western Pacific. Robert Gates, the US Secretary of Defense, spoke frankly for the maintenance of US hegemony: investments by China in new missiles and anti-ship weapons "could threaten America's primary way to project power and help allies in the Pacific" (Dyer and MacGregor 2011). In the same vein he cautioned that the new rivalry "could end the operational sanctuary our navy has enjoyed in the Western Pacific for the better part of six decades." The reaction of a Chinese military official, which reflects the sentiment in Beijing, has been expressed in a lively metaphor: "one person has a gun and the other a knife. But the one with the gun is accusing the one with the knife of behaving dangerously." It means that the disproportion of forces is so huge that US accusations look ridiculous. It is true that the balance in sea power tilts heavily towards the US (Table 8.2). But the imbalance in the armed forces is shrinking. Therefore US worries are logical

Table 8.2 Comparison in sea power

Items	China	US
Surface weapons:	*80*	*110*
Aircraft carriers	0	11
Cruisers	0	22
Destroyers	28	56
Frigates	52	21
Submarines	*65*	*71*
Amphibious vessels	*1*	*33*
Aircrafts	*290*	*900*
Active personnel	*255,000*	*335,822*

Source: International Institute for Strategic Studies, US Department of Defense

in conformity with the view that only hegemony can provide an international order and that the US is the "natural" hegemon.

It is true that, as long as there are no binding international rules that can guarantee the safety of trade routes, China must develop the military means to protect its primary resource imports and manufacturing trade. However, the US military establishment grossly exaggerates Chinese weapon capabilities for the purpose of getting a larger share of budget resources in time of fiscal stringency. China is not going to become a global military power in the pursuit of hegemony. In pretending the opposite, US strategists assimilate the rise of China with that of the USSR after World War II. For them the only way to deal with it is containment. This is a fatal error, no less because of the economic and financial ties. The US and the USSR were separated economies regulated by opposite principles. The US and China are tightly intertwined. If Congress tried unilaterally to override this reality, it would lose the trust of its allies and would stir opposition of business interests at home. Hegemony would be impaired and the whole world would suffer disruption and lower growth.

The problem, however, is how China's neighbors in Asia view China's military rise in the region, while there are unresolved territorial issues in the South China Sea. Their newly increased anxiety provides an opportunity for the US to reassert its military presence and get more active in Asian politics. In turn this makes relationships with China more tense. The danger is that the US can overplay its hand to take advantage of the mistrust of some countries of China with the result of strengthening hardliners in the Chinese Communist Party and increasing the influence of the military. To abate the tension a diplomatic move through regional groupings might reach mutual agreement for a legally binding code of conduct for which it would be necessary to build regional institutions that no one state has interest to cheat. However, according to ancient Chinese thinking, it would still be a fragile edifice if it is based solely upon national interests. The common interest must be cemented by moral values in international as well as in domestic affairs. This is the opportunity for international politics to move from the pursuit of hegemony to the building of "humane authority" in international politics.

The reason for China's neighbors to approve such a move is that they do not want to choose between their economic ties with China that bring prosperity and their need for security that leans toward keeping a US military presence in the region. As economic integration gets tighter and more complex, the dilemma becomes more acute. The only way to get both is to agree on a concept of international order that can guarantee lasting peaceful relations between the US and China. This cannot be under hegemony. For such a concept to work the parties must address the global challenge of the twenty-first century, which will be dominated by environmental issues.

Sustainability and the international political order

The Warring States era (476–221 BC) was rich in experiences in international relationships for ancient Chinese philosophers. Mencius and Xunzi were the main contributors in theorizing the variety of international configurations and in advising rulers how they should behave to attain a harmonious international order. They considered international relationships in continuity with social relationships. They viewed the ethic of the rulers as the main attribute of peaceful international relationships. For harmony of "all under heaven," rulers should not pursue hegemony but "humane authority." This is the essence of soft power.

Moral justification and modern tools of soft power

Mencius believed that morality impinged directly on politics. It is the basis of soft power. Only soft power can use economic, military, and cultural resources in conformity with equity in international relationships. He advocated rites and covenants among rulers to rectify attitudes, correct distorted relationships, and suppress conflicts. Xunzi was more circumspect because he believed that increase in wealth sustains the desire for more wealth and sharpens the competition for resources. He also believed that moral guidance fostered by the establishment of social norms can regulate human desires. A viable order can be achieved only if the sense of equity is shared, so that "all under heaven" can achieve more satisfaction with the same amount of resources. In international matters as well as in social matters there are hierarchies. To attain humane authority the norms should be the more demanding the higher people are in society, the richer and more powerful militarily are the states in the international system.

Contrary to present theories of international politics, ancient China's philosophy disputes that hegemony is the highest form of power in the international system. Hegemony refers to the power to influence or control other states to bind them to the interest of the hegemon. It has higher status than continuous rivalry among equal states. It might be stable if the hegemon is benevolent in the sense that it makes allowance for the interests of allies that are threatened by hostile states. In that sense hegemony has value. However, it has less value than humane authority, which refers to a common system of norms, not legitimated by conciliation of interest but by a sense of justice.

Soft power provides a raft of instruments to deal with the impediments facing China in its relationships with its neighbors and in its ascent into world politics. On the one hand, territorial disputes have shaped an image of China as an aggressive regional power looking for hegemony in Asia. While not competitive with the US, China has built up its military strength far ahead of the other countries in the region. On the other hand, Western propaganda has been keen to point out the authoritarian political regime and lack of concern for individual freedom of expression and property rights, as they are formally valued in representative democracies.

China's soft power diplomacy has for the time being mainly focused on confidence-building measures in Asia: resolving border disputes, investing in the region and building closer economic ties to demonstrate an enhanced economic engagement, and deploying a cultural outreach.

On the diplomatic side, soft power is induced by the paramount priority of stable relationships with Asian countries. Public diplomacy in China has powerful offices: the State Council Information Office, the Office of Foreign Propaganda of the Chinese Communist Party, and the Public Diplomacy Office in the Foreign Ministry. Chinese diplomacy has displayed a new security concept that has repackaged the principles of peaceful coexistence. It has been implemented in negotiating a web of bilateral and multilateral agreements. China is part of the following regional multilateral groupings: ASEAN+1, ASEAN+3, ASEAN regional forum, ASEAN vision group, ASEAN senior officials meeting, and East Asian Summit. China proposes to forge closer relationships for greater interdependence via those multilateral frameworks instead of transpacific groupings in view of weakening US influence.

The diplomatic offensive is backed by economic aid, which is provided without political strings. Aid is concerned with infrastructure development, trade facilities, and cross border investments all over the region. It has a large political impact on lower-income countries all over the region: Vietnam, Laos, Cambodia, Myanmar, Thailand, and the Philippines.

On the cultural side, there is the strong appeal of China's rich cultural heritage. Cultural diplomacy has become a strategic tool towards neighboring countries where people understand it. It is meant to neutralize the negative impact of South China Sea bickering and China's growing defense spending. Furthermore, the 2008 Beijing Olympics and the 2010 Shanghai world expo have enhanced China's prestige worldwide.

The other important tool of soft power is education and language learning. China is establishing a web of Confucian Institutes worldwide. Presently there are 295 institutes covering 78 countries; 21 are in South-east Asia and 13 in Thailand alone. Many more are planned. They aim at projecting China's cultural tradition abroad through language learning and education. Indeed, the teaching of Confucian tradition is appealing because it is based on secular values: humanity, education, and moral rules leading to harmony. The other way China is attracting more and more foreign students is through education programs and scholarships. Financial aid has been upgraded and visa policies relaxed with spectacular results in Cambodia, Vietnam, and Indonesia.

Conclusion: from hegemony to international regimes

Most Western theories of international relations do not make any distinction between the resources of power (hard power) and the political legitimization of power (soft power). They maintain that either the economy, or the military, or both, are the core factors for hegemony. Some see hegemony just in the domination of the armed forces; others in the share of the country in world GDP. Scholars of international regimes are more sophisticated. Keohane and Nye (2001) assign hegemony to the state capable of maintaining the rules governing interstate relations, changing the rules as it sees fit, preventing the adoption of rules it does not like and is more influential than others in creating new rules. They consider that military power has been weakened by globalization and plays a minor role now. Wallerstein (2012) thinks that economic power is vastly more important than the military. However, thinking with the concepts of game theory from fragmented groups of players, not in political terms from the point of view of the system, because in terms of interests none can take that point of view, they cannot conceive principles higher than hegemony. Political hegemony is seen as a strategy of working with allies, so that it can gain international recognition.

If China wants to leave the pursuit of hegemony aside and to direct its foreign policy under the banner of humane authority, it needs a moral universal ideal that it currently lacks. Mencius thought that humane authority establishes a model for the world and has attractive power, not because it is the model of the richest country, but because it proposes a political ideal and a model of social development founded on this ideal.

In the early twenty-first century the urgency of acting together to fight environmental perils the world has never faced before is mounting in public opinion throughout the international networks that link people in civil society. This type of concrete and interactive democracy has still to impinge upon politics. The stakes are so high that they rationalize a generalized principle of precaution. This principle provides the moral legitimation to attempt a radical transition in the course of world capitalism. If China takes the lead in the transition to the model of sustainable growth, and if it proposes international rules to combat climate change that are made credible by its own achievements, it might establish trust and reliability toward other countries on another basis than hegemony.

Meanwhile this international principle carries a new political model. Neither formal representative democracies, nor authoritarian regime, deprived of strong ethical foundation, are sufficient to organize the social debate necessary to legitimize the long-run view that will shape the right policies. Ethics must take over in the choice and the reproduction of elites. The criteria of social merit and recognition must change entirely. A deeper, more socially responsible, participative democracy must emerge.

Notes

1 The role of history and culture in the resilience of China's institutional framework

1 By the first century BC, the bureaucracy is said to have consisted of 130,285 officials, ranking in 18 grades (Fairbank and Reischauer 1979).
2 This is especially true with property ownership and in legal terms.
3 Ever since the beginning of Chinese history secular leaders also took the role of priest. Thus there were seldom the struggles between religious and secular powers.
4 In the Qin dynasty there were 36 commanderies.
5 For example, sales of offices were popular at the end of the Ming dynasty to supplement fiscal income in order to meet heavy national defense expenditures against the Manchu (Ho 1960).
6 Official positions could be obtained by wealth in times of dynastic decline or state fiscal difficulty. Professor Ping-tin Ho's research demonstrated the prevalence of the sales of office in the late Ming dynasty and throughout the Qing dynasty.

2 Growth regimes in capitalist history

1 The aggregate of Japanese and Boxer indemnities, without interest, was 650 million taels.

3 On the political economy of reform

1 There are different estimates about the number of casualties in this catastrophe. Aggregate death toll estimates in these three years range from 14 million to 26 million (Penny 1988).
2 The Hukou system is a Chinese household registration system which officially identifies a person as the resident of a geographical area. Even today it is difficult for a Chinese to change his or her hukou to an area other than his or her birth place.
3 Inspired by the theories of Schurmann (1966) and Bornstein (1977), some Chinese economists (Wu et al. 1986, Wu and Reynolds 1988, 2010) argued that the reforms before 1978 mainly addressed the allocation of power and decision rights between central and local governments. Using the terms invented by Bornstein, they called this kind of decentralization "administrative decentralization." Yet the reforms after 1978 applied the logic of "economic decentralization," which means giving the economic actors their rights to making economic decisions. Such kinds of reforms aims to lead the country into a regulated market economy which, according to them, is the real key for long-term economic prosperity.
4 Dependency ratio refers to the portion of dependants (population aged under 16 and over 65) to the active population (aged 16–64).

4 The second phase of Chinese reform

1 Admittedly, the income gap between rural and urban China was large. In 1978, average urban income was 2.7 times that of rural income.
2 Eighty percent of the active population worked for the state either as public servants or employees of SOEs. The unemployment rate in socialist China was extremely low.
3 "Jump into the sea" was a popular expression in the late 1980s and early 1990s referring to giving up a position in the state system and joining private economic activities.
4 VAT tax rate for industrial activities is set at 17 percent. A preferential rate of 13 percent also exists.
5 The 11 categories include: tobacco, wine and alcohol, cosmetics, skincare products, precious jewelry, jade jewelry, firecrackers and fireworks, gasoline, diesel, automobile tires, motorcycles and cars.
6 Corporate income tax rate was set at 33 percent.
7 Under the 1994 tax regime, central government also levied all consumption taxes, while local governments claimed all business tax and income taxes. Since 2003 income taxes have been shared between central and local governments on a 60/40 basis.
8 As the primary purpose of the 1994 fiscal reform was to strengthen the fiscal control of central government, the transfer scheme itself was not adequately designed. This is an incomplete component in the current tax-sharing system in China. In the following chapters, we will again discuss the shortcomings of the current transfer scheme and propose possible directions for future reform.
9 This definition of "strategic sector" was made official in the 4th Plenary Session of the 15th Central Committee, 1999.

7 A road map for the transformation of China's economic structure

1 Internationally, it is more common to charge royalty on mineral resource extraction based on sales or profit.
2 This estimation is based on the price level and exchange rate of 2007.
3 Estimations from PBoC, MoF, and other institutions varied mainly because of their disparate standards in defining local investment vehicles.
4 A calculation made by combining domestic VAT, domestic consumption, VAT and consumption tax on imports, business tax, tariff, and urban maintenance and construction.
5 Property taxes are usually important financial sources for local governments to provide local public goods and services. For instance, in some states in the US, they compose up to 80 percent of total local fiscal revenue.
6 Before the reform, Xinjiang charged 30 Yuan per ton of crude oil and 7–9 Yuan per cubic meter of natural gas.
7 Due to the widespread financial difficulties on the township level, expenditure responsibilities of townships, including the payrolls of rural teachers, were gradually centralized to county level, especially after 2006.
8 After 2004, farmers may transfer their land to other farmers in the same collective, but the land transferred is restricted to agricultural uses.
9 Replacement rate is the ratio between annual net salary in inactive years and annual net salary in active years.

Bibliography

Aghion, P., Hemous, D. and Veugelers, R. (2009) "No Green Growth without Innovation," *Bruegel Policy Brief*, no. 7, November.

Aglietta, M. (1980), *A Theory of Capitalist Regulation. The US Experience*, London: New Left Books.

Aglietta, M. (2007a) "Developing the Bond Market in China: The Next Step Forward in Financial Reform," *Economie Internationale*, Vol. 111, pp. 29–53.

Aglietta, M. (2007b) *La Chine vers la superpuissance*, Paris: Economica.

Aglietta, M. (2011a) "Internationalization of the Chinese Currency," *China Perspectives*, no. 3, pp. 79–83.

Aglietta, M. (2011b) "Sustainable Growth: Do we really Measure the Challenge?," in Measure for Measure, Proceedings of the 8th AFD-EUDN Conference, 2010 Paris, December.

Aglietta, M. and Lemoine, F. (2011) "La nouvelle frontière chinoise," in *L'économie mondiale 2011*, coll. Repères, La découverte, p. 35.

Allen, F., Qian, J. and Qian, M. (2008) "China's Financial System: Past, Present and Future," in L. Brandt and T. Rawski (eds) *China's Great Economic Transformation*, New York: Cambridge University Press, pp. 506–68.

Anand, S., Fan, V., Zhang, J., Zhang, L., Ke, Y., Dong, Z. and Chen, L. (2008) "China's Human Resources for Health: Quantity, Quality and Distribution," *The Lancet*, Vol. 372, no. 9651, pp. 1774–81.

Ao, X. and Fuginiti, L. (2003) "Productivity Growth in China: Evidence from Chinese Provinces," *Econ WPA Series Development and Comp Systems*, no. 0502024.

Arrighi, G. (2007) *Adam Smith in Beijing: Lineages of the Twenty-First Century*, London: Verso.

Arrow, K. (1950) "A Difficulty in the Concept of Social Welfare," *Journal of Political Economy*, Vol. 58, no. 4, 328–46.

Arrow, K., Dasgupta, P., Goulder, L., Mumford, K. and Oleson, K. (2007) "China, the US and Sustainability: Perspectives Based on Comprehensive Wealth," Stanford Center for International Development, Stanford US, January.

Aziz, J. and Suenwald, C. (2002) "Growth Financial Intermediation Nexus in China," IMF Working Paper, no.194.

Bahl, R. and Martinez-Vazquez, J. (2007) "The Property Tax in Developing Countries: Current Practice and Prospects," Lincoln Institute of Land Policy Working Paper.

Batson, A. and Zhang, J. (2011) "Managing the Debt Mountain," *China Economic Quarterly Review*, Vol. 15, no. 2, pp. 41–7.

Bell, D. (2008) *China's New Confucianism*, Princeton, NJ: Princeton University Press.

Belttrati, A. and Caccavaio, M. (2007) "Asset Float and Stock Prices: Evidence from the Chinese Stock Market," SSRN Working Paper, no. 971721.

Bensidoun, I., Lemoine, F. and Unal-Kesenci, D. (2009) "The Integration of China and India into the World Economy: A Comparison," *European Journal of Comparative Economics*, Vol. 6, no. 1, pp. 131–55.

Bergère, M. C. (2007) *Capitalismes et Capitalistes en Chine*, Paris: Perrin.

Bernanke, B. (2005) "The Global Saving Glut and the US Current Account Deficit," Board of Governors of the Federal Reserve System, Washington, DC, 10 March.

Bertaud, A. (2004) *The Spatial Organization of Cities*. Available at: http://alain-bertaud. com/, free site dedicated to spatial urban structures (accessed August 2011).

Bian, Y. (1994) *Work and Inequality in Urban China*, Albany, NY: State University of New York Press.

Bornstein, M. (1977) "Economic Reform in Eastern Europe," *Eastern European Economies Post-Helsinki*, Washington: USGPO, pp. 102–34.

Brandt, L. and Rawski, T. (eds) (2008) *China's Great Economic Transformation*, New York: Cambridge University Press.

Brandt, L. and Zhu, X. (2000) "Redistribution in a Decentralizing Economy: Growth and Inflation in Reform China," *Journal of Political Economy*, Vol. 108, no. 2, pp. 422–51.

Braudel F. (1985) *La dynamique du capitalisme*, Paris: Arthaud.

Brender, A. and Pisani, F. (2007) *Les déséquilibres financiers internationaux*, Paris: La Découverte.

Brueckner, J. K. (2000) "Urban Sprawl: Diagnosis and Remedies," *International Regional Science Review*, Vol. 23, pp. 160–71.

Cai, F., Park, A. and Zhao, Y. (2008) "The Chinese Labor Market in the Reform Era," in L. Brandt and T. Rawski (eds) *China's Great Economic Transformation*, New York: Cambridge University Press.

CCICED (2009) "Efficacité énergétique et développement urbain. Chine," Rapport du Conseil Chinois pour la Coopération Internationale sur l'Environnement et le Développement.

Chan, K.W. (2009) "Measuring the Urban Millions," *China Economic Quarterly*, March, pp. 21–46.

Chen, G. and Duan, W. (eds) (2009) *China's Experience: the Endogenous Path and Sustained Development*, Beijing: Economic Science Press.

Chen, H., Peng, W. and Shu, C. (2009) "Renminbi as an International Currency: Potential and Policy Considerations," HKIMR Working Paper, no. 18, May.

Cheng, A. (1997) *Histoire de la pensée chinoise*, Paris: Le Seuil.

Cheung, S. (2008) *The Economic System of China*, 2nd edn, Hong Kong: Arcadia Press.

Chieng, A. (2006) *La pratique de la Chine*, Paris: Grasset.

China Hand (2009) The Economist Intelligence Unit Limited.

Chow, G. (2002) *China's Economic Transformation*, Maiden, MA: Blackwell Publishing,

Chow, G. (2004) *Knowing China*, London: World Scientific.

Ch'u, T. (1962) *Local Government in China under the Ch'ing*, Cambridge: Harvard University Press.

CLSA (2010) "China's Energy Binge. Moving to a Greener, Low-carb Diet," Special Report, September.

CLSA (2011) "Getting Easier: China Starts Pumping the Economy," *China Strategy*, December.

Coale, A. J. and Chen, S. (1987) *Basic Data on Fertility in the Provinces of China, 1942–1982*, Honolulu, HI: East–West Population Institute Paper Series.

Confucius, *The Analects*, Chinese classics.

Corrado, A., Hulten, C. and Sichel, D. (2006) "Intangible Capital and Economic Growth," NBER Working Paper, no. 11948, January.

Dagongzhe Migrant Workers Centre (2009) "New Ongoing Violations after the Implementation of Labor Contract Law in China," Shenzhen: DMWC. Available at: http://www.workerempowerment.org/en/newsletter/18 (accessed 3 January 2010).

Davoodi, H. and Zou, H. (1998) "Fiscal Decentralization and Economic Growth – A Cross-Country Study," *Journal of Urban Economics*, Vol. 43, pp. 244–57.

Dooley, M., Folkerts-Landau, D. and Garber, P. (2003) "An Essay on the Revived Bretton Woods System," NBER Working Paper, no. 9971, September.

Dunaway, S., Leigh, L. and Xiangming Li (2006) "How Robust are Estimates of Equilibrium Exchange Rates: The Case of China," IMF Working Paper, no. 220, October.

Duttagupta, R., Fernandez, G. and Karasadag, C. (2004) "From Fixed to Float: Operational Aspects of Moving Toward Exchange Rate Flexibility," IMF Working Paper, no. 04/126, July.

Dyer, G. and MacGregor, R. (2011) "Beijing Builds to Hold US Power at Bay," *Financial Times*, January 19.

Ebrey, P. B. (1996) *Cambridge Illustrated History of China*, Cambridge: Cambridge University Press.

Eichengreen, B. (2004) "Chinese Currency Controversies," CEPR Discussion Paper Series, no. 4375.

Eichengreen B. (2006) *Global Imbalances and the Lessons of Bretton Woods*, Cambridge, MA: MIT Press.

Elvin, M. (1973) *The Pattern of the Chinese Past*, Stanford, CA: Stanford University Press.

Elvin, M. and Liu Ts'ui-jung (eds) (1998) *Sediments of Time: Environment and Society in Chinese History*, New York: Cambridge University Press.

Esping-Andersen, G. (1990) *The Three Worlds of Welfare Capitalism*, Cambridge: Polity Press, in association with Oxford: Blackwell Publishers.

Fairbank, J. K. and Reischauer, E. O. (1979) *China: Tradition and Transformation*, Sydney: George Allen & Unwin.

Fan, G. (1994) "Incremental Change and Dual-track Transition: Understanding the Case of China," *Economic Policy*, Vol. 19 (supp), pp. 99–122.

Fan, G., Zhang, X., Wei, Q., Liu, P. and Lv, Y. (2010) *Zhongguo Jingji Zaipingheng Zhilu: Neiwai Junheng yu Caishui Gaige*, Shanghai: Shanghai Far East Publishers.

Feng, Y. (1948) *A Short History of Chinese Philosophy*, New York: Macmillan Company.

Fong, T., Wong, F. and Yong, I. (2007) "Share Price Disparity in Chinese Stock Markets," HK Monetary Authority Working Paper, no. 11.

Frankel J. (1999) "No Single Currency Regime is Right for all Countries or at all Times," NBER Working Paper, no. 7338, September.

Fujita, M. and Thisse, J. F. (2000) "The Formation of Economic Agglomerations: Old Problems and New Perspectives," in J. M. Huriot and J. F. Thisse (eds) *Economics of Cities. Theoretical Perspectives*, Cambridge: Cambridge University Press, pp. 3–73.

Fukuyama, F. (2011) "Democracy in America has less than ever to Teach China," *Financial Times*, January 18.

Garnaut, R., Golley, J. and Song, L. (eds) (2010) *China: The Next Twenty Years of Reform and Development*, Beijing: Social Sciences Academic Press.

Gerber, H. (2006) *Exchange Rate Arrangements and Financial Integration in East Asia: On a Collision Course?*, Springer-Verlag: Berlin, pp. 359–77.

Girardin E. and Liu, Z. (2003) "The Chinese Stock Market: A Casino with Buffer Zones," *Journal of Chinese Economic and Business Studies*, Vol. 1, no. 1, pp. 57–70.

Glaeser, E. (2011) *Triumph of the City*, London: Macmillan.

Goldstein, M. (2004) "Adjusting China's Exchange Rate Policies," Institute for International Economics Working Paper, no. 04/1.

Gong, G. (2009) "The Formation and Evolution of China's Planning Economy," in G. F. Chen and W. B. Duan (eds) *China's Experience: the Endogenous Path and Sustained Development*, Beijing: Economic Science Press.

Goodhart, C. and Xu, C. (1996) "The Rise of China as an Economic Power," *National Institute Economic Review*, Vol. 155, no. 1, pp. 56–80.

Hale, G. (2007) "Prospects for China's Corporate Bond Markets," FRBSF Economic Letter, no. 2007-07, San Francisco.

Han Fei Zi (2010) *L'art de gouverner*, Paris: Presses du Châtelet.

Harvey, D. (2000) *Spaces of Hope*, Berkeley, CA: University of California Press.

Harvey, D. (2003) *The New Imperialism*, New York: Oxford University Press.

He, Z. (ed.) (2008) *Political Reform in China*, Beijing: Central Compilation & Translation Press.

Ho, P. (1960) *The Ladder of Success in Imperial China*, New York: Columbia University Press.

Holz, C. (2006) "China's Economic Growth Tomorrow," SSRN Working Paper, December, New York.

Hougaard, J. L., Osterdal, L. P. and Yu, Y. (2011) "The Chinese Health Care System: Structure, Problems and Challenges," *Applied Health Economics and Health Policy*, Vol. 9, no. 1, pp. 1–13.

Huang, P. (2002) "Development or Involution in 18th Century Britain or China? A Review of Kenneth Pomeranz's "The Great Divergence. China, Europe and the Making of the Modern World Economy"," *Journal of Asian Studies*, Vol. LXI, no. 2, pp. 501–38.

Huang, Y. (2010) "China's Great Ascendancy and Structural Risks: Consequences of Asymmetric Market Liberalization," *Asian-Pacific Economic Literature*, Vol. 24, no. 1, pp. 65–85.

Huang, Y. (2011) "Learn From Li Na," *Caixin*. Available at: http://english.caixin.com/2011-06-28/100273823.html (accessed 30 June 2011).

Islam, N., Dai, E. and Sakamoto, H. (2006) "Role of TFP in China's Growth," *Asian Economic Journal*, Vol. 20, no. 2, pp. 127–59.

Jefferson, G., Rawski, T. and Zhang, Y. (2008) "Productivity Growth and Convergence Across China's Industrial Economy," *Journal of Chinese and Business Economic Studies*, Vol. 6, no. 2, pp. 127–59.

Jiang, S., Liu, S. and Li, Q. (2010) *China's Land Policy Reform: Policy Evolution and Local Innovation*, Shanghai: Shanghai Joint Publishing Company.

Jullien, F. (2009) *Les transformations silencieuses*, Paris: Grasset.

Kalecki, M. (1943) "Political Aspects of Full Employment," *Political Quarterly*, Vol. 14, no. 4, pp. 322–30.

Kane, P. (1988) *Famine in China 1959–61: Demographic and Social Implications*, Basingstoke: Macmillan Press.

Keohane, R. (1984) *After Hegemony*, Princeton, NJ: Princeton University Press.

Keohane, R. and Nye, J. (2001) *Power and Interdependence*, London: Longman Pearson.

King, S., Henry, J., Qu Hongbin, Yetsenga, R. (2005) "China's Dilemma. Options for the Renminbi," *HSBC Global Research*, 20 May.

Knight, J. and Song, L. (1999) *The Rural–Urban Divide. Economic Disparities and Interactions in China*, Oxford: Oxford University Press.

Kracke, E. A. (1964) "The Chinese and the Art of Government," in R. Dawson (ed.) *The Legacy of China*, Oxford: Oxford University Press.

Krugman, P. (1995) *Development, Geography and Economic Theory*, Cambridge, MA: MIT Press.

Lardy, N. (1983) *Agriculture in China's Modern Economic Development*, New York: Cambridge University Press.

Lardy, N. (1998) *China's Unfinished Economic Revolution*, Washington, DC: Brookings Institution.

Lau, L., Qian, Y. and Roland, G. (2000) "Reform Without Losers: An Interpretation of China's Dual-Track Approach to Transition," *Journal of Political Economy*, Vol. 108, no. 1, 120–43.

Lemoine, F. (2006) *L'economie chinoise*, 4th edn, Paris: La Découverte.

Leonard, M. (2008) *What does China Think?*, London: Fourth Estate.

Levathes, L. (1994) *When China Ruled the Seas: the Treasure Fleet of the Dragon Thrones, 1405–1433*, London: Simon and Schuster.

Lewis, A. (1954) "Economic Development with Unlimited Supplies of Labor," *Manchester School of Economic and Social Studies*, Vol. 22, pp. 139–91.

Li, H. (2011) *Equity, Efficiency and Sustainable Development: China's Energy Subsidy Reform Theory and Policy Practice*, Beijing: China Economic Publishing House.

Li, W. (1957) *Zhongguo Jindai Nongyeshi Ziliao (Vol. 1)*, Beijing: Sanlian.

Li, W. and Yuan, Z. (2010) "Cujin Disan Chanye Jiuye Zengzhang de Zhengce Xuanze," *Journal of Shandong University of Finance*, Vol. 2, pp. 44–9.

Lim, M., Yang, H., Zhang, T., Zhou, Z., Feng, W. and Chen Y. (2002) "The Role and Scope of Private Medical Practice in China," Final Report to the World Health Organization and the United Nations Development Programme, UNDP, WHO and MOH China.

Ma, G. (2006) "Who Pays China's Bank Restructuring Bill?," Cepii Working Paper, no. 4, Paris.

Ma, G., Ho, C. and Mac Cauley, R. (2004) "The Market for Non-Deliverable Forwards in Asian Currencies," *BIS Quarterly Review*, June, pp. 81–94.

MacKinnon, R. (2005) "Exchange Rate or Wage Changes in International Adjustment? Japan and China Versus the United States," *China and World Economy*, Institute of World Economics and Politics, Pekin, Vol. 13, no. 5, September/October, pp. 11–27.

MacKinnon, R. and Schnabl, G. (2008) "China's Exchange Rate Impasse and the Weak US Dollar," CESIFO Working Paper, no. 2386, August.

McKinsey Global Institute (2011) *Urban World: Mapping the Economic Power Cities*, March.

Maddison A. (2003) *The World Economy: Historical Statistics*, Paris: OECD Publishing.

Maddison, A. (2007) *Contours of the World Economy, 1–2030 A.D.*, Oxford: Oxford University Press.

Man Kwong Leung (2011) "Hong Kong and the Internationalization of the RMB," *China Perspectives*, Vol. 2011, no. 3, pp. 67–77.

Marshall, A. (1920) *Principle of Economics*, 8th edn, reprinted 1966, London: Macmillan.

Meyer, C. (2010) *Chine ou Japon: quel leader pour l'Asie?*, Paris: Presses de Sciences Po.

Miller, T. (2009) "Big Cities, Small Cities," *China Quarterly Review*, 1st quarter, Dragonomics Research and GaveKal Research, pp. 28–35.

Ministry of Finance People's Republic of China (1987), *Zhongguo Caizheng Tongji 1950–1985*, Beijing: China Financial & Economic Publishing House.

Mooney, T. (2009) "Sticky Supply Chains," *China Economic Quarterly*, Vol. 13, no. 4, pp. 45–9.

Mozi, *Mozi*, Chinese classics.

Mu, H. (2006) "The Development of China's Bond Market," BIS Economic Paper, no. 26.

National Audit Office of China (2011) *Guanyu 2010 Niandu Zhongyang Yusuan Zhixing he Qita Caizheng Shouzhi de Shenji Gongzuo Baogao*, Beijing: National Audit Office. Available at: http://www.audit.gov.cn/n1992130/n1992165/n2032598/n2376391/2754043.html (accessed 6 September 2011).

National Bureau of Statistics of China (2003) *China Labor Statistical Yearbook 2002*, Beijing: China Statistics Press.

National Bureau of Statistics of China (2006) *China Labor Statistical Yearbook 2005*, Beijing: China Statistics Press.

National Bureau of Statistics of China (2008) *China Statistical Yearbook 2007*, Beijing: China Statistics Press.

National Bureau of Statistics of China (2011a) *2010 nian Diliuci Quanguo Renkou Pucha Zhuyao Shuju Gongbao (No.1)*, NBS, Beijing. Available at: http://www.stats.gov.cn/tjfx/jdfx/t20110428_402722253.htm (accessed 5 June 2011).

National Bureau of Statistics of China (2011b) *China Statistical Yearbook 2010*, Beijing: China Statistics Press.

National Development and Reform Commission (2009) "China's Policies and Actions for Addressing Climate Change," Beijing.

Naughton, B. (2007) *The Chinese Economy: Transition and Growth*, Cambridge and London: MIT Press.

Naughton, B. (2008) "A Political Economy of China's Economic Transition," in L. Brandt and T. Rawski (eds) *China's Great Economic Transformation*, New York: Cambridge University Press.

Needham, J., Wang, L. and Lu, G. (1971) *Science and Civilization in China* (Volume 4, Part 3), New York: Cambridge University Press.

Nordhaus, W. (2007) "A Review of the Stern Review on the Economics of Climate Change," *Journal of Economic Literature*, Vol. 45, no. 3, pp. 686–702.

North, D. C. (2005) *Understanding the Process of Economic Change*, Princeton, NJ: Princeton University Press.

OECD (2006) "Challenges for China's Public Spending," *Policy Brief*, March 2006, Paris: OECD.

OECD (2010) *Economic Survey of China 2010*, Paris: OECD.

Olson, M. (1982) *The Rise and Decline of Nations: Economic Growth, Stagflation, and Social Rigidities*, New Haven, CT, and London: Yale University Press.

Palit, P. S. and Palit, A. (2011) "Strategic Influence of Soft Power: Inferences for India from Chinese Engagement of South and South East Asia," ICRIER Policy Series, no. 3, August.

Park, A. and Cai, F. (2011) "The Informalization of the Chinese Labor Market," in S. Kuruvilla, C. K. Lee and M. Gallagher (eds) *From Iron Rice Bowl to Informalization: Markets, State and Workers in a Changing China*, Ithaca, NY: Cornell University Press.

PBoC (2011) *China Regional Financial Performance Report 2010*, PBoC, Beijing. Available at: http://www.pbc.gov.cn/image_public/UserFiles/zhengcehuobisi/upload/File/2010年中国区域金融运行报告主报告.pdf (accessed 3 June 2011).

Pearce, D. W. and Atkinson, G. (1993) "Capital Theory and the Measurement of Sustainable Development: An Indicator of Weak Sustainability," *Ecological Economics*, no. 8, pp. 103–8.

Peng, Z. (1983) *Shijiu Shiji Houbanqi de Zhongguo Caizheng yu Jingji*, Beijing: China Renmin University Press.

Penny, K. (1988) *Famine in China, 1959–61: Demographic and Social Implications*, New York: St. Martin's Press.

Perkins, D. and Rawski, T. (2008) "Forecasting China's Economic Growth to 2025," in L. Brandt and T. Rawski (eds) *The Great Transformation of China*, New York: Cambridge University Press.

Pomeranz, K. (2000) *The Great Divergence: China, Europe and the Making of the Modern World Economy*, Princeton, NJ: Princeton University Press.

Qiao, B. (2002) *The Trade-Off between Growth and Equity*, Beijing: People's Publishing House.

Rodrik, D. (2011) *The Globalization Paradox*, New York and London: W. W. Norton & Company.

Rodrik, D. and Subramanian, A. (2009) "Why Did Financial Globalization Disappoint," *IMF Staff Papers*, Vol. 56, no. 1, pp. 112–38.

Rosanvallon, P. (2008) *La Légitimité Démocratique*, Paris: Le Seuil.

Rosenthal, J.-L. and Wong, B. (2011) *Before and Beyond Divergence. The Politics of Economic Change in China and Europe*, Cambridge, MA: Harvard University Press.

Sassen, S. (1991) *The Global City*, Princeton, NJ: Princeton University Press.

Sassen, S. (2000) *Cities in a World Economy*, Thousand Oaks, CA: Sage, Pine Forge Press.

Schurmann, F. (1966) *Ideology and Organization in Communist China*, Berkeley and Los Angeles, CA: University of California Press.

Sen, A. (1976) "Real National Income," *Review of Economic Studies*, Vol. 43, no. 1, February, pp. 19–39.

Shi, R. (2009) *From Elite Education to Mass Education: Studies on Efficiency and Fairness Question in the Development of Higher Education*, Beijing: Higher Education Press.

Shih, V. (2010) "Big Rock Candy Mountain," *China Economic Quarterly Review*, Vol. 14, no. 2, June, pp. 26–32.

Solow, R. (1956) "A Contribution to the Theory of Economic Growth," *Quarterly Journal of Economics*, Vol. 70, no. 1, pp. 65–94.

Sin Y. (2005) "China: Pension Liabilities and Reform Options for the Old Age Insurance," Working Paper Series, no. 2005-1, Washington, DC: World Bank. Available at: http://www-wds.worldbank.org/external/default/WDSContentServer/WDSP/IB/2005/08/03/0 00090341_20050803142802/Rendered/PDF/331160CHA0Working0paper0P0583080P ension.pdf (accessed 5 January 2010).

Spitaes, G. (2007) *Chine–USA. La guerre aura-t-elle lieu?*, Paris: Luc Pire.

State Audit Bureau (2011), Zhonghua Renmin Gongheguo Shenjishu Shenji Jieguo Gonggao, no. 104, 35. Available at: http://www.audit.gov.cn/n1992130/n1992150/n1992500/2752208.html (accessed December 2011).

Statistic Bureau of Wuhan (1989) *Wuhan Sishi Nian*, Wuhan: Wuhan University Press.

Stern, N. (2007) *The Economics of Climate Change. The Stern Review*, New York: Cambridge University Press.

Stern, N. (2008) "The Economics of Climate Change," Richard T. Ely Lecture, *American Economic Review Papers and Proceedings*, Vol. 98, no. 2, pp. 1–37.

Stiglitz, J., Sen, A. and Fitoussi, J. P. (2009) *Rapport de la Commission sur la Mesure de la Performance Economique et du Progrès Social*, Paris: OFCE.

Stockholm Environment Institute (2009) *Going Clean. The Economics of China's Low-carbon Development*, Stockholm.

Stolper, W. and Samuelson, P. (1941) "Protection and Real Wages," *Review of Economic Studies*, Vol. 9, no. 1, pp. 58–73.

Sugihara, K. (2003) "The East Asian Path of Economic Development: A Long-Term Perspective," in G. Arrighi, T. Hamashita and M. Selden (eds) *The Resurgence of East Asia: 500, 150 and 50 Year Perspectives*, London: Routledge, pp. 78–123.

Tsai, L. L. (2007) *Accountability without Democracy: Solidary Groups and Public Goods Provision in Rural China*, Cambridge: Cambridge University Press.

Twitchett, D. and Mote, F. W. (1998) *The Cambridge History of China, 1368–1644*, Part 2, New York: Cambridge University Press.

Wallerstein I. (2012), "China and the US: Rivals, Enemies, Collaborators?," Commentary no. 321, 15 January. Available at: http://www.iwallerstein.com/commentaries/ (accessed August 2011).

Walter, C. and Howie, F. (2011) *Red Capitalism*, Singapore: John Wiley & Sons (Asia).

Wang, F. and Mason, A. (2008) "The Demographic Factor in China's Transition," in L. Brandt and T. Rawski (eds) *China's Great Economic Transformation*, New York: Cambridge University Press.

Wang, R. (2005) *China's Pension System Reform and Capital Market Development*, Cambridge, MA: Harvard University Asia Center.

Wang, S. and Hu, A. (2001) *The Chinese Economy in Crisis: State Capacity and Tax Reform*, Armonk: M.E. Sharpe.

Wang, Y. and Yao, Y. (2003) "Sources of China's Economic Growth 1952–99: Incorporating Human Capital Accumulation," *China Economic Review*, Vol.14, no. 1, pp. 32–52.

Weitzman, M. (2009) "On Modeling and Interpreting the Economics of Catastrophic Climate Change," *Review of Economics and Statistics*, Vol. XCI, no. 1, February, pp. 1–19.

Weizsäcker, E., Young, O. and Finger, M. (2005) *Limits to Privatization: How to Avoid Too Much of a Good Thing*, London: Earthscan.

Wensheng Peng, Chang Shu and Yip, R. (2006) "Renminbi Derivatives: Development and Issues," *China Economic Issues*, HK Monetary Authority, no. 5/06, November, pp. 1–17.

Will, P. and Wong, R. B. (1991) *Nourish the People: The State Civilian Granary System in China, 1650–1850*, Ann Arbor, MI: University of Michigan Center for Chinese Studies.

Williamson, J. (2005) "A Currency Basket for East Asia," *Policy Briefs in International Economics*, no. 1, Institute for International Economics, Washington, DC, July.

Woetzel, J., Devan, J., Dobbs, R., Eichner, A., Negri, S. and Rowland, M. (2009) "If You've Got it, Spend it: Unleashing the Chinese Consumer," McKinsey Global Institute Report. Available at: http://www.mckinsey.com/Insights/MGI/Research/Financial_Markets/Unleashing_the_Chinese_consumer (accessed June 2010).

Wong, C. P. W. and Bird, R. M. (2008) "China's Fiscal System: A Work in Progress," in L. Brandt and T. Rawski (eds) *China's Great Economic Transformation*, New York: Cambridge University Press.

Wong J. (1999) "China's Dynamic Economic Growth in the Context of East Asia," East Asian Institute, Singapore.

Wong, J. and Lu, D. (2002) *China's Economy into the New Century*, Singapore: Singapore University Press.

Wong, R. B. (1997) *China Transformed: Historical Change and the Limits of European Experience*, Ithaca, NY, and London: Cornell University Press.

Wong, R. B. (2009) "La Chine et l'économie politique de son empire agraire dans l'histoire globale, mondialisations et capitalisme," in Philippe Beaujard, Laurent Berger and Philippe Norel (eds) *Histoire globale, mondialisation et capitalisme*, Paris: La Découverte.

World Bank (2006) *Where is the Wealth of Nations? Measuring Capital for the 21ˢᵗ Century*, Washington, DC: World Bank, 188pp.

Wu, H. (2011) "Accounting for China's Growth in 1952–2008," Rieti Discussion Paper Series, 11-E-03.

Wu, J. (2010) *Understanding and Interpreting China's Economic Reform*, Shanghai: Shanghai Far East Publishers.

Wu, J. and Reynolds, B. L. (1988) "Choosing a Strategy for China's Economic Reform," *American Economic Review*, Vol. 78, no. 2, Papers and Proceedings of the One-Hundred Annual Meeting of the American Economic Association (May, 1988), pp. 461–6.

Wu, J., Lou, J., Zhou, X., Guo, S. and Li, J. (1986) *Zhongguo Jingji Gaige de Zhengti Sheji*, Beijing: China Social Sciences Press.

Wu, X. (2011) *Transformation and Rise of China: Exploring the Road to a Financial Power*, Beijing: China Financial Publishing House.

Wu, Y. (2008) "The Role of Productivity in China's Growth: New Estimates," *Journal of Chinese Economic and Business Studies*, Vol. 6, no. 2, pp. 141–56.

Xin, X. (1996) *Daguo Zhuhou – Zhongguo Zhongyang yu Difang Guanxi zhi Jie*, Beijing: China Social Sciences Press.

Xuetong, Y. (2011) *Ancient Chinese Thought, Modern Chinese Power*, Princeton, NJ: Princeton University Press.

Yang, Z., Ma, J., Yang, Z., Ma, C., Zhang, D. and Zhang, B. (2006) *Theory of Fiscal Decentralization and Reform of Local Public Finance in China*, Beijing: Economic Science Press.

Yao, Y. (2011) *Global Implications of the Chinese Experience*, Beijing: Peking University Press.

Yin-Wong Cheung, Menzie D. Chinn and Eiji Fujii (2009) "China's Current Account and Exchange Rate," NBER Working Paper Series, no. 14673, January.

Yueh, L. (2004) "Wage Reforms in China during the 1990s," *Asian Economic Journal*, Vol. 18, no. 2, pp. 149–64.

Zhang, T. and Zou, H. (1998) "Fiscal Decentralization, Public Spending and Economic Growth in China," *Journal of Public Economics*, Vol. 67, no. 2, pp. 221–40.

Zhang, W. and Wu, N. (2010) "Caizheng Jiaoyi, Yishixingtai Yuesu yu Jijin de Gongyouhua: Zhongguo 1950 Niandai de Zhengzhi Jingji Xue," *Economic Research Journal*, Vol. 2, pp. 137–51.

Zhang, Y. (2009) "Central–Local Governmental Relationship: A Theoretical Framework and its Application," *Comparison of Economic and Social System* [in Chinese], Vol. 2, pp. 65–71.

Zhao Ziyang (2009) *Prisoner of the State. The Secret Journal of Zhao Ziyang*, London: Simon & Schuster.

Zheng, J., Bigsten, A. and Hu, A. (2006) "Can China's Growth be Sustained? A Productivity Perspective," Scandinavian Working Paper in Economics, no. 236.

Zhou, T. (1984) *Dangdai Zhongguo de Jingji Tizhi Gaige*, Beijing: China Social Sciences Press.

Zhou, Y. and Tan, Y. (2008) *Zhongguo Jumin Shouru Fenpei Chaju Shizheng Fenxi*, Tianjin: Nankai University Press.

Index